Social Phobia

Social phobia is a disorder involving an intense fear of being judged by others and it affects the lives of many people. This book takes a critical stance toward the received view of social phobia as a disease of sorts, characterized by abnormal anxiety and caused by an inner mental or physical defective mechanism. Ariel Stravynski adopts an alternative approach to social phobia – as a purposeful interpersonal pattern protective against public humiliation or private rebuff. In this conception, fearfulness is the emotional facet of the socially phobic interpersonal pattern, rather than its driving force. This theoretical framework emphasizing dynamic transactions is articulated in terms of an anthropological psychology and Stravynski argues that social phobia can only be formulated and understood in interpersonal terms. He integrates all available knowledge on social phobia into his proposed framework and exemplifies its application by extending it to the assessment and treatment of the disorder.

ARIEL STRAVYNSKI is Professor of Clinical Psychology in the Department of Psychology at the University of Montreal and has been studying social phobia for more than thirty years. He is the author of *Fearing Others: The Nature and Treatment of Social Phobia* (Cambridge University Press, 2007).

Social Phobia

An Interpersonal Approach

Ariel Stravynski

University of Montreal

CAMBRIDGE
UNIVERSITY PRESS

CAMBRIDGE
UNIVERSITY PRESS

University Printing House, Cambridge CB2 8BS, United Kingdom

Cambridge University Press is part of the University of Cambridge.

It furthers the University's mission by disseminating knowledge in the pursuit of education, learning and research at the highest international levels of excellence.

www.cambridge.org
Information on this title: www.cambridge.org/9781316617939

© Ariel Stravynski 2014

First published 2014
First paperback edition 2016

A catalogue record for this publication is available from the British Library

Library of Congress Cataloguing in Publication data
Stravynski, Ariel, 1949–
Social phobia: an interpersonal approach / Ariel Stravynski.
   pages   cm
Includes bibliographical references and index.
ISBN 978-1-107-00719-2 (hardback)
1. Anxiety.   2. Social phobia.   3. Social phobia–Treatment.   I. Title.
BF575.A6S827 2014
616.85′225–dc23
2014004086

ISBN 978-1-107-00719-2 Hardback
ISBN 978-1-316-61793-9 Paperback

To Marsha

"[T]he secret of harvesting from existence the greatest fruitfulness and the greatest enjoyment is – to live dangerously!"

Nietzsche

Contents

viii   Contents

Figures

Tables

Preface

In the pages of this book, I shall state the case for approaching social phobia interpersonally. My main argument is simple: social phobia can be coherently described only in interpersonal terms. Furthermore, from that vantage point, everything known about social phobia coalesces into a coherent whole, meaningful and understandable.

Having, as I hope, successfully made that point at mid book, I shall go further and argue in the Conclusions (Part V) that social phobia can be understood only from that perspective. Perhaps recklessly, I hope to convince the reader of the value of that point of view.

If history teaches us anything, it is safe to say that all theories are doomed from the outset – bound to be proven wrong and superseded. Why then add another one? Perhaps this query is best answered by another question: is there any other way of advancing knowledge?

On a utilitarian level, this book is intended as a companion volume to *Fearing Others: the Nature and Treatment of Social Phobia* (2007).

Fearing Others was a study of social phobia in all its aspects. The natural upshot of engaging in such a wide-ranging overview was dealing with different bodies of theory and research on their own terms; most adhered to the received view of social phobia as a species of disease – a disorder of anxiety – that in turn is brought about by a defective inner mechanism – either physical or mental.

The untenable assumptions and conceptual flaws within each approach and the glaring incongruities between their claims allow – I daresay, call for – an alternative point of view, encompassing and harmonizing narrowly partial and blinkered perspectives.

In the final integrative chapter of *Fearing Others*, I outlined an alternative theoretical framework – interpersonal in nature – as one likely to provide the most comprehensive explanatory framework, integrating *all* current knowledge.

My purpose in writing this volume is to elaborate the integrative interpersonal theoretical framework for social phobia – presented in embryo form in *Fearing Others*. In the current volume, I seek to present a comprehensive argument for that point of view, set in, what I take to be, secure and defensible first principles. It is found in Part I.

Furthermore, in this volume, I consider the applied implications of the interpersonal approach, by extending its principles to assessment and treatment. By recasting social phobia, as well as the conceptual framework for alleviating or overcoming it, both are put on an integrated and coherent theoretical footing that accords with all current knowledge.

While the claim that the interpersonal approach clarifies social phobia best must rest mostly on its own merits, it is nevertheless justified, in part, by the conceptual flaws of currently received views of it. It is, however, the failure of research to give support to those notions that in my view decisively opens the door to a radically different kind of theorizing put forward in this book. Thus, I regard a critical scrutiny of the main contemporary body of ideas and the research it has generated as essential in providing a contrast against which the interpersonal theory of social phobia may be all the more sharply drawn. Questioning received ideas requires recasting these in alternative terms.

Substantively speaking, the second and third parts of the book are organized as an intellectual debate, pitting as it were, contrasting voices. On the one hand, we hear of social phobia construed as a disorder of anxiety. As a disease of sorts, caused by a putative inner malfunctioning, it is meant to be wholly distinct from "healthy" normality. On the other hand, social phobia is construed as a pragmatic construct, characterized by a fearful self-protective interpersonal pattern enacted for safety's sake; it is an exacerbation of social and emotional normality, distinct from it only functionally. It is evoked and modulated by (fearsome) social circumstances and individuals.

Needless to say, these divergent points of departure result in profoundly different ramifications. The differences are most glaringly apparent in matters of causality. Causality, however defined, is at the heart of any attempt to understand what is being studied. Two vocal lines, again, are heard.

While the received biomedical outlook (social phobia as disease) is resolutely reductionist (i.e. looking for malfunctioning elements within the person) and dualist (i.e. distinguishing sharply between body and mind), the (holistic) interpersonal perspective looks to the social life of undivided living individuals. It is seeking to understand social phobia in relational terms, as an extended pattern of transactions with others, in culturally fashioned social settings and mores. In this sense, social phobia will be identified as an extended fearful pattern of self-protection, enacted purposefully, against the threats embodied by other individuals in the social environment. Formulated in these terms, social phobia is enacted, not something one has.

Counterpoint – to borrow a musical notion – joins distinct voices, resonating against each other to create a richer texture of sound. By analogy, a richly textured picture of what is at stake necessitates, in my view, a substantive presentation (and critical consideration) of the biomedical outlook and – in keeping with its dualism and reductive mechanical logic – the research it generates.

As a consequence, the present book overlaps to some extent with *Fearing Others*. All the same, the relevant chapters or their parts, although covering similar ground, have been revised and updated. Furthermore, as elements in a different whole, these may be considered as having been, to a certain extent, transfigured. Practically, this has the additional advantage of allowing the current monograph to be self-contained and read on its own.

In that sense, it affords some independence gained painlessly. Every independent step, however small, furthers autonomy.

Autonomy – as I shall argue later – is to some extent a mirror image of the socially phobic pattern and, as such, a manner of being much prized by the interpersonal approach. From the interpersonal perspective, independence of thought and action are virtues highly recommended to those wishing to escape the narrow confines of a socially phobic life. By analogy, it may be beneficial to readers attuned to receive ideas as well.

Unlike Odysseus, who had to be attached to his ship's mast to resist the bewitching song of the sirens, we are fortunately not exposed to such beguiling and seductive singing. Autonomy, as practiced in this book, will be to turn away from the popular (received) refrain and to go one's own way. *Sapere aude!*

Autonomy, however, is not without its own risks. While challenging received ideas might be satisfying to the writer, shedding these could be disturbing to the reader. Taking it further, enacting new (and perhaps subversive) convictions might displease others and could possibly have – as the socially phobic have long suspected – unpleasant consequences. *Caveat emptor!*

At this point, the cautious reader might wonder as to what he or she has let themselves in for and wish to know something (perhaps reassuring) about the general orientation of the author. Briefly, I would describe my outlook as naturalistic. It is naturalistic in the sense of inclining towards observing life as it is lived – rooted in its natural, social and cultural habitat. In my view, any theorizing must accord with this; it is the only secure foundation for any conceptual enterprise. Such naturalism imposes a certain discipline: observation must take precedence over speculation;

observation has to take in everything within its purview and cannot be partial or arbitrary.

Substantively speaking and by extrapolation, I take it as axiomatic that only whole living beings – as opposed to minds or brains, for instance – engage in social life or conduct it fearfully. Similarly, fearful self-protection from harm (e.g. fleeing, "freezing") is made up of purposeful activities that only whole living creatures are capable of. Fearing and protecting oneself are features of the integrated activity of a whole individual; they are not separate, let alone independent activities. Nor do these occur in a vacuum.

Need it be emphasized that social life can only be engaged in with other people, in the social settings where they are to be found? Fearful and other emotional states permeating social behavior are elicited by and directed toward dangerous social circumstances – either tangible or foreseen. In the latter case, the fearful reaction is acted out imaginatively.

Social life is a human necessity; even the fearful pursue it relentlessly, albeit in a distinct mode. Without social life, such a relational pattern as social phobia is baffling, pointless and unintelligible.

Schopenhauer (2001, §396) saw it in this way:

On a cold winter's day, a group of porcupines huddled together to stay warm and keep from freezing. But soon they felt one another's quills and moved apart. When the need for warmth brought them closer together again, their quills again forced them apart. They were driven back and forth at the mercy of their discomforts until they found the distance from one another that provided both a maximum of warmth and a minimum of pain.

Fearsome (or prickly) others and fearfulness (pain) form an inextricable unity. Attempting to understand fearfulness without reference to the object of fear (i.e. the menacing context – individuals and the social setting) is misguided and unsatisfactory; if elevated to principle, it is willfully mystifying.

The title of this book (as well as its subject matter) is social phobia. This bucks current trends favoring the label of "social anxiety disorder," originating in the DSM-IV and continued in the DSM-5. In both, social phobia appears in parentheses, implying perhaps that the term (social phobia) has been eclipsed and superseded. My choice of the term, however, is deliberate, and therefore requires justification.

The historic term of "social phobia" hints at its genealogy (see Stravynski, 2007, pp. 16–24), tracing the rich intellectual trajectory of the hypothetical construct that it identifies and delineates. Crucially, the term relates to a description of the construct that it names. In other words, it tells us what social phobia is.

Abandoning such a conception has turned social phobia into a putative disease entity, and requiring, as such, no description but only criteria for its identification ("diagnosis"). Furthermore, by being proclaimed an "anxiety disorder," "social anxiety disorder" is saddled with a presumed "etiology" (anxiety). Taken together, this is what "social anxiety disorder" stands for.

By contrast with "social phobia," which emerged from an extended intellectual debate, "social anxiety disorder" is the creation of the DSM-IV task force, which "rebranded" social phobia by administrative fiat to align it better with "other anxiety disorders." This is perpetuated in the DSM-5.

If the above reasoning is accurate, the adoption of the term "social anxiety disorder" implicitly endorses the position of the DSM-IV and the DSM-5, construing social phobia as a disease entity caused by abnormal anxiety (itself brought on by some inner malfunctioning).

As I shall be persistently contesting these complacent assumptions in the pages of this book (while simultaneously putting forward an alternative position), I find I have no choice but to keep a critical distance from "social anxiety disorder." Bear with me, gentle reader.

Personal needs for self-expression aside, the writing of the book was sparked and sustained by the hope that the interpersonal theoretical framework presented in it will inspire researchers, clinicians and advanced students to adopt it so as to grapple with, investigate or disprove its main theses. The interpersonal perspective, I believe, allows the scaling of greater heights and affords a far better view, with a relatively undisturbed vista, of what social phobia is. For those seeking a deeper understanding, unfettered by intellectually irrelevant constraints, it points in a more promising direction, unseen from the lower ground.

As to the specific contents of the book, Part I (Chapter 1) presents a reasoned justification for the choice of an interpersonal level of analysis towards the understanding of social phobia, as well as its inevitable, somewhat philosophical foundations. On the basis of these first principles, the thesis of a relational social phobia is set out. This general formulation is broken up in several hypotheses; some supporting evidence is provided.

Part II concerns the search for the proper characterization of social phobia and its identity.

Chapter 2 analyzes the main assumptions underlying the received view of social phobia as a disorder of anxiety and finds them wanting. It argues, first of all, that social phobia cannot be characterized in terms of anxiety, however the term is defined. Secondly, social phobia cannot literally be considered a natural (disease) entity.

If this assessment is accurate, the current characterization of social phobia is ill-fitting. In those terms, social phobia remains a cipher and needs to be re-imagined. This is done in Chapter 3.

Chapter 3 provides an interpersonal characterization of social phobia. Rather than a breakdown in normal functioning due to abnormal anxiety, social phobia is understood in purposeful terms. It is envisaged as consisting of a web of self-protective, fearful transactions, enacted by the socially phobic in interactions with menacing individuals; all such transactions take place in culturally meaningful social settings.

Since the main features of social phobia are in continuity with normal traits, social phobia ought to be considered an exacerbation of normality. Nonetheless, a practical need for a categorical nomenclature exists. Such a category, however, ought to be explicitly declared as a "pragmatic" one, created to meet practical needs. The distinction between a "pragmatic" and a "natural" (disease) category is discussed.

Part III deals with matters of causality; it examines confusing and confused issues, fraught with difficulty. One wanders into this area at one's own peril; it is not for the faint-hearted.

In Chapters 4 and 5 our gaze turns inwards, as it were, in search of what makes social phobia tick. The former peers into the body or rather, the socially phobic brain, while the latter attempts to read the socially phobic "mind."

Chapter 4 presents the biomedical account of social phobia and concentrates on the main attempts to identify brain abnormalities: studies of neurotransmission and brain activity. A related issue, concerning genetic transmission (of the putative abnormalities), is also examined. Dimensions, on which the socially phobic, on average, differ statistically from contrast groups, are correlates of social phobia – not its causes. The "pathophysiology" of social phobia proves elusive.

Chapter 5 outlines the mental (malfunctioning) account of social phobia and surveys the resulting research. It argues that the "cognitive biases" and beliefs attendant on social phobia are some of its (many) features. These "cognitive" features of social phobia are its correlates, rather than its cause.

Chapter 6 presents a multi-causal analysis of social phobia, conducted at the interpersonal level. This analysis locates causality without. It emphasizes the purposeful nature of the socially phobic pattern of conduct, its defensive organization for the sake of safety, as well as the crucial role of the social context that evokes and molds the protean socially phobic pattern.

Although not directly dealing with causality, the historic nature of the emerging socially phobic pattern of conduct is very relevant to it. The factors contributing to the consolidation of the socially phobic pattern and its further evolution are identified and discussed.

Part IV presents the principles framing the applications of the interpersonal approach to assessment and treatment.

These follow closely the analysis of causality described in Chapter 6. Assessment and functional analysis (Chapter 7) and treatment (Chapter 8) are illustrated by means of three cases.

Part V (Chapter 9) makes the case, first of all, for the interpersonal level of analysis as being autonomous and not reducible to other "lower" levels of analysis. Secondly, it concentrates on the explanatory power of the interpersonal theory of social phobia. This framework is able to encompass all available knowledge touching on the nature of social phobia, its causal analysis and treatment. Thirdly, it argues that social phobia can only be characterized in interpersonal terms; all other accounts, narrowly focusing on the socially phobic state of anxiousness, fail to do so.

Acknowledgments

Much of the writing of this book (as well as most of my research) was carried out at the Research Centre of the Institut Universitaire de Santé Mentale de Montreal (IUSMM). I am much obliged to the directors of both Centre and Hospital for creating conditions propitious to such an intellectual endeavor.

Marc-Yvan Custeau and his colleagues at the library of the IUSMM were most helpful in tracing and providing me with articles from not always easily accessible journals.

Annette Maillet took on the daunting task of typing the references and matching them with a volatile text. I greatly appreciate her steadfast dedication and quiet competence.

In my attempt to assimilate a vast range of publications, I have been most ably assisted by Angela Kyparissis. Starting off as a doctoral student, she became a collaborator whose opinions I trust and value. Her involvement and interest blew wind into my sails.

From the ideas expressed in the book, it is obvious I owe much to many people. Put differently, if all ideas originating with others were taken away, not much would be left. Nevertheless, the responsibility for weaving the ideas together and all errors committed, either willfully or absent-mindedly, are mine alone.

Part I

The interpersonal approach

"All theory, dear friend, is gray, but the tree of life springs ever green."

Goethe

1 Social phobia in interpersonal perspective: a conceptual framework and theoretical statement

In this introductory chapter, I aim to present an explanatory theory of social phobia set in an interpersonal perspective. It presupposes a familiarity with social phobia, that some of the readers may not have. To such a reader I suggest starting with Chapter 3.

Chapter 3 describes social phobia in two ways. First of all, it presents it naturalistically and objectively, as if observed in its natural habitat. Secondly, it presents it empathetically, in an attempt to convey something of how it is experienced by individuals living it. What social phobia is and how it came to be that way are both illustrated by means of several cases and described analytically by pointing out its various features.

Having acquainted ourselves with social phobia either recently (after reading Chapter 3) or a long time ago, it is natural to wish to make sense of it. It is our final destination.

Before setting out, however, I shall consider the intellectual scaffolding necessary for the construction of the explanatory framework.

Choice of an appropriate level of analysis

Understanding in a scientific sense is, by necessity, advanced by means of theoretical statements. These create hypothetical constructs that postulate the grouping of certain observed phenomena and trace (hypothetical) links between them. Even if they appear to be supremely insightful or plainly plausible, such explanations remain speculative and their value uncertain. To gain validity, these constructs and their relationships need to be confirmed foremost by (natural) experience but also by (artificial) experimentation. A sound theory cannot be a-priori contrary to experience or reason; nor can it selectively focus on some of the relevant facts while glossing over others. Ultimately, a theory is an attempt to structure a boundless and amorphous natural reality and to reveal the (often hidden) processes accounting for what is being observed.

If done deliberately and reflectively, any attempt at understanding complex natural phenomena has to start with a preliminary theoretical choice of the most appropriate level of analysis. In principle, this could extend from astronomic (e.g. planetary positions at birth) to sub-atomic physics; the plausible range is probably narrower. The range to be considered could be represented as a funnel of ever-decreasing units of analysis or vice versa. In the present case concerning social phobia, the plausible range of where the explanation might be found would span the extra-personal, interpersonal and intra- (or sub-)personal factors.

At the sizeable end (in terms of scope of potential units of analysis) may be found the social world embedded in the physical environment in which humans dwell. This could mean group- or society-wide structures (sociology) and processes (anthropology). A narrower focus centered on the individual within the social environment would constitute an interpersonal level of analysis – the manner in which an individual engages with others and the resulting dynamic interplay. This would constitute the study of a person operating in his or her natural and social habitat in *relational* terms. Lower down along the continuum, are found intrapersonal explanatory notions, contemplating as it were processes within the body. These activities are typically separated into two kinds and identified as the "psychological" and "biological." Assuming further that these putative domains are relatively independent, a "psychological" perspective would deal with postulated mental systems (e.g. cognitive), whereas a "biological" perspective would be limited to investigating bodily structures and processes (e.g. anatomy, physiology) within the person. These in turn could be approached on various levels: systems (e.g. endocrine), organs (e.g. brain) or cells. Further reductions in the level of analysis are conceivable: the molecular, as in the case of genes and their products. Speculatively, a purely atomic or even sub-atomic level of analysis is conceivable but given the state of our knowledge, would make little sense.

By way of illustration of the dilemmas involved, how are we to understand, for example, the misleadingly labeled (as satisfying the patient) "placebo effect" – the oft reported observation of improvements in the state of the individual engaged in a culturally sanctioned healing process?

The question is this: what is the "placebo"? Is it the inert pill or the cultural transaction in which the pill serves as a "theatrical" prop?

If it is the former, is the sub-personal level of analysis appropriate? Does identifying the neurobiological (e.g. Benedetti, Mayberg, Wager, Stohler and Zubieta, 2005; Faria *et al.*, 2012) or "mental" (e.g. Colloca and Benedetti, 2005) processes involved, illuminate the placebo response?

Alternatively, would conceptualizing the phenomenon at an interpersonal level, emphasizing both the social transactions (e.g. Henderson, 1935) as well as the cultural settings in which these are embedded (Moerman, 2000), bring the placebo responses into sharper focus? Does the "placebo effect" in any way intersect with the equally well-documented effect of amulets and potions (see Chamberlain, 2007, and Donizetti's *L'Elisir d'amore*) on the one hand, and pilgrimage, prayer, confession and other religious rituals (see Scott, 2010) on the other?

The choice of level of conceptualization is not an empirical matter; the decision has to be taken deliberately, on theoretical grounds. This may not be easy, as certain set assumptions prevail.

The choice: intrapersonal versus interpersonal

The all-important issue of choice of level of analysis arises against the currently prevailing a-priori view favoring what might be termed "reductionism" – the metaphysical assumption, advocated by Descartes (see Cottingham, 1999, pp. 4–7), that causation is likely to run from lower to higher levels. Put differently, this doctrine maintains that the behavior of the whole person (or non-human organism), is best explained by the inherent characteristics of certain constituent elements or processes. This doctrine is widely considered to be the hallmark of science.

What processes would account for social phobia reductionistically? These processes are of two kinds, in keeping with another metaphysical assumption (Cottingham, 1999, pp. 4–7).

In the recesses of philosophical debate, reductionism (see Bennett and Hacker, 2003, pp. 355–377; Murphy and Brown, 2007, pp. 42–104) is intimately tied to the philosophical doctrine of mind–body dualism (Bennett and Hacker, 2003, pp. 111–114; Barendregt and van Rappard, 2004), its modern formulation identified with Descartes (see Sprigge, 1984, pp. 13–14). In a nutshell, it postulates that humans (and nothing else) are made of two utterly distinct substances: material and mental.

Dualism – the notion that human beings are a compound of body and soul, understood as separable entities – has roots in a religious outlook first expounded by Plato and refashioned by Augustine. In Descartes' view, all natural phenomena, with the exception of human thought and action, were to be understood in material and therefore mechanical terms. The human body, being material, was construed as machine-like. Nowadays, the brain and its workings are considered its main mechanism and wellspring. Although mind was characterized by Descartes in terms of "thought," thought was described as "everything in which we are aware of as happening within us" (quoted in Hacker, 2007, p. 24). This description would be characterized as consciousness today.

In contrast to the activities of the body, then, conscious experiences that do not lend themselves to be formulated as concrete occurrences (Sarbin, 1964, p. 631) were postulated as being made of a mental (i.e. a non-physical) substance – revealed by "introspection" alone. The exact nature of "introspection" and its subject matter is not clear.

Although existing nowhere, the mental – in its modern guise – is often spoken of as a kind of space (mind) where meanings are grasped and "cognitions" (i.e. desires, beliefs, memories, intentions, etc.) are (metaphorically) stored, retrieved and allegedly exert their influence (Lourenço, 2001). According to the Cartesian view, the mind is somehow contained in the body but does not necessarily have to be connected with it. How the mind influences the body, in seeming violation of the laws of nature, remains an unresolved puzzle.

Prior to Descartes, medieval scholastic Aristotelians considered mind narrowly as the possession of certain faculties, namely reasoning, exhibited only by humans. As Descartes redefined mind expansively to include anything to be caught in the net of "introspection," it came to encompass in addition to reasoning, emotions and sensations.

Wishing to make minds the exclusive preserve of humans, and in the process turning human emotions into states of mind, Descartes was led to assert – in today's terms – that animals lacked consciousness (and therefore sensations and emotions) and indeed were merely complex mechanisms (see Cottingham, 1978; Searle, 1994 for discussions). One can only wonder at the consequences for philosophy and by extension psychology, if Descartes had observed a house cat or a dog he cared for, or, at a distance, had marveled at animal migration.

Many animals (e.g. birds, butterflies and salmon) are able to perform feats of navigation (see Gould and Grant Gould, 2012) – let alone endurance and cooperation – unimaginable in humans without long and arduous training and imposed discipline. By means of internal "clocks" and "compasses," the earth's magnetic field, the position of the sun or the stars and internal (e.g. infrasound; see Hagstrum, 2013) maps refined through experience, animals are able to navigate distant trajectories (e.g. 6,000 miles of non-stop flight in formation by the curlew; a 2,000-mile journey from Canada to Mexico by the monarch butterfly), with astonishing precision (Gould and Grant Gould, 2012).

Whether sentient and intelligent behavior may be deemed "mindless" (see Gould and Grant Gould, 2007) is a moot point.

As it is, the doctrine of dualism has drawn much philosophical criticism (see Fesser, 2005, pp. 19–48 and Jaworski, 2011, pp. 34–67, for summaries), not least concerning the logical problems arising from the postulated interaction between the material and the mental domains (McGinn, 1982, pp. 24–25; Fesser, 2005, pp. 38–46; Phemister, 2006, pp. 147–165; Jaworski, 2011, pp. 55–59).

A contemporary of Descartes, the skeptical Pierre Gassendi, had this to say: "In a word, the general difficulty still remains of how the corporeal can communicate with the incorporeal and what relationship may be established between the two" (quoted in Phemister, 2006, p. 147).

Among modern objections to dualism is that it clashes with the theory of evolution that must maintain that mind comes from matter – something a dualist can hardly accept (McGinn, 1982, p. 25).

Centuries of philosophical criticism notwithstanding, dualism and its ramifications (e.g. the world as mechanism, the existence of mind without body and mind as the true self) remain woven into the prevailing "folk psychology" (Churchland and Haldane, 1988) – at least in the Western world. More worryingly, dualism is also widely and unquestioningly regarded as expressing the natural order in psychology/psychiatry.

This "mechanistic" world view – social phobia as defective clockwork, literally or figuratively – is reflected in the bulk of research on social phobia (see Stravynski, 2007). It mostly fits within the intrapersonal reductionist (and dualist) perspective. The reductive search operates on several levels. Its thrust is to identify either "mental" or bodily processes – or more precisely their aberrations – that would account for an "abnormal" anxious state allegedly characterizing social phobia. The "abnormal" anxious state, in turn, is presumed to account for the socially phobic pattern as a whole.

Needless to say, these assumptions are going to be challenged and an alternative perspective charted in the following chapters. The first step in this direction is the choice of a non-reductive level of analysis.

The interpersonal level of analysis

Bearing in mind all intellectual considerations involved, I shall make the case for an interpersonal level of analysis, invoking several justifications for that choice.

First of all, the interpersonal domain is the appropriate level of analysis since socially phobic behavior is other-oriented and played out in a social context even at a remove; this is where life takes place. Thus, socially phobic activity is complemented by the presence of others; even the most private preoccupations are characterized by this social aspect. Public and private behavior are both nested in current social and cultural practices (e.g. job interviews, courtship, dress, appearance).

Secondly, several decades of research have provided only tenuous support for an intrapersonal perspective. In other words, no intrapersonal factors can be shown to characterize social phobia; this calls for an alternative theoretical outlook integrating this most important fact. This perspective has to be broadly holistic and ecological; it is hardly conceivable that an exquisitely structured complex social behavior (e.g. dissembling, prevaricating), so well attuned to the complex social and institutional settings (Svyantek and Brown, 2000) in which it is displayed, can be accounted for reductionistically (Fan, 2007).

Thirdly, unlike a dualist perspective (that sustains reductionism) with its distinct two universes (a machine-like body animated by a ghost-like mind), an interpersonal level of theorization is integrative. This inclusive outlook is capable of accommodating all known facts about social phobia, regardless of their theoretical provenance.

Fourthly, and perhaps comfortingly, the interpersonal perspective – although resting on its own metaphysics (see below) – demystifies psychological understanding. In contrast to mind-reading or even gazing at brain imagery, sequences of interactions, if not plain at every particular moment, are tangible and observable and, when completed and set in context, perfectly intelligible.

Last but not least, the choice of the interpersonal level of analysis is apt because – as I shall argue – social phobia can only be characterized in interpersonal terms.

A few words are in order to lay bare the metaphysical principles underlying the interpersonal perspective I am favoring. This perspective has strong affinities with an "organicist" – or in a modern idiom – a systemic outlook (e.g. Noble, 2008; Gatherer, 2010) drawing on Aristotle. It maintains that living organisms are best understood as a fully integrated organic whole. This holistic view lays stress on the organization of an organism and the structure of its activities, rather than its composition (e.g. Strohman, 2000). Seen holistically, the unitary organic whole determines the activities of the parts and their interrelationships. In this sense, it is a mirror image of the (reductionistic) mechanistic perspective in which any part has an impact and therefore determines the functioning of the whole.

Furthermore, as all life is embedded in an environment and sustained by interactions with it, the holistic view is also ecological. The Aristotelian organicist/systemic outlook will be developed fully in Chapter 6, concerning causality.

The critical stance inherent in the interpersonal approach towards Cartesian dualism and the concomitant reductionism draws mostly on the anthropological psychology, refined and elaborated by Wittgenstein. This is part of what is usually called analytical philosophy (see Jost, 1995; Kenny, 2005). Various aspects of these ideas have been also advanced by other earlier (e.g. Dewey, 1930; Mead, 1934) and contemporary (e.g. Ryle, 1949) theorists (see Brinkmann, 2011 for a discussion).

Wittgenstein rejected outright all Cartesian doctrines, including the mind–body dichotomy positioning the mind as an independent agent (see also Ryle, 1949). According to Hacker (1996, p. 117), Wittgenstein maintained that:

It is a confusion to suppose that there are two domains, the physical and the mental, each comparable to the other, each populated by objects, properties, states, processes and events, which differ only in that in the first domain they are material and in the second immaterial. And it is equally erroneous, on the rebound from dualism, to suppose that the mental domain is really the neural in disguise, let alone to suppose that in the fullness of time, psychology will achieve maturity and be able to replace gross qualitative psychological descriptions with quantitative neurological descriptions.

Like Aristotle, Wittgenstein "held that such attributes as consciousness, perception, cognition and volition are attributes of the living animal, not of its material parts, such as the brain, let alone of its allegedly immaterial parts such as the mind" (Hacker, 2007, p. 28). Contrary to the Cartesian representation of behavior as bodily motion and speech activated from an "inner" realm, "Wittgenstein emphasized that human behavior is, and is experienced as being, suffused with meaning, thought, passion and will" (Hacker, 1997, p. 5).

"Wittgenstein put the human being – a psychophysical unity, not an embodied *anima* – a living creature in the stream of life" (Hacker, 1997, p. 5). A cardinal upshot of this outlook is that an individualistic psychological account, be it "mental," behavioral or somatic, cannot be intelligible. There are two reasons for this.

First of all, persons are whole and unified organisms. Human activities therefore are not an expression of an inner realm. Nothing hidden from view (but observable privately) goes on "behind" the behavior. Rather, in action all human powers combine together in a meaningful way. Human conduct is permeated with thought, emotion and desire; these are manifest in it.

Secondly, and most importantly, humans are social beings. Put more forcefully, human beings live their lives through relationships. As Godelier (quoted in Carrithers, 1992, p. 1) strikingly puts it: "human beings in contrast to other social animals, do not just live in society, they produce society in order to live." Human relationships, then, are the soil in which human life flourishes; human survival in its absence is unimaginable. Our very sense of who we are emerges from considering ourselves in relation to others.

Human relationships are nested in a large variety of social systems (all based in diverse physical environments) embedded in larger societal and cultural systems (see Carrithers, 1992). These encompass language, ideas about the nature of the universe, a system of morals often embedded in a religious outlook, a political and economic organization, kinship, dress, diet, and so on. Human existence is inextricably woven into a certain form (or mode or way) of life (see Gier, 1980; Rudder Baker, 1984; Scheman, 1996; Schatzki, 2000).

A mode of life is a system of relationships, exhibiting regularities of patterns and configurations of social conduct organized and informed by formal and informal frameworks. It is evident from the fabric of human existence within it (e.g. Ledeneva, 2008). A way of life is thus simultaneously the extent of its practices and the norms governing (i.e. meanings attached to) it. Thus, all human attributes are involved in a dialectical interaction with their social environment and fashioned by it. "Individuals are socially constituted and the social context within which this occurs is a complex of practices" (Schatzki, 2000, p. 103).

Social practices (e.g. worship, commerce, food, education, courtship) are a set of considerations that govern actions (Schatzki, 1996, p. 96). Among social practices, communicative behavior (especially language) is of supreme importance (Schatzki, 1996, pp. 88–132), blended as it is, in socially patterned ways ("language games"; see Kenny, 1995, pp. 126–140), into almost every activity – including thought. Words in themselves are actions, affecting other people as well as the utterer. As such they are constitutive of reality. Through language, the individual is impregnated with societal processes permeating words and manner of speech. We think in words (and therefore language patterns); language is the vehicle of human thought (Budd, 1989, p. 128). Language provides us with the framework from which we build up our understanding of the world.

Socially, typical ways of saying things (e.g. flippantly) are integrated with an intonation, a bearing and a manner of behaving (and dress and grooming) fitting, or sometimes at odds with, a social occasion. Action is purposeful in being attuned to the social setting and therefore to the cultural context manifest in it. Stated differently, every action is embedded in a social role or arrays of roles (one's place in society as one's part in a play) anchored in institutions (see Zurcher, 1983). Consequently, meaningful action fulfils a function within a certain way or form of life (i.e. cultural community) at a certain period (see Sarbin, 1986, pp. 88–97).

Socially instituted ways of being envelop every activity. Furthermore, life activities unfold as a continuous stream not necessarily clearly demarcated (e.g. passionately vs. placidly).

Properties allegedly of mind (e.g. courage, fortitude, prudence) are attributes of an individual, enacted in activities displayed in the social environment; whatever mind is, it cannot be manifest apart from the body. Consciousness and purposefulness are properties of persons not of minds (or brains); thinking is not carried out in the head, but by a person. It is not hands that play the piano, nor are sexual activities engaged in by the sex organs.

Any attempt at understanding a person must take account of the social context in which he or she functions. Social customs (e.g. fasting, sending flowers, honor killings) and practices (e.g. pursuing profit or ritual purity, safeguarding virginity, seeking pleasure) are bound up with human institutions (e.g. religion, law, honor, markets, marriage, illegitimacy) and customs (e.g. hospitality); actions are meaningful only against this backdrop. Distinctive individual features are a narrow range of idiosyncratic variations on common practices. Their meaning lies not in the individual activity, but in the general pattern of life, of which it is an exemplar.

Within society, various ways of life interlock. Remaining unruffled, standing on honor (e.g. dueling or going to war) and displaying conspicuous carelessness (e.g. about losses and debts from gambling), for example, were aspects of a noble demeanor in Europe of the eighteenth century (see Kiernan, 1988; Doyle, 2010). Carriages carrying their aristocratic owners from all-night revelry crossed laborers on their way to work at dawn, who stood aside respectfully and prudently – so as not to be overrun. Domestic servants in nineteenth-century Britain were answerable to the mistress of the house. Daily interactions, involved numerous rituals of servility and deference (e.g. bowing, curtsying); carelessness about these would result in being condescendingly "put in one's place" (see Delap, 2011). Contemptuously, Lord Chesterfield (quoted in Harré, 1991a, p. 158) considered that only the "awkward and ill bred" (i.e. members of the lower orders) could be flustered and embarrassed. Members of the upper classes, by implication, would remain unperturbed and dignified under any set of circumstances. Codes of condescension and deference sustained the domination.

Rituals of self-abasement – public sessions of self-criticism – prevailed in the ruling body of the Communist party of the Soviet Union under the dictatorship of Stalin (see Getty, 1999).

A final example is from ancient Lacedaemon (Sparta), where an enslaved stratum of society (the Helots) both cultivated the land of the peers who formed the warrior caste and served as their weapon carriers.

According to Myron of Priena (a historian of the third century BC, quoted in Vidal-Naquet, 1992), in order to keep them in a state of submission:

The Helots are made to perform the most ignominious and degrading tasks. They are forced to wear a dog skin cap and dress in animal hides; each year they receive a certain number of blows, without having committed any infraction, in order to remind them that they are slaves; worse yet, if there are any who exceed in strength the measure appropriate to slaves, they are punished by death and their masters receive a fine for not having impeded their development.

Institutionalized contempt proclaimed symbolically the inferior position of the Helots. As a further measure of domination, assassinations of Helots were carried out in secret assignments (*krypteia*) by young warriors in training, for whom it constituted an initiation rite into the ruling class of peers (Ducat, 1974, p. 1454).

These examples illustrate the fact that conduct within each class and relationships between classes are tied to the general power structure (relationship of domination and subordination) within the society at the time and the gestures and feelings associated with them are intelligible only within that context (see Elias, 1987). The – by now arcane – dispute between the Peers of France and the Princes of the Blood over precedence at a coronation is a case in point (Jackson, 1971).

Many of these may be likened to rule-based scripts establishing a prescribed sequence and structure (e.g. Getty, 1999). Within the general framework, as in a spider's web, a beaver's dam or a flock of migrating geese flying in formation, variations occur, taking into account prevailing conditions.

Resentment or rebelliousness cannot come to the fore without disparagement or oppression. Followers' dedication to utopian goals leading to an intensification of communal bonds, accompanied by feelings of exaltation, reverence and devotion, flourish in "religious" collective movements (see Riis and Woodhead, 2010), inspired by a messianic leader (usually a man of providence endowed with charismatic authority) on a sacred mission, as in Nazi Germany under Hitler (see Kershaw, 1993).

It is the context that evokes as well as shades feelings (e.g. fear or anger). Fear, to take it as an example, cannot be described as an inner state (either of mind or the body) independently of the actions of the person and the circumstances evoking it. Therefore the same label (e.g. fear), abstracted from the relationship giving rise to it, misleadingly suggests a spurious uniformity of reaction. Fear of humiliation, for example, may bear only a distant relation to fear of losing a cherished spouse to illness. Subjective experiences are inseparable from the sequences of actions that constitute interdependent relations and the social environment in which these are embedded. What gives offence is culturally constituted; so is the response to it – angry, resentful or otherwise.

Smiles, in a similar vein, have a variety of cultural meanings, although the facial expression always involves a curving of the corners of the mouth. Depending on the context, it may express among others, friendliness, amusement, irony or contempt.

A final historic example illustrates the paramount importance of the social and cultural context. Among the members of the Samurai class of Japan between the twelfth and nineteenth centuries, one could arguably maintain that social anxieties (and perhaps fear altogether) did not exist. Within such a warrior caste (King, 1993, pp. 37–60), the very experience of fear would be disgraceful; giving expression to it unthinkable. Through years of drilling and training in swordsmanship and other martial skills, the provision of example and encouragement of lording it over the lower orders (who could be killed with impunity for being less than obsequiously deferential), the treatment of one's equals with utmost consideration, and unquestioning obedience to one's superiors, fear might be said to have been banished from this way of life. Although seemingly contrary to nature, it would neither be shown objectively nor acknowledged subjectively. This example suggests that while fear is undeniably an important human emotion, it may be modulated in important ways by the social form of life and culture of the individual.

In summary, an understanding of individual actions is impossible without taking into account other individuals involved within the matrix of the social practices that are woven into the actors' form of life (e.g. courtship, offering or taking bribes). Forms of life are established patterns of action shared by members of a community (Winch, 1977, p. 90). Membership in a community (e.g. class, caste) is a powerful determinant of behavior. Several examples would serve to illustrate the importance of this wider societal/cultural context.

First of all, in the Western nuclear family in which usually only the mother is available as a caregiver, much rides on the attachment relationship. It might be different in a social life based on an extended family (or a collective life of sharing with neighbors), where many adults might be available physically as well as emotionally to the child. Thus, the unavailable and fearful mother, who shares the burden of raising the children with some other adults, belonging to several generations, would exert far less influence with probably a different outcome in terms of attachment and subsequently social anxiety for the growing child.

Secondly, the way of life prevalent in the industrialized West today (organized as a marketplace) is relatively lightly structured, thus affording relatively great freedom to the individual to participate in what amounts to numerous competitions. This begins at a relatively young age (being accepted at school, making the grade) and never stops. The process also includes personal relationships (finding and keeping a mate) as well as a way of being (making a living), acquiring and keeping positions, and making a success of them. This might account for the fact that, although quite secure, life in Western countries is, nevertheless, attended by many anxieties, as reported by surveys. Might social anxiety be greater in individualistic and highly competitive societies in which no social positions are guaranteed, no alliances permanent, than in societies more rigidly stratified, in which one's way through life and one's social standing are to a large extent determined by kinship (i.e. on being the member of a family in a larger social structure)?

Group membership dictates decorum and important decisions, for example, the choice of marriage partner (see Rendle, 2008, concerning former nobles after the Soviet revolution) or an ancestral occupation determined by caste (e.g. a girl becoming a Hindu temple-dancer in the Devadasi tradition in Tamil Nadu; see Srinivasan, 1983).

Indeed, most social facts that constitute a way of life (e.g. property, authority, class, caste, nation) are established communally by being enacted (e.g. that paper money has value, that members of a "nation" are a tribal family of sorts, sharing a common descent and fate; see Searle, 1995).

As all activities (and psychological concepts) are inextricably related to the social context and social roles (see Zurcher, 1983) embedded in it, their meaning emerges from interactions rather than from individual experiences. Marx put it thus: "It is not the consciousness of men that determines their being, but on the contrary, their social being determines their consciousness" (quoted in McLellan, 1975, p. 40).

The significance of actions resides in the functional role they fulfill in social life (McLelland, 1975, p. 44). Explaining an action is ultimately an analysis of patterns of social activities on a cultural backdrop (Rubinstein, 1986, p. 304), some relatively short lived, others extending into the distant past. Even covert action (e.g. withholding information) is a phase in a sequence which ultimately concerns overt action (e.g. resistance, protecting others). Such analysis follows a dialectical logic. Actions are neither ready-made and clear-cut, nor independent; their definitive character emerges relationally, from sequences of interactions with the actions of others. Theoretically this outcome is best considered an emergent process (see Thompson, 2007, pp. 60–65), one that arises from a collective self-organization. In such a dynamic and spontaneous co-emergence, no single segment is decisive; part and whole mutually specify each other.

Two illustrative thought experiments

Examples may be useful at this point to illustrate the above abstract principles.

Imagine we can observe a scene through a contraption acting as a telephoto lens, allowing us to focus on a distant object by a narrowing of the angle (zoom in) or vice versa. Let us say that we focus on the face of a person but cannot see anything else. We can see his head inclined, his expression tense, lips twitching and the forehead glistening. What is happening? It is impossible to say. If we widen the angle, moving backwards so to speak, we would see the whole person. In this position we observe a man in his mid twenties, dressed casually and appearing somewhat disheveled. He is sitting slightly hunched, looking at his feet, fidgeting while holding his slightly shaky hands and his lips are moving. We realize at this stage that without hearing his speech (and understanding what is being said) we have no hope of figuring out what is taking place. Through our mastery of magic (this is an imaginative experiment), let us add sound. Although we are able to hear our protagonist, whose language we happen to understand, it is with great difficulty. He is barely audible; his speech is halting and meandering, delivered in a monotonous fashion. What is taking place? It is still incomprehensible. It seems clear by now that the solution to our bewilderment is to widen our angle of observation. Indeed, this allows us to see that the individual sitting in the chair is facing three men, in their shirtsleeves and wearing ties, across a large table in a bare and nondescript room lit by neon lights and shoddily constructed of cheap synthetic materials, typical of North American office decor of the early twenty-first century. As we linger on for a time, we grasp that he is responding to their questions and comments about his background, his studies, experience, strengths and weaknesses. From the content of the exchanges and the way they ended and our familiarity with the customs of the place, we realize that what took place is a job interview, following an application from the candidate. Strikingly, the interviewee acted as a supplicant, as if at the mercy of the selection committee, rather than a negotiator in possession of worthwhile assets, of value to the firm. Seemingly, he is attempting, against the odds, to make a good impression but in a disheartened sort of way, as if having concluded in advance that the struggle is futile and rejection almost a certainty.

Let us take another example and, since we are free to roam anywhere, why not seventeenth-century Rome? Starting in a similar manner, as with the previous example (it is a didactic exercise), we see a man's head only. His facial muscles are tense, his eyes are bulging and sweat is dripping from his brow to his beard. His lips are moving rapidly but, without hearing what is being said, we are incapable of making sense of the event. As we add the sound allowing us to hear the speech (simultaneously translated), we realize that the man is pleading vigorously and repeatedly that "he knew nothing and had no inkling of what took place." Although we are able to hear him plead ignorance, we are still baffled. We know by now the remedy for this, and in widening our angle of observation, we see that our sweaty protagonist sits facing three men behind a large oak desk on an elevated podium in an imposing audience hall lit by candles and torches. The walls are of chiseled stone and paneled wood, decorated with tapestries. The three men are dressed in identical black coats over white habits with crucifixes hanging from a chain on their chests; a large crucifix is found on the wall behind them. Who are they? Being all knowing, we immediately recognize their dress and the ceremony unfolding: these are Dominican friars conducting an inquisition (a "holy office"). From the exchanges, we understand that our man, who is dressed in his best clothes, is a bookseller allegedly carrying proscribed books (such as those of René Descartes, whom we have encountered earlier), propounding doctrines contradictory to the teachings of the church and therefore on the Index as heretical. He is fearfully at pains to convince the tribunal that the anonymous denunciation against him is slanderous, as he is ignorant of such transactions and certainly not party to them. Convincing the tribunal of his good faith is vital, as being found guilty could result in being given over to the secular authorities to be thrown into a dungeon, his property confiscated or, if he were obdurate enough, being burnt at the stake. The protagonist's nervousness, his desire to come across as respectable, his pressured speech, deferential manner to the court and indignation at being wrongly accused by malevolent enemies, all coalesce into an extended attempt to extricate himself from a situation fraught with danger.

But wait! There is some room left to widen the angle of our instrument a little bit more to gain an even larger perspective. This takes us beyond the solemn and somber audience hall to a stage with a theatre audience looking on. This new context reconfigures entirely the significance of what took place. The nervous man desperately pleading and the stern members of the tribunal are actors in period costumes, impersonating fictitious characters in a recreated imaginary scene from seventeenth-century Rome in the shadow of the Holy See.

In summary, in both examples, the extended interpersonal pattern (submissive) acquires its meaning from the social context in which it is displayed. Fear and interpersonal performance are rolled into one; the interpersonal conduct is not disrupted by fear, but is propelled by it. The submissive pattern and fearfulness on display was odd and inappropriate (i.e. socially phobic) in the first example. It was so both in terms of its contrast with what is needed in such situations (e.g. talking up one's abilities and credentials) as well as the – at worst disappointing – consequences of lack of success. By contrast, groveling while protesting one's innocence seems fitting and may have proven helpful (if anything could), in the second example. If one is at the mercy of the representatives of a leading institution charged with enforcing a certain way of life, being found guilty of breaching its rules could have nothing less than catastrophic consequences.

What is "interpersonal"?

Although I have argued for the appropriateness of an interpersonal outlook for an account of social phobia, from abstract principles, the term itself has so far remained undefined. The dictionary definition of "interpersonal" is obvious, but how is it actually used?

The term "interpersonal" appears in a variety of publications concerning psychopathology (e.g. McLemore and Benjamin, 1979) to draw attention to the interpersonally problematic nature of psychopathology. Historically, Sullivan (1953) appears to have coined the term "interpersonal relations," by which he meant behavior but also thoughts or dreams of someone. In keeping with this, anxiety – being rooted in expectations of rejection and derogation by others – was treated by Sullivan as an interpersonal construct.

The term "interpersonal" may be interpreted in two ways, which I shall consider. Its most common use in keeping with Sullivan (1953) is to argue that unsatisfactory or problematic social functioning is an important facet of psychopathology (e.g. Adams, 1964). In that spirit, Stangier, Esser, Leber, Risch and Heidenreich (2006), for example, have compared the "interpersonal problems" of socially phobic and depressed individuals. Crucially, such "interpersonal problems" are considered the *consequences* of processes within the person. Thus, Stangier *et al.* (2006, p. 418) assert that: "Interpersonal relationships are impaired in both disorders as a consequence of negative self-esteem, social skills deficits and dysfunctional social behavior." In a similar vein, Alden and Taylor (2004, p. 857) write: "Social phobia involves more than anxiety related symptoms. It is also an interpersonal disorder, a condition in which anxiety disrupts the individual's relationship with other people." Fernandez and Rodebaugh (2011, p. 326) concur, asserting that "Many studies indicate that maladaptive social anxiety has detrimental interpersonal effects."

In terms of units of analysis put forward earlier, the conception of social phobia that can be inferred from these writings is actually intrapersonal, as the pernicious social consequences are considered the result of defective hypothetical structures or processes (e.g. perceptions, expectations, interpretations; see Alden, 2005, pp. 168–169) within the person generating the allegedly pathological anxious state.

Strictly speaking, the term "interpersonal" seems inappropriate for such a designation, as the formulation neither includes interlocutors in the proceedings involving socially phobic individuals nor refers to a dynamic set of exchanges between participants. Inadvertently, viewing difficulties in the social domain as a breakdown in normal functioning renders them – as any mechanical failure – senseless.

In sum, such an *intrapersonal* reading of the term *interpersonal,* although historically sanctioned, is inappropriate at best and perverse at worst, for it fails to identify processes *between* persons to which the prefix "inter-" refers.

That particular use would be akin – to take a historic example from world affairs – to saying that Czechoslovakia in 1938, bullied by Great Britain to give up some of its territory (the Sudetenland), betrayed by France (its nominal ally), while cowering before a thrusting and menacing Nazi Germany that had recently swallowed up Austria – had international problems. Such a bland formulation – while not entirely wrong – would be both inaccurate and uninformative. Worse still, it would occlude understanding.

A proper reading of the term "interpersonal" ought to be literal – to designate a relational analysis of transactions or a series of interactions between persons (e.g. Hinde, 1976, p. 2). Needless to say, such a definition fits the interpersonal level of analysis chosen earlier. As one would expect, a true *inter*personal analysis ought to enable one to characterize the *relationship* between the participants as revealed in sequences of patterned exchanges. Crucially, that would entail viewing the actions and reactions of the socially phobic individual and the other participants as complementary and interdependent (Hinde, 1976, pp. 5–7). This would also make these extended transactions meaningful and purposeful (i.e. means to an end).

To conclude, what narrowly (or intrapersonally) appear to be the characteristics of an individual, seen dialectically, are the results of a dynamic interaction. Thus, the socially phobic pattern enacted by an individual is determined by his or her exchanges or relationships with other individuals in various social settings.

An interpersonal characterization of social phobia has further conceptual ramifications. Foremost, it concerns whole persons, who are agents in pursuit of their goals in the social world they inhabit. This social world (i.e. rule-bound institutions, practices and individuals that constitute it) frames the activities of the socially phobic individuals and gives them meaning. Social and therefore cultural context is an integral part of an interpersonal analysis. An interpersonal outlook, therefore, is necessarily both an ethological (Hinde, 1987) and an ecological one (Wicker, 2002).

Social phobia viewed interpersonally

How can we tell whether someone is socially phobic? From a reductionist/dualist position the answer ought to be obtained by the following reductive (and figuratively mechanical) reasoning. Socially phobic individuals are prone to be in a fearful state, commonly understood as a state of anxiety; I shall treat fearfulness and anxiousness as rough equivalents and use the terms interchangeably (the justification for this and an extensive discussion may be found in Chapter 2). Furthermore, the rather fearful socially phobic individuals display varying degrees of impaired social functioning. These difficulties are regarded as the consequence of a state of anxiety (or disarray), disruptive of social functioning. The state of anxiety in turn, is regarded, as we go down the causality chain, as the consequence of a defect within the person.

In keeping with a dualist outlook, the defect must be either of a somatic or a mental nature; the former obtained by observation, the latter by "introspection." Practically speaking, it would be a unique characteristic that would itself or by means of a derivative – as in pregnancy testing – serve as a marker flagging social phobia whenever apparent.

Needless to say, the existence of such a characteristic would have been a vindication of the reductionist intrapersonal outlook. Tellingly, despite considerable efforts deployed to that end, no such characteristic has been identified to my knowledge. At the conclusion of a comprehensive overview, I wrote (Stravynski, 2007, p. 349) the following:

no characteristics on any level of analysis (social e.g. skills deficits; mental e.g. cognitive biases or biological e.g. neuro-transmission) are typical of and exclusive to socially phobic individuals. Although at times (but not always) higher in degree, socially phobic responding is within normal-range. Similarly, no developmental characteristic, fraught as it might seem, in itself irrevocably leads to social phobia. In sum, regardless of the dimension examined at any particular moment, socially phobic individuals are more alike those who are normal than different from them.

This conclusion is still valid today.

Indeed, in a tacit acknowledgment of this fact, social phobia in clinical practice is established by means of an interview during which the patients' complaints (in medical terminology – "symptoms") are matched with a set of behavioral and experiential criteria deemed to identify social phobia as a "significant behavioral or psychological pattern." The main defining criteria of social phobia may be seen in Chapter 2.

Despite the medical discourse, the failure in identifying such a marker is meaningful in that it throws doubt on the widely accepted construction of social phobia as a disease of sorts. Consequently, intrapersonal commonplaces such as studying brain activity (body), or being privy to confidences (allegedly revelatory of mind) – although absorbing – are unsatisfactory, as their accuracy, let alone meaningfulness, is uncertain.

An interpersonal outlook postulates first and foremost that social phobia is an overall distinct interpersonal pattern (made up of manifold subpatterns) that can be characterized relationally. If that is the case, can such a composite pattern, which is likely to be complex, be recognized readily?

The somewhat complicated answer is that for patterns of actions to become discernible, an extended period of observation is indispensable. Put differently, patterns are extended and enacted in time. In terms of tools borrowed from the world of spying, long sequences of surreptitious filming are required; photographic pictures of momentary occurrences will fail in revealing interactive patterns.

Under such a type of continuous observation, seemingly unrelated activities coalesce and acquire a unity of purpose. Insider trading – an economic crime – is defined in terms of suspicious sales patterns around significant corporate events such as takeovers or earnings reports. For the discerning, patterns may be found in a host of meaningful events, for example financial crises in the USA (Madrick, 2011) and Napoleonic victorious battles (Chandler, 1966). Luckily for those intent on observing them, established patterns tend to recur (Chandler, 1966).

In the case of individuals, patterns of conduct are established in a similar manner; none other is available. In our private lives, we are able to characterize (i.e. get to know) those we come into contact with (e.g. spouses, friends, children, parents and pets) only to a limited extent. We accomplish this by attending mostly to mutually extended and repeated patterns of interactions; these are the bedrock of any relationship. However, reactions of each participant to other people as well as to the other's absence, although more difficult to obtain (and therefore precious), would be highly instructive. It is precisely this information that we typically lack. However that may be, the coherence of the relational pattern integrates its constituent elements into a meaningful whole; its effect on the other participants hints at its purposeful nature.

A non-human example may illustrate this relational outlook in which interactions and related activities, prompted by triggering events, are the main units of analysis. Cats are highly sociable animals with a proclivity towards forming social bonds (Turner, 2000). Domestic cats engage in extensive interactions with other members of the household. Most sleep and eat with their owners and greet them by the door (Bernstein and Strack, 1996). Cats are expressive (e.g. purring in contentment) and communicate their wishes (e.g. to be fed, groomed or let out) by vocalizing, posturing and positioning in specific contexts (Moelk, 1944; Bradshaw and Cameron-Beaumont, 2000). Given cats' propensity to form attachments with humans (Edwards, Heiblum, Tejeda and Galindo, 2007) and vice versa (Serpell, 1996), cats can be disturbed by a separation from their owners. Some, in fact, are unsettled even by household activities leading to an imminent departure (e.g. packing of suitcases).

Reactions include soiling (inappropriate urination or defecation), piteous vocalizations, states of prostration and fearfulness (hiding) alternating with destructiveness (Schwartz, 2003, p.1528). Seen as a sequel to a disrupted established affective bond, this cluster of reactions is labeled by veterinarians "separation anxiety syndrome" (Schwartz, 2002). Taken together, these responses are not unlike the human variety (e.g. Wijeratne and Manicavasagar, 2003).

In sum, "separation anxiety syndrome" is easily recognizable as a fearful relational pattern enacted by cats. It is precipitated by a threatening specific event: the involuntary disruption of a previous relational configuration (of dependency?). The attendant loss and uncertainty open up a range of threatening possibilities. It is relevant, I believe, to note that it is not in the power of the cat to prevent such outcomes. The accuracy of this interpretation is debatable. Cats cannot help in this respect as they are not keen on being interviewed (by strangers) and are positively averse to filling out questionnaires. However that may be, experimentation along the lines of establishing utility functions (e.g. Rachlin, Battalio, Kagel and Green, 1981) used to study preferences under imposed constraints, would undoubtedly demonstrate that the separation was not of the cat's choosing. Moreover, in a relational context, their reaction may be seen as a deterrent against further separations. When these take place they are imposed on them by the more powerful party or by unfortunate circumstances; the cats must bear the consequences as well as they can.

After this brief excursion into cat–human relationships, we are ready to apply similar analytical logic to elucidate social phobia. Our first step has to do with identifying such a group of individuals. To this end, let us carry out another thought experiment. In keeping with a naturalistic version of ecological psychology (Barker, 1968), imagine we could observe – undetected – anyone constantly, around the clock, day in and day out, even in their most private and unguarded moments. Blessed with sufficient leisure and omniscience, after a time – under stable conditions – we would find that saturation has been reached, as no new information has been forthcoming. At this point, patterns that have already begun to emerge earlier would consolidate, as various relational activities would begin to coalesce in clusters and repeat themselves, some tightly woven into contexts and others in distal relation to them. Imagine further, that unencumbered by any practical or ethical consideration, we could observe in a similar fashion countless numbers of people. At the end of this process, if we were to attempt to group these large numbers of observations, we would probably discover that the great majority of individuals lead an undifferentiated sort of life from their fellow humans, resembling members of similar social groupings. We could call the patterns of life displayed by the large majority group – the norm. We could name – by extension – the remaining and outlying minority groups as tending towards (statistical) abnormality.

How shall we choose, from the doubtlessly mixed bag of abnormalities, the one of most interest to us? As a focal point at this stage, the dimension most useful to our concerns would be social fearfulness – both as a pattern of behavior and the associated emotion (see below). Social fearfulness is a universal feature, especially among adults (see Chapter 3). For this reason, it is likely that on this feature we shall find two sharply contrasted sub-groups, each congregating at the opposite ends of the continuum.

At one end of the continuum, there will be those characterized by an intense sociability and (perhaps glib) charm, combined with bold self-assertion and flashes of ruthless deceitfulness, with scant concern for the sensitivities of others. The best term for this group is "psychopathic" (a construct put forward by Cleckley, 1941, and elaborated by Hare, 1993); to be found at the high end of the dimension of psychopathy denoting a characteristic distributed in the population rather than a synonym of criminality (Levenson, 1992). Crucially, the relationship between psychopathy and criminality is tenuous (Levenson, 1992); psychopathy – in varying degrees – is on display in normal life.

From our point of view, two important features of psychopathy stand out: intense sociability and a seemingly fearless, rather callous and manipulative pursuit of domination (e.g. Salekin, Trobst and Krioukova, 2001). Meaningfully, psychopathy generally bears an inverse relationship to anxiety (e.g. Hofmann, Korte and Suvak, 2009).

At the other end of the continuum, will cluster those characterized by a fearful self-effacement, reticence and passivity – let us call this end timidity – a mirror image of high-end psychopathy. These individuals would tend to keep a distance, but when cornered would choose conciliation and accommodation for fear of criticism and acrimonious exchanges. Such tendencies, in the face of situations where the dreaded exchanges are likely, are enacted and experienced fearfully.

The traits that these admittedly extreme tendencies exemplify are not in themselves abnormal, and are probably distributed normally. These tendencies become abnormal, not just statistically but also clinically, when generating distress and affecting (at times seriously handicapping) social functioning and undermining the realization of personal goals, either in the public or private domain.

We now must tear ourselves away from the glittering charm and promising excitement generated by the socially fearless and domineering (i.e. psychopathic) and keep company with the duller and less immediately rewarding socially fearful and reticent. Let us observe them at close range.

From our continuous but unobtrusive observation of all social activities, extended relational patterns would begin to emerge, coalesce in clusters and soon repeat themselves. We would then notice that these would be firmly anchored in certain social settings (e.g. the work place, university) and structured by social practices (e.g. team meetings, presentations to classmates) embedded in time cycles. Patterns could be relatively short (e.g. a brief presentation) or extended (e.g. the actual presentation preceded by numerous written versions, rehearsals, but also disturbed sleep, intestinal cramps with diarrhea, etc.).

Within the working period (or academic year), for example, patterns of exchanges would also repeat themselves at some stage, differentiated perhaps by the position of the interlocutors in the institutional hierarchy, possibly modulated by their personal manner (e.g. warmly affable or chilly and domineering) and by the type of relationship (e.g. impersonal or personal). Thus, within this period, patterns of interaction might be differentiated further by whether the individual relates to others formally as incarnating an institutional role within a hierarchy (e.g. a person chairing a meeting, a teaching assistant or a lecturer) or informally, as an individual with whom one is acquainted.

Similarly, during non-working periods, activities would cluster in relation to various social contexts. Patterns of interactions related to making a living, securing a dwelling place, daily living (e.g. getting to work; buying and preparing food) would be fairly repetitive and therefore well defined. Other patterns less frequently manifest (or in the extreme – mostly absent) – may be usefully grouped under headings such as leisure, family life, intimacy (emotional and sexual) and friendships; the pattern in these social domains would require longer periods of observation to emerge.

Clearly, observations of such scope and quality are impossible to realize practically. Realistically, only limited observations in clinical settings and partial self-monitoring by socially phobic patients in consultation are available. We shall generalize from the latter in the spirit of the former to flesh out the thesis that social phobia is best understood interpersonally. This will be presented in a series of propositions accompanied by supporting arguments.

An interpersonal formulation of social phobia

Social phobia – an extended fearful social activity of the whole person

Although a coherent whole, for analytic purposes, social phobia may be described as having an interpersonal as well as a somatic (anxious or fearful) locus. The former refers to the various interpersonal patterns comprising social phobia, the latter to the labile "emotional" state of the organism permeating the social behavior.

Within the extended overall pattern, these twofold systems of responding – although integrated – are imperfectly synchronized and loosely coordinated. The fluctuating state of anxiousness is future oriented, best seen as a tense mode of vigilance and readiness for action, arising out of a self-protective orientation towards the threat, shaping and sustaining the activity subsequently. Avoidance of threatening circumstances, in which one risks becoming entrapped, diminishes anxiousness; whereas evasive action, immobility, dissembling or other attempts at concealment are deployed in a state of heightened anxiety.

Arising in conjunction with the self-protective interpersonal patterns, the state of anxiousness inadvertently interferes with incompatible types of activities (requiring concentration, articulation, fine manipulation or acting with stylish elegance or abandon).

Both aspects of the overall social phobic pattern are best seen as processes and therefore extended in time in relation to the menacing social setting or event, modulated by the proximity and imminence of social danger. Evoked by and enacted in social contexts, the interpersonal patterns serve a self-protective function. Anxiousness – the all-purpose state of alarm permeating the defensive behavior and arising out of its interaction with the menacing social context – undergirds the self-protective tactics, while readying the individual to respond to further threats that may arise.

In the previous paragraphs, I have been at pains to describe social phobia as a unified fearful interpersonal activity in face of threatening social circumstances. Within this activity, two constitutive elements were discernible: interpersonal activity suffused with anxiety. It raises the question: what is the relationship between the two?

Seen interpersonally, anxiousness does not arise within the person (as a state of body or mind), supplying, as it were, the energy that drives the interpersonal action. Rather, the whole organism is in a state of fear while engaging in social transactions (and responding to them). Anxiousness, then, as is the case for any other feeling, arises out of the recognition of cues inherent in the interpersonal patterns of behaviors (enacted in or directed towards the menacing social settings). The anxious feeling, therefore, is responsive to both behavior and the context towards which it is oriented (see the theoretical argument for this in Laird, 2007, pp. 183–232).

Fearfulness arises with (and is involved in shaping) the interpersonal self-protective activity (while sustaining the process of its unfolding). To paraphrase Laird (2007, p. 4), fearfulness does not precede action, nor does anxiety cause behavior. On the contrary, there is strong evidence for the induction of the appropriate feeling by a variety of patterns of behavior (2007, pp. 49–63, 114–124). Boasting, for example, makes one feel more confident, as does standing erect (2007, p. 122).

In summary, anxiety cannot be described as an inner state (either of mind or the body) independent of the actions of the person and the circumstances evoking it. Rather, anxiousness is a dynamic process, reflecting the variations in the maneuvering of the individual in the face of ceaselessly evolving threatening circumstances.

Interpersonal transactions evoking fearful self-protective responses

If the fearfulness of the socially phobic individual is embedded in certain kinds of interpersonal transactions (in the face of certain circumstances), what are these?

As a general observation, humans are responsive to others; dealings with them induce powerful and complex emotional states, such as infatuation, anger, joy or fear. Fearful responses bear a close relationship to the dimensions of *power* and *status* (Kemper, 2000, p. 46) that are inherent in social interactions (see Kemper and Collins, 1990 for the evidence supporting these dimensions). Power and status are relational notions, describing the dynamic connection between two individuals or a pattern of relationships between an individual and others that form a group. Power is a construct tightly associated with the ability to control through force (i.e. to constrain, to thwart, to harm, to inflict pain and ultimately death). To accord status, by contrast, is to hold someone in awe as possessing superior qualities (e.g. integrity, beauty, knowledge, courage) or to single someone out – as in courtship – by means of high regard, rewards and attention. Correspondingly, to suffer diminished regard, or losing it altogether, is experienced painfully as loss. An authority inspires both fear and awe; it wields power and has high status.

Dominance (the enactment of power) and submission (the enactment of relative powerlessness) are played out in sequences of symbolic "scripted" reciprocal behaviors in humans and non-humans (see Barash, 1977, pp. 209–246). In humans, for example, a direct fixed stare is met with lowered eyes and an averted gaze, a fierce expression with a smile, criticisms (or orders) delivered in a loud and imperious voice are acknowledged (or obeyed) with bowed head, a submissive posture and softly spoken and apologetic tones (see Keltner and Buswell, 1997, p. 263). Dominance is recognized by deference; the dominant party is not challenged, contradicted or ignored. In many cultures (e.g. Cambodian), such exchanges are ritualized as marks of rank and are part of proper etiquette.

Although dominance might be difficult to determine objectively at every specific point as the sequence unfolds – it becomes plain who influences (e.g. compels or charms) whom and, correspondingly, who yields (if they do). Briefly stated, insufficient power or an erosion or loss of it in the present, or previously established disparities of power, are typically associated with feelings of fear or anxiety (Kemper, 2000, pp. 46–47). The degradation of status, as manifested by the manner in which one is treated, is associated with shame (e.g. one does not count for much) and humiliation (e.g. disdain from others). The worst cases of humiliation are those in which the perpetrator seeks, by degrading the victim, to exclude him or her from the group (Statman, 2000, p. 531) or deny their humanity.

In addition to yielding specific and immediate power and status estimates, even circumscribed social interactions convey wider implications (e.g. reflecting a deteriorating social environment, such as at the work place). The recognition of one's weakness for not having been able to prevent or soften the blow in a specific encounter, insinuates the possibility of similar defeats in future confrontations. One is thereby placed at the mercy of the powerful party. Such dependency counsels caution; keeping a safe distance if possible, submission to superior force, if not.

In sum, if the realization of cherished plans depends on individuals indifferent to one's well-being, or if one is made to endure certain experiences or to do things one does not wish to do, while being ignored or worse (say treated with contempt or one's discomfiture mocked) – one feels threatened, ashamed and humiliated. Unsurprisingly, this is the sort of social encounter most dreaded by socially phobic individuals. It could equally involve a fierce bully and his acolytes, a child who might insolently disobey a command or a sexually alluring ("overpowering") and fickle relative stranger. Needless to say such transactions involve fearful self-protective responses on the part of the socially phobic.

Social settings evoking socially phobic responses

Socially phobic responses are evoked by social settings where the above described risks predominate; what are these? It may be useful in characterizing the situations evoking socially phobic responses to construe the social environment as consisting of many social settings on a continuum. At one extreme are institutions and environments involving individuals enacting (often hierarchic) social roles publicly and impersonally, according to formal rules; these have a theatrical aspect and require a certain degree of stage acting and appropriate costumes and props (see Beeman, 1993).

At the other extreme are social settings in which the encounters and relationships are of a personal and purely private nature, enacted to more loosely defined social norms (e.g. friendship). The middle ground, then, would consist of public social settings in which aspects of private life take place (e.g. places of worship, weddings and celebrations at the work place). These combine formal actors acting according to prescribed rules (e.g. members of the clergy), others acting informally as guests, and yet others (e.g. friends of the bride and groom) led by their own lights within that cultural context.

The greatest threat is experienced by the socially phobic individual in a formal and impersonal setting; here they have to deal satisfactorily with powerful members of the hierarchy, while enacting a public role, under critical and widespread scrutiny, to specified exacting standards.

Public events of a private nature that concern membership in communities are moderately threatening. These often involve public rituals (de Coppet, 1992) and play (Huizinga, 1955), affirming membership in communities. During such events, the socially phobic individual is uncertain as to what to do and fearful that, despite their best efforts, they might be called upon to perform in public (e.g. a religious ritual, dance, sing) while all eyes are upon them. Thus, membership in groups that give so many individuals a sense of worth and connectedness is, in the case of the socially phobic individual, tenuous and marginal. Within the group hierarchy – formal or not – they usually remain low-ranking.

The least threatening setting is private life – encounters one on one with people known personally – especially intimate friendships and love relations that are obviously requited. Nevertheless, dangers lurk there as well. Parties with a number of people congregating (e.g. to celebrate birthdays), especially those involving strangers, are fraught with dangers. Among these, dominant individuals (highly attractive and/or confident) are liable to be unpredictable, haughty and possibly hurtful. Members of the family (or even friends) may be insensitive and try to impose unwanted obligations.

To generalize over and above specific settings, the socially phobic are at their most vulnerable when in a position of seeking recognition for who they are and/or whether they fit in. The experience is humiliating when, by words or other actions, the recognition is explicitly or implicitly denied and the respect they wish for is withheld.

In summary, social phobia is a fear of public humiliation or degradation and personal rejection that one is powerless to prevent. It is embedded in a comprehensive network of defensive interpersonal patterns, minimizing the risk of being hurtfully treated by others and the subsequent loss of standing or even membership in various social communities. The most common interpersonal patterns, the underlying fearful somatic state of alarm as well as the typical evoking social contexts are described in detail in Chapter 3.

Self-protection patterns I (acts of commission): active safety seeking

The overall self-protective interpersonal strategy is enacted by two inter-related defensive tactics (patterns of behavior): distancing, as a precaution against being trapped, and submission, as a precaution against being mistreated by powerful interlocutors or groups. As a general rule, the socially phobic individual establishes a safety perimeter, keeping the safest distance possible under the circumstances or staying away altogether – if practicable – from potential social danger. When by necessity finding oneself in inhospitable social surroundings, the socially phobic individual tries to keep safe by minimizing contact, staying at a distance, attempting to attract as little notice as possible (invisibility, immobility, concealment, propriety). Nonetheless, even with all precautions in place, he or she is all the while in readiness to take evasive action if danger materializes.

When involved in interactions with others, the socially phobic individual tends to act reactively (i.e. responding to the initiatives of others) and submissively (i.e. passively, humbly and deferentially). When cornered, with neither distancing nor submissiveness of much help, a flash of fearful self-protective aggression (e.g. exasperated anger) may be displayed – in the manner of a fighting retreat – as a means of escape from entrapment.

Over and above the content of the specific behaviors involved, the reactive conduct of socially phobic individuals in interactions with others tends to the complementary (withdraws when approached, offers justifications and apologies when criticized, grins and blushes when praised), rather than reciprocal (exchange of banter, compliments or threats, titillating gossip, teasing).

Self-protection patterns II (acts of omission): safety in inactivity

Social phobia has been so far been characterized positively, as an amalgam of self-protective interpersonal patterns (typically reactive distancing and various modes of submission), attended by episodes of fearful somatic arousal, enacted in and modulated by various social contexts. Less conspicuous, but necessary for a full relational account of social phobia, is the corresponding relative absence of active risk-taking (e.g. seeking the limelight, competing for the attention of high-status individuals, considering events complacently) and dominant behavior (e.g. negotiating, organizing others, issuing orders or threats, speaking plainly, decisively or deceptively, boasting, reacting angrily at being treated disrespectfully, being dismissive or fickle).

This does not make socially phobic individuals necessarily always subordinate and docile. Powerful behavior (e.g. deceit, subversion) is displayed occasionally. This is usually indirect, mostly through acts of omission rather commission. Thus, various passive acts of non-collaboration or obstruction, subvert or at least undo some aspects of unwanted schemes foisted on them by dominant others. Slanderous allegations go some way towards taking revenge for slights (i.e. belittling their tormentors in the eyes of sympathetic listeners). Their critical stance, however, usually remains furtive and is cautiously not made public. Competition, either in earnest (i.e. involving dominance and a degree of aggression for position or resources in a formal public setting or for the attentions of a desirable individual) or playful (i.e. games carried out publicly, dancing and displaying oneself), is a threatening activity as it exposes one to potential ridicule and is typically shunned.

Moreover, socially phobic individuals do not typically seek institutional power (although it is at times thrust on them); they tend to shun activities leading to grasping it (e.g. use of force, astutely manipulating others through outright lies or subtler forms of deception, running for office, exercising authority, cultivating the patronage of powerful backers) or extending it (e.g. building coalitions, engaging in deal making, plotting the undoing of opponents, dealing viciously and treacherously with former allies) (see Emerson, 1962). Whether the reticence about exercising power also extends to personal life and whether it is relative or absolute is not clear. Do socially phobic individuals, for example, tend to dominate the obviously powerless (e.g. young children) through coercion and deceit?

Overall then, the comprehensive socially phobic pattern may be depicted as one of fearful (relative) powerlessness, resulting in a some-what disengaged social life, lived for safety's sake at a remove, and therefore on the periphery. The socially phobic individual is highly self-conscious, prone to withdraw into oneself to ruminate, calculate and ponder the possible consequences of various actions, or feel resentful and conscience-stricken when things go wrong. Although relatively free from danger, such a life is limited in opportunity, for fortuitous openings and risk go hand in hand. Furthermore, as opportunities do not last, the prudence, irresolution and self-restraint of the socially phobic individual reduce the possibility of timely bold action. Seen in this light, socially phobic individuals are not failing to realize conventional social goals, but are primarily in pursuit of different goals altogether.

The impoverished (social) functioning of the socially phobic

That social phobia is characterized by a diminished social functioning is self-evident. The question is: what accounts for it?

The impaired social functioning of the socially phobic is viewed con-ventionally as occasioned by the anxiety that is a prominent feature of social phobia. Put differently, this suggests that socially phobic individ-uals are inhibited from acting proficiently or that they are deficient in or lack altogether the social skills necessary in order to function adequately. Although different theoretically, both notions amount to the same thing in practice.

On the face of it, this is consistent with the fact that social phobia might be typified by what socially phobic individuals fail to do (e.g. take a stand or take charge) and achieve socially (e.g. partners, friends, spouses). However, experimentation has produced results that go against the grain of the above-stated explanation.

This hypothesis has been discussed extensively in Stravynski (2007, pp. 225–245). A salient fact has emerged: in comparison with normal individuals, the laboratory enactments of public speaking or getting acquainted did not consistently point to definite deficiencies in social skills, however broadly construed. On the contrary, many elements of performance of the two experimental groups largely overlapped. Thus the statistically significant differences – where found – seemed more indicative of differences in degree, rather than in kind, of skillfulness and anxiousness. Nonetheless, socially phobic individuals were perceived as functioning less adequately than their normal counterparts (Stravynski, 2007, pp. 234–236), while not being altogether different from them in either skill or anxiousness. The puzzlement is resolved if the explanation is not sought intrapersonally, but interpersonally.

The impaired social functioning of the socially phobic is the indirect consequence of their typical manner of relating to others, described in previous sections. A widespread reliance on the defensive tactics described earlier, makes them narrow specialists in defensive self-protection. Fearful distance keeping, submission and passive dependence, clash with and interfere in the enactment of social and cultural roles that require different modes of relating to others.

Why this is so, is readily clarified by means of theatrical metaphor, considering social life through the perspective of dramaturgy (see, e.g., Brissett and Edgley, 1990).

It is immortalized by Shakespeare in verses from *As You Like It*:

> All the world's a stage,
> And all the men and women merely players:
> They have their exits and their entrances;
> And one man in his time plays many parts ...

The modern dramaturgical outlook on social life originates with Goffman (1956). As its name implies, it considers social life from the vantage point of theatrical performance, emphasizing *symbolic interactions* (e.g. Shott, 1979). Specifically, it relies on the observation that human beings reliably and predictably display patterns of behavior consistent with social *roles* typical of their social identities, within specific settings. Roles are best understood as designating a social position within a social and cultural system, as well as providing a script for its enactment (Biddle, 1986, p. 68). Roles, therefore, acquire their meaning from the network of other – complementary – roles within the system (Biddle, 1986, p. 70). Put interpersonally, a role is created and constituted by means of a web of enacted relationships with other roles, within the same social system (Walsh-Bowers, 2006, p. 669). Thus, plot and roles (or personal character permeating the role) are indivisible. While roles (or character) are revealed in the vicissitudes of the action, plot becomes intelligible only when roles or characters are enacted in predictable ways.

Within this perspective, performances are viewed as depending largely on context, the performers on stage as it were and an audience.

Performances on this view emerge from interactions with others and are constantly modified in light of the ongoing dynamic transactions.

Within the dramaturgical framework, role means both a part in a play as well as a script supplying the words and other non-verbal actions.

The theatrical outlook also illuminates other aspects of social life. First of all, it points to the manipulative tendency towards mystification in public life and its equivalent – deceit – in personal life, all done for effect. Secondly, it draws attention to the importance of costumes and staging venues as well as the desirability of careful preparations (e.g. rehearsals) to achieve the right effect. Finally, there is the distinction between actors and audience and between "front-stage" and "back-stage" conduct.

Of the three considerations guiding performance, the main one is how to act in a manner likely to lead towards a desired outcome. Another consideration is how to stay in character without making the role incoherent. Finally, an issue of some importance in the case of the reflexively self-effacing socially phobic, is how to project social status in one's appearance, as well as manner of conduct.

A theatrical perspective illuminates, like no other, what is wrong with the performance of socially phobic individuals when enacting various social roles. Nonetheless, it is a metaphor and as such has its limitations (see Wilshire, 1982, pp. 258–281; Walsh-Bowers, 2006, pp. 676–679). Theoretically, an additional account of self is necessary for a complete understanding of personhood (see Harré, 1991b).

Seen as an actor, the socially phobic individual is highly successful in a narrow range of supporting roles: usually of the self-effacing, stiffly reticent and intense, but ultimately amenable individual. Unfortunately, there is little demand for this kind of performance, however virtuosic; very few plots call for this type of acting. Occasionally, when unexpectedly thrust into the limelight, the socially phobic excel in the "shy role" – dramatically projecting an intense fear of doing or saying the wrong thing (see Scott, 2005), thereby wrecking the plot and moving the audience to writhe in embarrassment.

As a rule, such individuals take on leading roles only with the greatest reluctance. Requiring a projection of power, while remaining at the center of the action for long stretches of time, such roles (e.g. figures of authority or desire, romantic or moral heroes) are not their forte and their record of success in these is patchy.

When taking on these roles despite everything, the socially phobic – although over-rehearsed – are nevertheless poorly prepared, chiefly concerned with concealing their supposed weaknesses, rather than creating a dramatic effect. For this reason, although familiar with their lines, the socially phobic have no firm grasp of the play overall and tend to ignore the other actors and their parts.

When on center-stage, they tend to fluff their lines and be barely audible or otherwise expressive. Moreover, although occasionally their face reveals emotional states (e.g. pallor, blush or twitch) these do not fit the plot, and, at times, are at odds with it. Worse still, the socially phobic often appear in the wrong costume and tend to act out of character. Although inadvertent, the carelessness tends to undermine the plot, rather than advance it.

Being narrowly preoccupied with their own part and fears, and only dimly aware of what is happening on stage, the socially phobic actor is often deficient in empathy and fits poorly with the other actors, giving them neither support nor the possibility of integrating his or her performance with theirs into a cohesive ensemble playing. Nor is the socially phobic actor strictly playing to the gallery; he or she is mindful of the audience only as a threatening mass.

Little wonder, then, that the critics, although finding the play of some interest, consider that the socially phobic acting – lacking in credibility and commitment – fails to do it justice. The audience – although less demanding and not unsympathetic – is not quite won over. It finds the overall performance less than riveting and its attention wanders. Although it is more tolerant than the critics of the rather wooden and inexpressive acting – the public leaves the theatre with mixed feelings, many wondering why they have chosen this play.

The socially phobic conduct off stage is as awkward as the acting on stage. Instead of thanking the supporting staff, exchanging compliments and other pleasantries with the other actors, as well as receiving appreciative members of the audience, the socially phobic actor is tensely self-critical and wishes to flee to a zone of safety as soon as an opening emerges.

In summary, fearful submission and passive dependence as the main interpersonal characteristics leave the socially phobic individual ill prepared for social roles requiring confident dominance (e.g. stiff integrity, commanding or charming presence, seductiveness, generosity), self-assertion, as well as unself-conscious participation in ambiguously defined roles (e.g. guest at a wedding) in culturally meaningful group events.

This disposition, however, has further and wider consequences on the manner in which the socially phobic lead their lives. The inadequate participation in social life, combining relative powerlessness with dependency is also experienced as not being quite competent enough in meeting life demands in general, and therefore living at the sufferance of others.

Competence (an aspect of power), the ability to have the desired effect, is highly related to emotional states. High competence is associated with pride and confidence (e.g. Pleskac and Busemeyer, 2010), while doubts about one's competence, which are typical of the socially phobic, go hand in hand with retrenchment, resignation and fear tinged with despair (e.g. McCauley Ohannessian, Lerner, Lerner and von Eye, 1999). Needless to say, these shape (or distort) to varying degrees choices or decision-making (Dörner and Schaub, 1994; Klein, 2008), from setting goals to considering means, and finally selecting an alternative and implementing it.

The heterogeneity of social phobia

Social phobia is highly heterogeneous and cannot be otherwise. The integrated network of fearful somatic responding to threat with self-protective interpersonal patterns develops historically and emerges gradually, from potentiality to actuality, through an individual trajectory involving a great variety of life circumstances.

The abnormality of social phobia

Social phobia, as a fully fledged amalgam of fearful somatic responding to threat and self-protective interpersonal patterns, is distinct from normal interpersonal life. The constituent self-protective interpersonal patterns, as well as the fearful bodily state of arousal, however, are in continuity with and within the range of normal conduct and bodily alarm responses in a state of fear.

Supporting evidence

The main hypotheses find support in three studies.

In a series of case studies (Amado, 2005) conducted "anthropologically" with an emphasis on ecological validity, four socially phobic individuals were studied in their natural environment while carrying out their normal activities. Two shy and two normal individuals served as control participants.

Information was obtained by means of in-vivo observation, diaries and interviews with each participant, as well as two informants who knew them well. The spheres of social life covered by the study were as follows: work, friendships and leisure, family and marital relations. In other words the social functioning under observation spanned both social activities conducted formally and in public settings, as well as varying degrees of private life, conducted rather informally, sometimes in public and sometimes in private intimacy.

Overall the socially phobic tended to evasiveness, fleeing or outright avoiding social situations whenever possible. When feeling compelled to take part in an activity or remain in a situation, their presence was muted and self-effacing.

When pushed into a corner and elusive tactics were to no avail, the socially phobic individual could become belligerent – as a last resort. This bout of aggressiveness, however, was quick to fizzle out, and seemed defensive rather than offensive in nature – a means towards putting an end to acrimonious exchanges and to disengage, rather than towards intimidating for the sake of domination.

Altogether, the frequency of self-protective patterns was found to be in proportion to the degree of formality of the setting, and in inverse proportion to the degree of intimacy of the relationship with the people involved.

By contrast, both shy and normal participants tended consistently to seek people out rather than to keep them at a distance. In social situations involving groups, both normal and shy individuals would seek to integrate themselves into the main activity rather than staying on the periphery and looking on from a distance, as the socially phobic did.

In Kyparissis, Stravynski and Lachance (2013a), 132 socially phobic individuals, 85 single sexually dysfunctional and 105 normal participants filled out an Interpersonal Circumplex (see Plutchik and Conte, 1997) type of measure, adapted from the Interpersonal Check List (LaForge and Suczek, 1955). The answers to 88 interpersonal statements were subsequently arranged in a two-dimensional (axes) interpersonal space, reflecting power and affiliation. Each axis is defined by two ends: dominance–submissiveness and aggressiveness–agreeableness. Combinations of the two axes are divided into octants.

The main results (see Figure 1.1) were as expected: the socially phobic reported less power than did both contrast groups. As predicted by theory, the socially phobic were less dominant, more submissive and more self-effacing than were both control groups.

The comparison of the socially phobic group to the normal one on the power axis brings other aspects of social phobia into sharper focus. The socially phobic were less competitive, more mistrustful and more docile than the normal subjects.

In absolute terms, both abnormal groups, namely the socially phobic and the sexually dysfunctional, characterized themselves as powerless. However, whereas the sexually dysfunctional singles were in the adaptive area of the Interpersonal Circumplex, the socially phobic were located

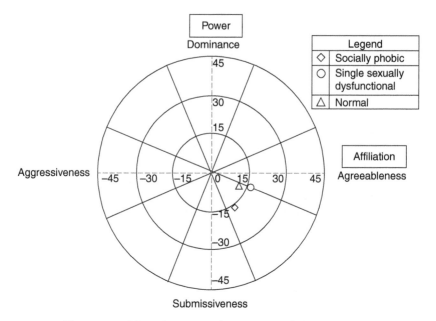

Figure 1.1. *Mean interpersonal axes scores of the socially phobic, single sexually dysfunctional and normal groups, plotted onto the Interpersonal Circumplex*

in the non-adaptive end, indicative of impaired social functioning, as predicted by theory. The normal subjects' characterization of themselves was a mirror image of both abnormal groups; describing themselves as powerful, they were located in the adaptive area.

It is noteworthy that in terms of affiliation, the socially phobic were similar to the normal group along the dimension of agreeableness–aggressiveness. They were distinguished from the normal subjects only in being less friendly (one octant). Compared with the sexually dysfunctional singles, who seemed to be rather energetically amiable, the socially phobic were consistently less agreeable, generous and friendly.

In absolute terms, all three groups tended towards the agreeable mode of relating to others (affiliation). However, while the socially phobic and normal groups were clustered together in the adaptive area, the sexually dysfunctional singles' mode of relating – although agreeable – might be described as excessive and non-adaptive.

A study carried out by another research group (Russell *et al.*, 2011), provides support for the link between anxiousness and powerlessness postulated by the interpersonal theory of social phobia as well as other aspects of the theory.

Forty socially phobic and 40 normal individuals monitored their social interactions in real life, rating these in terms of an interpersonal checklist and levels of anxiety. The results were plotted on a categorical version of the Circumplex and similarly defined by two dimensions (dominant–submissive and agreeable–quarrelsome), giving rise to four distinct interpersonal patterns.

On the power dimension, the socially phobic reported significantly higher levels of submissiveness than did the normal participants in anxiety-eliciting situations. Moreover, no submissiveness was reported by either group in a state of little or no anxiety.

In terms of affiliation, the normal subjects were either more agreeable or more quarrelsome when highly anxious. The socially phobic, by contrast, were only more agreeable and not quarrelsome at all.

In conclusion, it is worthy of note that the socially phobic did not report being ever dominant – even under the most favorable conditions. This fact lends additional support to the interpersonal theory of social phobia.

In summary, these studies, in aggregate, corroborate the main hypotheses derived from the interpersonal theory of social phobia.

Part II

What is social phobia and what is its nature?

"*Truth seldom lives where temples have been built for it and priests ordained.*"

Schopenhauer

2   The received view: social phobia construed as a disorder (disease) of anxiety

Social phobia as a disorder of anxiety

In Chapter 1, I presented a conceptual analysis of social phobia within an interpersonal framework. The main feature of this analysis is that it allows an understanding of social phobia relationally. It construes social phobia as having been woven (as it were) from, and kept in being by, extended interactions taking place within the context of various social settings, embedded in the way of life of the socially phobic individual. Seen in this light, what defines social phobia is the organization of the relationship with the social environment characteristic of such individuals.

Having argued in the abstract on the basis of certain premises, it is no wonder that one reaches wished-for conclusions. Are those the right ones, however? Does the theory fit reality snugly? Before finally making a commitment, it is prudent to consider alternatives.

The obvious contrast to the interpersonal and, for the time being, dissident perspective is the intrapersonal, at this time, the received view of social phobia.

For the sake of structuring an eventual comparison and rendering it meaningful, two related questions will be asked. First of all, what is social phobia? Secondly, what is its "identity," or as I will call it, its nature? Put differently, what is the category or class of phenomena under which social phobia can be best subsumed?

While the first question seems to require little justification, the question of categorization, narrowly viewed, might be regarded as overly pedantic and of little interest. I will argue that to the contrary, especially when considered practically, the issue is of great consequence.

Categorization is a fateful first step; once taken, it commits one a priori to a decided way of looking at almost everything. It will predetermine research goals, appropriate research methods and, finally, treatment strategies.

Perhaps the most accessible entry into the issue is to consider how social phobia is construed in public discourse and in practice. Three notions I deem central will be subjected to critical analysis.

The first two, relate to what social phobia is: a distinct entity characterized by an allegedly "disordered" (abnormal) sort of anxiety. The third, underpinning both, concerns the nature of social phobia: a type of disease.

As the issues concerning social phobia as an entity and a disease of sorts are formal and rather abstract, it seems best to start with the very essence of what social phobia is putatively "made of" – anxiety.

Social anxiety – normal and abnormal

Disease is a general and undifferentiated designation. In professional circles, social phobia is talked of as a disorder or a diagnostic entity, a sub-set within a large class of disorders characterized by complaints considered as indicative of anxiety. To clinicians, socially phobic individuals are familiar as those who typically seek help for an inability to control shaking (e.g. hand tremor), blushing or incapacitating surges of fear (e.g. panic), that are likely to occur when attention is on them, making it embarrassing and at times all but impossible to, say, eat, drink or speak in public.

Over and above such acute modes of distress, socially phobic individuals – when asked – report muscular (e.g. neck, shoulders) stiffness, headaches and cramps. Ahead of a dreaded event and while taking part in it, the socially phobic experience palpitations, heat and sweating, tightening of the chest, rapid breathing and a pressing need to urinate or to have a bowel movement. Some feel nauseous and vomit.

Adding insult to injury, such an overwrought state exposes them to the increased risk of drawing attention to themselves and giving away their turmoil and embarrassment, leading to loss of standing and perhaps disgrace.

A widely held opinion considers the various features of social phobia, described above, as manifestations (in medical terminology – symptoms) of anxiety (e.g. Mersch, Hildebrand, Mavy, Wessel and van Hout, 1992; Scholing and Emmelkamp, 1993). According to the DSM-IV, "Individuals with social phobia almost always experience symptoms of anxiety (e.g. palpitations, tremors, sweating, blushing) in the feared social situations" (APA, 1994, p. 412).

Although not always specifically stated, the anxiety is viewed as a clinical (i.e. abnormal) sort (e.g. Noyes and Hoehn-Saric, 1998, p. ix). In an official endorsement of this view, social phobia is to be found among the "anxiety disorders" in contemporary classification manuals (e.g. DSM-5, ICD-10).

The view that social phobia is characterized by an intense anxiety state, extends to treating self-reportedly highly socially anxious normal participants (typically undergraduate students) as a near equivalent of social phobia in many studies (e.g. Gee, Antony and Koerner, 2012).

From this "anxious" perspective, anxiety is a disturbing state of the organism, acting as a kind of driving force propelling experiences and behavior. Seen in that light, avoidance of fear-evoking situations would be understood as an anxiety-reducing maneuver (see Goodwin, 1986) performed in order to lessen the "immediate psychological instability" that "permeates all anxiety disorders" (Putman, 1997, p. 4). Similarly, the rather disorganized execution of verbal, manual or other tasks might be seen as illustrating a dramatic drop in performance typically associated with high degrees of anxiety (see Lader and Marks, 1971, p. 7).

While the hypothesis of disordered (or is it disordering?) anxiety is not implausible, it is, nonetheless, noteworthy that the presumed entities found among the anxiety disorders relate strikingly to four classes of *common* and therefore normal fears that have been highlighted in numerous surveys (Ohman, 2000, p. 575). These are (in descending order of prominence) fears of interpersonal strife, criticism, rejection; death, disease, injuries, pain; animals; finding oneself alone and/or trapped or amidst strangers far from a secure and familiar base (Arrindell, Pickersgill, Merckelbach, Ardon and Cornet, 1991).

The various hypothetical entities found in the cluster of anxiety disorders are viewed as having in common a predominantly abnormal anxious response albeit to differing evoking situations. Intriguingly, other patterns of abnormality (e.g. irritable bowel syndrome, dysmorphophobia, sexual aversion, bulimia–anorexia nervosa), however, that might be considered plausibly as anxiety-driven, have not found their way into the category of anxiety disorders and are classified elsewhere (e.g. somatoform, sexual or eating disorders).

Social phobia is obviously related to the interpersonal cluster of fears, highlighted in Arrindell *et al.* (1991), as the fear-eliciting situations triggering it are predominantly in the social domain. As is the case with other phobias, it might be also narrowly defined as a "a fear of a situation that is out of proportion to its danger, can neither be explained nor reasoned away, is largely beyond voluntary control, and leads to avoidance of the feared situation" (Marks, 1987, p. 5).

The view that social phobia is a "disorder of anxiety" has had a profound impact on treatment development in that most attempts at psychological treatment and pharmacotherapy have sought to provide help to patients by means of various methods aiming directly or indirectly at anxiety reduction. In keeping with this, reduction of anxiety serves also as the primary measure of outcome.

What is anxiety?

What, then, is anxiety and what is the meaning of its being "disordered" or abnormal? A striking fact about much psychological and psychiatric research of anxiety is that the term – although widely in use – is seldom defined (e.g. MacLeod, 1991). Nevertheless, a variety of inventories constructed for the purpose claim to measure "anxiety." Are they all assessing the same conceptual structure? If not, what constructs then are being assessed?

Dictionaries define anxiety as "A painful or apprehensive uneasiness of mind usually over an impending or anticipated ill" (*Webster's New Collegiate Dictionary*, 1962) or "A condition of agitation and depression with a sensation of tightness and distress in the praecordial region" (*Shorter Oxford English Dictionary*, 1972).

According to Lader and Marks (1971), "Anxiety is an emotion which is usually unpleasant. Subjectively it has the quality of fear or of closely related emotions. Implicit in anxiety is the feeling of impending danger, but there is no recognizable threat or the threat is, by reasonable standards, disproportionate to the emotion it seemingly evokes" (p. 1).

Almost identically, Goodwin (1986, p. 3) defines anxiety as "an emotion that signifies the presence of danger that cannot be identified, or, if identified, is not sufficiently threatening to justify the intensity of emotion." Fear by contrast, "signifies a known danger ... the strength of which is proportionate to the degree of danger" (1986, p. 3). Fear in this view represents a response to actual danger, whereas anxiety a response to a potential danger whose degree of likelihood is slim. Nevertheless, the anxious response may arise in anticipation to potential pain and suffering vividly imagined, however improbable their occurrence might seem.

The glossary of DSM-5 (APA, 2013) defines anxiety as: "the apprehensive anticipation of future danger or misfortune accompanied by a feeling of worry, distress and/or somatic symptoms of tension" (p. 818). Fear by contrast has an identifiable eliciting stimulus (p. 820).

Exceptionally among theoreticians, Izard and Youngstrom (1996) maintain that anxiety is a compound of fear (constituting a permanent component) and other shifting emotional states (e.g. sadness, guilt): "Although fear may represent a common element in anxiety's permutations, it is inappropriate to equate anxiety with fear" (p. 35).

The term "anxiety" is used in two distinct ways: either *restrictively* as a label for an emotional state akin to fear or *expansively*, as a hypothetical construct with agency. When used descriptively, anxiety is spoken of as an emotion, unifying its various phenomena and giving them coherence. When used in an explanatory fashion (i.e. typically positioning anxiety as a proximate cause), anxiety is likely to be presented as a hypothetical construct. I shall consider each in turn.

Anxiety as an emotion

What is an emotion? Conceptually, emotions are part of the passive powers – the ability to be affected – with which humans are endowed (see Hacker, 2004, pp. 90–121). The affections are usually taken to include agitations (e.g. being upset, surprised, thrilled by something), emotions (e.g. fear, anger, envy, shame, pride) and moods (e.g. feeling low, elated, irritable). Affections are not produced at will but can be checked, enhanced or diminished. Affections, if prominent, take on the guise of traits of character. These in turn doubtlessly reflect the way the person has lived so far.

Emotions are felt and, as in the case of fear, have quite definite somatic dimensions, both subjectively experienced and objectively observable. What makes these sensations into specific emotions is the transactional context with the specific individuals that evokes it. The evoking context identifies the emotion and determines for instance, that the slight tremor is experienced as fear, and not as anger. The feelings themselves do not have a precise location. Although linked with typical sensations (e.g. mouth dryness in a state of fear) emotions are not located in a particular area but are experienced by the whole human organism. Emotions may be manifested directly in typical expressive facial features (e.g. blanching) or behavior (e.g. frozen immobility) or indirectly, such as a life (re) organized so as to steer clear of fear-inducing interactions. Altogether, the human face is a key locus of emotional expression and, as such, a prominent means of social interaction. Emotions, then, are not sharply defined or independent occurrences. Rather, they are manifest as a synthetic fusion. *Strictly speaking, there are no emotions, only ways of feeling and acting emotionally.*

Emotions have a definite duration and cannot be interrupted and resumed at will. Emotions, typically, take a characteristic course. Emotions arise in context, in relation to specific situations, institutions and individuals. Emotions are therefore part of a relational process. Detaching emotions from that process reifies and subsequently mystifies them. Emotions reflect an evaluative appraisal of the world – especially the social world that includes judgment and standards – from the perspective of the individual's well-being. As emotions are evoked by transactions with a definite object, they are subtly influenced by what the individual knows or believes (e.g. jealousy, contempt). In that sense emotions (e.g. regarding infidelity or birth (origins)) and their display (e.g. giving vent or keeping a dignified reserve) are highly conditioned by social conventions. Although it is likely that that there is a natural foundation for emotionality in general, expressivity varies from society to society, between different historic periods and between classes within the same society. This suggests that human emotions are tied to specific cultural patterns of life. Certain emotions presuppose use of language and highly complex social and cultural arrangements. Remorse and regret, for example, are hardly imaginable in non-human beings.

"Paradigmatic emotions are such things as love, hate, hope, fear, anger, gratitude, resentment, indignation, envy, jealousy, pity, compassion, grief as well as emotions of self–assessment such as pride, shame, humiliation, regret, remorse and guilt" (Hacker, 2004, p. 200). They are experienced as pleasant or painful in varying degrees.

In summary, human transactions with others evoke powerful emotions. Emotions are meaningful only relationally. As such they register forcibly, both as communications to others and to oneself (Oatley and Jenkins, 1992, p. 59), indicating the way one is situated at a certain point in a trajectory of a given relational pattern. Emotions are ineluctable, strongly embodied and moving (i.e. closely geared to action). In recognition of their vital role in social life, emotions are artfully simulated (e.g. compassion) and painstakingly dissembled (e.g. resentment, envy).

Fear and anxiety – different emotional states?

As we have seen earlier, the mainstream distinction between fear and anxiety seems to rest on the salience of the trigger context evoking the reaction, the specificity of the reaction and its proportionality. McNeil, Turk and Ries (1994) by contrast see anxiety as "associated with more cognitive symptoms and less visceral activation and cues for its manifestation are more diffuse and changeable, relative to fear" (p. 151). Chorpita and Barlow (1998, p. 3) consider anxiety as the initial phase in an unfolding response, concerned with detection and preparation for danger, while fear arises at the "actual confrontation with danger." Bowlby (1981b, pp. 151–152) by contrast, regards fear as constituting the appraisal phase, itself a prelude to action. Rosen and Schulkin (1998, p. 325) similarly divide the extended pattern into a schematic "fear or anxious apprehension" phase – the terms are used interchangeably – when the first whiff of danger is identified, perhaps to be followed by a "defensive" phase, displayed in the face of actual danger. Ohman (2000, p. 574) recasts the difference as one between a "prestimulus" (anxiety) and "poststimulus" (fear) reaction. Epstein (1972), however, doubts that the nature of the external stimuli determines the difference between fear and anxiety. Rather, fear is tightly bound to action (i.e. flight). When acting on the fear (e.g. escaping) is not possible, the resulting emotion is one of anxiety, that is, an unresolved or undirected fear. In the final analysis, how the above-enumerated distinctions can be made practically and whether they hold up under rigorous and sustained scrutiny is not altogether clear.

The social context – most relevant to our concerns – illustrates well the ambiguities involved. Social settings, the participants and what they do (e.g. talking, listening, dancing) are very concrete indeed; we can hear, see, touch and smell them. The interactive processes, however, are not easy to characterize. With the exception of being brutally pounded into submission, it is usually difficult to point to specific moments when the social threat (eroding capacity to stand one's own ground, maintain one's dignity) actually becomes manifest. Social transactions are an unfolding sequence that can be clearly spotted only when complete. Is the queasy feeling then one of fear or anxiety? Does one worry about an unwanted pregnancy or the break–up of a marriage in a state of fear or anxiety? Does one wake up from a nightmare, bathed in sweat with one's heart racing, anxiously or fearfully?

The impossibility of resolving ambiguities such as these without resorting to dogmatic pronouncements, has led Levitt (1980, p. 9) to conclude that: "it seems prudent to eliminate, for the most part, any distinction between anxiety and fear and regard them as interchangeable terms with perhaps minor shades of meaning."

Anxiety as an agent

Anxiety as an intrapersonal construct is typically used to account for behavior. Within this perspective, the term "anxiety" has a dual meaning. Anxiety, on the one hand, is used descriptively ("narrow" anxiety); as designating an emotional state, linking various phenomena. On the other hand, this narrowly defined anxiety is considered only a surface manifestation of an underlying process (the "expansive" anxiety) hidden from view, endowed with causal powers. Such an anxiety is assumed to be a proximate cause, driving and therefore explaining conduct.

Such use of the term is widespread. Anxiety as an explanation of socially phobic conduct is prominent in the DSM-5 and is considered self-evident. Noyes and Hoehn-Saric (1998, p. 2), for example, speak of "somatic manifestations of anxiety." Alden and Taylor (2004, p. 857) state that: "Social phobia is a condition in which anxiety impairs the person's ability to relate to others." In a similar vein, Heerey and Kring (2007) investigate the "interpersonal consequences of social anxiety."

As a final example, Fernandez and Rodebaugh (2011, p. 326) assert that: "Many studies indicate that maladaptive social anxiety has detrimental interpersonal effects." One wonders where these demonstrations – as opposed to claims – are to be found?

How justifiable is it, then, to use the term "anxiety" as referring to an explanatory hypothetical construct?

Let me start with anxiety as designating an alarming and alarmed fearful emotional state, oriented towards the source of danger. Its salient manifestations are a bodily activation with its consequences, expressions of distress and related self-protective behavior.

The physiological arousal that is seemingly such a predominant part of anxiety, however, is non-specific and occurs in many "exciting" situations (e.g. parachuting for sport, dancing, gambling, attempting an elaborate deception, narrowly avoiding being hit by a car, an angry row, getting intimate with an alluring and sexually receptive partner); the state of anxiety cannot provide an explanation for it.

Furthermore, are self-protective actions, such as keeping a vigilant watch, literally jumping to conclusions (i.e. fleeing while taking evasive action or, "freezing" into immobility in an attempt to make oneself unnoticeable, and if everything else fails, appeasing or fighting when cornered), made any clearer by postulating an intrapersonal anxious state? Rather, considering these activities in context renders them transparently meaningful; the state of anxiety, while permeating the behavior, adds little to understanding.

On the face of it, this preliminary discussion of anxiety does not recommend it strongly.

Let me now consider anxiety as a construct identifying a hypothetical process or rather, an unseen system, postulated to underlie and give rise to observable conduct. It must be remembered that constructs are hypothetical abstractions, attempts at understanding by delineating and linking phenomena. Eventually it may be shown that what was hypothesized as a hypothetical construct is no more than an intellectual tool (i.e. an intervening variable) and therefore may not refer to anything definite in nature at all. Nevertheless, anxiety and other constructs are spoken of as if they were "things" actually existing within a person. Indeed the very existence of a label is in itself suggestive to many of a corresponding "object" in the world.

Needless to say, an autopsy will not locate anxiety or for that matter intelligence or introversion within the brain or any other organ of a person. Furthermore, attempts to identify specific biological correlates ("markers" – Hoes, 1986) or processes of anxiety (e.g. salivary cortisol, carbon dioxide inhalation, lactate infusion, levels of monoamine oxidase, among others) have failed to yield such an "essential or non-reducible component" (Friman, Hayes and Wilson, 1998, p. 139).

These results suggest that the naive attempts to find correlates of "anxiety" by a purely empirical approach are misguided, for such research is bereft of theoretical bearings. It naively and perhaps cheerfully assumes that anxiety is something lurking in the deep, ultimately to be caught in the net. This reveals the weakness of the hypothetical construct of anxiety to be found both at a conceptual and a theoretical (linking concepts) level.

The conceptual difficulty is the main one, as a theoretical network of concepts, at the heart of which is an ill-defined notion, is intellectually pointless. It may have its practical uses, however, if considered theatrically – as a rhetorical flourish – hollow but rousing.

First things first, to have scientific merit, a construct must be defined in concrete terms (acts), not words alone (Levitt, 1980, p. 5). Word definitions of anxiety are typically made up of constructs in need of definition themselves (e.g. danger, threat, arousal). Thus, such verbal refinements do not add much clarity to the meaning of the construct of anxiety. It is therefore a commonplace that there is no unequivocal operational definition of anxiety (Sarbin, 1964, p. 630).

It is, in part, the absence of such referents as well as the fact that most measurements of anxiety in practice rely solely on subjective estimates (even of objectively measurable features such as bodily reactivity) that leads some authors to question the standing of anxiety as a scientific construct.

In his thorough analysis of the construct of anxiety, Hallam (1985, pp. 2–3) lays stress on the fact that it does not have a unique and stable set of referents. On this view it is rather a *lay* construct redefined afresh by every user in pursuit of an idiosyncratic purpose in expressing complaints or providing information about his or her state of anxiety. Thus according to Hallam (1985), anxiety has no objective standing, but the (social) practice of complaining of it, for example, might have purposes such as deflecting social obligations (1985, p. 175).

In an earlier critique of the term "anxiety," Sarbin (1964) called for its discontinuation for scientific purposes. His key argument was that anxiety must not be regarded a scientific construct but rather a literal rendering of a metaphor. Etymologically (Lewis, 1967) the term "anxiety" stems from the ancient Greek root *angh* meaning to press tightly or strangle (p. 105). It was transmitted into medieval English as *anguish* (suffering of a spiritual kind) via the French *anguisse* (preceded by the Latin *angustus*), which denoted an oppressing or choking sensation. The modern word "anxiety" is a translation of Freud's German term *Angst* (that kept the original Latin spelling), denoting a hypothetical state of mind (Sarbin, 1964, p. 634) of unconscious origins and arising from inner conflict (Michels, Frances and Shear, 1985, p. 598). Thus, it is very much unlike fear that is presumably set off only by objectively dangerous events. First of all, the word that originally denoted an oppressive physical sensation came by analogy to be used for a spiritual (religious) distress. Eventually, the inner state of disquiet shorn of its religious connotation came to be seen as causing the sensation. It is for this reason that Sarbin (1964) considers anxiety – the state of mind of no definite referents but possessing *agency* – a reified metaphor.

On this reading, far from describing the workings of nature, that is, a mental structure with agency underpinned by brain structures and neuropsychological processes (e.g. Gray and McNaughton, 2004), anxiety might be considered better as the product of a historic and social process of (mis)use of words (Sarbin, 1964). In consequence, the term "anxiety" – although always the same word – will carry many meanings, determined by the particular definitions attached to it. As such, it is liable to be highly misleading. This applies with special force to attempts to measure "anxiety" and the interpretation of the ensuing results.

In sum the use of the term "anxiety" – normal or abnormal – as an explanatory intrapersonal agency is beset by conceptual pitfalls and unwarranted. Not least, such use creates a dichotomy separating the actor (anxiety) from the activity (anxious conduct).

These difficulties notwithstanding, the call for the abolition of anxiety, particularly in its explanatory role, has not been heeded so far. Despite the doomsayers, it is still leading a vigorous and charmed life.

Social anxiety or fear

Social fear might be defined abstractly as an apprehensive response to individuals or to social situations involving a number of people. Chapter 1 presented the case for considering social fears as tightly bound to situations where one is liable to be exposed to interactions where disparities of power predominate. These circumstances are determined by a confluence of interpersonal, institutional and cultural factors (see Parkinson, 1996, p. 663). This raises the question: is it legitimate to separate social fear from what might be an overall propensity towards timidity (i.e. responding anxiously to a host of dangers)? Several arguments – I believe – justify such a distinction.

First of all, "social shyness" is the largest and the most common factor extracted from responses to multidimensional personality inventories (Howarth, 1980). Similarly, factor analytic studies of various inventories of fears, consistently yield a factor (at times two) concerning social fears in relation to conflict, criticism, rejection (Arrindell, Pickersgill *et al.*, 1991). These are typically elicited by meeting new people, being interviewed for a position, addressing a group, taking charge or speaking in public (e.g. Gursky and Reiss, 1987).

Adult concerns are prefigured in studies of children's fears – adjusted for age – e.g. being called to the blackboard or reading in front of the class, being ridiculed or bullied, making people angry (e.g. Spence, Rapee, McDonald, and Ingram, 2001; Rose and Ditto, 1983). Thus, phobic patients of all stripes report similar fears to varying degrees; these are not exclusive to social phobia (Stravynski, Basoglu, Marks, Sengun and Marks, 1995a).

Secondly, social anxieties in the guise of fears of separation from caregivers (or familiar figures) and fears of strangers appear at an early stage in development (the second half of the first year) and persist – albeit in different form – in most adults (see Marks, 1987, p. 139).

Thirdly, fear arising from interactions with members of the same species (conspecifics) is a fundamental fear in non-humans (Boissy, 1995) and humans alike (e.g. in competitive interactions with peers or dealings with powerful members of a group).

The dangers inherent in social life

Is Goodwin's (1986) definition of anxiety – to take it as an example – as an "emotion that signifies the presence of danger that cannot be identified, or, if identified is not sufficiently threatening to justify the intensity of emotion" (p. 3) appropriate in a social context? It seems not. At issue is what is meant by "sufficiently threatening" danger.

"In nature," for instance, "the most important threats of injury that an individual encounters during its lifetime come from predators or competing or attacking conspecifics" (Boissy, 1995, p. 166). Thus, in animal societies (unlike in the laboratory where it is artificially induced by means of noise or electric shock – see LeDoux, 1996) fearful behavior is exhibited typically in response to a threat arising from their conspecific group members (Boissy, 1995, p. 182). In light of this, the main question to be answered is this: are there any grounds for suspecting that humans might injure or cause harm to fellow humans?

Personal experience and a daily perusal of newspapers from the most high-minded to the lowliest offer an unequivocal answer. Harmful acts ranging from the viciously criminal (e.g. murder, assault, rape, theft, fraud), via the immoral (e.g. deceit, slander, breach of faith) to the unscrupulous ill use of others (e.g. manipulative exploitation; shifting the blame) are daily occurrences affecting numerous people directly or at one remove. Although aberrations statistically, such experiences are nevertheless commonplace enough.

Some of the worst acts, either criminal (e.g. arson, massacres) or not (e.g. ritual humiliations, turning on members who question profoundly held beliefs, hostility to strangers), are carried out by bands. Bands are composed of members acting together (Canetti, 1981, p. 385), often organized and led by individuals who assume a position of leadership – formal or not. Men acting under orders are capable of the most appalling deeds (e.g. Kelman and Hamilton, 1989).

Human societies and their various institutions (e.g. places of work, government) are almost universally organized hierarchically (Mousnier, 1969; Hawley, 1999). At different levels of social stratification (Barber, 1957), much power resides in the hands of small ruling groups (Sidanius and Pratto, 1999, pp. 31–33); these may change or perpetually cling to power. Within that system – where this is permitted or even encouraged – intense competitions for power and resources ensue. The structures expressing and enforcing such systems of power may either encourage and reward collaboration or alternatively, through intimidation or even brutality – discourage and punish challenges to it (e.g. Corner, 2002).

Although not necessarily visible, these structures of power are manifest and exert tight control (e.g. as contingencies determining consequences or matrices of cost-benefit) over behavior (Gerth and Mills, 1953, pp. 185–374). A vast majority of adults (let alone children) are often subordinates to whom commands are issued, depending on the goodwill of those holding power over them. Furthermore, millions find themselves daily in situations in which a hastily spoken word or a misplaced gesture might have dire consequences (e.g. Conquest, 1990). The displeasure of the mighty may be expressed as anger (suggestive of darkening prospects), scorn (put-downs, questioning one's standing) and other methods of intimidation and manipulation (Kemper, 2000, p. 46), for "anyone who wants to rule men, first tries to humiliate them" (Canetti, 1981, p. 245; see Sofsky, 1997, pp. 82–85). Concrete sanctions in addition to symbolic threats might follow. Obviously, the consequences of crossing high-ranking individuals (e.g. employer, manager) who hire and fire, control access to resources and privileges as well as punitive sanctions by those belonging to a lower stratum (i.e. status) group (e.g. employee), may prove to be costly (e.g. Donkin, 2000). The actual consequences depend on the range of arrangements prevailing in particular countries or sections of society at a given time. In fascist Italy a favorite form of intimidation through humiliation was shaving off half a moustache or forcibly administering large quantities of castor oil to those who overstepped the limits (Paxton, 2004, pp. 61–64). Grimmer fates awaited the recalcitrant: beatings, loss of employment, torture, prison, camps and death (Corner, 2002).

Military society, for instance, "makes dissatisfaction with a superior, once expressed, a criminal offence; even 'dumb insolence' attracts confinement, while fomenting dissent is mutiny, in times of war an act punishable by death" (Keegan, 1988, p. 335). Needless to say, not being duly appreciative of or openly disagreeing with tyrants, let alone conspiring against them, puts one in quite a delicate position (e.g. Sebag Montefiore, 2003).

Unlike earlier examples (e.g. crime) that might be considered as touching on the exceptional, life in human societies involving stratification (i.e. power flowing from the top) with all its ramifications in terms of the hazards involved, are woven into the very fabric of social life.

In the interest of comprehensiveness, to the previous account must be added the occurrence of various organized (or impersonal) social systems of discrimination favoring the interests of some to the detriment of others. Thus, the dominance hierarchy represents the crystallization of an unequal distribution of benefits. Furthermore, no less organized brutalities and violence directed against members of its own society designated as enemies or foreigners are rife. These take the form of atrocities, mass executions, torture, war, dispossession, deportation, slavery as well as political, ethnic and religious persecutions and campaigns of exterminations that are sanctioned by the state (or competing political organizations as in civil war) and enacted by its officials (see Mazower, 2002; Pedersen, 2002). Within such political contexts, spying on and denunciations of individuals considered members of "enemy" groups by those (e.g. neighbors, colleagues) making a show of their loyalty are commonplace (Paxton, 2004, p. 230). Such occurrences, although not part of life in the rich industrialized West at the present and viewed as an aberration, were pervasive in it in previous (and not too distant) times (see Naimark, 2002) and could conceivably return. However that may be, this is very much part of the plight of humanity elsewhere at the present (see for example Green, 1994), let alone in the past.

Unlike the powerful inhibitions against killing conspecifics in evidence in most animals, humans engage in murder on both an individual and collective scale, often accompanied by the infliction of torture and degradation.

If such is the potential inherent in possible dealings with others, either as individuals or in an official capacity (enacting social roles embedded in a social structure), it is little wonder that most humans approach them warily.

Russell (1958, p. 122) put it thus: "We are accustomed to being the Lords of Creation; we no longer have the occasion, like cave men, to fear lions and tigers, mammoth and wild boars. Except against each other, we feel safe." The fact that among humans, "the weakest has strength enough to kill the strongest, either by secret machination, or by confederacy with others," Hobbes wrote, is sufficient to make everyone afraid of everyone else.

Social life as a necessity

Human life is universally organized in societies (subdivided into communities and other groupings) and within these frameworks it is intensely social. People seek safety in groups, as do many other species (see Marks, 1987, pp. 83–89). Fitting in and being part of groups is a necessity dictated by survival, but also brings ample rewards. It provides pleasure; it is protective, enriching (culture, higher standards of living) and the source of most human companionship (mates, allies), comfort and joy. Group membership is a fundamental social category, second only to gender, and the demarcation between the social group(s) to which one belongs and members of other groups is vital. Conformity with the group in dress, manners and opinions is an important social force (Bond and Smith, 1996). Standing out (e.g. by challenging customs or cherished beliefs) evokes resentment and hostility. This is especially true when the group feels threatened (Rothgerber, 1997). Being cast out from community restricts access to resources and diminishes prospects of reproduction (Buss, 1990) and survival. Excommunication and forced exile, nowadays in disuse, were once among the harshest of punishments. Membership in groups, however, extracts a high cost. Groups impose demands and diminish freedom. Invariably, group life involves conflict. As Buss (1990) put it, others "will injure you, steal your cattle, covet your mate and slander your reputation" (p. 199).

Nevertheless, sociability comes naturally to humans. Seeking to establish durable affectional bonds "is as intrinsic a system of behavior, as feeding and sex" (Lader and Marks, 1971, p. 13). Quintessential human characteristics such as language and self-consciousness are likely to have evolved in the process of social living (Humphrey, 1976) and have sustained it. Fearful behavior, for example, or at least some acts related to it, might be considered communicatively, say as means of raising the alarm and thus instigating the coordination of an appropriate communal response.

The survival of newborns depends on careful long-term nurturing by others. Conversely, the restriction of social contact during infancy and childhood (as well as other forms of inadequate care) exerts powerful effects on psychopathology across the life span. "Disruptions of personal ties, through ridicule, discrimination, separation, divorce, bereavement, are among the most stressful events people must endure" (Cacioppo, Bernston, Sheridan and McClintock, 2000, p. 831).

Thus the selfish striving of every individual in the ceaseless struggle to promote its well-being and existence, often in competition with others or at their expense, is mitigated by the thoroughgoing sociability and propensity to cooperate of humans (Glassman, 2000).

Social danger as an erosion in environmental conditions

Social dangers are concrete in terms of the very real harmful consequence they entail. On the one hand, it may mean being compelled to do what one does not wish to do. On the other hand, it may mean making enemies, becoming the target of violence, being vilified, suffering diminished standing, being driven out as well as being denied access to resources with an attendant loss of opportunity. The consequences of these might not necessarily register strongly at once; rather, these expand almost imperceptibly in time. Such a ripple effect unfolds gradually while gaining strength in the manner of countrywide economic decline, for instance (falling of hours worked, rising unemployment, rising number of unemployment benefits claims, jump in welfare spending, collapse of tax revenues). In that sense these might be signs of *deteriorating environmental conditions* in train. In the face of these, existence becomes increasingly precarious. Historic experiences, for example the mass Stalinist repressions of 1937–1938 in the Soviet Union (the "Great Terror"; see Conquest, 1990), provide a wealth of illustrations. In the face of worsening prospects, many strove to find some safety in detecting predictable patterns. In the words of a survivor: "We never asked, on hearing about the latest arrest, what was he arrested for? But we were exceptional. Most people, crazed by fear, asked this question just to give themselves a little hope: if others were arrested for some reason, then they wouldn't be arrested because they hadn't done anything wrong" (Mandelstam, 1970, p. 10).

Similarly to humans, anxiety in non-human animals increases markedly when environmental events of vital importance to them become unpredictable and uncontrollable (Mineka and Kihlstrom, 1978, p. 257). This observation suggests that although danger may not be specific or salient (e.g. a fire, a predator on the prowl), environmental patterns conveying dynamic information of an unfolding threat through distal clues (e.g. smell, moving noise, staring eyes) are detectable nevertheless (Bowlby, 1981b, pp. 109–111). This information would be inherent in the *patterning* of various elements foreshadowing deteriorating environmental conditions or responsiveness. In the long haul, the assessment of one's environment (and by extension one's prospects in it) as poor may lead to a general decrease in activity, including socialization and reproduction in a variety of animals (Lima and Dill, 1989) and doubtless in humans (Williams, 1998).

Thus, the dangers inherent in social life are varied and might not be, on every count, like losing one's footing on a high cliff. Nor are social dangers like being under well-aimed artillery fire, when sensing the earth shake with deafening explosions, being showered with falling debris, mouth parched, stomach in knots, bladder emptying, bowels loosened and legs gelatinous, one experiences a mind-shattering terror suffused with fear of pain, injury and death.

Social fears, however seemingly different, nevertheless speak of the implications of diminished prospects and capacities of survival, and, as is the case for any fears, ultimately concern suffering and death. On the battlefield, however, where armies function in small fighting units of strongly bonded men (Holmes, 1985, pp. 290–315), the social consequences of letting one's comrades down often outweigh fear of mutilation, pain and death (1985, pp. 138–142).

Bridging the two sets of fears (the social and of pain and death) is Darwin's (1872, quoted in Marks, 1987, p. 3) imaginative reconstruction of the origins of social fears.

Men during numberless generations have endeavored to escape from their enemies or danger by headlong flight, or by violent struggling with them, and such great exertions will have caused the heart to beat rapidly, the breathing to be hurried, the chest to heave and the nostrils to be dilated. As the exertions have been prolonged to the last extremity, the final result would have been utter prostration, pallor, perspiration, trembling of all muscles ... Now, whenever the emotion of fear is strongly felt, though it may not lead to any exertion, the same results tend to reappear, through the force of inheritance or association.

This example leaves one in no doubt that social dangers were once and still are very real and concrete indeed. Thus, fearing others to a degree that does not overall interfere with other activities is *normal*, and the attendant anxieties might be expected to be highly pervasive in the overall population. As we shall see shortly, much evidence supports the view that social anxiety is not the exclusive province of social phobia (albeit such individuals report it subjectively to a higher degree). Normal individuals (e.g. Purdon, Antony, Monteiro and Swinson, 2001) and patients meeting criteria for a variety of psychiatric disorders (and not only those that primarily concern anxiety) also report social anxiety. So do individuals suffering from highly visible medical conditions such as essential tremor (spasmodic torticollis; Gündel, Wolf, Xidara, Busch and Ceballos-Baumann, 2001), loss of hair (alopecia; Hunt and McHale, 2005) or disfigurement (Newell and Marks, 2000). These examples suggest strongly that there is a continuity of social anxiety between various groups and individuals. The differences between them are differences of degree, rather than of kind. The upshot of this is that the dividing line between a justified (i.e. proportional to the danger) degree of social anxiety and an excessive one is to an extent arbitrary, depending on what is taken to be the norm.

Furthermore, this would also suggest that social anxiety tends to arise in reference to and from concrete transactions with the social environment. On this reasoning, the view that social anxiety is, for example, solely or primarily a state of mind, e.g. "a subjective cognitive-affective experience" (Leary, 1983, p. 67), is unjustifiable. Social fear abstracted from its relationship to the social world is unintelligible; fear cannot be meaningfully divorced from what evokes it (Gerth and Mills, 1953, p. 184). The concrete social situations feared as well as the range of the appropriate responses to them would be embedded in a pattern of life or culture, typical of a time and place.

Individual differences

Given the importance of social life to humans and the dangers inherent in it, it is hardly surprising that social anxiety is a permanent fixture of human life. Individuals, however, do not exhibit such fears to the same degree. Undeniably, the subjectively experienced (but not necessarily the objectively measured; see Edelmann and Baker, 2002) levels of anxiety of socially phobic individuals stand out in their severity. How are we to understand such differences?

Underlying social anxiety and fearfulness in general is in all likelihood a broad genetic propensity, perhaps best described as emotionality; Marks, 1987, p. 153). Fearfulness is not a ready-made and enduring characteristic evident at the onset of life. Fear is not present in the repertoire of newborns and appears to emerge as the result of maturation (Izard and Youngstrom, 1996, p. 41). Furthermore, "in all mammals, friendly, affiliative, or positive approach behaviors emerge developmentally before fearful (and thus also aggressive) behaviors. Human infants, for example, typically first evidence clearly positive, affiliative behavior at around 6 to 8 weeks when the social smile appears; they first show clear signs of social fear at around 8 months when fear of strangers ordinarily appears" (Chisholm, 1999, pp. 31–32).

Thus, "emotions are socialized as they emerge in development; therefore, the possible configurations of any pattern are limited both by what society (and particularly the family) dictates and by which basic emotions are developmentally available" (Izard and Youngstrom, 1996, p. 41). Fear (or anxiety) therefore, is not a unitary characteristic but an amalgam of various features without any fixed relationship to the other. It is on the individual propensity – the raw material as it were – that the environment acts and which would mold the propensity from birth (or even before) and subsequently, in the course of development. The differences in the potential endowment as well as life histories (the process of molding the individual propensity including learning as well as unlearning) translate into individual differences in social fears.

Social anxiety viewed developmentally   The distress occasioned by separation from a caregiver is in all likelihood the earliest form of social anxiety experienced by a child (age range between 8 and 24 months, peaking at 9 to 12 months; Marks, 1987, p. 139). It is the first instance of a variety of experiences in a child's life as a supplicant, depending entirely on the goodwill of his or her caregivers.

Closely allied to this is a fear of strangers – mostly of adults but also of children – occurring about the same time (Marks, 1987, p. 134). "Despite widely varying patterns of child-rearing, fears of strangers and of separation are seen in children all over the world" (Marks, 1987, p. 109). While both fears (of strangers and separation from the caregiver) appear almost simultaneously, they are nonetheless different. At the appropriate age a child reacts with alarm to strangers even in the arms of the caregiver. Anxiety at separation from the caregiver is manifest even in the absence of strangers. The two fears are compounded when the child is separated from the caregiver in the presence of a stranger (Marks, 1987, p. 142). These two complementary fears are the raw material that, further transformed through life's vicissitudes within a particular society (and its culture) at a given time, will make up social anxiety.

Abnormal social anxiety   Although it is a commonplace to describe social phobia as characterized by abnormal anxiety and patients seeking treatment describe themselves as prey to it, it is surprisingly difficult to verify that assertion.

First of all, we face the uncertainty of whether clinical (to be used interchangeably with abnormal) anxiety is different in kind or only in degree from normal social anxiety or shyness. The first possibility is more or less unimaginable for we would not know how to define, let alone measure, clinical anxiety in isolation. The second option is intelligible conceptually and some means to assess social anxiety conceived as a continuum are available. Here another difficulty arises: where and how to set the demarcation point between normal and abnormal social anxiety?

Two examples illustrate the dilemma. Within various groups of subjects (socially phobic, normal community residents) there is a wide variation in self-reported social anxiety scores. Although, statistically, socially phobic subjects as a group on average score significantly higher than normal subjects, there is an overlap between the two score distributions. The upshot of this is that some socially phobic subjects report only moderate levels of social anxiety, whereas some fairly socially anxious normal individuals do not satisfy defining criteria for social phobia. The reason for this is that the criteria that matter most in order to satisfy the definition of social phobia are those concerning social functioning in various spheres of life. That is where the distinction between the highly anxious normal subjects and moderately anxious socially phobic subjects lies; the former function adequately in the absolute sense and far better than the latter, relatively speaking.

Furthermore, in a study of single cases of socially phobic patients undergoing treatment (Stravynski, Arbel, Lachance and Todorov, 2000), striking individual differences in scores of social anxiety emerged. For instance, the initial anxiety levels of some of the patients were lower than those reported by other patients at follow-up who, at that stage, were in remission. Both examples suggest that the relationship between social anxiety, social functioning and social phobia is not a simple one.

What do the above imply as to the definition of abnormal anxiety? An immediate conclusion seems to be that whatever definition and its corresponding demarcation point we adopt, it is bound to be arbitrary to some extent. This is not without consequences, for even minute methodological variations in "cut-off" levels tend to have considerable repercussions, for example, on prevalence estimates in epidemiological studies (Furmark et al., 1999).

The functional standard (i.e. one taking into account the wider patterns of social behavior) is far more significant than the severity of anxiety experienced at any point. Practically, the severity of anxiety notwithstanding, a "significant restriction on the ability to engage in deliberate action ... and to participate in the social practices of the community"

(Bergner, 1997, p. 241) appears the more meaningful definition of psychopathology, socially phobic or other (see also Adams, 1964).

Implications for the measurement of social anxiety

As we have seen earlier a variety of meanings are attached to the term "anxiety" (and "fear"). This implies that there could be substantive variations in one construct of anxiety or even a variety of quite different scientific constructs of anxiety. Inevitably, these would have been reflected in the different rating scales devised to assess the construct. Nevertheless, "there is often a general assumption that all of them assess the same construct of anxiety and that selection of a scale is purely a matter of personal preference or convenience" (Keedwell and Snaith, 1996, p. 177).

A clinician, for example, might be interested in whether patients' social anxiety is diffused and all-encompassing or arises in reference to specific social situations; whether it is pervasive or occurs in sudden surges (panic); whether it is long-standing or of recent onset; or whether it is proportional – normatively speaking – to the difficulty inherent in the evoking situation(s) or not. Typically, an inventory cannot provide answers to all these queries; it will usually privilege some limited aspects at most.

Furthermore, the phenomena that might fit the term "social anxiety" range widely. These could include "a specific mood equivalent to fear, feelings of insecurity and apprehensive anticipation, content of thought dominated by disaster or personal incompetence, increased arousal or vigilance, a sense of constriction leading to hyperventilation and its consequences, muscular tension causing pain, tremor and restlessness, and a variety of somatic discomforts based upon over activity of the nervous system" (Keedwell and Snaith, 1996, p. 177). To this list, a variety of associated fearful (e.g. self-protective) behavioral patterns might be added if assessment of fear might be understood as involving "three systems" (Eifert and Wilson, 1991). These might be measured at a given point or monitored at length to capture patterns extended in time. An assessment of the three systems might include verbal reports of subjective distress, behavior (e.g. startle, immobility and escape) and physiologic activation (e.g. increased heart rate, sweating – electrodermal activity measured as skin conductance).

Ideally, if the construct of anxiety or fear were fairly valid, the sampling of its different facets would converge. As it is, most "three systems" measurement of anxiety show rather disconcerting "desynchrony" among the different aspects of what a priori is thought of as a unitary fear response (Eifert and Wilson, 1991).

Is it any different in the case of anxiety in social context? Only one study attempted to trace the links among the three factors. In Douglas, Lindsey and Brooks (1988), 28 subjects complaining of being anxious in a wide range of social situations but who did not fulfill diagnostic criteria, subjectively reported assessments of autonomic, behavioral and cognitive systems. Objective measurements were obtained from observations of a social task performed in the laboratory: a short (5 min.) conversation with a stranger that was video-recorded and then rated. Pulse rate was also taken, while subjective distress was self-reported. Heart rate correlated significantly at .41 with self-report of autonomic arousal. It correlated, however, neither with self-reported subjective distress, nor with behavioral difficulties of any kind (verbal as well as non-verbal). The cognitive score correlated significantly with difficulties in verbal self-expression at .73, but correlated neither with non-verbal behavior nor with heart rate. It is interesting to note that there was a fairly high correlation (.73) between both objective and subjective measures of the bodily, but not with the other two systems.

In sum, the disharmony between the three factors observed in various anxious subjects has been found to occur also in the context of social anxiety. Especially striking, is the lack of association between behavior and bodily activation. Perhaps what these results reflect, is an artifact of the specific methods employed (laboratory simulation). Thus, the proper unit of observation might be that of behavioral patterns extended in time, rather than discrete observations of reactions at one specific point. Such studies with socially phobic subjects are still to be carried out. All the same, the results of available studies comparing socially phobic and normal subjects are in agreement and consistently suggest desynchrony. For example, specific socially phobic subjects (concerned only with public speaking) have a higher heart rate than generalized socially phobic or normal subjects. However, generalized socially phobic subjects overall behave far more anxiously than their specific or normal counterparts (e.g. Heimberg, Hope, Dodge and Becker, 1990; Levin et al., 1993).

Whether at stake is the measurement model of an ultimately sound construct or, alternatively, the very conception of anxiety itself, or both, is difficult to state with certainty. However that maybe, the slipperiness of the term "anxiety" and the lack of a theoretical framework to support it are important conceptual obstacles.

In view of the differences of outlook as to what constitutes social anxiety (e.g. does it include or exclude fearful or self-protective behavior?), there are bound to arise meaningful differences in the choice of kinds of observable events – the *referents* (McFall and Townsend, 1998, p. 317) – that will provide the concrete grounding for the abstract construct.

Whether in the different cases and despite the similar label – social anxiety – the assessment procedure or more likely the self-report inventory, would provide a measurement of the same construct is rather doubtful. Furthermore, as in most inventories behavior and bodily activation – while observable in principle – are estimated subjectively by the participants (as is distress), it is not clear what relationship these ratings bear to the same phenomena were they objectively assessed.

With these reservations in mind I shall turn to examining the relationship between social anxiety and social phobia. It is well to reiterate at this point that the studies that have attempted to shed light on the relationship between social anxiety and social phobia make little use of instruments with known psychometric properties designed to assess a *scientific construct* of anxiety. Rather, and for the most part, participants in those studies were instructed to rate situations in terms of anxiety (as well as fear, nervousness, etc.) that they had to define idiosyncratically – guided by their own lights and that they subsequently graded. Thus either by design or inadvertently the *lay construct* of anxiety is assessed in most studies. How the ratings based on it might be related to any scientific construct of social anxiety is unknown and remains to be clarified.

The relationship between social anxiety and social phobia

Are socially phobic individuals characterized by abnormal (debilitating) levels of social anxiety?

While it is a commonplace of clinical lore that socially phobic individuals are typically in the grips of severe anxiety, this assumption has been little investigated. The best way of approaching the question is by means of controlled studies providing a benchmark for comparison. Only a few are available.

Beidel, Rao, Scharfstein, Wong and Alfano (2010) compared 200 normal individuals with 119 generalized and 60 non-generalized socially phobic participants in terms of simulations of speech giving and social interaction. Anxiety was both observed and self-reported. During the simulations, the two socially phobic sub-groups had significantly higher anxiety scores than the normal group. Before the simulations, however, the anxiety levels of non-generalized socially phobic and normal groups were equivalent, while the generalized group anxiety score was significantly higher.

During simulation, the generalized socially phobic group had consistently higher anxiety scores than the non-generalized one, except for the self-reported anxiety during the speech task.

Hofmann and Roth (1996) recruited 24 (public-speaking) socially phobic and 22 control subjects by means of advertisements in newspapers. In both groups, participants who reported experiencing distress in either a single or multiple situations were separated. While participants who were categorized as "generalized social phobia" reported higher levels of anxiety than did patients identified as "single-situation phobia" (and similar controls), there was no difference in the degree of reported anxiety between the non-generalized socially phobic and the normal subjects, who typically reported distress in several situations. Altogether a gradation of degrees of anxiety was in evidence. Socially phobic individuals were not excessively anxious, nor were the normal participants entirely free of anxiety. Even when statistically significant differences obtained between groups, these were rather modest, judging from the average scores.

In Beidel, Turner and Morris (1999), 55 anxious children (mean age 10) identified as "socially phobic" were compared to 22 normal control children (mean age 12) on a social phobia and anxiety inventory for children (SPAI-C) and on a behavioral assessment task. This included an interaction with a peer, as well as reading aloud in front of an audience. On the SPAI-C specifically, socially phobic children scored six times as high as the control group (26 vs. 4), with the normal children reporting few social fears.

Similarly, "blind" judges observing the behavioral assessment tasks, rated the socially phobic children as highly anxious while normal subjects were considered little anxious. It is interesting to note that the phobic children rated themselves, as less anxious than did the judges. All the same, the difference in self-ratings of the socially phobic and the normal children was still significant.

In the previous studies, social anxiety or fear were considered states of mind and measured accordingly – as subjective experiences. Would the same conclusions obtain if social anxiety were conceptualized as a construct also designating a somatic process of gearing up for danger and in some manner measured objectively?

Stevens et al. (2010) compared 103 socially phobic to 23 normal individuals in a simulation involving initiating and maintaining a conversation with a stranger of the opposite sex. On a scale ranging from 0 – "no anxiety" and 100 – "worst anxiety I can imagine," the socially phobic participants reported higher levels of subjective anxiety than did their normal counterparts. Although statistically significantly apart, in absolute terms, both groups reported mild to low levels of subjective anxiety.

The mean for the socially phobic group was 37 out of 100 and for the normal group, 19 out of 100. The same pattern was observed in subjective reports of bodily activation and anxious social behaviors.

When heart rate was actually measured, however, no difference was found. In both groups, heart rate was above the normal resting heart rate (72) but within the normal range: socially phobic – 83; normal – 85 (*sic*).

In a similar study to Beidel *et al.* (2010) described earlier, but with slightly different categories of participants (Heiser, Turner, Beidel and Robertson-Nay, 2009), 25 generalized socially phobic and 26 shy (determined by a cut-off score on the Cheek, 1983 shyness scale) and 27 normal individuals were compared on simulations of speech-giving and social interaction. Anxiety was measured subjectively as well as objectively (e.g. heart rate).

Crucially, in terms of objective measurements, no differences were observed between the groups either before or after the experimental tasks.

With the exception of the speech task, during which the socially phobic reported higher anxiety levels than did the shy and the normal subjects, in all other tasks and measurements, anxiety levels of the socially phobic and the shy were equivalent but higher than those of the normal participants.

In Edelmann and Baker (2002), 18 socially phobic, 18 anxious but not socially phobic patients and 18 non-anxious individuals took part in four tasks: a physically demanding activity (riding an exercise bicycle); a mentally demanding activity (calculation); imagining a personally relevant anxiety-provoking situation; and a simulated (getting to know someone) social interaction. There were no group differences on any of the objective measures (i.e. heart rate, sweating, facial temperature) that could be construed as gauging aspects of anxiety.

Some differences, however, were noted on subjective ratings of bodily sensations. Both clinical groups, for example, rated their heart rate as significantly higher during the imagery phase, while the socially phobic group rated its anxiety higher than did both contrast groups during the simulation of social interaction. Similarly, both clinical groups rated their hands as more sweaty during the simulation phase. Altogether, subjective ratings of anxiety of all participants accorded poorly with objective "indices of anxiety."

Levin *et al.* (1993) compared the reactions of 28 generalized and eight discrete socially phobic to 14 normal participants, while giving a simulated 10-minute speech. Before giving the speech (baseline), the discrete socially phobic participants rated their anxiety (average 15 out of 37) as significantly higher than did the normal subjects (1 out of 37). The ratings of generalized socially phobic participants, although higher (9 out of 37), were not significantly different from those of the normal individuals.

At the end of the speech, the generalized socially phobic participants rated their anxiety as significantly higher (27 out of 37) than did both the discrete (11) and normal subjects (3 out of 37). By contrast, the discrete socially phobic participants had a significantly higher heart rate than did the other two groups. Still, heart rates peaked at 95. However, when baseline levels were controlled for, no differences in heart rates between the three groups were found.

In summary, on average the degree of social anxiety reported by socially phobic subjects was higher than that of the normal control subjects. Altogether reported anxiety levels were moderate. Where statistically significant differences were noted, these were differences in degree, not in kind.

Furthermore, when parameters of what might be construed as anxiety were objectively assessed, the differences vanished. While unlikely, it is impossible at this stage to rule out the possibility that the above results are an artifact of highly contrived experiments, bearing little resemblance to highly fluid real-life situations where much is at stake. However that may be, it seems appropriate to conclude that socially phobic individuals neither experience unique kinds of anxiety, nor react in alarm in extraordinary ways.

In contrast to adults, qualitative differences in anxious responses were observed in children. The meaning of these, however, is questionable. As will be seen below, social fears rise to prominence in adolescence. This is likely in response to new social demands placed on young people finding themselves on the threshold of adulthood. For this reason it is very much to be doubted that the socially phobic pattern is found in children. This, of course, does not exclude anxious states.

Altogether, the studies surveyed suggest that anxiousness, although a feature of social phobia, is not its defining element, let alone its cause. That this is the case is illustrated by an epidemiological study (Cox, MacPherson and Enns, 2005) of social phobia in relation to shyness – a rough equivalent to the lay construct of social anxiety, not lack of sociability. As the socially anxious, the shy are less socially active than the non-shy, while tending to be more reactive inwardly. In a sample representative of the population of the USA, approximately 50% of individuals meeting criteria for social phobia (lifetime) did not consider themselves shy when growing up. Moreover, only 28% of the shy women and 21% of the shy men reported social phobia over the lifetime (2005, p. 1024).

Is social anxiety unique to social phobia? Social fears among normal populations

Children and adolescents Bell-Dolan, Last and Strauss (1990) interviewed a selected a sample of 62 children (mean age 11; range 5 to 18) from the area of Pittsburgh without any psychiatric history. In regards to social fears, 22% reported a fear of public speaking, 11% a fear of blushing; 15% feared dressing in front of others and 15% were apprehensive about social contacts. At the 1-year follow-up, none of the subjects met diagnostic criteria for any of the anxiety disorders.

In Ollendick, Matson and Helsel (1985), 126 subjects (from the USA) filled out the fear survey schedule and were divided in four age groups: 7–9, 10–12, 13–15 and 16–18. Social fears (as well as other fears) remained stable across age groups. Among the 10 most feared situations, only one (number 8 – looking foolish) was social. This stability in the degree of fears, may mask, however, the fact that the content of fears change.

In a later study (Ollendick, Neville and Frary, 1989) involving a mixed sample from Australia (n=591) and the USA (n=594), subjects ranging from 7 to 16 years of age filled out the Fear Survey Schedule. With the exception of fearing poor grades that might be construed as a fear concerning low social rank, other most feared events concerned mostly physical harm.

The paucity of social fears (with prominence of fears of being harmed) among the 10 most feared situations reported by children and adolescents was also observed by Gullone and King (1993) from Australia, and Muris, Merckelbach, Meesters and van Lier (1997) from the Netherlands.

Westenberg, Drewes, Goedhart, Siebelink and Treffers (2004), in a study of 882 children (aged 8 to 18) from Holland, found that an overall decrease in fearfulness masked two contradictory processes. On the one hand, fears of harm and punishment decreased with age while, on the other hand, social fears of evaluation and falling behind in achievement were on the rise – especially in adolescence.

In Poulton *et al.* (1997) (conducted in New Zealand), only 2% of the children reported the same categories of fears after 2 years (from 13 to 15). The top four fears in this sample did include three social fears: speaking in front of the class, speaking to strangers and meeting new people.

In Brown and Crawford (1988), 1,119 university students (mean age 19) responded to a fear survey schedule. Fifty-nine percent of the men and 78% of the women reported one or more extreme fears. Of these, 18% reported an extreme fear of speaking in public and between 12 and 15% reported fearing being rejected, disapproved of or looking foolish. More women consistently reported extreme fears, both social and not.

Strikingly similar results have been also reported by Bryant and Trower (1974) from the UK, as well as Essau, Conradt and Petermann (1999), and Wittchen, Stein and Kessler (1999) from Germany. A factor analysis of the latter results yielded several factors, the most important (accounting for 70 percent of the variance) was one of interpersonal fears (e.g. being teased, criticized, disapproved of).

The dynamic as well as transitional aspects of fears are well highlighted in Gullone and King (1997), who carried out a longitudinal study on 273 subjects aged 7 to 18 from Australia. This is a sub-set of the 918 subjects described in Gullone and King (1993). The participants in the study who had been followed for 3 years, while reporting a decline level of fear overall, experienced an increased discomfort about talking in front of the class. The same trend was also apparent in a cross-sectional study of various age groups (Gullone and King, 1993) in which 7- to 10-year-olds reported a much lower degree of distress about talking in front of the class than did 15- to 18-year-olds.

In summary, the evidence regarding social fears in childhood is inconsistent. On the available evidence, social anxieties in children are slight. These become more prominent in studies involving adolescents and young adults, prefiguring adult sensitivities regarding loss of face and standing among one's peers and superiors.

Adults   In Costello (1982), a random sample of 449 women (age range 18–65) drawn from the community (Calgary) underwent the Present State Examination interview. Fears were rated for intensity and avoidance. A continuity of severity combined with a tendency to avoid was established. Twenty-six percent reported mild social fears without avoidance, 8% reported mild social fears with avoidance, 4% reported intense fears without avoidance and 2% reported intense social fears and avoidance. The highest prevalence of social fears (all intensities confounded) was reported between the ages of 18 and 25.

In Stein, Walker and Forde (1994), a random sample of 3,000 telephone subscribers in Winnipeg were contacted for a telephone interview of 32 minutes; the 519 who accepted were representative of the population of the city. During the interview the subjects were presented with six situations: speaking in public (either to a large or a small group), meeting new people, writing or eating in front of others, attending social gatherings and dealing with people in authority. They were asked to rate the degree of distress these might evoke as well as to identify the worst situation and what impact the problem had on their lives.

Approximately 61% of the respondents were of the opinion that their distress ("nervousness") was average or more in at least one situation; the most frequently mentioned situation was public speaking in front of larger groups (55%), followed by speaking in front of a small group of familiar people (25%). Consistently with these results, 85% of the subjects reported public speaking to be the worst situation in terms of "nervousness." Forty-seven percent of the subjects, however, reported difficulties in other situations in addition to public speaking. For example, approximately 15% found that they are apprehensive ("somewhat" or "much more than other people") attending social gatherings. But fully 46% reported nervousness about dealing with people in positions of authority. However, only a quarter (26%) of those feeling nervous reported a moderate (19%) or marked (7%) distress that interfered with their daily life. It is the latter that the authors considered as equivalent of those who satisfy criteria for social phobia.

In a reanalysis of the previous study, Stein, Walker and Forde (1996) found that speaking in front of a large audience as opposed to a small group of people evoked a different anxious self-reported response. Thus, 34% of the subjects reported being "much more nervous than other people" with regard to public speaking. Less than 12% of these subjects, however, rated themselves as "much more nervous than other people" in small groups.

Pollard and Henderson (1988) surveyed by telephone a sample of 500 subjects (half men, half women) in the St. Louis area. Twenty-three percent of the sample was identified as meeting criteria for social phobia (DSM-III), with fears of public speaking predominating (21%). When the criterion of significant distress and interference with daily life was applied, however, the prevalence rate fell to 2%. This finding implies that the bulk of subjects experiencing lesser degrees of distress and interference represent, on a continuum, various degrees of normality. As do the Stein *et al.* (1996.) studies, it does also suggest that the norm is a varying degree of social anxiety rather than none at all.

In Pélissolo *et al.* (2000), 12,873 subjects (15 years and older, representative of the population of France) responded to a mailed questionnaire concerning social phobia. Two sets of definitions were used (broad and narrow) distinguished by the persistence of avoidance and impairment of daily life. Fully 67% of the sample reported at least one strong fear in social situations, while between 3 and 8% (according to the definition) reported that such fears interfered with daily life. Clearly, the severity of the criteria is in inverse relationship to the proportion of subjects meeting these criteria.

In summary, social anxieties are widespread in the normal population. In terms of abnormalities, social anxieties are reported among those with visible dermatological conditions (e.g. acne; see Bez, Yesilova, Kaya and Sir, 2011). Nor are these absent in other psychopathologies than social phobia. Social anxieties are in evidence, among others, in psychosis (Romm, Melle, Thoresen, Anreassen and Rossberg, 2012), eating disorders (Sawaoka, Barnes, Blomquist, Masheb and Grilo, 2012; Pallister and Waller, 2008) and body dysmorphic disorder (Pinto and Phillips, 2005; Fang and Hoffmann, 2010).

Single-situation fears (e.g. speaking in public) are reported by roughly ⅔ to ¾ of the individuals questioned. Public speaking and handling individuals in position of authority are normally anxiety-evoking situations. Thus, social fearlessness is exceptional and, by statistical standards, abnormal. At the other end of the continuum, a similar principle applies: the greater the extent of anxiousness and the number of situations evoking such responses (and in parallel the severity of the functional handicap), the rarer the phenomenon. Nevertheless, even this severe amalgam lies on a continuous spectrum with normality. However defined, it can only be marked off it in a somewhat arbitrary manner.

Discussion

Considering social phobia a disorder of anxiety, or alternatively, a consequence of "disordered" (i.e. "abnormal") social anxiety, does not accord with the available facts. While, undeniably, socially phobic individuals lead, to varying degrees, a fearful social life, concentrating on this narrow perspective neither adequately characterizes social phobia, nor advances our understanding appreciably.

It is a commonplace that socially phobic individuals are prone to a fearful gearing up for a desperate (and losing) figurative struggle, either during various actual social interactions or while imagining them from the remove of relative safety. Specifically, this way of being is usually associated with a looming sense of threat, accompanied by a heightened self-reported activation of bodily processes (see Sapolsky, 1992) readied for self-protective action (e.g. fleeing or feigning), without actually engaging in either most of the time. Without exception, relevant studies show that socially phobic individuals, compared to either normal or other phobic participants, do not experience unique physiological reactions during threatening social situations, judging by their measurement (objectively and subjectively) in the laboratory (see section on "psycho-physiological responding" Stravynski, 2007, pp. 91–93; the Edelmann and Baker, 2002 study, is illustrative).

Although marked by exacerbations, these are within the range of normal reactions to threat. While statistically significant, the average difference between the socially phobic and various contrast groups is one of degree. Furthermore, the score distributions typically overlap to a considerable extent.

In sum, the socially phobic, either as a group or individually, cannot be characterized or identified in anxiety terms.

As a consequence, with the exception of perhaps avoidance of social interactions, neither specific socially phobic behaviors nor complex patterns are brought into sharper relief by the construct of anxiety. Even avoidance (or lack of it) must be interpreted with caution. For little avoidance or none does not (as is implicit in many assessment inventories) mean little or no fear; nor does it imply well-adjusted social behavior.

The dearth of dominant behavior in the repertoire of socially phobic individuals is another case in point. How would one conceive of this observation in terms of anxiety? Maintaining that anxiety inhibits social assertion would be tautological and redundant. The same reservations might be raised regarding anger and its display. How does anxiety seemingly inhibit anger (at being dominated and consequently mistreated) in some socially phobic individuals, but not in others, who are just as anxious (Kachin, Newman and Pincus, 2001)?

By contrast, setting the behavior (or its absence) in an interpersonal context is more helpful. Angry behavior (to be distinguished from stifled emotion) is a display of power, conveying a threat (as a mobilization for fighting). It fits the proposition that insufficiency of (social) power is at the root of social fear (Kemper, 1978a, p. 56). The interpersonal perspective, considering social phobia relationally (i.e. analyzing its transactions with other people within the social environment, in terms of power and status) transfigures the term anxiety altogether. From an *intrapersonal* concept, it becomes an *inter*personal or a relational one, embedded in a relational pattern. As such, it would inevitably be woven into the social life of a specific individual (within a definite society and its culture at a given time and place).

Be that as it may, anxiety understood intrapersonally (i.e. reductively and dualistically) involves assumptions that need to be questioned. The construct of anxiety – either as a state of mind or of the brain – is reified from the activities and experiences of the living human organism, engaged in unceasing dynamic transactions with its social environment. Similarly, intelligence (see Richardson, 2000) is used as a hypothetical construct with agency, driving, as it were, intelligent behavior. In both cases something located within is set up as causing behavior. Through this, the environment becomes an inert stage on which a plot, dictated from within, unfolds.

Such a conception is obviously inadequate. With the exception of some behaviors (taking alcohol and/or medication) that might be conceived of as attempts to self-regulate, most socially phobic behaviors (and certainly broader patterns such as submission) are attempts to come to grips with threats in the environment. These would be actions directed towards others, either as individuals or as social actors (i.e. performing social roles), nested in social structures and in reference to interpersonal (e.g. power or status) processes embedded in them.

Perhaps the most questionable assumption is one that considers social anxiety as a *fixed* characteristic that may be accurately and repeatedly measured. Since being socially anxious is an actively emergent process, it should be properly expressed as a verb. Instead, it is regarded as a *thing,* and accordingly expressed as a noun. Fittingly, it is often spoken of as something one has.

This is a highly inadequate characterization. Going about social transactions fearfully is the product of a process; it emerges from specific circumstances and is firmly embedded the dynamic shifts (in say power and status) in relationships and the context in which these interactions take place. It is therefore highly sensitive to situational variations and the danger inherent in them. Nonetheless, social anxiety is typically considered a fixed quality within the individual, regulated by a (figurative) mechanism that, when functioning properly, can be turned on and off (as well as modulated). In morbid conditions, this putative mechanism is presumed malfunctioning. In sum, various instances of a fluid process of social interactions, taking place on different occasions, are abstracted, reified and located inside the individual. Thus, the actor as it were, is oddly cut off from the activity.

Why does the notion of social anxiety as the hallmark of social phobia endure, despite its evident conceptual flaws and rather slight empirical support? Perhaps the outlook that assigns a central place to anxiety (social phobia as an anxiety disorder) is not formed in response to evidence alone. It draws its strength from being consistent with "an intuitive concept of disorder that underlies medical judgment and is widely shared by health professionals – that the symptoms of disorder are due to an internal process that is not functioning as expected (i.e. an internal dysfunction)" (Wakefield, Pottick and Kirk, 2002, p. 380).

On this view (social) anxiety is the expression of the dysfunction of certain (as yet unknown) regulatory mechanisms *within* the individual;

social phobia would be its ultimate consequence. It is consistent with a Cartesian model of the human body as a machine (Shepherd, 1993, p. 569), inhabited by a ghostly mind.

The most important practical consequence of the construction of social phobia as a disorder of anxiety is that the remedies that have been devised for it, on the whole, seek to reduce anxiety. Consequently, outcomes are assessed and claims to efficacy are formulated mainly in terms of anxiety. This flows from the rationale that difficulties in social functioning are the consequence of morbid anxiety. Anxiety is, in turn, considered a consequence of a malfunctioning, either physical (i.e. neurobiological) or mental (i.e. cognitive). This way of construing social phobia is in keeping with a medical view, separating the disease (within) from the resulting social impairment (measured as a diminished quality of life) displayed in the environment. Whether a reified social phobia may be detached from the manifest problematic social functioning of such individuals is questionable.

In the final analysis, although the view that social phobia is a *disorder* of anxiety might appear plausible on the face of it, the evidence in support of it is slim at best, even when taking the subjective estimates (of uncertain validity) at face value. In absolute terms, no specific sort of socially phobic (or abnormal) anxiety has been identified. Palpitations, trembling, sweating and blushing, for example, are self-reported not only by socially phobic subjects, but also by various other categories of individuals (e.g. normal, shy, other anxiety disorders). In quantitative terms, no specific demarcation point cuts abnormal social anxiety off from the normal sort. Thus, although socially phobic individuals typically rate themselves subjectively as more anxious than do normal individuals, the difference between the two is one of degree rather than of kind. This also applies to the various subtypes of social phobia. Additionally, if intermediate degrees of severity (sub-clinical fears) are taken into account (Chavira, Stein and Malcarne, 2002), the results become consistent with a continuum of social fears, with socially phobic individuals as a group at its high end. Furthermore, when physiological indices of anxiety (admittedly evoked by somewhat artificial social tasks) are objectively measured in the laboratory, the differences – significant on the continuum of subjective anxiety – blur (e.g. Gerlach, Wilhelm, Gruber and Roth, 2001) and in some studies vanish altogether (e.g. Edelmann and Baker, 2002).

In a survey seen earlier (Stein *et al.*, 1994), 85% of the 519 subjects (a sample representative of the population of Winnipeg) identified public speaking – a typical socially phobic concern – as the worst situation in terms of "nervousness." While the degree of distress varied, it is obvious that "nervousness" in such social situations is the norm. Similarly, musicians and singers for instance, commonly report "stage fright" (performance anxiety) and so do other artists; for a minority, the problem is handicapping (see Lederman, 1989).

Thus, social anxiety, unlike social phobia, is commonplace. It is prefigured to some extent in childhood, increasingly evident in adolescence and fully manifest in adulthood, evoked by dealings with authorities and a variety of socially competitive activities. Given its ubiquity, social anxiety could plausibly be considered an adaptive trait, conferring a protective advantage from an evolutionary point of view (see Gilbert, 2001). Social anxiety or sensitivity (Stravynski, Basoglu, Marks, Sengun and Marks, 1995b) about evoking displeasure in others is protective of the individual and doubtless plays a role in reducing strife and hence increases cohesion within the group. Viewed from that vantage point, the maladaptive interpersonal pattern of social phobia might be seen as the extended misuse of highly adaptive short-term defensive tactics.

Altogether, socially phobic individuals do not strike one as obviously abnormal in any specific comparison, either in their anxious responses conceived either narrowly (e.g. tremor, pallor, sweat) or broadly (e.g. avoidance, hiding, immobility). Nor are the threatening social situations evoking these abnormal. The differences that have been identified (in self-reported subjective distress) are exacerbations (at times extreme) of apparently normal tendencies. Socially phobic individuals differ markedly from normal ones not so much in terms of the anxiety reactions as such or fear in concrete interactions (e.g. when evaluated) but cumulatively, as a sequence of various self-protective patterns of conduct displayed at different times in various spheres of social life. As proposed in Chapter 1, this web of many continuous acts combines in an extended pattern of maladjustment and fearful distress we identify as social phobia. Only socially phobic individuals enact this overall pattern; the various elements constituting the socially phobic pattern are within normal range.

In conclusion, rather than being the cause of social phobia, anxiety construed interpersonally is its emotional facet. It emanates from, suffuses and supports the socially phobic pattern of behavior, rather than generating it. As such, it is not unique to the socially phobic. These can neither be described nor identified in anxiety terms.

Social phobia as an entity

Both the *International Classification of Disease* (10th edition), compiled by the World Health Organization (1992), and the *Diagnostic and Statistical Manual* (5th edition), published by the American Psychiatric Association

Table 2.1. *Main defining criteria of social phobia in the International Classification of Diseases (ICD-10) (World Health Organization, 1992) and the Diagnostic and Statistical Manual of Mental Disorders (DSM-5) (APA, 2013)*

ICD-10	DSM-5
Either (1) marked fear of drawing attention to oneself, or fear of behaving in a way that is embarrassing or humiliating or (2) marked avoidance of situations such as eating/speaking in public, meeting unknown people in public, dealing with authority.	Marked and persistent fear of one or more social situations in which the person is exposed to unfamiliar people or scrutiny by others that might attract negative evaluation.
At least two complaints out of the following list: palpitations, sweating, trembling, dry mouth, difficulty in breathing, choking feelings, chest pain, nausea, dizziness, unreality, fear of losing control or dying, hot flushes, numbness or tingling; and at least one of the following: blushing, shaking, fear of vomiting, micturition or defecation.	Exposure to social situations elicits anxious responses. The feared social situations are avoided or endured with intense anxiety.
Complaints restricted to, or predominate in, feared situations or when envisaging those. Significant emotional distress created by avoidance or anxious experiences.	Fear, anxiety and avoidance in feared situations impair social functioning. Fear or anxiety is disproportionate to the actual social threat.
Significant emotional distress is engendered by anxious experiences or avoidance; these are recognized to be excessive and unreasonable.	

(2013), list social phobia as one of the "mental disorders." (The defining criteria may be found in Table 2.1.)

Although the titles of these field manuals would suggest that social phobia is a disease among others, bafflingly mental disorders are defined as a "significant behavioral or psychological pattern" associated with *distress* and *impaired functioning*.

Be that as it may, this would signify that social phobia is an independent entity found in nature, sharply defined, clearly demarcated, internally consistent and running a "natural course." Although I shall argue later that social phobia cannot be considered literally a disease, the question nevertheless remains: is it a natural and coherent entity?

The necessity of asking such questions arises from the somewhat uncertain nature of what is actually found in the classification manuals (see Boysen, 2007 for a searching discussion).

According to Frances and some of his fellow creators of the DSM-IV (Frances *et al.*, 1994), "Most, if not all, mental disorders are better conceived as no more than (but also no less than) valuable heuristic constructs. Psychiatric constructs as we know them are not well-defined entities that describe nature on the hoof" (1994, p. 210).

Social phobia then, as one of the hypothetical entities found in the diagnostic manuals, is best seen as a tentative "heuristic construct." Although the fact that it is listed in diagnostic manuals since the advent of DSM-III lends it a certain dignity, it does not, however, confer on it a seal of validity. It is best construed as a hypothesis considered by a group of experts to be worthwhile and, on current evidence, promising enough to be put to further tests.

The fact that there is a readily available label while what it identifies is uncertain, poses its own dangers. Namely, according to J. S. Mill (2002), it is of committing the fallacy "to believe that whatever received a name must be an entity or a being, having an independent existence of its own. And if no real entity answering to the name could be found, men did not for that reason suppose that none existed, but imagined that it was something peculiarly abstruse and mysterious." Anxiety, as an explanatory construct, may be a case in point.

The validation of a construct

How can we tell if a hypothetical construct denotes a valid entity? Various strategies have been proposed for the validation of hypothetical constructs (e.g. Blashfield and Livesley, 1991; Nelson-Gray, 1991; Gorenstein, 1992). All draw on the indispensable work of Cronbach and Meehl (1955), who have outlined the rationale as well as the methods to be used for the purpose of validation of instruments (tests) measuring psychological characteristics (constructs). Such an approach may be usefully applied to psychopathological entities (Morey, 1991), for in both cases the end is the same: developing, measuring and validating a concept denoting a pattern of psychological functioning.

A somewhat different approach to validation identified as "clinical" (Kendell, 1989) or "diagnostic" (Robins and Guze, 1970) has been outlined from a medical perspective. It does share some features with the psychological approach to construct validation, but differs from it in its relative unconcern with the issue of validity of measurement and its emphasis on "etiology" as the ultimate step in validation. This is hardly a practical strategy; what causes social phobia is likely to be both elusive and contentious as it depends on various philosophical assumptions. Furthermore, an entity of uncertain validity can hardly be expected to yield clear-cut causes. It seems necessary and prudent therefore, to separate the question of whether social phobia is indeed an entity, from that of what may cause it.

To answer the question, most published research on social phobia up to 2006 has been examined and synthesized. The procedure, the analytical framework and the results are described in Stravynski (2007, pp. 75–139). Subsequent publications since then broadly support the conclusions reached.[1]

The main conclusions of this survey were fitted into three categories: supporting, ambiguous and undermining evidence.

Supporting evidence

A self-reported socially phobic pattern of responding can be fairly accurately agreed on from interviewing the subject by either unstructured (as typical to clinical practice) or structured interviews incorporating standard questions based on the defining criteria found in manuals.

As a construct, social phobia was consistently associated with difficulties in more social situations with more severely anxious reactions to them, regardless of measuring instrument.

On the one hand, the social fears characterizing social phobia are in varying degrees widely shared with normal individuals and other anxiety disorders, especially agoraphobia. On the other hand, these are, nevertheless, highly distinguishable not only in degree but as a kind whose configuration of fears represents a pattern. I consider this the strongest unequivocal single finding.

As expected, lower employment and marriage rates and fewer friends characterize social phobia; these are the gross features of an unsatisfactory pattern of social functioning. In the past lurk more than common difficulties at school.

Social phobia has a fairly distinctive age range of onset (15 to 18) and equal sex distribution; it usually precedes other anxiety, affective and alcoholism disorders with which it has affinities.

---

[1] Content validity (e.g. Crippa et al., 2008); criterion validity – concurrent (e.g. Garner, Baldwin, Bradley and Mogg, 2009); criterion validity – predictive (e.g. Chronis-Tuscano et al., 2009); construct validity (e.g. Chou, 2009; Leray et al., 2011; Ohayon and Schatzberg, 2010).

Ambiguous supporting evidence

Disconcertingly, concordance rates between different ways of identifying social phobia (e.g. clinical interview vs. structured interview) are rather modest. Furthermore, the accuracy of observation of specific features of social phobia (as opposed to gross patterns) was rather low.

Similarly, the accuracy in identifying social phobia over time was less than that obtained by two interviewers operating simultaneously. Although acceptable, this is worrisome. This inconsistency might indicate an error of measurement.

Alternatively, and in my opinion more likely, it might be interpreted as questioning the stability of socially phobic features and perhaps of the socially phobic pattern altogether. Another clue to this may be found in the difference between present and lifetime rates of prevalence (Stravynski, 2007, pp. 125–133). The far greater rate over the lifespan would imply that there are numerous former socially phobic individuals. A protean social phobia, suggested by these results, runs counter to the received view of it as an entity.

The socially phobic pattern or its main features have close links with other hypothetical entities with pronounced anxious features (e.g. agoraphobia/panic) as well as those of alcoholism and depression. It is important to emphasize that these interrelationships obtain both with individuals seeking treatment and those in the general populations, who do not. These findings could be interpreted as suggesting that the socially phobic construct might be an element in an even larger pattern encompassing, for example, also other anxieties, depression and wider interpersonal difficulties (e.g. general neurotic syndrome; Tyrer, 1985).

An alternative theoretical possibility, already alluded to earlier and not based on the assumption of stable multiple independent entities inherent in the DSM (III, III-R, IV and 5), might be that social phobia is a loosely defined multi-tiered protean pattern extended in time, sometimes fading out of existence and reincarnated in various guises in response to the vicissitudes of circumstances.

While social phobia is distinguishable from normality, it is typically only in terms of a (higher) degree of distress in certain situations or dimensions of experience. For this reason, it is plausible that the individual interpersonal patterns and the anxious responses woven into them that make up the overall socially phobic pattern are exacerbations of normal self-protective responses and associated social fears.

Finally, the fact that no feature or psychological construct pertaining to childhood predicted social phobia specifically, bolsters the above interpretation to some extent.

Undermining evidence

Social phobia cannot be separated from the (clearly related) hypothetical entity of avoidance personality disorder (APD). On the face of it, this fact undermines the validity of social phobia (or APD) as currently conceived. It may, however, be interpreted as questioning the distinction between phobic and interpersonal difficulties that in theory belong to two different realms of psychopathology expressed in Axes I ("performing in situations") and II ("relating to persons") of the DSM-III and upwards (Millon and Martinez, 1995, p. 222). Subversively, social phobia straddles both; it is simultaneously an anxiety disorder and a personality disorder.

It seems hardly daring, therefore, to suggest that the two (or three, if social phobia is separated into the specific and generalized subtypes) hypothetical constructs are degrees of severity of the same problematic overall interpersonal pattern.

Looming large by its absence is the fact that no specific factors on any level of analysis (social, psychological, biological) have been firmly established as characterizing the socially phobic hypothetical entity, despite considerable research efforts, driven by the reductionist and dualist outlook framing the quest for "etiology." This issues another challenge to the unspoken assumption inherent in the classification schemes, such as DSM-5, that social phobia would be clearly marked off – in this case by some constituent element or inner part – from normality on the one hand and other abnormal hypothetical entities on the other hand.

Large discrepancies in the prevalence of social phobia reported by various studies cast a serious doubt on what is being measured by the defining criteria. Regarding social phobia as a natural entity would lead one to expect a certain (rather high given the broad definition) prevalence rate that would fluctuate to a degree in view of the somewhat different life-demands that various cultures make on members in terms of the social roles they fulfill. International and same-country (e.g. the USA) discrepancies, however, are of such magnitude as to throw into question what is being measured each time. Similar problems were encountered when co-occurring hypothetical entities were delineated. The variability and incomparability of rates of prevalence across studies throw into doubt the very measurement and ultimately the meaningfulness of social phobia, entity or not.

In summary, this overview of the process of construct validation of social phobia has ended rather ambiguously. On the credit side, some evidence such as inter-rater reliability and especially the demonstration that social phobia has definable features that are well distinguished from those of other phobias with whom it stands in a close relationship. Although not specifically evidence of an entity, it nevertheless suggests that a concrete pattern with distinguishable characteristics occurs.

Two entries have to be made on the debit side. First of all, what is notable by its absence. Intensive research efforts have not been able to show that social phobia consists of a well-integrated and unified structure, made up of characteristic elements reliably on evidence. Secondly, the results concerning generalizability are so inconsistent as to undermine seriously our confidence in both what we consider social phobia to be, as well as in the means available towards identifying it (defining indicators anchored in structured interviews administered by lay interviewers).

The remaining results are of a middling kind, tentatively pointing in the right direction but not contributing meaningfully to strengthening the validity of social phobia as a hypothetical construct and would-be entity.

In conclusion, the available evidence considered so far dissolves the presumption of unity and stability inherent in the view that social phobia is a natural (i.e. disease) entity. Altogether, social phobia does not appear to be an entity with highly regular features and internally consistent in all instances (see Zachar, 2001, p. 167) and sharply distinct from normality on the one hand and various forms of abnormality on the other hand.

Social phobia as a disease

Numerous publications – lay and professional – make clear that social phobia is regarded by many (most?) physicians and other clinicians (e.g. psychologists) a disease.

In a Cochran review of the outcome of pharmacotherapy for social phobia, Stein, Ipser and van Balkom (2009), for instance, state: "Skepticism about social phobia comes from those who do not see it as a medical disorder, and from those who believe it is best understood as a form of personality disorder" (p. 9). Perhaps taking a cue from Soviet psychiatry, the authors suggest that against that kind of skepticism the remedy is "robust education emphasizing the chronic and impairing nature of socially phobic symptoms and their response to pharmacotherapy" (p. 9). One wonders what fate is reserved for those unconvinced by such evidence?

Tellingly, an introduction to a series of articles published in *International Clinical Pharmacology* (James, 1997) – for instance – had as its title: "Social phobia – a debilitating disease with a new treatment option."

More expansively, Sipila *et al.* (2010) claim that "Anxiety disorders are complex diseases" (p. 1163). Going even further, Insel and Quirion

(2005), in a programmatic article bearing the title "Psychiatry as a clinical neuroscience discipline," argue that "mental disorders be understood and treated as brain disorders" (p. 2221).

That social phobia is a disease is also implied by the vocabulary in use. Typically, individuals seeking help are "diagnosed" as "suffering from" social phobia – "a debilitating condition with an etiology that has yet to be established." Fearfulness of, and an inclination towards avoidance of social occasions, are said to be its "symptoms." In various comparative studies (e.g. Baur *et al.*, 2011, p. 1366) control subjects are described as healthy, insinuating that the socially phobic experimental subjects are ill.

In a formal manner of great legal importance, social phobia is at least implicitly recognized as a disease by international official authorities and by some national professional bodies. It is listed in both the *International Classification of Diseases* (ICD-10; Classification of Mental and Behavioral Disorders), compiled by the World Health Organization (1992), as well as in the *Diagnostic and Statistical Manual* (DSM-5), published by the American Psychiatric Association (2013).

Do these official positions then establish social phobia as a disease? On the face of it, the answer appears beguilingly clear. In fact, it is bedeviled by complex conceptual issues and the fact that there is rather little evidence to rely on.

The arguments for considering social phobia a disease are mostly rhetorical and abstract, rooted in how psychiatric problems are construed in general. For this reason, I shall have to take a roundabout route and – before coming to a conclusion – examine the notion of disease and whether it might be applicable to social phobia.

Disease or disorder?

Disease, illness and sickness are fundamental constructs of theoretical medicine. Disease is by definition an organic phenomenon independent of subjective experience or social conventions. It is measured objectively; such measurements are the *signs* of disease. Illness refers to the subjective experience of the individual (e.g. complaints of pain, discomfort); these are known as *symptoms*. Sickness is a social phenomenon; it refers to the individuals' performance of various social roles and the manner of his or her participation in the life of their community (see Hofmann, 2002, pp. 652–653).

In the ICD-10 and DSM-5 diagnostic manuals the term "social phobia" is found under the heading of anxiety disorders. What is a disorder? Is it a synonym of disease?

In its introductory note on terminology, the ICD-10 (World Health Organization, 1992, p. 5) explains:

The term "disorder" is used throughout the classification, so as to avoid even greater problems inherent in the use of terms such as "disease" and "illness." "Disorder" is not an exact term, but it is used here to imply the existence of a clinically recognizable set of symptoms or behaviors associated in most cases with distress and with interference with personal functions.

A similar line is taken in the DSM-III and subsequent revisions. In the DSM-IV (p. xxi). there is a caveat stating,

although this manual provides a classification of mental disorders, it must be admitted that no definition adequately specifies precise boundaries for the concept of mental disorder ... In DSM-IV, each of the mental disorders is conceptualized as a clinically significant behavioral or psychological syndrome or pattern exhibited by an individual and that is associated with present distress (e.g. a painful symptom) or disability (i.e. impairment in one or more important areas of functioning) or with a significantly increased risk of suffering death, pain, disability, or an important loss of freedom.

Significantly, however, it is argued elsewhere (by some of the individuals who have been in the forefront of the creation of the DSM-III): "a mental disorder is a medical disorder whose manifestations are primarily signs and symptoms of a psychological (behavioral) nature" (Spitzer and Endicott, 1978, p. 18).

While the ICD is reticent in coming to grips with the issue and shies away from providing a definition of disease or disorder, the DSM (from III to 5) appears to be having it both ways; it provides no real definition of disease but insinuates it is dealing with them nevertheless. It explains that "all medical conditions are defined on various levels of abstraction – for example, structural pathology (e.g. ulcerative colitis), symptom presentation (e.g. migraine), deviance from a physiological norm (e.g. hypertension) and etiology (e.g. pneumococcal pneumonia). Mental disorders have also been defined by a variety of concepts (e.g. distress, dyscontrol, disadvantage, disability, inflexibility, irrationality, syndromal pattern, etiology and statistical deviation). Each is a useful indicator for a mental disorder, but none is equivalent to the concept, and different situations call for different definitions" (p. xxi).

As the final step I shall turn to pathology – the medical authority on disease – for its applied understanding of the terms of disease and disorder. According to the *Robbins and Cotran Pathologic Basis of Disease*, pathology is "devoted to the study of the structural and the functional changes in cells, tissues and organs that underlie disease" (Kumar, Abbas, Fausto and Astor, 2010, p. 1). Disease then, spans the anatomy (structure) and the physiology (function) of the human organism. In other words it is "the structural alterations induced in the cells and organs of the body (morphologic changes), and the functional consequences of the morphologic changes" (2010). By functional Kumar *et al.* (2010) mean that "the nature of the morphological changes and their distribution in different organs or tissues influence normal function and determine the clinical features (symptoms and signs), course and prognosis of the disease" (p. 1). In other words, in disease functional abnormalities flow from structural changes; they are not independent of them.

As functional abnormalities are the consequence of the structural ones, the structural/functional perspectives on disease must not be seen either as a dichotomy or as mutually exclusive. In some circumscribed instances, however, one would be able to separate the two perspectives as during the period when the structure – say of an organ – is abnormal while it is still functioning adequately.

In summary, disease is viewed materialistically in terms of (observable) lesions to cells, tissues or organs, identifiable biochemical imbalances, and so on. These manifest themselves through signs (e.g. fever), symptoms (e.g. expressions of suffering) or a combination of the two. These indicators are used to arrive at a tentative diagnosis. In practice, some diagnoses may never be validated independently. As a matter of principle, however, there is a concrete disease independent of its manifest indicators. In the absence of disease the use of the related terms of diagnosis, symptoms, and so forth is hardly justified and lends them a rhetorical or theatrical quality.

Mental disorder – a metaphoric disease?

For the reasons evoked above, Szasz (1987, pp. 135–169) considers the use of the term "mental illness" or its modern equivalent – disorder – fallacious and misleading. In his view the use of the term "disease" ought to be limited to material disease only. The definition of disease by distress and maladjustment is, according to him, figurative, arrived at by analogy.

The underlying reasoning is as follows: since individuals with a bodily (i.e. material) disease are ill (i.e. suffer) and sick (i.e. may have trouble leading well-adjusted lives), those who resemble them in being ill and sick, may – by inference – be deemed to be diseased as well. An example would be "lovesickness" (diagnosis: *febris erotica*) – an affliction of the lovelorn (see Sobel, 2009). Another is the melancholic pining for home (diagnosis: *nostalgia*) among Swiss mercenaries observed in the seventeenth century (see Illbruck, 2012).

As one might look at disease functionally (in terms of physiology) (e.g. when no lesions are observed), poor psychological functioning by an inverse logic could be also conceived along the lines of a disease (disorder). According to Szasz (1987), if such patients may be said to be diseased at all, it is figuratively, as when saying "it makes me sick" to express disgust and disapproval.

In a similar vein, Lenin, whose chief preoccupation after seizing power in October 1917 was to hold on to it, diagnosed (some) of his more scrupulous comrades' concerns about abandoning principle for expediency, as being afflicted with "left-wing communism – an infantile disease."

Social phobia – a neurological disease?

Recent decades have been characterized by an intensification of a biologizing trend in the search for explanations of abnormality – still unabated – especially in US psychiatry. Consequently, some authors have come to denounce and reject the distinction made between the two kinds of disease – mental and otherwise (described above) – striving to show that mental disorder (defined psychologically) is a medical (i.e. material) disease after all. This quest – despite its thoroughgoing modern ring and tools (see Chapter 4) – actually has a long pedigree as suggested by Griesinger's (1845) maxim: "Geisteskrankheiten sind Gehirnkrankheiten" (mental diseases are diseases of the brain, quoted in Mooij, 1995, p. 26).

As a working hypothesis, such a possibility is eminently plausible – either for social phobia or for any other problem. Andreasen (1984, p. 29), for example, asserts the following: "The major psychiatric illnesses are diseases. They should be considered medical illnesses just as diabetes, heart disease and cancer are." On what grounds? Because, "the various forms of mental illness are due to many different types of brain abnormalities, including the loss of nerve cells and excesses and deficits in chemical transmissions between neurons; sometimes the fault may be in the pattern of the wiring or circuitry, sometimes in the command centers and sometimes in the way messages move along the wires" (1984, p. 221). To sum it up, "mental illnesses are diseases that affect the brain, which is an organ of the body just as the heart or the stomach is. People who suffer from mental illness suffer from a sick or broken brain."

What evidence is there to bolster such claims? Concerning anxiety disorders as a group (social phobia is not discussed on its own), the author first expresses the hope that "anxiolytic" medication might shed light on the neurochemistry of anxiety. As to actual evidence, we are told that there is a possibility of a genetic component to anxiousness, that panic may be induced in certain patients with the infusion of lactate and that there is a link between panic and mitral-valve prolapse (see Andreasen (1984, pp. 239–243). These hardly give support to the rather sweeping assertions of "brain abnormalities." Comprehensive surveys of studies of socially phobic individuals offer little support to these claims (e.g. Sutterby and Bedwell, 2012).

Sheehan (1986) advocates a broadly similar approach. Although in his book, "the anxiety disease" social phobia is broached tangentially – as a stage in the development of what he terms the anxiety disease – his views have a bearing on our topic.

"The proposed model suggests that at the center of this disease, feeding it like a spring, is a biological and probably a biochemical disorder" (1986, p. 90). Secondary (exacerbatory) roles are accorded, however, to psychological (i.e. conditioning processes) and environmental stresses.

In support of his views, Sheehan (1986, pp. 91–92) asserts that there is evidence that vulnerability to the disease may be genetically inherited, and that it is

possible that such a genetic weakness could give rise to biochemical abnormalities ... What are the precise biochemical abnormalities in this disease? No one yet knows with certainty ... The best guesses so far involve certain nerve endings and receptors in the central nervous system which receive and produce chemical messengers and excite the brain. These nerve endings manufacture naturally occurring stimulants called catecholamines. It is believed that in the anxiety disease, the nerve endings are overfiring. They are working too hard, overproducing these stimulants and perhaps others ... At the same time there are nerve endings that have the opposite effect: they produce naturally occurring tranquilizers, called inhibitory neurotransmitters that inhibit, calm down and dampen the nerve firing of the brain. It appears that the neurotransmitters or the receptors may be deficient, either in quality or quantity.

In summary, "a chain of events apparently runs from the inherited gene or genes through the cell nucleus to the cell membrane to the nerve ending and the chemicals it uses, involving some or all of the above mechanisms" (Sheehan (1986, pp. 91–92).

Even without carefully examining each argument introduced by both authors conceptually and methodologically at this point (this is done in Chapter 4, critically reviewing key areas of research), it is clear that the insubstantial and tangential proof provided hardly makes the case that social phobia is an instance of neurological disease. In an early but comprehensive review of all studies having a bearing on the neurobiology of social phobia, Nickell and Uhde (1995, p. 128) had already concluded that: "what available data have been collected across different laboratories suggest that tests of biological function in patients with social phobia are more typically similar to, rather than different from, those of normal control subjects." More recent reviews (Dewar and Stravynski, 2001; Stravynski, 2007) concurred. Indirect evidence such as the lack neuropsychological abnormalities (see Sutterby and Bedwell, 2012) is consistent with the failure to identify neurobiological abnormalities.

The implications of this are far reaching. Either the paradigm and methodologies used in this research program are inadequate and need to be rethought radically, or there is no neurobiological deficit or excess underlying social phobia to be found. By all appearances, the brain physiology of socially phobic individuals is in continuity with normal functioning (see Chapter 4).

In summary, to quote Nickell and Uhde (1995) again, "While this continuum view of social anxiety to social phobia might appear self-evident in some scientific circles, it is, in truth, a different theoretical construct from the disease model" (p. 128).

The social and cultural context of the disease model

The frank use of the term "disease" in reference to social phobia occurs mostly in publications describing and (wittingly or not) promoting the use of psychotropic medication as its treatment. It is disconnected from its scientific basis and used rhetorically, insinuating that in the face of disease, only medication will do.

Clinicians, according to Lipowski (1989, p. 252),

tell patients that they suffer from a chemical imbalance in the brain. The explanatory power of this statement is about of the same order as if you said to the patient "you are alive". It confuses the distinction between etiology and correlation, and cause and mechanism, a common confusion in our field. It gives the patient a misleading impression that his or her imbalance is the cause of his or her illness, that it needs to be fixed by purely chemical means, that psychotherapy is useless and that personal efforts and responsibility have no part to play in getting better.

Thus the notion of disease complements the designation of certain compounds (which have many other applications) as indicated for social phobia. These are typically elements in marketing campaigns orchestrated by pharmaceutical companies ("chronic pain" provides another example of this process; Spence, 2014, p. 39). Pharmaceutical Marketing, a trade publication, "singled out social phobia as a positive example of drug marketers' shaping medical and public opinion about a disease" (Moynihan, Heath and Henry, 2002, p. 888).

Disease or not?

Ultimately, as the absence of supporting facts is not considered inimical to the construction of social phobia as a disease, we are left wrestling with definitions and working out the implications.

According to Kendell (1986, pp. 41–42), the possibilities are as follows:

most physicians, when they give the matter any thought at all, believe that disease is a scientific term whose sphere of application should be determined by doctors on technical or scientific grounds, but that in practice, they apply the term inconsistently, often in response to what are quite clearly social or political considerations of various kinds. What should the architects of a classification of diseases or a classification of psychiatric disorders do in this unsatisfactory and confusing situation? A total of four alternative strategies are available. The first, adopted by the World Health Organization, is to ignore the problem, perhaps in the hope that others will do the same, and to make no attempt to define the term disease or any of its analogues. The second, adopted by the task force responsible for DSM-III, is to provide a definition, which is vaguely worded to allow any term with medical connotations to be either included or excluded in conformity with contemporary medical opinion. (A subsidiary strategy, adopted by both WHO and the APA, is to refer throughout to mental disorders rather than diseases, on the assumption that the undefined term disorder will be both less contentious and broader in scope than the similarly undefined term disease.) The third strategy, which so far as I am aware has never yet been adopted, at least for a psychiatric classification, is to provide an operational definition of disease (or disorder), which provides unambiguous rules of application, and then abide by the unsatisfactory constraints imposed by that definition. The fourth is to concede openly that psychiatric classifications are not classifications of diseases or disorders, but simply of the problems psychiatrists are currently consulted about, and that the justification for including such categories as oppositional disorder or pyromania (DSM-III) or specific reading retardation (ICD-9) is merely that in practice psychiatrists are consulted by, or about, people with such problems.

My own view is that this is probably the best course, at least until we have resolved some of the problems discussed above. It avoids the ambiguity and intellectual dishonesty of the first two options and the serious constraints of the third. It does, of course, leave unresolved the question of which of the conditions listed in the glossary is a disease and which merely a problem resulting in a psychiatric consultation, but the use of the term "mental disorder" does that anyway.

In the final analysis, if disease is an organic problem, soundly demonstrated – social phobia cannot possibly be considered one. If any problem attended to by a physician becomes thereby a disease, social phobia may be labeled – pragmatically – as such. Although puzzling by strict logical standards, such a practice is part and parcel of a general tendency towards the medicalization of distressing aspects of life evident in modern life (Conrad, 2007). This includes excessive "shyness" (Scott, 2006) but also unsatisfactory and unsatisfying sexuality (Moynihan, 2003, 2010; Sadeghi-Nejad and Watson, 2008; IsHak, Bokarius, Jeffrey, Davis and Bakhta, 2010), among others.

General conclusions

Social phobia, styled as a social anxiety disorder, rests on shaky foundations. There are two facets to the question of what social phobia is, and a corresponding twofold answer.

Substantively speaking, the abnormal anxiety allegedly characterizing social phobia has been proven elusive, both as notion and substance. Even when taken as indicating only subjective experience, as it does in most studies, socially phobic anxiety has been shown to be in continuity with normal anxiety and within the normal range. Similarly, while being quantitatively different, the anxiety of the socially phobic has strong affinities with the anxiety experienced by individuals with other abnormalities. Most importantly, this evidence can hardly support anxiety as a proximate cause of social phobia. If anything, these results undermine anxiety as a hypothetical construct and raise additional quibbles.

First of all, why are there such variations in anxiety levels between different socially phobic individuals? Should not anxiety levels be relatively high and rather uniform?

Secondly, what accounts for the variations in anxiety levels reported by the same individual on different occasions?

Thirdly, why does the same social anxiety (but in different degrees) give rise to social phobia in some, while remaining a short-lived state in normal individuals?

Finally, why does a more severe degree of anxiety result in social phobia, rather than say agoraphobia or bulimia?

The likely answer to these questions is that social anxiety itself varies with other factors on which it depends; the dynamic combinations of these factors account for all of the above examples.

Formally speaking, in terms of the structure containing the anxiety, the assumption that social phobia is a distinct entity, internally coherent and externally sharply defined and differentiated, has not much support. On the contrary, social phobia, studied over time, is variable and internally labile, with blurry and permeable external boundaries. As discussed earlier (in the section considering social phobia as an entity), social phobia is distinguishable from normality and other abnormalities only functionally. The predominance of contradictory evidence challenging the construal of social phobia as an entity is already prefigured in the comments regarding anxiety in the previous paragraphs.

As to the nature of social phobia as a disorder of social anxiety, its styling as a literal disease cannot withstand critical scrutiny. To claim it nevertheless is arbitrary, in defiance as it were, of both reason and evidence contradicting its key theses (see Chapter 4).

Needless to say, such a stretching of the construct of disease distorts it and is liable to confuse the unwary. Cynics will retort – this is what it is meant to do.

3 The interpersonal outlook: social phobia construed as an extended fearful interpersonal pattern

What is social phobia?

What is social phobia? We have seen in Chapter 2, that social phobia, construed intrapersonally, remains to a large extent an enigma.

First of all, it cannot be characterized in terms of anxiety – however that term is defined. The socially phobic mode of anxiousness is neither of a unique sort, nor of a particularly severe degree.

Secondly, social phobia is not obviously and demonstrably an entity, nor, in the final analysis, can it be claimed to be literally a disease.

Of what, then, could the significant clinical pattern that the term social phobia designates, consist? As a stop-gap solution, it is tempting to seek guidance in diagnostic manuals – the authoritative compilations of what are currently deemed to be various patterns of psychological abnormality.

Disappointingly, the relief obtained in this way can only be short-lived, for it is well to remember that the "criteria" found in diagnostic manuals neither describe social phobia, nor any other abnormality.

Rather, these list indicators: features considered prominent and therefore potentially useful for purposes of identification. The indicators are typically applied during an interview, against someone's self-representation, in a process resembling means-testing. As is the case with the DSM and the ICD (see Chapter 2, Table 2.1), in principle, there could be several sets of indicators (overlapping to an extent), possibly all useful (not necessarily to the same degree), in identifying social phobia. However apparently useful in detecting socially phobic individuals, these putative aids leave unsettled the question of what social phobia is.

It is the aim of this chapter to provide such a substantive description. Beforehand, however, I shall set out the conditions I believe a description of social phobia ought to satisfy.

First of all, to be considered an abnormal condition, social phobia has to be a distinct behavioral or psychological pattern, associated with considerable distress and impaired functioning, substantially compromising the ability of such individuals to pursue desired goals and to participate fully in the life of the community (or communities) to which they belong.

Secondly, while the overall socially phobic pattern – narrowly construed – does indeed involve a heightened state of anxious distress in the face of looming social threats, it is only a facet of the overall pattern. Unnaturally, the narrow focus detaches the state of the acting organism from the activity, as if the two were separable.

A comprehensive description has to include the individual's attempts to deal with the threat while in the grip of fear. These attempts are varied and not necessarily reflexive and stereotypical. While the wish to avoid or flee the threatening circumstances is commonplace, it is not necessarily always acted on. Nor is it the only fearful response to threat. The undue emphasis on avoidance conceals the fact, among others, that socially phobic individuals often enter and stay in menacing environments. In these, for example, they take great pains to remain as little noticeable as possible. When detected or otherwise compelled to participate, socially phobic individuals engage in intricate attempts at concealment and dissimulation and maneuver deftly (and submissively) to stay out of trouble.

Needless to say, all such defensive tactics straddle both somatic and interpersonal aspects of the socially phobic pattern. Therefore, a description of the socially phobic pattern needs to encompass the activity of the whole human organism, not the workings of a putative system (e.g. state of mind) or organ (e.g. brain) or system (i.e. the autonomic) within it. But even such a description still remains incomplete; a comprehensive account requires the setting, without which the socially phobic conduct would not be in play.

In consequence and thirdly, the description needs to give prominence to the social (or interpersonal) environment within which the socially phobic pattern unfolds. Fearsome circumstances and fearful activity are intertwined and form a dynamic system; socially phobic conduct arises in response to (or is evoked by the prospect of) definite activities set in social or interpersonal contexts. Both fearful activities and the fearsome settings in which they occur become meaningful only as embedded in a culture or a way of life; otherwise they remain a denatured abstraction.

As in my view all intellectual constructions must draw from and accord with life as observed, the best way of fleshing out social phobia and breathing life into a notion, is to present several cases illustrating it.

Case descriptions

A is a 36-year-old homemaker and a mother of two children aged 12 and 7. When consulting, she reports dreading going to parent–teacher meetings at school and to outings with her husband's friends and their wives. In company, especially when seated at a table in a well-lit room, she feels trapped and longs to escape. While trying to endure it, she feels remote and unfocused, attending to the conversation and participating only fitfully. She feels most threatened by the possibility of being addressed, doubting that she could respond appropriately without betraying her disarray and blushing. While dreading such a possibility, in a state of mounting tension, she experiences an oppressive sensation in her chest that makes it difficult to breathe, and occasionally has intestinal cramps followed by diarrhea. Normally, her social life is restricted to the home and family, and she stays away from the above-mentioned threatening situations, whenever possible.

When going out, she takes considerable precautions against the possibility of being seen blushing (i.e. flushing spread over portions of the face, neck and chest). To minimize the likelihood of this happening, she accepts only invitations to events taking place outdoors. These she attends wearing turtleneck blouses, wide-brimmed hats and large sunglasses, eating only cold food and declining alcoholic drinks. She does, however, take fitness classes without too much difficulty, as she is surrounded with relative strangers, unconcerned with her presence.

She worked briefly in a clerical capacity before marrying, and had found doing anything in the presence of others difficult; dealings with persons in position of authority were particularly disconcerting.

She finds her married life satisfactory and her husband supportive and understanding. She feels confident with him and able to express her point of view.

In private life – with the exception of her husband – she has difficulties in initiating or maintaining a conversation, expressing an opinion or receiving a compliment for fear of blushing, even with familiar persons. Furthermore, she complains of being unable to set limits to the interference of different family members who tend to take decisions affecting her, without prior consultation.

She feels incapable of developing new contacts and friendships, although she would like to.

In retrospect, her difficulties began in early adolescence when her early sexual maturity set her apart from classmates who teased her. The repeated taunts provoked blushing, which in turn intensified the teasing.

It was then that she started wearing loose-fitting turtleneck blouses and found speaking in class increasingly difficult, although she tended to be self-effacing even beforehand.

These long-standing difficulties were exacerbated by the death of her father 3 years before consulting. She was very attached to him and still feels his loss very keenly. She finds her mother, by contrast, cold, harsh and controlling.

B is 41-year-old married father of two children, aged 16 and 14, who dreads business-related meetings with clients and/or their representatives, particularly when he is the center of attention. In such encounters, he attends to what is being said erratically and is sometimes hard put to come up with appropriate answers, especially when challenged. Ahead of such meetings, his heart races, pressure builds up in his chest and he feels hot, sweaty and flushed.

During meetings, he dreads the possibility that the other participants find him nervous and insecure and possibly incompetent. To avoid confrontations, he tends to adopt a conciliatory posture towards wayward clients (e.g. delays in payments, rude and unappreciative comments). He can, however, become disproportionately angry after long periods of self-restraint. While at times longing to escape this part of his life, he feels compelled by necessity to soldier on, hoping to expand his business.

Occasionally in the past, when put on the spot in front of many people, he experienced episodes of panic that rendered him speechless. Although milder fluctuating instances of these difficulties had occurred before, they have been exacerbated in the last few years by his attempts to shift his business from individual customers to companies. He finds dealing with representatives of companies or their management more difficult, as their negotiating tactics are harsher and at times underhand.

He finds leading his company and overseeing his employees trying, although to a lesser extent. He lurches from being over-controlling and irritable, to ignoring non-pressing issues (e.g. overseeing the training of employees) that demand attention nevertheless. Since the shift in his customers began, he had felt increasingly anxious and low, sleeping poorly.

On the advice of a friend, he has made a point of attending social functions with a potential for business contacts. During these events, he keeps mostly to himself and is ill-at-ease. When seated at a table, he remains silent, speaking only when addressed directly. He perseveres, although no business opportunities have materialized.

These anxieties also extend to his personal life. He is apprehensive of social situations in crowded and hot spaces (e.g. family celebrations), during which he is tied down to one spot, unable to get away without being noticed. Frequent family gatherings make him uncomfortable, as he hardly participates in the jovial bantering and dreads being made fun of by the more boisterous members. When such teasing takes place, he remains silent and looks away, hoping his discomfort will pass unnoticed. Although he would preferr not to attend such get-togethers, he has so far resisted the temptation.

Although he gathers that his wife has an inkling of his suffering, he has never mentioned it. He is reticent to confide in her – convinced she will not understand and will think less of him. Although he appreciates her as a capable and confident person, she overwhelms him at times. On occasion, he finds her disregard for his views, or her outspoken comments, bruising. When this takes place, he feels low and withdraws, sulking for days.

The "anti-depressant" medication prescribed by his physician, while taking the edge off his anxious distress, does not meaningfully improve his overall condition.

He describes himself as having always been timid. His mother worried about everything, while his father was a harsh authoritarian. Although quiet and withdrawn, he demanded strict obedience and imposed collective punishments on the children. The patient was scared of his father, who would violently strike his turbulent brother (who nevertheless remained defiant).

He became self-conscious in his teens because of acne; he would repeatedly examine his face for new eruptions and would be upset about his appearance. Consequently, he missed classes and failed several courses; this excluded the possibility of pursuing a higher level of studies.

C is a man of 42, married and father of two children, who works in the public sector. He is ambitious to make the most of the expertise that he has developed in his field, but is held back and troubled by the public speaking that this entails.

On such occasions, he is intermittently seized by panic, feeling uncertain about where he is, unable to articulate, hands unsteady, legs weak, heart pounding, flushed and in a sweat. When in front of an audience, he feels uncertain and imagines being sized up and found wanting as pretentious and not convincingly competent. The size of the audience and the presence of figures of authority are aggravating factors. By contrast, he is generally comfortable in small groups or with individual interlocutors. However, he is intimidated by self-assured individuals in positions of authority or women he finds attractive, and shrinks in their presence and finally withdraws.

Although still suffering and struggling (and therefore seeking help), he describes himself as much better now than he was years ago, since he is able to present in public, however inadequately.

Nevertheless, the weeks preceding a presentation are a torment to him. He experiences a fluctuating and at times disorganizing level of anxiousness without let up. While in the grip of this, he cannot concentrate on anything else and engages repeatedly in the preparation and constant revisions of his texts and supporting graphics. The typically successful conclusion of the presentation brings only brief relief, as he finds many faults in it and himself. He experiences a lesser degree of dread when engaged in the task of producing written material; he imagines how it will be read by others, who undoubtedly will find it incomprehensible and intellectually shoddy. Such activity consumes an inordinate amount of time, in part because it is typically interspersed with periods of procrastination.

Since his early days at school, he found it impossible to answer the teacher when questioned; feeling trapped, he would become "paralyzed and incoherent." Nevertheless, he was a very good student, especially in scientific subjects, but had great difficulty in writing essays or compositions, which proved a major handicap at university.

He describes himself as always having been rather inhibited. Despite his powerful physique, he let himself be mistreated by other children at school and was terrorized by threats made by a classmate with a reputation for delinquency.

His father was a tough manual laborer who set great store by force and aggressive self-assertion. He found his son woefully lacking in these manly qualities and treated him brutally and with derision. A forceful and turbulent sister won the father's approval, while the patient tried to keep out of their way. His mother was a fearful and sickly individual who paid little attention to him and wished not to be disturbed.

I shall now – at last – turn to the interpersonal characterization of social phobia.

The socially phobic pattern

Although yearning to be accepted and approved of, socially phobic individuals incline to keep a safe distance from social situations altogether or, even when present, remain aloof from the main activity. However, when outright avoidance is unaffordable, they take part fearfully and tentatively, gearing up – if evasive tactics are to no avail – for a losing struggle with "threatening" individuals (e.g. attractive members of the opposite sex, confident persons or those occupying position of authority) during various social interactions.

The overall socially phobic pattern has therefore simultaneously an interpersonal and a fearful somatic locus. The interpersonal pattern is enacted, and the fearful state that permeates it is realized somatically. Fluctuating anxiousness of varying degrees is best seen as a process permeating socially phobic behavior.

In sum, both the interpersonal conduct and the fearful emotional state welling up from it are constitutive aspects of social phobia. The socially phobic pattern is an organic whole, enacted by an indivisible living individual.

Fearful interpersonal patterns: a defensive strategy and its tactics Although longing to escape the frightening aspects of social life while at times actually steering clear of threatening social situations, few socially phobic individuals literally choose seclusion. Although weary, they recognize the opportunities that social life provides (e.g. for a mate, companionship, advancement), as well as the harsh necessity (e.g. making a living) dictating taking part. While specific challenges (e.g. public speaking or eating, joining a group) might be desperately avoided, socially phobic individuals do participate in social life, but exceedingly cautiously. In addition to avoiding outright certain situations or steering clear of certain individuals as well as dissembling (e.g. concealing their fearfulness or blushing), four interpersonal patterns, which are woven into an overall strategy minimizing risk-taking, stand out.

First of all, socially phobic individuals seek security in being approved of and appreciated. To this end, they make themselves agreeable, smiling and nodding with interest and support to those they know. When not preoccupied with themselves, they can be well attuned to the needs of others, and readily lend an attentive ear or a helping hand. To put it negatively, they are not unresponsive, demanding, critical, capricious or petulant.

They are conciliatory, and tend to give in or take the blame for mishaps, so as to minimize frictions. Resentment and disappointment are carefully dissimulated, for fear of retaliation. A matter-of-fact, impersonal exchange (i.e. without pleasantries) is experienced as chilly and potentially hostile, and, as such, disquieting. Relationships of any kind, therefore, tend to be personalized with much effort invested in being likable and gaining approval or, at the very least, forestalling disapproval.

Secondly, to minimize strife and the possibility of loss of face in a conflict they feel they are bound to lose, socially phobic individuals choose to propitiate and appease. They are soft-spoken, docile and mild; not challenging or provocative. They keep out of power struggles, preferring not to take sides. Nor are they masterful and eager to take charge. Rather, they readily fall in with the initiatives of others and tend to give in to pressure or intimidation – or at least give that impression. When not complying, they resort to elaborate justifications so as not to give offence; when in opposition they remain silent and resist passively. When embarrassed (e.g. blundering, being teased or praised), they turn their head away, bow it, avert their eyes, grin or giggle, and some blush. This disarming pattern is best considered an appeasement or a submission display (Stein and Bouwer 1997), indicating that one is not a threat to potentially domineering or hostile others. Blushing, considered narrowly as the reddening of the skin, is baffling; when understood relationally and contextually, its meaning is rather obvious.

Thirdly, to stay out of trouble socially phobic individuals strive to lead a blameless public life. For this, they adopt stringent standards of propriety and scruple, striving but not necessarily succeeding, to be beyond reproach. Despite being eager to please, they refrain from making promises lightly or manipulatively, as these might come to haunt them. In a similar vein, various activities (e.g. working; grooming) are carried out in a somewhat obsessive search for "perfection," aimed at eliminating mistakes or the possibility of being found in the wrong.

Fourthly, socially phobic individuals tend to lead a shadowy and furtive existence. Although yearning for recognition, they prefer escaping notice and staying out of the limelight at all costs. They dread the possibility that, as all attention is on them, embarrassment will disable them from performing the required social activity (e.g. speaking in public, responding graciously to praise, courting, dancing) to standards they find mandatory; looking silly or foolish – must be guarded against at all costs.

Socially phobic individuals are rather self-effacing and pliant. Being singled out for praise in front of a group, evokes anxiousness to the same degree as does criticism (Rodebaugh, Weeks, Gordon, Langer and Heimberg, 2012). It is experienced as an ordeal, with so many witnessing their potential discomfiture (e.g. blushing or standing speechless) and the ensuing disgrace.

Finally, socially phobic individuals are rather passive participants in social life, given more to studying others and ruminating about their own shortcomings and unfortunate lot. Those with whom they come into contact find them uninvolved, reserved and inscrutable. They shun novelty (e.g. attractive strangers), as the upredictability is perceived as being too dangerous. Imposed changes (e.g. new neighbors) are experienced as menacing unless experience proves otherwise. Faults of commission (e.g. blundering) are guarded against as far more dangerous than faults of omission (i.e. missing out on opportunities).

In summary, the main interpersonal patterns, described earlier, are best seen as a host of tactics embedded in a defensive strategy organized for the sake of self-protection (i.e. safety from harm). To this end, risk-taking is minimized by keeping a safe distance from (dangerous) social events whenever possible, and engaging social activities in fearful submission and passive dependence – refraining from any provocation as it were – when necessary.

This mostly defensive "campaign," extended in time, ranging over various settings and involving multiple activities of varying degrees of intensity, is often waged, to pursue the military metaphor, in a heightened condition of anxiousness – a mixture of alarm, vigilance and extraordinary state of preparedness and exertion. The degree of anxiousness fluctuates in line with the constantly updated intelligence estimates, as it were, of the solidity of one's defensive position (at best considered vulnerable and, in the final analysis, untenable) in the face of the offensive onslaught that the massed enemy (i.e. the other participants in the transaction) might unleash. Benefitting from all the advantages of ruthlessness, surprise and initiative, the fatal outcome of any conflict with such an enemy is preordained. Although inextricable from the self-protective pattern of conduct, of what does the state of anxiousness consist?

A state of fearful (anxious) mobilization   In the face of a threatening emergency, as well as in the midst of it, the body enters a state of alarm ("stress response" involving major autonomic and endocrine changes; see Rodrigues, LeDoux and Sapolsky, 2009), leading to heightened activation of the processes readying it for vigorous self-protective action (fleeing, if possible; fighting as last resort, if not). In such state of readiness for action, all relevant systems are on "high alert," resulting in:

1. Palpitations – the heart pumps faster; for the more blood circulates, the greater the energy. Blood is shifted from the skin to where it is needed most: muscles and brain. This results in cool extremities and pallor.
2. Fast breathing – supplies more oxygen.
3. Tensing up of muscles, as readying for intensive action occurs. The natural impulses of fleeing (if possible) or fighting (if not) are not of much use to the socially phobic individual and typically resisted. At peak, this keyed-up state results in trembling, an impoverished coordination of limbs and a mask-like rigidity of the face.
4. Sweating – evaporation cools off hot straining muscles.
5. An urge to urinate (in some an inability to do so), with intestinal cramps and alternating diarrhea and constipation and sometimes vomiting. Needless processes in an emergency are aborted and waste evacuated.
6. Speech difficulties due to labored breathing and poor coordination of the muscles involved in articulation (being "tongue-tied").

7. Otherwise diminished responsiveness and blunted perceptiveness, as vigilance is narrowly focused on identifying danger before it arises, and reacting to it as soon as it does.
8. Dilated pupils to increase visual acuity.
9. Hair standing on end. Disappointingly, it is of little practical use. Unlike cats' enemies, those of humans are usually not taken aback by such displays.

As a consequence, socially phobic individuals frequently report neck and shoulder stiffness and headaches. Ahead of feared situations they experience palpitations, rapid breathing, tightening of the chest, heat and sweating, a queasy sensation in the stomach and gut and a pressing need to have a bowel movement or urinate. Some paradoxically are unable to relieve themselves in public.

Subjectively, these individuals describe experiencing an almost unrelieved dread, uncertainty and helplessness, with much rumination directed towards guessing various conjunctures that may arise in the future, and what various important people might be thinking of them. All the while, they would also be brooding over their own awkwardness, unattractiveness, incompetence and cowardliness. These are contemplated with a sense of impending doom. Periods of discouragement and hopelessness, especially following setbacks, punctuate a fluctuating but uninterrupted sense of menace.

Some socially phobic individuals dread blushing. Although this reddening of the face, ears, neck and upper chest is a psychosomatic manifestation, it is unlikely to be one of anxiety. Blanching rather than blushing prevails in a state of fearfulness. The facial expressions accompanying blushing (e.g. smiling, averting one's gaze and lowering one's head) are unlike the strained vigilance typical of fear. Finally, blushing occurs in a state of passivity and immobility, in contrast to the restlessness and agitation common to anxious states. Consequently, I consider blushing as a facet of a wider submissive interpersonal pattern, described earlier.

All anxious disorders might be said to involve an exacerbation of the above normal "stress-response," chronically extended. Social phobia is marked off from other such anxious states by the insistent attempts of such individuals to hide visible manifestations of fearfulness from the critical gaze of others. Some adopt a disguise: dark glasses, wide-brimmed hats, make-up and turtlenecks to conceal blushing, for example. The surest means to safety, however, is keeping a distance from danger (i.e. avoiding fraught social encounters altogether) or, if it cannot be helped, escaping and hiding (i.e. remaining out of sight or refraining from drawing attention to oneself, by saying little). As the cumulative social cost of such actions might be very high indeed (e.g. none are compatible with working), most attempt concealment and dissembling. This is a "hair-raising" strategy: feigning poise while dreading exposure as an impostor; the "nervousness" (detailed above) or blushing threatening to let slip how sensitive and vulnerable one really is. Use of alcohol or medication as anxiolytics is common. The taking of these substances, acting as inhibitors of a fearfully overexcited nervous system, induces a decrease in palpitations, hand tremors, and so on. It offers, therefore, some relief from the fear of drawing unwelcome attention for being out of control.

While simultaneously seeking to master the unruly (but normal) bodily facets of a state of fearfulness, dissembling is essentially an interpersonal act, aiming at creating a positive impression or at the very least to conceal or minimize what is presumed to elicit an unfavorable one. It hints at the paramount importance, for safety's sake, of being in the good graces of others, and the necessity to conform to their alleged expectations – typical of the socially phobic. Additionally, dissembling illustrates the inextricable connection between the self-protective interpersonal tactics and the state of anxiousness that pervades this activity in the face of threatening circumstances.

In summary, anxiousness – the all-purpose state of alarm permeating the defensive socially phobic pattern and arising out of its interaction with menacing social situations, undergirds the self-protective tactics, while readying the individual to respond to further threats that may arise.

Overall then, the comprehensive socially phobic pattern may be depicted as one of fearful (relative) powerlessness resulting in a somewhat stunted social life, lived at a remove for safety's sake. Keeping a safe distance if possible, and if not, fearful submission and passive dependence, are its main interpersonal characteristics during engagements with others.

Threatening social settings

Socially phobic behavior (or any extended pattern of conduct), considered in isolation, is baffling. It acquires meaningfulness by being set in physical and cultural contexts. Four categories of evocative situations highlight most socially phobic responses.

First of all, publicly enacting a social role elicits the most intense somatic reactions of fearfulness, as well as the greatest associated subjective distress. Thus, interacting with individuals in sanctioned, authoritative and powerful positions (embedded in hierarchical structures) presents the most threatening challenges to the socially phobic individual.

For most, these difficulties occur in formal/institutional situations (e.g. meetings, presentations at work), and concern acting authoritatively and dealings with people occupying positions of power. When facing authorities, socially phobic individuals assume a passively obedient and overall submissive posture, designed to placate and pacify, fearing otherwise to be found in the wrong, the butt of criticism and ridicule, their presumption cut down to size.

Objectionable demands are resisted passively and stealthily. When exercising authority (e.g. instructing or leading), the socially phobic are hesitant to assert themselves and to impose their views for fear of being challenged, fomenting mutiny or sullenly resented. Concerned about fanning discontent, the socially phobic attempt to satisfy all involved.

Yearning for approval while dreading criticism and dissatisfaction, socially phobic individuals feel unable to argue their case, defend their point of view against critics, expose weaknesses in contending arguments, convince and carry the day. Rather, they feel powerlessly at the mercy of others, having to humor them and depend on their goodwill. When thing go badly, they feel they have only themselves to blame for their shortcomings.

Given their heightened anxiousness while participating in meetings or presenting, such individuals typically fear shaking (e.g. hand tremor) or incapacitating surges of anxiety (i.e. panic), that would make it all but impossible to speak in public. Their embarrassing lack of poise, at times punctuated by blushing, combined with what they consider a lackluster performance, adds insult to injury. During meetings, formal or not, they tend to remain silent. If addressed directly and made to speak, they are obviously reluctant to refuse – but do not quite comply either. When attempting to communicate, they are liable to meander inarticulately and inexpressively, talk rapidly in a strained and barely audible voice – usually failing to make an impact.

When faced with complex tasks to be performed in the presence of others (e.g. while instructed), socially phobic individuals are prone to being distracted, failing to understand or even remember information or operations they have been shown recently.

Secondly, group membership and participation in its activities form an uncertain area of social life for the socially phobic individual. Collaborative activities as a group (e.g. a dinner party) are entered upon defensively. During these, self-effacement (e.g. silence) is far more prominent than participation (e.g. describing an amusing incident, expressing an opinion). Such passive involvement marginalizes socially phobic individuals.

Relationships among members of a group are not equal. All groups (e.g. family, peers, community) naturally involve ranking. Some members personifying the highest values of their community are more admired than others; some exercise leading roles. Unless otherwise organized, group life involves, in addition to collaboration, a fair amount of rivalry, among others, for standing within it. Socially phobic individuals find competitive activities, either symbolic (e.g. games) or in earnest (e.g. for a position or a desirable mate), threatening and tend to forgo them. Consequently, they also shun self-promotion (as well as denigrating others, often its flip side), alliances with like-minded people in the furtherance of their interests, and the company of authoritative, glamorous, decisive and seemingly self-assured people.

Unsure of their ability to impress and be chosen, they fear that attempts to gain recognition might attract contempt and ridicule instead, further diminishing their rather uncertain standing within the group. Concerned about both losing and winning – not being able to make the most of it, or stoking the resentment of other competitors – they find keeping out of the running to be safer.

Performing symbolic rituals (e.g. leading a prayer, toasting the bride and groom, performing a ritual dance at a wedding), affirming group membership (e.g. sharing a meal or a drink with colleagues at work, while participating in the conversation), are experienced as ordeals to be performed to the satisfaction of others, on which one's uncertain standing hinges. Failure to satisfy or, worse, ridicule if one is not up to standard, bring closer the possibility of becoming an outcast or being banished from the group in disgrace.

Thirdly, strangers as unfathomable sources of threat are watched warily, and studiously kept at a distance. An attempt at establishing contact with an individual or joining a group after all might be greeted with indifference or end in rebuff, confirming the socially phobic individual's insignificance. Accepting strangers' attentions might be exciting, but it opens the door to potentially disastrous entanglements, as their interest is likely to wane, turn to disappointment, and finally rejection. Strangers among a group of familiar people (at a party, at work), although less threatening, are nevertheless assessed for their potential of being dismissive and overbearing, especially if sounding and looking confident or particularly attractive (and presumed to be capricious and conceited).

Such diffidence with relative strangers, typical of social phobia, is a major handicap for personal life in the countries of the industrialized world, where meeting potential partners, and subsequent courtship, depends entirely on individuals' initiative and ability to win someone over (sometimes against keen competition). Many socially phobic individuals are chosen, rather than actively pursuing somebody they have singled out. Men are at a greater disadvantage under such arrangements, as they are culturally expected to take the initiative, and be the driving force in courtship. Furthermore, the choices open even to the more adventurous socially phobic individuals are rather restricted, for they consider the more attractive potential mates in great demand. Having considerable choice, they are more likely to be dismissive, or soon lose interest and pursue brighter prospects elsewhere.

Fourthly, intimate relations set in relief both strengths and weaknesses in the socially phobic interpersonal pattern. A certain eagerness to please and gain the appreciation of others, while dreading disapproval, is one of the threads running through the description of social phobia so far. If striving for the liking and high regard of someone while wishing to satisfy them, is at the core of relations of intimacy and love; it might be said that socially phobic individuals are driven to try to establish various forms of intimacy as a rule, even where they are unlikely to be found, as in group and institutional life, normally characterized by rivalry (as well as cooperation) and impersonal power relationships. Such misdirected efforts undermine adequate social functioning based on the enactment of social roles, in the public sphere.

However, the longing to be liked and treated with consideration and kindness common to social phobia brings a great strength to love relationships or intimate friendships – once they are formed. Socially phobic individuals are not unscrupulous, scheming and ruthless. They are in their element in relationships where affection, respect and dependency are reciprocated. In such a secure context, they may learn to drop their guard, take initiative or even charge, become less calculating, more spontaneous and adventurous (e.g. more reckless and powerful) and therefore less than perfect. However, even in close intimacy, socially phobic individuals are not entirely trusting; nor do they come across as warm and generous.

Domineering partners tend to exacerbate the anxieties and frustrations of submissive, socially phobic individuals, stoking their insecurities. Emotional expressivity (e.g. of affection but especially anger) is circumscribed. Socially phobic individuals are cautiously calculating. Passive/aggressive gestures of omission or commission – enacted surreptitiously – abound instead.

The muted expressivity and inept communication, inevitably, adversely affect various areas of intimacy such as sexual satisfaction.

It is important to note that fearful and self-protective responses are not monolithic. The specific dispositions within the general socially phobic interpersonal pattern are sharply articulated and dynamically enacted in response to the minutest gradations and changes. Socially phobic individuals are most discerning; their responses are highly differentiated from situation to situation, the danger inherent in it, depending on the category of threat and various relevant parameters.

The most dangerous situations are those concerning competitive performances as a social actor, in front of a discerning and demanding audience, on public occasions. The formality of the occasion, what is at stake, the kind of participants (e.g. authorities, known detractors) and their numbers, act as exacerbating factors. The least dangerous situations would be engaging in an intimate relationship that is obviously requited, under conditions guaranteeing privacy.

In summary, abstracted from the specific responses to myriad social dangers (personified by individuals and settings), social phobia is a fearful and powerless web (or interpersonal pattern constituted of various sub-patterns), protective against the threat of humiliation – be it public degradation or private personal rejection.

At its worst, humiliation is experienced when one is brutally or hurtfully exposed as an impostor, as it were, pretending to be what one cannot possibly be, laying claim to an undeserved dignity. Less demeaning, but hurtful nevertheless, is the absence of acknowledgment, regard and respect.

The integrated pattern is abnormal, in being grievously distressing and in seriously compromising the ability of the individual to carry out desired personal goals and to participate fully in the life of the groups, institutions and communities to which she or he belongs.

If this narrowly pure definition of social phobia were to be widened, it might also include other types of fearfulness, intermittent or chronic depressed mood and dependency on substances used towards self-medication. Which is the true social phobia? The question might be somewhat evasively but truthfully answered: that it is a matter of perspective and definitions; where the boundaries are drawn is, to some extent, artificial.

Cultural differences

Are socially phobic individuals the same the world over? It is difficult to answer this question with any certainty, for relevant descriptions are scarce.

If separating the integrated socially phobic pattern analytically, into an anxiously somatic and an interpersonal dimension, one could take for granted that the alarmed (and alarming for the socially phobic) bodily activation accompanying and supporting self-protective action in the face of threat, has to be similar. In all humans, the "stress-response" is orchestrated by various systems in the brain involved in emotional regulation and triggering an array of autonomic and endocrine changes.

The powerlessly defensive behavior, however, being culturally molded, is likely to be altogether different. The self-protective interpersonal patterns issued from culturally constituted social roles embedded in social structures organized into a way of life, might in principle vary a lot, although not necessarily in all particulars. Everywhere, the socially phobic pattern makes itself evident by disrupting to a considerable degree the ability to enact social roles, and participate in the life of the community.

An informal comparison between the Canadian socially phobic individuals described earlier and those described in Stravynski, Arbel, Lachance *et al.* (2000) and the socially phobic, ultra-orthodox-Jewish men residing in the state of Israel (Greenberg, Stravynski and Bilu, 2004) is illustrative.

First of all, in contrast to the Canadian cohort, only men are included in the Israeli orthodox-Jewish one. As marriages are arranged, women are confined to the private sphere in orthodox-Jewish life, raising children and in contact mostly with other women in a private capacity; social phobia in such a cultural context is hardly imaginable. Neither is agoraphobia in housebound, pious Muslim women (El-Islam, 1994).

Secondly, as marriages are arranged, it is almost impossible to fail to secure a spouse among orthodox men, no matter how bashful and lacking in drive and social graces they might be. In other cultures where marriages are also arranged, the requirements might be somewhat more onerous. These, however, would not be of a personal nature. Among most Indians, matching language, caste, status and horoscope are indispensable. By contrast, the Canadian socially phobic male is at a considerable disadvantage within a culture placing the onus of courtship on men, reliant mostly on their ability to charm and sustain a relationship, often in the face of competition. Although admittedly an extreme example, one of the cases in Stravynski, Arbel, Lachance *et al.* (2000), while pining for a life companion, remained alone.

Things were easier in this respect for the Canadian socially phobic woman (described earlier). She was spotted as a desirable partner and courted by her future husband, having only to go along and provide some encouragement.

Thirdly, both Canadian and Israeli orthodox-Jewish socially phobic individuals were principally handicapped in the performance of public social roles, feeling uncertain of satisfying requisite standards and ultimately fearing failure and ensuing disgrace. For the Canadians, it was, for example, acting as a lecturer, a self-employed businessman or as a mother in charge of her children's education.

The orthodox-Jewish men, by contrast, could not lead a prayer or preside over a religious ritual. This was true either in the presence of other worshippers in the synagogue, or at home, and interfered with the performance of religious duties. Most hurtful, however, was their inability to act authoritatively as teachers and interpreters, expounding on matters of observance and faith. Not daring to conduct themselves as befitting a religious authority, fearful of asserting claims to the prestige reserved to the religious scholar, they forwent an exalted status in their community, keeping out of the limelight and out of danger.

In summary, socially phobic individuals, living very different ways of life, share a similar fearfulness, suffusing a variety of defensive, self-protecting interpersonal patterns. Whether these are activated depends on the social demands placed on the individual by the way of life of their community; this in turn is determined by the culture in which the community is embedded. These determine the situational contexts evocative of the socially phobic responses. For example, the Canadian woman (case A) withdrew from the work place to homemaking and raising children. Such an outlet was not available to the men. Case B, regardless of the duration and extent of his torment, felt compelled to provide for his family and remained at his post.

Individual differences

Even within the same culture, socially phobic individuals are not made in the same mold. Individual cases of social phobia are variations on the theme of fearful self-protection against possible interpersonal injury, public and/or private. Some differences among such individuals are of degree, for instance in the level of anxiousness arising with, and supporting self-protective action in the face of threat. Another difference in degree is in the severity of the subjective experience of distress and the manner in which it is reported. Similarly, the number of triggering social situations might provide a crude index of severity.

Some differences, however, are differences of kind. First of all, there are the somatic aspects of anxiousness (e.g. shaking, panicking) and powerlessness (e.g. blushing). Secondly, there is the prominence of certain interpersonal sub-patterns described earlier, and their proportion in making up the socially phobic pattern as a whole.

As the socially phobic response and the situations evoking it are inseparable, some individual differences are embedded in circumstances, both present and past. Gender and changes in position, occupation or personal status (e.g. marriage) modulate the socially phobic response considerably.

Altogether, it is likely that personal history is the most important source of individual differences (see Chapter 6). Underlying fearfulness is, in all likelihood, a broad genetic propensity, perhaps best described as emotionality (see Chapter 2). Anxiousness is not a ready-made and enduring characteristic, evident at the onset of life (see Chapter 2). For instance, fearfulness is not present in the repertoire of newborns and appears to emerge as the result of maturation. It is on the individual propensity – the raw material as it were – that the social environment acts; it will mold the propensity from birth (or even before) and subsequently, in the course of development; the end result is the ongoing interaction between the two.

In summary, the differences in the potential endowment as well as life histories (the process of molding the individual propensity including learning as well as unlearning), translate into individual differences in the integrated socially phobic pattern of fearfulness and interpersonal self-protection. While various social fears might precede it in childhood, the socially phobic pattern is forged by adult demands made on the individual by the way of life of the community to which he or she belongs. These crystallize in late adolescence or early adulthood; so does the onset of social phobia (see Stravynski, 2007, pp. 88–89).

What is the nature of social phobia?

As we have seen in Chapter 2, social phobia is not demonstrably an entity, let alone a disease entity. An entity, by definition, is stably coherent within, with a core of necessary properties and well differentiated from other entities, near (i.e. other anxiety or personality disorders) or far (i.e. normality).

As the hallmarks of a natural entity (e.g. a leaf – see Vogel, 2012) are highly regular features combined with an internal consistency, manifest in all instances (see Zachar, 2001, p. 167; Haslam, 1998, pp. 293–294), it has great inductive potential. Knowing that something is an instance of a natural kind allows many inferences to be drawn (and generalizations to be made) about the fairly identical members of the category. For that very reason, treating social phobia as a natural entity is highly misleading.

As we have seen earlier, social phobia is quite obviously not a natural entity, existing independently of the social and cultural world. Nor are the socially phobic – the members of this putative category – identical. Rather, social phobia is characterized by a great heterogeneity, both in degree but also in kind, especially when it is associated with other co-occurring disorders or some of their features (e.g. inordinate concerns about appearance).

An inescapable fact is that every feature of social phobia can be located on a continuum; none is a discrete and unique characteristic of social phobia. In that sense, social phobia is an exacerbation of, but in continuity with, normality.

In purely scientific terms, then, no strong argument justifies considering social phobia a categorical entity, as its taxonomic classification currently implies. Practicality, however, argues in favor of using the term "social phobia" as designating a category of sorts. This offers several advantages.

First of all, it allows an economical means of communicating. Secondly, it organizes the investigation of social phobia, in all its variations. Finally, it allows social phobia to be linked to methods of intervention that reliably produce positive outcomes (with most cases).

In the final analysis, and bearing in mind all the above considerations, it is most fitting to consider social phobia a pragmatic category. The main strength of this kind of category is flexibility and therefore usefulness, both practical and theoretical. Although a practical kind is a fuzzier category (see also Lilienfeld and Marino, 1995) than a natural kind, it is not necessarily an admission of arbitrariness (Zachar, 2001).

The designation of a practical category has two main advantages.

First of all, such a pragmatic category considers the membership within it as distributed on a continuum, and varying in degree of resemblance, with no members being necessarily identical. Furthermore, the category itself could be on a continuum with normality, with distinctions at times blurred and made on practical grounds (i.e. social functioning).

Such a pragmatic framework fits, without strain, the reality of social phobia. It acknowledges (without blushing) the resemblance of socially phobic features with normality and acknowledges their considerable variability. Moreover, it accommodates a dynamic social phobia, extended in time and permanently in flux, both in terms of the elements making up the various interpersonal patterns, as well the web of patterns constituting the overall socially phobic cluster, in relation to specific situations and life circumstances.

Secondly, a pragmatic category is rich in theoretical potential. Without any preconceived ideas, it admits the possibility of different ways of conceptualizing the nature of social phobia. Casting social phobia in relational (rather than medical) terms, for example, frees social phobia from the straitjacket of being a stable and unvarying medical "condition." Additionally, a pragmatic category accommodates a social phobia that combines features of both a disorder of anxiety and of personality. In this sense, the use of a pragmatic category is liberating, or at the very least, less constraining. Nothing illustrates this better than dropping the misguided quest for "etiology," the touchstone that will presumably establish what social phobia is "really" like.

A pragmatic approach to the identity of social phobia, by being unprejudiced, allows the relative merits of different perspectives (the interpersonal, but also others), to be judged by the only standard that matters – their explanatory power; namely, the ability to assimilate and illuminate most – if not all – known facts about social phobia.

Part III

What causes social phobia?
General introduction

In an enquiry into the nature of social phobia conducted in Chapter 2, it was found that there are no firm grounds for considering social phobia to be either a disease or, indeed, an entity characterized by abnormal anxiety. This preliminary conclusion allows one – in the quest for understanding – to shed the narrow framework dictated by these notions, in the grip of which one would have languished otherwise.

What is this framework? It is well to restate it. It is commonly considered (e.g. in the DSM-5) that socially phobic behavior stems from abnormal levels (or kinds) of anxiety. An attempt to understand social phobia from a disease perspective implies identifying the processes causing such abnormal anxiety. Where should one direct one's gaze?

Within the medical outlook prevails "an intuitive concept of disorder that underlies medical judgment and is widely shared by health professionals – that the symptoms of disorder are due to an internal process that is not functioning as expected (i.e. an internal dysfunction)" (Wakefield *et al.*, 2002, p. 380). On this view (social) anxiety is the expression of the dysfunction of certain (unknown) regulatory mechanisms *within* the individual; social phobia, then, would be its ultimate consequence.

Such an intrapersonal outlook would necessarily be reductionist, that is, bent on finding an explanation for the socially phobic behavior of the whole human organism in terms of the malfunctioning of some of its constituent elements.

In the currently received view, the reductionist construal of the human is bound to be dualist with a machine-like human body (Shepherd, 1993, p. 569; Taylor, 1970, p. 62), in which dwells a non-material "ghostly" mind. In keeping with this, malfunctioning processes could be envisaged as either physical (typically neurophysiologic) or "mental" (as in mental disease) – however defined.

However that may be, in both domains causality is envisaged as an antecedent event (Taylor, 1970, p. 49), a transmittal of force (or its failure) from one contiguous element to another. The action of each element is explained by the "force" exerted by the element lower down the chain of transmission. Although in the material domain, a mechanical system is literally possible, in the mental "realm" the chain can only be meta-phorical, with expectations, intentions, interpretations, and so on, acting as figurative links in a chain and metaphorically satisfying the require-ment of contiguity. Social phobia, then, construed as a faulty mechan-ism, would be the result of defects in, malfunction of, or altogether a breakdown of such an orderly transmission.

As an alternative approach to explanation, compatible with an inter-personal outlook, I shall propose a framework that is neither reductionist nor dualist. This emphasizes, on the one hand, the organic integration of a living organism (human and otherwise), and, on the other hand, the mutuality and indeed the purposeful nature of the activities of a person within his or her social and cultural environment. For this I shall rely on the Aristotelian analytical framework of explanation (Hocutt, 1974; Ross, 1995, pp. 74–77; Hankinson, 2009). This, contrary to the mechan-istic Cartesian universe, is compatible with a biological and a systemic or holistic outlook, emphasizing organization, functionality and, therefore, purpose as inherent in the activities of live beings in their natural settings (Nussbaum, 1978, pp. 59–99). Purpose – it must be emphasized – does not entail providential design or, indeed, conscious intention. Natural processes are goal directed. They are inherent in the self-maintaining nature of the living organism (Nussbaum, 1978, pp. 76–80).

I shall argue that this framework offers the appropriate analytical tools for understanding social phobia and present it in detail later. The reason for this delay is as follows.

As my justification for the adoption of such a conceptual framework rests in part, on the unsatisfactory record (if judged leniently) or indeed failure (if judged sternly) of the reductionist accounts, I shall start with a survey of two lines of research carried out within the reductionist and dualist perspective. Adopting empathetically (and provisionally) the Cartesian world view, I shall concentrate, within the physical domain (Chapter 4), on a search for brain defects, and within the "mental" domain (Chapter 5), for faulty mental (cognitive) structures or processes as providing possible accounts for the allegedly abnormal state of anxiety that, in turn, gives rise to social phobia.

4   Reductive dualism I: social phobia as a consequence of bodily (brain) defects

Individuals who are identified as socially phobic often complain of various physical sensations (e.g. sweating, blushing, tachycardia and tremulousness) they experience, when, for example, entering a cafeteria or a classroom, meeting strangers at a party or imagining an interview lying ahead. At their peak, a vast range of somatic reactions include among others: (1) palpitations and cool extremities and pallor (peripheral vasoconstriction); (2) respiratory difficulties; (3) an urge to urinate, intestinal cramps and alternating diarrhea and constipation and vomiting; (4) muscle tension in the face, trembling and incoordination of the hands; and (5) speech difficulties due to troubled breathing and lack of coordination of muscles involved in articulation (being "tongue-tied"). These are also accompanied by blunted perceptiveness and diminished responsiveness.

Although reported subjectively, these are not confabulations; many of these somatic responses can be independently measured and verified. What could account for this very physical anxiousness experienced powerfully and bafflingly in seemingly anodyne circumstances?

A possible account could be that the brain processes involved in the regulation of the above anxious reactions are defective. In this spirit, Liebowitz, Gorman, Fyer and Klein, 1985, p. 729) have suggested that, "it is tempting to speculate that social phobics either experience greater or more sustained increases or are more sensitive to normal stress-mediated catecholamine elevations."

Background

With the exception of Liebowitz et al.'s (1985) brief, speculative statement, a more definite neurobiological formulation of social phobia has – to my knowledge – never been published. Rather, it is held loosely that social phobia is a valid disease entity – the upshot of excessive anxiety, itself the consequence of putative abnormalities in brain neurological circuitry, triggered by some genetic defect.

111

Although offering no specific content (i.e. theoretical postulates providing guidance for research), these unarticulated theses hold sway over a considerable number of researchers and clinicians who uphold them in practice. These draw on a general biomedical outlook that, in its search for explanatory models, accords ontological primacy to (lesions in) biological structures and (malfunctioning in) physiology. Such a perspective – in turn – is the logical extension of construing social phobia as a disease (see Chapter 2).

The principles of this perspective may be summarized in the following propositions:

(1) The socially phobic pattern of behavior is the ultimate result of (molecular or cellular) events in particular brain regions of the individual exhibiting it. These events may be localized, and are associated with quantitative changes in particular neurobiological or biochemical substances. In other words, both morphological (structural) and physiological (functional) abnormalities (both unspecified) ought to be detected in the brains of individuals identified as socially phobic. This, however, begs a related question: how do the above abnormalities come into being? The answer is found in the second proposition.

(2) Something coded in the genes of the individual displaying the socially phobic pattern predisposes him or her to the above-mentioned brain abnormalities and, hence, anxiety and social phobia.

Overall, then, this implicit model presumes that social phobia, while being a distinct disease entity, is something as yet unspecified – on the biological level of analysis – which the afflicted individual actually and concretely carries within. Materially and figuratively, social phobia – as construed within the biomedical model – is something that one has (or lacks). It is assumed, therefore, that the presence or absence of whatever is causing social phobia, although unknown, can be detected "naturalistically" by observing and probing. Theory, viewed from such a "naturalistic" cum medical vantage point, is not really necessary, and its absence is not a hindrance (if not a deliverance).

In the following pages I shall review the available evidence providing a test of the above propositions.

Neurobiological abnormalities

A research program seeking to show that the socially phobic pattern of behavior and experience is the consequence of brain defects has first to postulate the brain abnormalities theoretically and then identify these experimentally. A subsequent demonstration of their causal role needs to be carried out independently.

The "naturalist" outlook notwithstanding, the absence of a theoretical framework has been the main obstacle on the path towards the realization of such a program. The formulation of such a theory is a tall order and not only in the case of social phobia (e.g. depression). For this reason, although such a theory is sorely needed, it is unlikely that the void will be filled quickly.

This conceptual hurdle is being sidestepped by approaching social phobia "naturalistically," as it were. Presuming that social phobia is a (valid) disease entity, the resulting research has – strictly speaking – attempted to identify biological features (or correlates) of social phobia. This is not, however, how it is viewed by those who have been carrying out and interpreting the studies.

Such research has been carried out assuming that a *quantitative* difference (i.e. one of degree) between group averages of socially phobic subjects and a matched control group on a neurobiological parameter indicates a *qualitative* difference. In other words, such studies presume to unveil an underlying abnormality, characteristic of social phobia. Whether this bold assumption is warranted is very much in doubt and we shall return to it subsequently.

Be that as it may, in order to identify such disparities, the bulk of available research took one of three approaches: (1) measuring brain function and structure (by means of brain-imaging techniques); (2) measuring (either directly or indirectly) neurotransmission; and (3) considering responses to pharmacological treatment as indications of underlying neurobiological mechanisms.

A previous comprehensive review (Stravynski, 2007, pp. 143–183) found that on the whole: "The bulk of the results surveyed are consistent with the fact that on any measure, socially phobic individuals are much alike their normal counterparts than different from them" (p. 183).

In this update to the earlier review, I have chosen to concentrate on what we consider to be the main tests of the notion of brain defects: the brain functions and structure as well as the neurotransmission of the socially phobic.

As the main development between the 2007 and the present survey has been the surge in use of functional neuroimaging (fMRI), I shall begin with it.

Structural and functional neuroimaging studies

Continuing developments in magnetic resonance imaging (i.e. structural MRI; functional MRI and diffusion tensor imaging – DTI) and radionuclide imaging (i.e. Positron Emission Tomography – PET – and Single Photon Emission Computed Tomography – SPECT) allow direct, non-invasive, measurement of activity in the living human brain. The functional neuroimaging methods measure changes in the consumption of glucose and oxygen in brain tissues. This allows the observation of active parts of the brain, while performing a task compatible with the very narrow constraint of lying within a scanner (e.g. responding to images of angry faces).

These technologies have been applied extensively to the study of structural and functional neural correlates of aspects of social phobia.

Table 4.1 summarizes studies conducted between 2006 and 2013. Earlier studies (up to 2006) may be found in Stravynski (2007, pp. 157–165).

Neuroimaging studies can be divided in two according to the method used: structural and functional MRI.

Structural MRI studies of social phobia are few and the results rather non-specific. Irle *et al.* (2010), for example, found that the socially phobic participants' hippocampus and amygdala had diminished volumes relative to those of normal control subjects (see Table 4.1). The meaning of these findings, however, is not evident; is it the consequence or the cause? However that may be, similar results have been now observed in other anxiety disorders, as well as mood disorders and even psychotic disorders (Brambilla, Barale, Caverzasi and Soares, 2002; Caetano *et al.*, 2007; Keller *et al.*, 2008; Hayano *et al.*, 2009; Lorenzetti, Allen, Fornito and Yücel, 2009; Atmaca, Sirlier, Yildirim and Kayali, 2011; Morey *et al.*, 2012; Watson *et al.*, 2012).

In contrast to the limited number of structural MRI studies, the use of functional MRI (fMRI) has been quite extensive. Most of these consisted of experiments involving the presentation to the participants of what are presumed to be 'anxiety-inducing' stimuli: fearful and angry faces (e.g. Phan, Fitzgerald, Nathan and Tancer, 2006; Campbell *et al.*, 2007; Yoon, Fitzgerald, Angstadt, McCarron and Phan, 2007; Evans *et al.*, 2008), or angry-sounding voices (Quadflieg, Mohr, Mentzel, Miltner and Straube, 2008).

Taken as whole, neuroimaging findings have been interpreted as characterizing social phobia with a predominantly subcortical/automatic pattern of emotion processing with insufficient cortical control (Tillfors, 2004; Freitas-Ferrari *et al.*, 2010). This interpretation raises a number of difficulties.

First of all, the experiments do not allow one to tell whether the enhanced amygdala activity is a consequence of an inadequate cortical control, or whether it reflects a primary hyperactivity of this subcortical

Table 4.1. *Neuroimaging studies*

Study	Subjects	Methods	Results
Structural MRI			
Phan et al. (2009)	30 SP 30 NC	Diffusor tensor imaging was used to assess fractional anisotropy within white matter of the whole brain.	Fractional anisotropy localized to the right uncinate fasciculus white matter near the orbitofrontal cortex; SP<NC
Irle et al. (2010)	24 SP 24 NC	3-dimensional structural magnetic resonance imaging of the amygdala and hippocampus and a clinical investigation.	Amygdala and hippocampus; SP<NC. Reduction in the size of the amygdala was statistically significant for men but not women. Smaller right-sided hippocampal volumes of SP significantly related to severity of SP.
Functional MRI (fMRI)			
Campbell et al. (2007)	14 SP 14 NC	Participants performed a facial emotion processing task consisting of blocks of neutral, fear, contempt, anger and happy faces. Analyses focused on the temporal dynamics of the amygdala, prefrontal cortex and fusiform face area.	Amygdala responses in SP occurred later than the NC participants to fear, angry and happy faces. Parallel prefrontal cortex responses were found for happy and fearful faces. No group differences in temporal response patterns in the fusiform face area.
Cooney et al. (2006)	10 SP 10 NC	Participants viewed fearful, angry, sad, happy and neutral facial expressions as well as an oval with a cross-hair in the middle that was the same size as the faces and were asked to make valence ratings.	Activations in right amygdala for neutral face vs. oval contrast; SP>NC. Activations in left amygdala for neutral face vs. oval contrast; NC>SP. Right amygdala for the neutral face vs. oval contrast correlated significantly with anxiety scores.
Phan et al. (2006)	10 SP 10 NC	Participants viewed blocks of emotionally salient facial expressions.	Activations in right amygdala in response to harsh vs. happy faces and in response to harsh vs. neutral faces; SP>NC. Activation to harsh faces within the right amygdala correlated with the intensity of social anxiety.

Table 4.1. (*cont.*)

Study	Subjects	Methods	Results
Sareen *et al.* (2007)	10 SP 10 NC	Participants underwent an fMRI task while performing an implicit sequence learning task.	Activation in bilateral amygdala, insula, lingual gyrus, superior parietal and middle frontal gyrus to the high-intensity emotional faces *vs.* baseline; SP>NC. Bilateral amygdala activation to the low-intensity emotional faces *vs.* baseline; SP<NC.
Quadflieg *et al.* (2008)	12 SP 12 NC	Brain responses to neutral and angry voices were assessed when emotional prosody was either task-relevant or task-irrelevant.	Orbitofrontal activation in response to angry *vs.* neutral voices under both task conditions; SP>NC.
Gentili *et al.* (2009)	18 SP 7 NC	Participants performed a face perception task with emotional and neutral stimuli. The "default mode network" was assessed.	Deactivations in precuneus/posterior cingulate gyrus during task condition; SP<NC.
Goldin, Manber *et al.* (2009)	15 SP 17 NC	Participants implemented a cognitive-linguistic regulation of emotional reactivity induced by images of social (harsh facial expressions) and physical (violent scenes) threat.	Emotional reactivity: • Brain activations in prefrontal cortex, parahippocampal gyrus, postcentral gyrus, superior parietal lobule and occipital regions during social threat stimuli *vs.* neutral scenes; SP>NC. • Brain activations in precuneus, inferior parietal lobule and supramarginal gyrus during social threat *vs.* neutral scenes; SP<NC. • No significant group differences for physical threat condition. Emotional regulation: • Brain activations in regions of the prefrontal cortex, occipital cortex and parietal and temporal lobes for regulate *vs.* social threat contrast; SP<NC. • Brain activations in dorsolateral prefrontal cortex and subcortical structures for regulate *vs.* physical threat contrast; SP>NC. • Brain activations in middle frontal gyrus and superior temporal gyrus for regulate *vs.* physical threat contrast; SP<NC.

Study	N	Task	Findings
Goldin, Manber-Ball et al., (2009)	27 SP 27 NC	Participants reacted to and implemented cognitive reappraisal to down-regulate negative emotional reactivity to negative self-beliefs.	Emotional reactivity: • Early brain responses in bilateral dorsolateral prefrontal cortex, left superior temporal gyrus and right supramarginal gyrus; SP<NC. • Late responses in bilateral inferior parietal lobule; SP>NC. Cognitive reappraisal: • Early brain responses in regions of the prefrontal cortex, dorsal anterior cingulate cortex, temporal lobe, parietal cortex and subcortical regions; SP<NC. • Late responses in brain regions of the dorsolateral and ventrolateral PFC, insular cortex and parietal cortex; SP>NC.
Blair, Geraci et al. (2008)	17 SP 17 NC	Participants read positive, negative and neutral comments concerning either self or somebody else.	Activations in medical prefrontal cortex and bilateral amygdala in response to negative comments (criticism) referring to themselves; SP>NC.
Blair, Shaywitz et al. (2008)	17 SP (without GAD) 17 GAD (without SP) 17 NC	Participants viewed neutral, fearful and angry facial expressions while making a gender judgment.	Activations in regions of the prefrontal cortex, anterior cingulate and temporal cortex to fearful relative to neutral expressions; SP>NC>GAD. Activations in middle frontal gyrus, inferior temporal cortex and culmen to angry relative to neutral expressions; GAD>NC. Activations in middle frontal gyrus and inferior temporal cortex to angry relative to neutral expressions; SP>NC.
Evans et al. (2008)	11 SP 11 NC	Participants passively viewed angry, happy and neutral schematic faces.	Activations in right amygdala, supramarginal and superior frontal gyrus for the angry vs. neutral contrast; SP>NC. Activation in the anterior cingulate gyrus; SP<NC.
Gentili et al. (2008)	8 SP 7 NC	Participants viewed angry, fearful, disgusted, happy and neutral faces and scrambled pictures (visual baseline).	Activations in left amygdala, insula and bilateral superior temporal sulcus in response to emotional and neutral pictures vs. baseline; SP>NC. Activations in left fusiform gyrus, left dorsolateral prefrontal cortex and bilateral intraparietal sulcus in response to emotional and neutral pictures vs. baseline; SP<NC.

Table 4.1. (*cont.*)

Study	Subjects	Methods	Results
Schmidt *et al.* (2010)	19 SP 18 NC	Participants attended either to social meaning (direct task) or to grammatical category (indirect task) of phobia-related vs. phobia-unrelated words.	Indirect task: Activation of the amygdala and orbitofrontal cortex in response to phobia-related vs. phobia-unrelated words; SP>NC. Direct task: No difference between SP and NC. Activation in insula to phobia-related vs. phobia-unrelated words was positively correlated with symptom severity of SP patients.
Blair *et al.* (2010)	16 SP 16 NC	fMRI scans while reading stories that involved neutral social events, unintentional social transgressions (e.g. choking on food at a party and coughing it up), or intentional social transgressions (e.g. disliking food at a party and spitting it out).	Increased brain activations in ventro- and dorsomedial prefrontal cortex, insula, amygdala/parahippocampal gyrus for all transgression types; SP>NC. Increased brain activations in ventro- and dorsomedial prefrontal cortex in response to unintentional relative to intentional transgressions; SP>NC.
Danti *et al.* (2010)	8 SP 7 NC	Participants were asked to perform a one-back repetition detection task based on face identity of differing emotional expressions. Functional connectivity analysis was used between seed regions of interest and voxels in the whole brain.	Fusiform gyrus: Negative correlation with precuneus, posterior cingulate gyrus, sensorimotor cortical areas; SP<NC. Right superior temporal sulcus: Negative correlation with inferior parietal, anterior intraparietal cortex and precuneus; SP<NC. Positive correlation in ventral premotor/inferior frontal areas; SP>NC. Left amygdala: Negative correlation in superior temporal cortex, inferior parietal, anterior middle prefrontal and postcentral gyrus; SP>NC. Positive correlation in inferior frontal regions; SP>NC. Negative correlation in paracentral sensorimotor cortex; SP<NC.

Study	Sample	Task	Results
Klumpp et al. (2010)	12 SP 12 NC	Participants performed a facial emotion processing task with threatening stimuli morphed at low, moderate and high intensities.	Activity in left amygdala for threatening faces at moderate and high intensity; SP>NC. Activity in right amygdala for threatening faces at high intensity; SP>NC. Whole brain results: High threat intensity: Brain activations in parahippocampal gyrus, inferior frontal and orbitofrontal cortex; SP>NC. Moderate threat intensity: Brain activations in insula, cerebellum, midbrain and putamen; SP>NC. Low threat intensity: Brain activations in cuneus, thalamus, parahippocampal gyrus and insula; SP>NC. Brain activations in middle frontal gyrus; SP<NC.
Blair, Geraci, Korelitz et al. (2011)	39 SP – unmedicated (25 adults, 14 adolescents) 39 NC (23 adults, 16 adolescents)	While in the fMRI scan, participants viewed angry, fearful and neutral facial expressions while making a gender judgment.	Activations in the amygdala while viewing fearful faces and activations in the rostral anterior cingulate cortex in response to fearful and angry faces; SP>NC. No enhanced neural response in SP vs. NC in response to neutral facial expressions. Increased neural responses to angry and fearful expressions within the anterior cingulate positively correlated with complaint severity in adults with SP.
Blair, Geraci, Otero et al. (2011)	15 SP (unmedicated) 15 NC	fMRI bold responses recorded while participants read 1st (e.g., I'm ugly) and 2nd (e.g., you're ugly) person viewpoints comments.	Increased activation in medial prefrontal cortex in response to 1st relative to 2nd person viewpoints; NC. Increased activation in medial prefrontal cortex in response to 2nd relative to 1st person viewpoints; SP. Increased activations in SP significantly correlated with severity of social anxiety.
Brühl et al. (2011)	16 SP 18 NC	Subjects completed a task involving the anticipation of cued visual stimuli with prior known emotional valence (positive, negative and neutral) or prior unknown/ambiguous emotional content. The anticipated stimuli had no specific socially phobic content.	Increased activations in the upper midbrain/dorsal thalamus, the amygdala and in temporo-occipital and parietal regions during the anticipation of prior known negative and prior ambiguous emotional valence; SP>NC. Activations in the amygdala and in occipital regions correlated with trait anxiety and social anxiety measures. Decreased activations in orbitofrontal cortex; SP<NC.

Table 4.1. (*cont.*)

Study	Subjects	Methods	Results
Nakao *et al.* (2011)	6 SP 9 NC	While in the fMRI scanner, participants were presented with photographs of various social situations (e.g. going to a restaurant) and were asked to imagine themselves in those situations.	Brain activations in posterior cingulate gyrus, cerebellum and precuneus during the task trial; SP<NC.
Schneier *et al.* (2011)	16 SP (unmedicated) 16 NC	fMRI to assess neural response to viewed images of neutral faces simulating movement into eye contact vs. away from eye contact. Patients treated 8 weeks with paroxetine and then re-imaged.	Baseline: Neural response to eye contact in parahippocampal cortex, inferior parietal lobule, supramarginal gyrus, posterior cingulate and middle occipital cortex; SP>NC. After paroxetine: Improvement was associated with decreased neural response to eye contact in regions including inferior and middle frontal gyri, anterior cingulate, posterior cingulate, precuneus and inferior parietal lobule.
Klumpp *et al.* (2012)	29 SP 26 NC	Participants performed an emotional face matching task involving the processing of fear, angry and happy facial expressions; A "psychophysiological interaction analysis" was used to examine functional "coupling" between the insula and prefrontal cortex.	Bilateral anterior insula activation for fearful vs. happy faces; SP>NC. Right anterior insula and dorsal anterior cingulate coupling; SP<NC.

Note: NC: normal control
SP: social phobia
GAD: generalized anxiety disorder

structure, with the consequent insufficiency of an otherwise normal cortical function.

Secondly, enhanced amygdala activation (as well as that of other limbic structures) is typical of fear states in general, as observed in numerous imaging studies of human (Costafreda, Brammer, David and Fu, 2008; Sehlmeyer *et al.*, 2009; Herry *et al.*, 2010) and non-human organisms (Delgado, Olsson and Phelps, 2006).

Thirdly, hyperactive amygdala and cortical dysfunction have been observed in other anxiety disorders, including panic (Eren, Tukel, Polat, Karaman and Unal, 2003), generalized anxiety disorder (Thomas *et al.*, 2001; Bremner, 2004) and post-traumatic stress disorder (Liberzon and Phan, 2003; Shin *et al.*, 2005;). Additionally, it has been observed in affective disorders (Townsend and Altshuler, 2012).

Overall, then, amygdala hyperactivity is a common aspect of fear states. As such it is an element of the overall fear response of the living organism.

To reiterate: the overall tenor of these findings is a greater reactivity of the limbic and corticolimbic system (in most cases amygdala, but also anterior cingulate, insula, orbitofrontal cortex) of the socially phobic in comparison to normal control subjects.

Typically, this "over"-activation of the amygdala and the medial prefrontal cortex are interpreted as flagging a neurological "abnormality" (e.g. "a neurocircuitry dysfunction," "pathological neural responses" (Blair, Shaywitz *et al.*, 2008, p. 1193) in social phobia. As the greater brain reactivity of the socially phobic is part of stronger overall organismic and behavioral response (i.e. greater fearfulness of the socially phobic in comparison to control participants), the conclusion seems rather forced and unwarranted. Qualitatively speaking, normal individuals exhibit mostly similar brain activation, but to a lesser degree than the socially phobic.

The claims that statistical differences between group averages represent "abnormalities" (e.g. Freitas-Ferrari *et al.*, 2010) are unjustified at best and misleading at worst. If the term "abnormality" were defined as a controlling factor with predictable consequences, no support for it was in evidence (Freitas-Ferrari *et al.*, 2010). As seen previously, in all studies making such claims, socially phobic individuals indeed showed a higher degree of the brain activity being measured than the normal control participants. The point, however, is that all participants, not just the socially phobic, displayed the same brain activity to varying degrees.

How would such a difference in scale between experimental groups square with the proposition that it reflects an "abnormality," and, by inference, plays a causal role in social phobia? Need not effect be present when the cause is manifest (and vice versa)? In light of the above, why were only the socially phobic individuals socially phobic? Perhaps a counterargument to the objection could be that only a certain critical threshold of this brain activity is causal, but then what is it?

Be that as it may, even in the studies where significant statistical differences between group averages occurred, a sizeable overlap between the score distributions of each group was in evidence. Given the great individual variability found on every dimension of social phobia, it is most likely that some of the socially phobic participants would fall below such a hypothetical threshold, while some of the normal control individuals would score above it. Thus, the likelihood that some participants in all experimental groups overlap to some extent, further undermines the possibility that the presumed "abnormality," if that is what it is, plays a causal role in social phobia.

Speaking figuratively, abnormality in this context, rather than referring to any process characterizing social phobia, fits much better the spurious and complacent conclusions drawn from the statistical differences observed. Is it not odd that one group of individuals is singled out for a universal pattern of brain activity? This strongly suggests that the conclusions regarding abnormality are foreshadowed in the a-priori assumptions of the biomedical outlook. Lacking any theoretical notion to guide them, confusing correlation with causality, the experiments fail to put its central thesis – social phobia as a disease – to the test.

For all the above reasons, considering the "excessive" socially phobic brain activity as arising out of abnormal brain circuitry is arbitrary. It is more likely empirically, and more prudent (as well as conceptually economical – mindful of "Occam's razor"), to consider the difference in degree of brain activation between the socially phobic and control subjects as representing the difference between the intensity of the fearful response of the whole organism, in each group. Functional neuroimaging provides a glimpse into some of the processes involved in socially phobic as well as normal fearfulness; it does not identify brain "abnormalities" causing social phobia.

Direct measurements of neurotransmitter systems

Direct measurement of central and peripheral receptor and transporter functions is a research paradigm that has been commonly used in the study of anxiety and mood disorders as a means to assess indirectly the less accessible central neurotransmission. The rationale of extending this general approach to socially phobic individuals is based on the expectation that they would display similar alterations in markers of monoaminergic function that are known to be present in other conditions with prominent anxious components such as mood, panic and generalized anxiety disorders (Millan, 2003). As with the neuroimaging studies, I shall update the Stravynski (2007) survey. Studies using this paradigm are summarized in Table 4.2.

Although the number of functional neuroimaging investigations has risen exponentially over the past few years, studies of neurotransmitter systems, either direct or indirect, have been on the wane. No wonder, as can be seen in the earlier (Stravynski, 2007, pp. 145–153) review, the findings were mostly negative and some contradictory.

While some suggestions have been made (Tiihonen *et al.*, 1997) that social phobia may be associated with abnormal central dopamine function, the recent findings, summarized below, do not support this contention.

Dopamine (DA) and serotonin (5-HT) are monoamine neurotransmitters with widespread distributions and wide-ranging functional implications in the brain. The principal DA pathways include: (1) the nigrostriatal pathway, which links the dopaminegic cell bodies found in the substantia nigra to the basal ganglia neurons and regulates locomotor events; (2) the mesolimbic circuit, which arises in the ventral tegmental area (VTA) and projects to the limbic cortices, nucleus accumbens and amygdala, where it regulates emotional events (e.g. reinforcement, natural rewards and drug addiction); (3) the mesocortical pathway, which also arises in VTA but projects further into the neocortex (especially prefrontal regions), where it modulates cognitive function (e.g. working memory, attention, executive function). Serotonin (5-HT) cell bodies are found mainly in the raphe nuclei and project extensively to the limbic structures and the cerebral cortex. Serotonin is involved in the modulation of mood, sleep, appetite and pain. Depression, suicide, impulsive behaviour and aggressiveness, for instance, all appear to be associated with certain imbalances in serotonin.

Dopaminergic (DA) pathways – Using single photon emission computerized tomography (SPECT) neuroreceptor imaging, Tiihonen *et al.* (1997) reported low striatal dopamine transporter (DAT) binding (a presynaptic measure of dopaminergic innervation). Conversely, van der Wee *et al.* (2008) found the same measure to be increased in social phobia.

Schneier *et al.* (2000, 2008) used positron emission tomography (PET) to investigate dopaminergic neurotransmission and reported low availability of striatal D2 receptors (a primarily postsynaptic measure) in social phobia and in social phobia concurrent with obsessive-compulsive disorder. In the most recent, carefully designed study by the same group, socially phobic and control participants completed a

Table 4.2. *Neurotransmission studies*

Study	Subjects	Methods	Results
Position emission tomography (PET)			
Lanzenberger et al. (2007)	12 SP (unmedicated) 18 NC	Using PET and the radioligand [carbonyl-11C] WAY-100625, the 5-HT1A receptor was quantified.	5-HT1A binding potential in amygdala, anterior cingulate cortex, insula and dorsal raphe nuclei; SP<NC.
Schneier et al. (2009)	12 SP 13 NC	Participants completed baseline assessment of D2 receptor availability using PET with the radiotracer [11C]raclopride. A repeat scan after intravenous administration of d-amphetamine to study dopamine release was performed (12 SP, 13 NC). Participants also completed SPECT with the radiotracer [123I]methyl 3ß-(4-iodophenyl) tropane-2ß-carboxylate ([123I]ß-CIT) to assess DAT availability (12 SP, 12 NC).	Striatal DAT availability, the overall striatal or striatal sub-region D2 receptor availability at baseline, or change in D2 receptor availability after d-amphetamine; SP=NC.
Lanzenberger et al. (2010)	12 SP 18 NC	Using PET and the radioligand [carbonyl-11C]WAY-100635, the 5-HT1A receptor was quantified. Partial correlation analysis was performed to test the association between cortisol plasma levels and 50HT1A receptor binding.	Cortisol plasma levels; SP<NC. Negative correlations between cortisol plasma levels and 5-HT1A binding in the amygdala, hippocampus and retrosplenial cortex; SP only.
Peripheral (blood sample) studies			
Barkan et al. (2006)	15 SP (drug-free) 18 NC	Blood sample collected in the morning for measures of serotonin transporter (5-HTT), as determined by [3H]5-HT uptake to blood lymphocytes.	[3H]5-HT maximum uptake velocity (Vmax); SP=NC 5-HTT affinity (Km); SP=NC.
Laufer, Zucker et al. (2005)	20 SP (drug-free) 15 NC	Blood sample collected in the morning for measures of vesicular monoamine transporter (VMAT2) using high-affinity [(3)H] dihydrotetrabenazine ([(3)H]TBZOH) binding.	VMAT2 density (B[max]); SP=NC. VMAT2 affinity constants (K[d]); SP=NC.

Study	Sample	Method	Results
Laufer, Maayan et al. (2005)	26 SP (drug-free) 21 NC	Blood sample collected in the morning for measures of dehydroepiandrosterone (DHEA), its sulfate ester (DHEA-S), pregnenolone and cortisol.	SP=NC on all measures.
Peripheral (blood sample) studies			
Barkan et al. (2006)	15 SP (drug-free) 18 NC	Blood sample collected in the morning for measures of serotonin transporter (5-HTT), as determined by [3H]5-HTT uptake to blood lymphocytes.	[3H]5-HT maximum uptake velocity (Vmax); SP=NC. 5-HTT affinity (Km); SP=NC.
Laufer, Zucker et al. (2005)	20 SP (drug-free) 15 NC	Blood sample collected in the morning for measures of vesicular monoamine transporter (VMAT2) characterized using high-affinity [(3)H] dihydrotetrabenazine ([(3)H]TBZOH) binding.	VMAT2 density (B(max)); SP=NC. VMAT2 affinity constants (K(d)); SP=NC.
Laufer, Maayan et al. (2005)	26 SP (drug-free) 21 NC	Blood sample collected in the morning for measures of dehydroepiandrosterone (DHEA), its sulphate ester (DHEA-S), pregnenolone and cortisol.	SP=NC on all measures.
Bell et al. (2013)	23 SP 23 NC	Challenge with 400 mg of selective D2 antagonist, sulpride, in a randomized, placebo-controlled, crossover design.	Prolactin response to sulpride; SP=NC. Social anxiety, mood and ability to experience pleasure; SP=NC.
Nardi et al. (2009)	26 NC 19 SP 28 PD 25 GAD All participants psychotropic drug-free for at least 4 weeks	Challenge with 480 mg of oral caffeine in a randomized double-blind experiment performed on 2 occasions, 7 days apart.	Number of induced episodes of panic and features of anxiety; NC<GAD<PD and SP.

Note: NC: normal control
SP: social phobia
GAD: generalized anxiety disorder
PD: panic disorder

baseline assessment of D2 receptor availability using PET and then a repeated scan after intravenous administration of d-amphetamine to study dopamine release (Schneier et al., 2009). In addition, SPECT was employed to assess DAT availability. Striatal DAT availability, the overall striatal D2 receptor availability at baseline, or change in D2 receptor availability after d-amphetamine, did not differ between the two groups.

In the same vein, an indirect challenge study with 400 mg of selective D2 antagonist-sulpiride, in a randomized, placebo-controlled, crossover design, did not show any significant difference between socially phobic and control participants (Bell et al., 2013).

Serotonergic (5-HT) pathways – The studies concentrating on 5-HT neurotransmission and the 5-HT1A binding potential (BP) in social phobia (and other anxiety disorders) are based on the following rationale. First of all, serotonin (5-HT) has been shown to be implicated in the regulation of mood and affective states. Secondly, drugs modulating the serotonergic system are widely used in the treatment of anxiety disorders and depression. Thirdly, agonists of the 5-HT1A receptor have modest anxiolytic properties (Blier and Abbott, 2001).

Thus, Lanzenberger et al. (2007) employed PET and the highly specific and selective 5-HT1A receptor radioligand to investigate the regional 5-HT1A BP in socially phobic and matched control participants. The study focused on the limbic and paralimbic system and the results revealed a significantly lower 5-HT1A receptor BP in the amygdala, the anterior cingulate cortex and insula of the socially phobic relative to the control participants.

In a subsequent study (Lanzenberger et al., 2010), the relationship between 5-HT1A binding and plasma cortisol levels was examined. The main finding was an overall negative correlation between cortisol plasma levels and regional 5-HT1A receptor binding in all participants. In the socially phobic group, the negative correlation between cortisol plasma levels and 5-HT1A receptor binding in the amygdala and the hippocampus was stronger than in the normal group. However, as the authors point out, the fact that the significance of correlations from the control subjects did not survive correction for multiple comparisons might be attributed to the small sample size. In other words, the statistical differences between the socially phobic and the normal groups may be an artifact.

In addition to PET and SPECT studies of central nervous system neurotransmission, the peripheral studies of serotonin transporter (5-HTT) (Barkan et al., 2006), vesicular monoamine transporter (VMAT2) (Laufer, Zucker et al., 2005), or corticosteroids (Laufer, Maayan et al.,

2005), have not revealed any significant differences between the socially phobic and comparison participants.

These mostly negative results are consistent with the non-specificity of 5-HT overall. This neurotransmitter serotonin (5-HT) is widely involved in the regulation of mood and affective states. For example, Sullivan *et al.* (2005) reported an association between lower 5-HT1A binding potential and depression. In the same vein, a widespread reduction in 5-HT1A receptor binding has been observed in anxious patients identified as "chronic fatigue syndrome" (Bailer *et al.*, 2005).

In summary, the overall trend found in these studies is that the neurotransmission of the socially phobic and the normal is very much alike.

Pharmacological treatments and the neurobiology of social phobia

The demonstrated efficacy of various pharmacological compounds reducing distress and avoidance has been on occasion invoked as evidence for a neurobiological mechanism underlying – as it were – social phobia. For instance, Nutt, Bell and Malizia (1998, p. 7) have expressed the opinion that "the clinical effectiveness of SSRI's (see section II below) in the treatment of social anxiety disorder indicates that serotonin (5-HT) has a role in the etiology of social anxiety disorder."

While serotonin could be considered – speculatively – as a candidate for playing such a role, the evidence reviewed earlier contradicts this. However that may be, response to treatment cannot be regarded as providing evidence for it. For in addition to reacting to SSRIs, socially phobic patients are also equally responsive to other classes of medication, and to alcohol as well as various psychological treatments in like manner (see Stravynski, 2007, pp. 289–334).

Psychotropic medication, in general, achieves its effect by affecting the central nervous system. When the medication is taken or administered, it is absorbed into the blood and carried by the circulatory system to the brain. These drugs bind with a specific receptor that has been targeted. Electrochemical changes that occur then release the drug from the receptor site where it exerts its effects, some desired, others not. A psychotropic medication typically interferes with, and therefore transforms, the transmission of nerve impulses. This is achieved by modulating the availability of the neurotransmitter required for proper impulse transmission or modifying properties of cell membranes. A therapeutic effect is achieved by saturating the receptors; this also provokes undesired or adverse effects.

Four different classes of psychopharmacological agents, each involving distinct molecular targets, have been extensively evaluated for their anxiety-reducing properties in the treatment of social phobia (see, e.g., Stein *et al.*, 2009). These are as follows:

I. Monoamine oxidase inhibitors (MAOI) – these block the metabolism of the catecholamines and serotonin through inactivation of their catabolic enzyme, monoamine oxidase. A refinement within the same class is the reversible inhibitors of monoamine oxidase (RIMAs). Both target the catabolic enzyme; while the MAOIs bind permanently, the RIMAs do so reversibly. Practically this broadens the restrictive diet required under the MAOIs. A typical use for this type of medication (e.g. moclobemide) is for the treatment of depression.

II. Selective serotonin reuptake inhibitors (SSRIs) – these inhibit the transport of serotonin back into the neuron where it is subsequently metabolized, thus increasing the synaptic concentration of this neurotransmitter. At this time, this type of medication is considered first-choice treatment for depression and most of the anxiety disorders (see Clinical Practice Guidelines: Social Anxiety Disorder, 2006, pp. 37S-41S).

III. Other regulators of monoaminergic synaptic activity (e.g. buspirone) – this type of medication is used occasionally as an anxiolytic; olanzapine, however, is primarily used as an anti-psychotic.

IV. Suppressants of neural excitability that regulate gabaergic transmission:
   a. Agonists of aminobutyric acid (GABA) receptors (e.g. benzodiazepines) – this type of medication is commonly used as a treatment of anxiety and insomnia.
   b. Stimulators of GABA release (e.g. gabapentin) – this type of medication is used as an anti-convulsant and more recently as a mood stabilizer.

It is remarkable that, despite their distinct molecular targets, most pharmacological treatments are of equivalent efficacy, and result – in the short term and/or as long as the treatment lasts – in a similar degree of improvement. This may have something to do with the fact that inert ("placebo") pills also have not negligible therapeutic effects in social phobia. The difference between the effects of medication and the inert ("placebo") pills, although statistically significant, is usually modest (e.g. Kirsch, Moore, Scoboria and Nicholls, 2002). By way of illustration, in two out of four controlled studies of moclobemide, its effects were equivalent to those of placebo.

Altogether, it is most unlikely that any of the pharmacological processes inherent in the medications reveal anything about the etiology of
social phobia.

The implausibility is compounded by the fact that psychological
therapies result in a rather similar outcome in the short run, while –
unlike medication – maintaining gains subsequently, after treatment has
stopped (see Stravynski, 2007, pp. 289–334). Altogether, the generalized
decrease in anxiety observed as a result of a diversity of pharmacological
and psychological treatments cannot be seen as providing evidence for
the involvement of any one of the putative processes invoked by any of
the approaches, either pharmacological or psychological.

In summary, the inference of malfunctioning neurobiological processes
allegedly implicated in social phobia from pharmacological treatments,
is unwarranted. The unspoken presumption that the pharmacological
agent directly affects a putative biological substrate of social phobia is
speculative at best; the therapeutic response is in all likelihood only a
facet of a wider underlying neurobiological activity. On current evidence,
it is probable that the impact of pharmacological treatments is wide and
diffuse rather than narrow and specific. All result in functional improvement, by dampening the activity of the systems involved in emotional
regulation and therefore without actually influencing any putative underlying neurobiological defect. This is quite likely to be the case in social
phobia since pharmacological agents with very different pharmacological
profiles have been shown to be equipotent in reducing anxious distress.

Conclusions

In the face of sustained efforts yielding a large body of research, no
neurobiological malfunctioning underpinning social phobia has come to
light. Overall, research has been exploratory and "naturalistic" in nature.
It has yielded results that are inconclusive at best. With the possible
exception of some functional imaging findings (Blair *et al.*, 2010; Blair,
Geraci, Otero *et al.*, 2011) where the socially phobic brain activations
were quantitatively opposite to those observed in the normal group, no
other reports highlighting significant differences from normal subjects
are available.

Overall and on current evidence, I reach the conclusion that no major
structural or functional brain abnormalities are inherent in social phobia
as such. This conclusion is in agreement with earlier reviews (Tancer,
Lewis and Stein, 1995; Nickell and Uhde 1995). It is also consistent with
the normal biological functioning of socially phobic individuals in evidence in various areas (e.g. general psychophysiological responding – see

Stravynski, 2007, pp. 91–93; sleep – see Papadimitriou and Linkowski, 2005).

Functional neuroimaging studies have repeatedly shown that the activation of the amygdala is stronger in socially phobic than in normal individuals. Whether this is an exacerbation of the normal fear response – as is most likely – or evidence of a qualitative difference remains to a certain extent an open question. In the absence of any other abnormality, however, a structural defect or a malfunctioning of the brain seems highly implausible.

Ultimately, on current evidence, it is most likely that in fact there is no specific neurobiology or pathophysiology of social phobia. An intense reactivity of the "fear-network" is after all within normal range; it is hardly specific to social phobia (see Gorman, Kent, Sullivan and Coplan, 2000). Such a state of overexcitement of the brain would be associated with social phobia not specifically, but indirectly, as an instance of intense fearfulness. An intensified brain activity is involved in and sustains the active process of fearing of the whole living organism in the face of threat, be it phobic or not.

Genetic transmission of social phobia

Before turning to the question of whether social phobia is transmitted genetically, it is well to ask as a preliminary: what are genes and what is that they do? I am relying on Noble (2006) and Coen (1999) for enlightenment.

A genome designates all the chromosomes in a cell. A chromosome designates a long DNA molecule and its associated proteins. A gene is a section of DNA used in producing a certain protein. DNA is composed of four chemicals (nucleotides): adenine, thymine, guanine and cytosine, usually referred to by the letters A, T, G and C. There are two strands of DNA in each chromosome coiled round each other. The nucleotides on one strand are always found opposite those on the other in the following order: A opposite T, G opposite C (Noble, 2006, pp. 3–4; see also Coen, 1999, pp. 82–96).

Altogether the approximately 20,000–30,000 genes found in humans encode the sequences of roughly 100,000 proteins making up the human body (Coen, 1999, pp. 82–96).

How do the genes function? "Genes by themselves are dead; it is only in the fertilized egg cell, with all the proteins, lipids and other cellular machinery ... that the process of reading the genome to initiate development can get going. At least 100 different proteins are involved in this machinery without which the genome would express nothing" (Coen, 1999, p. 45). Thus function in biological systems depends on other factors that those specified genetically (Coen, 1999, p. 10). For this reason, it is impossible to recreate a living creature from a DNA code (Coen, 1999, p. 29). The outcome (phenotype) is powerfully influenced by a systems level of interactions of proteins (Coen, 1999, p. 17), with higher levels also triggering and influencing action at lower levels.

Assuming that hundreds of genes are necessary as a template for a biological function, the resulting number of possible combinations would be 10^{289} (Coen, 1999, p. 28). In the case of an organ like the brain approximately a third of the genome (approximately 10,000 genes) may be expressed (Coen, 1999, p. 43). The interactive possibilities in such numbers are staggering. For this reason, patterns and not individual genes are of consequence, while gene expression is influenced by both factors within the organism and the outside world (Coen, 1999, p. 17). Gene expression is characterized by a certain plasticity. Although set within definite boundaries, gene expression is modulated by circumstances in the environment (Kupiec and Sonigo, 2000, pp. 63–65; see also Coen, 1999, pp. 207–229 for a general discussion). For example, "the sex of all crocodilians, most turtles and some lizards depends on the temperature at which they develop" (Coen, 1999, p. 210). This principle is also illustrated, according to Noble, (2006, p. 93), by the fact that:

all cells in the same body have the same complement of genes inherited from the original gene combination formed from the sperm–egg fusion. Yet they are remarkably different. Bone cells differ from nerve cells, pancreatic cells from skin cells and liver cells from heart cells. How are these inheritable differences explained? It all comes down to the fact that, although the DNA code is the same in every cell, different genes come into play in each type of cell and genes are also expressed differently – which genes get expressed when is different, and how they are expressed is also different.

Configurations matter, not individual genes.

This point is further illustrated by the fact that 99 percent of human genes have a related copy in the mouse. While this might be understood as indicating that humans are gigantic mice in disguise (or vice versa), this fact rather suggests that minute differences in sequence may encode vast differences in function (Noble, 2006, p. 104). The fact that the differences found in human "racial" features are estimated to be encoded by only 0.1 percent of the human genome, emphasizes this further.

Coen (1999, p. 343) puts it thus: "organisms are not manufactured according to a set of instructions. There is no easy way of separating instructions from the process of carrying them out, to distinguish plan from execution." Or metaphorically, "There is a continual interaction between the tinkerer and his materials, rather than a tinkerer following a definite plan" (1999, p. 343).

In summary, the genome construed as an immutable program (see Dar-Nimrod and Heine, 2011) driving the "mechanical" process of the creation of the organism – is a metaphor. Put more bluntly, "the view that genes dictate the organism is silly" (Noble, 2006, p. 33).

In principle, the most satisfactory demonstration of the hereditary nature of social phobia would have been the identification of a gene or rather an array of genes controlling it. All other methods are by contrast speculative estimates. These indirect attempts to show genetic heritability attempt first to demonstrate that social phobia runs in families. This is a precondition for a further search for supporting evidence in favor of genetic inheritance. As usual in scientific practice, it has to be done while simultaneously controlling for rival explanations, that is, that family agglomeration is a result of shared environmental processes.

Genes versus environment

A comprehensive review (Stravynski, 2007, pp. 169–171) suggests that social phobia – only when considered over the life span – might run to a certain extent in families (defined somewhat ambiguously as first-degree relatives). The prevalence of social phobia in them is at any rate significantly higher than the morbidity in the families of normal individuals: 2.2, 5, 6 and 2.7% for generalized and 14% for discrete social phobia in Stein, Chartier, Hazen *et al.* (1998). With the exception of the latter, however, these prevalence rates are in line with the known range of estimates of prevalence of social phobia within the general population in the USA. However, it is noteworthy that the greatest association was typically with depression – not social phobia. Finally, studies looking specifically at children of parents with anxiety disorders (e.g. Beidel and Turner, 1997) contradict, however, the hypothesis of agglomeration.

Be that as it may, some are tempted to see genetic factors at work in some of the results above, as do, for example, Gelder, Gath, Mayou and Cowen (1996, p. 172). This is imprudent. Nothing much may be concluded about such inheritance, as members of a family not only share genes, but also share and have a hand in creating the family environment as well, as they also do – but to a lesser extent – the world outside it.

One way around this difficulty would be to differentiate family members according to their genetic similarity or closeness and to demonstrate that liability to social phobia increases with genetic likeness.

An additional scientific constraint when wishing to highlight heritability is somehow contriving to keep the influence of environment and experience from confounding the results. Can this be done?

There are two schools of thought on the matter. One – a minority view (e.g. Rose, Kamin and Lewontin, 1984) – would argue that the socially phobic pattern of conduct is an ongoing process that had been fusing (and continuing to do so) certain genetically determined characteristics with inputs from the environment. As a result of that historic process – still operative in the present – linking interactively genetic capabilities and environmental influences, the two are inextricably intertwined and would prove impossible to disentangle – as are, say, the ingredients of a cake and the ambient heat. All attempts to separate the constituent elements of an interactive process at a particular point in time are bound to fail to convince and in the final analysis futile (see also Noble, 2006, pp. 44–45; Richardson, 2000, pp. 65–69).

The second, by far the received point of view (e.g. Dawkins, 1976; Plomin, DeFries and McClearn, 1990) – allied closely with the disease model – regards certain (all?) abnormalities as fixed in the gene – manifesting themselves according to a rather implacable logic and to which the environment serves at most as backdrop or as evoking opportunity. As such, the effects of both factors are assumed to be rather independent of each other and therefore – in principle – quantifiable and amenable to being parceled out according to certain statistical models resting on numerous assumptions (e.g. Kendler, Neale, Kessler, Heath and Eaves, 1992).

Demonstration of genetic transmission

In principle, had we been able to assume that the socially phobic pattern of conduct is under complete genetic control, the most powerful and convincing way to demonstrate it would be to identify the genetic markers that correlate perfectly with the presence of social phobia and then, armed with this knowledge, predict what member of a family would develop the disorder in adolescence or young adulthood.

As the above assumption would be in all likelihood unwarranted and, furthermore, as the relevant technical knowledge is lacking (the steps entailed are discussed in Rutter and Plomin, 1997, p. 215), such demonstrations are for the time being at least, beyond our reach.

Table 4.3. *Approaches to the study of genetic transmission and respective quality of evidence*

Approach	Design	Quality of evidence
Study of twins	Monozygotic (MZ) vs. dizygotic (DZ) same-sex twins	Inconclusive
	Concordance rates for MZ twins reared apart	Impressive but impractical
Genetic marker studies	Association of a genetic marker with social phobia	Impressive
	Presence of marker in childhood successfully predicts social phobia in adulthood	Conclusive

What additional (lesser) kind of evidence could be invoked to help to settle the matter? Table 4.3 provides a summary of the main approaches.

Twin studies   Four twin studies have been reported; all compared concordance rates of social phobia between monozygotic (MZ) and same-sex dizygotic (DZ) twins.

The rationale of this particular paradigm rests on the fact that the MZ twins are genetically identical whereas the DZ twins – like other siblings – share (on average) 50 percent of their genes.

The fact that DZ twins are only half as similar as the MZ twins would imply that the resemblance of any trait in the MZ twins ought to be far greater than in the DZ twins. The comparisons typically are restricted to same-sex DZ twins since MZ are all of the same sex.

The degree of heritability, in theory might be estimated from the magnitude of the difference between the MZ and the DZ correlation (see Plomin *et al.*, 1990, pp. 207–253).

Let me now turn from discussing theory to examining evidence. The first two studies use countrywide samples of patients treated in psychiatric institutions. Torgersen's (1983) study involved a sample of adult same-sex twins treated for neurotic disorders in a psychiatric institution in Norway. A structured interview and a developmental history were used as the basis for establishing a lifetime (i.e. not current) DSM-III diagnosis. Zygosity was determined by blood analysis (of 10 genetic markers) in three-quarters of the sample and by questionnaire (all subjects).

Eighty-five (out of 318) met the criteria for various anxiety disorders; one identical (MZ) twin and three fraternal (DZ) twins met the criteria for social phobia. The analysis (following the "proband concordance wise method" whereby the number of twins both satisfying criteria for social phobia is divided by the total number of pairs – also used in all other studies) found that no MZ pairs had the same anxiety disorder and that no twin pairs were concordant for social phobia.

In a similar study from Norway (Skre, Onstad, Torgersen, Lygren and Kringlen, 1993), that is, subjects recruited from the same source (mostly psychiatric in-patients), in addition to the sample of probands with anxiety disorders, there was also a contrast group of probands with other conditions (e.g. mood and substance abuse disorders). Lifetime diagnoses (DSM-III-R) were determined following a structured interview and zygosity by means of a questionnaire with the assessors aware of who the subjects were.

As to social phobia, there were two identical (MZ) twins compared to four fraternal (DZ) twins among the anxiety disorders probands in comparison to no MZ and three DZ twins in the comparison group. No significant difference was found between the two sets of twins. Furthermore, a similar prevalence of social phobia was observed in twins with anxiety disorders as in the comparison co-twins. The authors' conclusion that "the predisposition to social phobia is caused by environmental experiences" (p. 91) illustrates a dichotomy pervading much of the theorizing in this area – if the cause is not to be found in the genes it must reside in the environment.

Studies drawing on twin registries from the general population (and established for research purposes), that is, subjects who are not individuals seeking help, end this survey. Such studies are of great importance as they allow a far greater scope for drawing general conclusions.

The first (Andrews, Stewart, Allen and Henderson, 1990), from Sydney, interviewed 462 pairs. Lifetime diagnosis (DSM-III) was established by means of a structured interview while zygosity was determined by questionnaire. The final sample included the following five groups of twins: 104 MZ-female, 82 MZ-male, 86 DZ-f, 71 DZ-m and 103 DZ-opposite sexes. This is a strength of this exemplary study, as typically – because of the need to compare same-sex twins – only women or men would be included (see next study).

The results showed that MZ twin-pairs were no more concordant than the DZ pairs for either social phobia or – for that matter – any other category of anxiety disorders.

In the second study (Kendler *et al.*, 1992) from Virginia (USA), of 2,163 female twins, 654 met DSM-III-R criteria for phobias.

The proband-wise concordance for social phobia was 24% for MZ twins compared with 15% for DZ; the concordance for a lifetime diagnosis was identical in both sets of twins – 12%. The proband-wise concordance rates – although different – were not significantly so for either social or any other phobia.

In a subsequent and complex statistical analysis, heritability and environmental influences were partitioned off (see Brown, 1996, p. 393 for a critical assessment of this procedure). Heritability for social phobia was estimated at 31%; 68% was put down to environmental influences of a "traumatic conditioning" rather than that of a "social learning" (i.e. in the family environment) kind.

Genetic contributions (i.e. liability) were then separated into specific (i.e. social phobia alone) and common (i.e. any phobia). Specific genetic factors were estimated to contribute 21% of the variation in liability to social phobia and the common factors 10%.

The latter results (and theoretical logic) are contradicted by Fyer, Mannuzza, Chapman, Martin and Klein (1995), who found a rather moderate but specific agglomeration of social phobia in families of socially phobic probands, but without an increased liability for other types of phobia.

Behind the dazzling statistical apparatus deployed in this oft-quoted aspect of the study, various perplexing features may be found.

First of all, it is not clear what evidence supports the conclusions concerning the environment. Neither individual nor family environments – key variables in the study – are given an operational definition; nor are the corresponding measurements that quantify them described. That factors of such complexity are actually validly summarized by a single valuation (a score) needs to be demonstrated (see Medawar, 1977). The failure to provide a description of the conception guiding the measurement of the environment, as well as some proof of the validity of the measuring instruments in use, is a serious flaw limiting the drawing of any conclusions from this study.

Secondly, dichotomies are created (e.g. traumatic conditioning vs. social learning, heredity vs. environment) that rely on an a-priori assumption of the independence of each factor. Whether such assumptions are warranted is doubtful. For "this procedure is only satisfactory if there is no gene–environment interaction" (Brown, 1996, p. 393). Even if the case for interaction is not ironclad, it is the likelier assumption for humans (see Mayr, 1974 on "open" vs. "closed" genetic programs). The notion of independence of genes and environment in the case of social phobia seems implausible in the extreme and needs – if one wishes to assume it – to be at the very least systematically defended. These aspects of the results, however, are presented as naturalistic observations rather than theory driven.

Thirdly, an alternative statistical model, resting on quite different assumption, was found to fit the results just as well (Kendler *et al.*, 1992, p. 280) but little was made of it.

Fourthly, the meaning of the very notion of heritability and consequently the figure attached to it remain shrouded in obscurity.

Fifthly, the relationship of the degree of heritability (whatever it may mean) to the finding that the prevalence rates of social phobia are not significantly different in both groups of twins, is of the greatest theoretical importance, and yet was not explicitly discussed in the paper. Moreover, it is not entirely clear what is the value of estimating a somewhat abstract notion of heritability, while the rather similar rates of morbidity in the two groups of twins, do not support the hypothesis of a greater liability for social phobia due to genetic influences.

The case that the somewhat recondite statistical approach, although not as intuitively graspable as the relatively simple comparison of the degree to which MZ and DZ twins share the disorder, affords greater or different insights has not been made.

Finally, the general notion of heritability itself surely refers to an abstract underlying liability to a certain and unspecified behavioral disposition (trait), not necessarily to the disorder as such.

It is, therefore, all the more important to remember, in interpreting the results, that these calculations do not highlight universal characteristics of the trait in question, because inheritance is not fixed. Rather, it says something about the specific population investigated under a very specific set of circumstances. If these were to change, so would the result.

To paraphrase Rutter and Plomin (1997, pp. 209–210), the true meaning of heritability is that the estimate indicates how much of the individual liability to a socially phobic trait (whatever this might be) in a particular population at a particular time, is due to genetic influences. Crucially, if circumstances change, so will the heritability.

Genetic marker studies Whereas the previous studies are inconclusive at best, a more impressive demonstration of the possibly hereditary nature of a disorder would be correlating a genetic marker with the presence of social phobia. For such a type of investigation to be meaningful (i.e. driven by a clear hypothesis), prior knowledge of the neurobiology of the disorder as well as a familial pattern of transmission is necessary. As we have seen earlier neither is available in social phobia.

Nevertheless, two different exploratory approaches have been used in order to identify potential genes for social phobia: linkage analysis and association studies.

Close proximity of genes on a chromosome ensures that they are passed on together from generation to generation. This fact is exploited by "linkage analysis," so as to study the association between the presence of a given phenotype – in our case social phobia – and a marker gene whose location on a given chromosome is accurately known.

Technically, the term "linkage" refers to alleles (forms of a gene) from two different loci (locations of the gene in the chromosome) passed on as a single unit from parent to child. Consequently, genetic linkage requires family studies. Thus, if the frequency with which the association between a given marker and social phobia manifest in family members is higher than what would have been expected from both genes being located in completely different chromosomes, one could conclude that it is likely that the gene for the phenotype (i.e. social phobia) is in close proximity to the marker.

In an elegant study using this method, Gelernter, Page, Stein and Woods (2004) highlighted evidence linking social phobia to markers in chromosome 16. That would imply that if social phobia is genetically determined, a contributing gene (for the time being unknown) is located in this chromosome.

Other studies of a similar nature have assessed linkage between social phobia and the DA transporter, the 5-HT transporter or different subtypes of monoaminergic receptors, all yielding negative results (Stein, Chartier, Kozak, King and Kennedy, 1998; Kennedy et al., 2001).

The second approach towards identifying potential genes for social phobia compares the incidence of social phobia in people with distinct forms of a candidate gene thought to have the potential to contribute to it. This allows the establishment of an association between social phobia and the presence of a specific allele. The 5-HT transporter, for example, is encoded by a polymorphic gene that has a short and a long allele (Heils et al., 1996; Lesch et al., 1996). The presence of the short allele is associated with reduced transporter expression and 5-HT uptake (Lesch et al., 1996). Individuals in the general population with a short polymorphism for the 5-HT transporter gene report higher levels of anxiousness than those with long forms of the gene (Melke et al., 2001). This observation has prompted several studies evaluating the association between the short allele and various anxiety disorders (e.g. panic disorder – Ishiguro et al., 1997) as well as social phobia. As with findings from linkage analysis, no associations between 5-HT transporter polymorphisms and social phobia were found (Samochowiec et al., 2004).

However, a study of socially phobic individuals in which the short allele genotype was associated to state or trait anxiety showed that individuals homozygous for this form of the gene reported higher levels of both types of anxiety (Furmark et al., 2004). This is in keeping with the fact that, in the general population, short alleles are related to increased self-reported anxiety (Melke *et al.*, 2001). Unfortunately, the lack of a control group in Furmark *et al.* (2004) prevents one from ascertaining whether the frequency of association between anxiety levels and short alleles in socially phobic individuals is different from that of normal controls. Associations between social phobia and polymorphisms for monoamine degradation enzymes like MAO-A and COMT have also been sought, but no specific genotype for either of these enzymes was associated with social phobia.

In a study carried out in South Africa (Lochner *et al.*, 2007), 63 socially phobic participants and 150 normal individuals were assessed for specific personality dimensions and their DNA extracted. The socially phobic scored significantly higher on harm avoidance but lower on novelty seeking and self-directedness compared to controls. Meaningfully, these characteristics were not related to any genetic variations. The DNA analysis revealed that in the Caucasian sub-set, but not in the black one, there was a statistical difference between the socially phobic and the normal participants in terms of the 5-HT(2A)T102C polymorphism, with significantly more socially phobic participants harbouring T-containing genotypes. While there was a significant statistical difference between the socially phobic and control groups of participants on average, no one-to-one correspondence between this polymorphism and social phobia was found. The conclusion of the authors that the results suggest "a possible role for the 5-HT(2A)T102C polymorphism in the development of social phobia," is hardly justified.

In summary, the studies under review have failed to establish a clear association between genes encoding for functional proteins of different monoaminergic systems and social phobia. Unsurprisingly, genetic polymorphisms proved to be unrelated to (long-term) response to treatment (Anderson, Ruck, Levebratt, Hedman *et al.* 2013). These findings are consistent with results from neurotransmission studies reviewed earlier, in which no major abnormality in monoaminergic function could be found.

Conclusions

No systematic evidence supporting the hypothesis that social phobia (as a fully fledged pattern of conduct) might be genetically transmitted has been brought to light. The number of studies to have looked at the question was limited and the chosen paradigms of the bulk were not the most powerful. For these reasons, corroboration – if obtained – would have been, in any case, inconclusive. Furthermore, the fact that social phobia is to a high degree associated with numerous co-occurring disorders (see

Stravynski, 2007, pp. 105–111) makes the hypothesis that all are under specific and separate genetic control even less plausible. In the final analysis, it is unlikely that the hypothesis of the genetic transmission of social phobia has bright prospects.

Broad propensities manifested in universal phenomena, such as fear of strangers (Marks, 1987 pp. 133–147), sociability (e.g. intraversion--extraversion) and emotionality (Gray, 1970) or "temperament" (Kagan and Zentner, 1996) are highly likely to be in some sense inherited. These factors, however, constitute only one of the risk factors for social phobia, as "expression of a genetic program depends on the environment" (Marks, 1987, p. 110).

The reason for this is made forcefully clear by Rose *et al.* (1984, p. 95):

The critical distinction in biology is between the phenotype of an organism, which may be taken to mean the total of its morphological, physiological, and behavioral properties, and its genotype, the state of its genes. It is the genotype, not the phenotype that is inherited. The genotype is fixed; the phenotype develops and changes constantly. The organism itself is at every stage the consequence of a developmental process that occurs in some historical sequence of environments. At every instant in development (and development goes on until death) the next step is a consequence of the organism's present biological state, which includes both its genes and the physical and social environment in which it finds itself.

The other forces involved in shaping the individual might be generally termed developmental (Sroufe, 1997, pp. 253–255), that is, embedded in a historic process that the organism undergoes, simultaneously biological and social.

Kagan and Zentner (1996, p. 347) describe the "propitious" environment, as one that continuously amplifies the psychological vulnerability of the fearfully reticent individual, while subjecting him or her to repeated social demands eliciting the pattern.

To paraphrase Rose (1995, p. 382) the shorthand gene "for" a condition is profoundly misleading – after all there are not even genes for blue or brown eyes, let alone such complex historically and socially shaped features of human existence as shyness, anxiousness or social phobia. The process that leads to social phobia (and away from it, as in cases of therapeutic or marital success) clearly involves genes (e.g. Shumyatsky *et al.*, 2005) but cannot be regarded abstractly as embodied in them.

General conclusion

The causal view of the biomedical outlook on social phobia was represented in this review by two interlinked propositions postulating the following: (1) the socially phobic pattern of behavior is caused by unspecified (molecular or cellular) events in particular regions of the brain of the individual exhibiting it; (2) something coded in the genes of the individual predisposes him or her to brain malfunction.

Both general propositions, but especially the first, have proven a great stimulus to research. The findings they gave rise to, however, provide little support for either thesis. Consequently, there is little ground for considering socially phobic conduct the consequence of a malfunctioning in the brain, itself inherited.

It is not impossible that this rather unsatisfactory record may be the upshot of various methodological shortcomings; these may be overcome in time, as new tools (e.g. genetic neuroimaging) become available. Another possibility is that this disappointing outcome was foreshadowed by the absence of a neurobiological theory of social phobia and hence, the lack of specific hypotheses to steer research. In that case, the formulation of such a theory (or better still) theories is of the highest priority. Given the state of current knowledge, it is not likely that one will be forthcoming soon.

Over and above methods and theory, a more substantive alternative must not be overlooked. Likely, no defects or anomalies in the brain have been highlighted or "pathophysiology" delineated because there are none to be found.

The bulk of the results surveyed is consistent with the fact that on any measure, socially phobic individuals are far more like their normal counterparts than different from them. Startlingly, this state of affairs has neither thrown into doubt the view of social phobia as a neurological disease of sorts, nor diminished its influence. Rather, it seems acceptable, in this field of inquiry, to be following the inferential logic that if hypotheses have not been conclusively refuted, there is no pressing need to question them.

Seen in context, the reason for this might be found in the fact that the biomedical outlook also fulfills an important extra-scientific function. It provides a justification for the pharmacotherapy of social phobia, in lockstep with the marketing efforts of the pharmaceutical companies (see Crews, 2007; Lane, 2008; Angell, 2011; Scull, 2011, pp. 118–124).

First of all, a potential disease entity is identified. Secondly, it is legitimized by inclusion in a diagnostic manual and reified, its validity no longer questioned. Thirdly, pharmacological compounds are matched with it. The circular logic justifying this seems to be: if social phobia responds to medication, something biological must be wrong; since it is "biological" (i.e. a disease), it needs to be treated pharmacologically.

Thus, the commercial availability of an ever expanding number of psychotropic medications capable of lessening anxious distress is – in itself – impetus enough to drive an incessant intellectual effort to rationalize their use. The wider disease model (with its biological deterministic perspective) in which this effort is embedded (e.g. Hyman, 2007, p. 731), continues to provide the concepts and their logical organization for the task of rationalization.

5 Reductive dualism II: social phobia as a consequence of mental (cognitive) defects

It is a commonplace that the socially phobic complain of varying degrees of anxiousness in various guises – this has been amply described in previous chapters. It is furthermore widely assumed that the abnormal state of anxiety causes social phobia. What accounts for the anxiousness, however, remains contentious.

Defects of body or mind remain favorite candidates. Chapter 4 described the unsuccessful search for brain abnormalities; this chapter concern itself with the search for mental defects.

That socially phobic individuals tend to describe seemingly mundane events in startling ways offers a cue. A former military officer describes attending an oral examination at university as more frightening than going into battle. A landscape designer dreads that an unsteady grip on a cup of coffee might suggest that he is a former alcoholic. A lawyer, who carefully concealed his fears from his wife, is convinced that she would leave him, if she knew.

Assuming that these narratives are an expression of what the socially phobic individuals perceive and believe, a possible account would hold that the mental processes of the socially phobic are distorted, and that anxiousness and ultimately socially phobic behavior are their products.

What is cognition?

The somewhat arcane (see Malcolm, 1977, p. 385) philosophical term "cognition" is today familiar-sounding in psychology. Cognition is defined by the *Concise Oxford Dictionary* as the faculty of knowing, perceiving and conceiving in contrast, for example, with emotion and volition – a distinction inherited from Plato.

Its general modern use is in reference to the experimental study ("cognitive science") of reasoning on its own terms (e.g. memory, decision-making), often with a view to duplicating these processes by machines ("artificial intelligence"). It bears repeating that such a

143

"mechanistic" outlook is in sharp contrast to considering the person as a whole being – involved in dynamic relationships with a human and physical environment.

A particular, clinical, use of the term has originated with Beck (1976), who came to advocate a psychotherapy that he branded as cognitive. This aimed at "correcting" certain hypothetical structures or operations – assumed to be faulty – of the mind of patients. This framework, first applied generally and in the abstract to a broad range of psychopathology, has been subsequently refined and extended to social phobia as well (Beck, Emery and Greenberg, 1985, pp. 146–164).

It is baffling that there is little meeting of minds between the two cognitive domains (the "science" and the "therapy"). Both methodology and theory divide them (McFall and Townsend, 1998, pp. 325–327).

Whereas "cognitive science" uses mostly objective measures (i.e. acts of choice, classification, detection, etc.), the therapy relies on "introspection," for both therapy material as well as assessment by means of questionnaires. Even the implicit notion of cognition is not necessarily a shared one (Looren de Jong, 1997). Attempts to reconcile the two have been made, e.g. McFall, Treat and Viken (1998), but have failed to achieve wide currency.

Although numerous other "cognitive" models have been put forward (e.g. Meichenbaum, 1977), most have been eclipsed ultimately by that of Beck and his collaborators (e.g. Clark, 1999).

The cognitive formulation of social phobia

Despite numerous statements of the therapeutic implications of the cognitive outlook, the key term "cognition" remains undefined (e.g. Beck *et al.*, 1985). It is probably not unreasonable to say that cognition is used as a label for either a hypothetical, information-processing system, or the product of such a process, or both. A lay interpretation of the word might be that it refers to that portion of our consciousness in which the kind of thinking that may be put in words takes place.

In essence, proponents of the cognitive school hold the view that faulty thinking results in emotional distress (anxiety) and, subsequently, inadequate (i.e. socially phobic) behavior. This, in turn, generates more distress.

Although these authors take pains to point out that "the cognitive model does not postulate a sequential unidirectional relationship in which cognition always precedes emotion" (Clark and Steer, 1996, p. 76), it is plain that, for all intents and purposes, the cognitive perspective is suggestive of precisely this sort of causal relationship. The assertion that "social phobics become anxious when anticipating or participating in social situations *because* they hold beliefs (dysfunctional assumptions) which *lead them* to" (my italics; Stopa and Clark, 1993, p. 255), serves as a case in point. Fodor (1983), a foremost proponent of cognitivism, is unequivocal: "the structure of behavior stands to mental structure as an effect stands to its cause" (p. 8).

Cognition then – as a generic description of mental structures with agency – is at the center of the theoretical discourse of cognitive therapy (hence the name). It is for this reason that cognitive factors are regarded as "maintaining" social phobia (e.g. Hackmann, Surawy and Clark, 1998, p. 9); that is, they are its efficient cause. Altogether, the cognitive outlook is an outgrowth of the fertile mental domain of the Cartesian philosophical universe.

On the most simple level, faulty thinking ("cognitions"; e.g. Clark and Steer, 1996, p. 79) implies various kinds of irrational inference drawings. Exaggerating or ignoring counter-evidence, as gathered from the justifications patients offer for what they did or felt, could serve as examples. On a somewhat loftier plane, inadequate thinking implies broad beliefs ("schemas") expressing a whole outlook (e.g. the importance of being in the good graces of others). Finally, various cognitive processes are said to be operative (e.g. focus on self), presumably driven by the overarching cognitive structures.

Stopa and Clark (1993, p. 255) summarize the cognitive view of social phobia in these terms:

According to this [the cognitive] model, social phobics become anxious when anticipating, or participating in, social situations because they hold beliefs (dysfunctional assumptions) which lead them to predict they will behave in a way which results in their rejection or loss of status. Once triggered these negative social evaluation thoughts are said to contribute to a series of vicious circles, which maintain the social phobia. First, the somatic and behavioral symptoms of anxiety become further sources of perceived danger and anxiety (e.g. blushing is interpreted as evidence that one is making a fool of oneself). Second, social phobics become preoccupied with their negative thoughts, and this preoccupation interferes with their ability to process social cues, leading to an objective deterioration in performance. Some of the changes in the social phobic's behavior (for example, behaving in a less warm and outgoing fashion) may then elicit less friendly behavior from others and hence partly confirm the phobic's fears. Third, an attentional bias towards threat cues means that when not preoccupied with their internal dialogue, social phobics are particularly likely to notice aspects of their behavior, and the behavior of others, which could be interpreted as evidence of actual, or impending, negative social evaluation.

An elaboration of the above outline may be found in Clark and Wells (1995, pp. 69–93).

An immediate problem in this line of theoretical analysis is the nature of consciousness. Although our own is accessible to us to some extent, that of others is obviously (and frustratingly for any model relying on it) accessible only in a refracted way – and at specific moments, not at all. Therefore, whatever one may hazard to say about it must remain derivative and tentative, reliant on whatever the participants in the experiment or patients in consultation choose to say, or else inferred from their general account of their way of being.

A skeptic, Père Malagride (in Voltaire's correspondence with Frederick, King of Prussia) – put it thus: "La parole a été donnée à l'homme pour cacher sa pensée."[1]

Ultimately, whether what people say reflects what they think or, rather, is their manner of communicating and transacting with particular others in specific social settings, is impossible to establish with any certainty at a given moment. Only observations extended in time might provide decisive cumulative evidence.

Regardless of what "cognitions" might be, as is always the case with hypothetical constructions, they present a danger of reification. In principle, "cognitions" have to be viewed as hypothetical constructs or processes standing for predispositions to act in a certain way. In other words, these constructs represent an underlying principle that may be said to manifest itself in, or may be inferred from, actual behavior.

The main attraction of such point of view is in the kind of inference it seems to allow: the mental construct within drives hypothetically the action without. In such a quest for explanatory leverage, however, lurks the danger of tautology. If cognitions and beliefs are inferred from what the individual says and does, these activities cannot be seen as resulting from the operations of dysfunctional cognitions. An inferred mental structure from a certain conduct could hardly be invoked as a causal explanation for the same behavior. For a hypothetical structure to be considered as endowed with explanatory power, it has to be shown to be valid (i.e. to make a difference and to have myriad predictable consequences), in a series of independent studies.

Before delving into the studies testing aspects of the ideas described earlier, however, a few words are in order regarding the intricate issue of how to assess and to quantify thought (dysfunctional or otherwise).

Despite thorny conceptual and to a lesser extent practical difficulties in measuring thought processes, a variety of scales have been developed. All boldly assume, for all intents and purposes, that what people say

---

[1] "Speech has been given to man to hide his thoughts."

about themselves reflects their "cognitions." Whether this is warranted must remain shrouded in doubt.

The various methods used in assessing cognitions have been reviewed by Heimberg (1994) and others. Typically, the measures have attempted to quantify either enduring cognitive dispositions (traits) or thoughts that happen to occur through either endorsement of ready-made statements, or the listing by the subjects of idiosyncratic thoughts they experienced on occasion.

A critical overview of some measures in use with socially phobic subjects may be found in Stravynski (2007, pp. 189–194). Whatever qualms there might be about the validity of such measures, I shall put them aside and take the measures at their own valuation as valid. This allows the seeking of answers to several key questions.

Are the socially phobic characterized by different cognitive processes than normal individuals?

The cognitive processes of socially phobic individuals ought to be according to the cognitive model systematically and typically dysfunctional. The relevant available studies testing this proposition in relation to several processes (e.g. memory) have been reviewed in detail (Stravynski, 2007, pp. 194–205) and I shall only summarize the conclusions.

These will be rendered more meaningful if we distinguish between two kinds of measures quantifying cognitive processes. The first kind was objective, that is, allowing an objective quantification of perform-ance (such as those used in the experiments of "cognitive science"). The second kind was subjective, that is, reliant on self-report questionnaires alone. Typically, the questionnaires ask the participants in the experi-ment to estimate subjectively some features of their own state of con-sciousness (e.g. degree of occurrence of negative thoughts), quantified in terms such as "very often" or "hardly ever," to which a numerical value is attached.

Do specific cognitive processes, then, characterize socially phobic indi-viduals? In terms of objective measures, the results are equivocal. First of all, socially phobic individuals perform no differently from control subjects in terms of memory. Secondly, in terms of attention, socially phobic individuals were either no different than controls (homographs) or showed a *slightly* delayed response (modified Stroop task) in compari-son to that of normal and panic disorder subjects.

Overall, in some experiments socially phobic subjects showed responses that differed – to some degree – from those of other subjects. The source of this difference remains obscure. There is no evidence, however, to support the claim that it reflects an inherently socially phobic "cognitive bias." Crucially, in absolute terms, no "cognitive" activity – objectively measured – inherently and exclusively typifies social phobia.

As to the results obtained by means of self-reported subjective estimates of uncertain validity, these seem to amount to no more than various ratings of anxious distress, expressed by the socially phobic participants within the constraints of the metaphors imposed on them, by different questionnaires. These point, for instance, to the fact that, under certain conditions, socially phobic individuals report being more self-deprecating than do control subjects. Ultimately, these measurements are no more revealing than a casual interview. What they highlight of alleged cognitive processes remains uncertain at best. In most studies under review, socially phobic subjects' responses to experimental tasks were indeed somewhat different from those of contrast subjects. However, since all subjects in those studies seem to be exhibiting the hypothetical cognitive quality to some extent, these results cannot be regarded as compelling proof of specific socially phobic cognitive processes in play.

Are the socially phobic characterized by different cognitive processes than individuals with other anxiety disorders?

According to cognitive theory, different disorders ought to be characterized by specific cognitive distortions and overarching beliefs (see Clark, 1999, p. S5). Does the evidence support this thesis?

Rapee, Mattick and Murrell (1986) compared the thoughts listed by 16 panic disorder (PD) participants to those of 16 socially phobic (without panic) subjects, after an experience of panic provoked by CO_2 inhalation.

The socially phobic subjects reported a much lower proportion of "catastrophic thoughts" than did the PD ones. The rates of "catastrophic thoughts" reported by socially phobic participants – unlike those of the PD subjects – were not influenced by reassuring instructions.

The former results seem to question the received view holding socially phobic individuals as particularly vulnerable while being in a state of high anxiety (see Amir, Foa and Coles, 1998).

Hope, Rapee, Heimberg and Dombeck (1990) compared the responses of 16 socially phobic subjects to a modified Stroop task described earlier with those of 15 PD (without agoraphobia) subjects. Socially phobic participants took longer to read the social "threat" (compared to control) words, than did those in the panic group. The latter, by contrast, took longer to read words describing physical threat. No differences in reaction to the unmodified part of the test (color naming) were observed.

Altogether, these results are somewhat questionable as they were obtained by multiple statistical comparisons (t-tests), rather than by a single analysis of variance. Even if the statistical analyses were beyond reproach, the fact that socially phobic individuals take somewhat longer (about 8 seconds) to read words of "social threat" than "control" words hardly bears out the authors' conclusion (p. 185) that a specific cognitive process purported to explain this rather anodyne fact has been revealed.

In Harvey, Richards, Dziadosz and Swindell (1993), socially phobic and panic disorder participants were compared to control subjects (12 subjects each), in terms of their interpretation of ambiguous stimuli.

The experiment required the rating of 14 brief scenarios in terms of harmfulness and anxiety. The underlying assumption being that the higher score reflects a bias in interpretation. The two clinical groups had higher scores than the controls but (with the exception of one result) did not differ from each other.

Although the conclusion that the anxious patients tend to interpret ambiguous events in a more alarming fashion seems uncontroversial, the overall interpretation that "These results lend support to the theory that interpretive biases are a function of schema which require activation by salient stimuli" (p. 246) has nothing in the study to support it.

In Amir et al. (1998), 32 generalized socially phobic subjects were compared to 13 obsessive-compulsive patients and 15 normal controls. The propensity to negative interpretation was studied by the responses of the subjects to social and non-social ambiguous scenarios. The questionnaire had a forced choice between positive, negative and neutral interpretations that the subjects had to rank in terms of plausibility. Participants were also asked to rate the questionnaire twice: as concerning them personally and in general.

When subjects rated the questionnaires as if it concerned them, generalized socially phobic individuals interpreted social situations more negatively than the other two groups; there were, however, no differences in the non-social situations. When rating the situations in general, there were no differences between the groups regardless of scenario (either social or not).

The authors concluded from this that generalized socially phobic individuals have a negative bias in interpreting social situations in which they are involved. This conclusion is rather doubtful for several reasons. First of all, the unknown validity of its scenarios and the limited comparisons with other pathologies leaves it uncertain as to what is really being measured.

The statistical analysis in this study further undermines the credibility of its conclusions. Ranking order results are transformed into a score by summation, and the data are subsequently treated as if originating in a scale of equal intervals. This violates the basic postulates of the analysis of variance. The relevant data ought to have been properly treated by means of some form of non-parametric ranking analysis.

In summary, with the possible exception of having less catastrophic thoughts induced by CO_2 inhalation than did PD participants, there seems to be little that is specific and distinct in the cognitive processes of socially phobic individuals when compared to those with other anxiety disorders.

Do cognitive factors cause (maintain) social phobia?

Some studies have put forward the claim of having uncovered cognitive factors implicated in the causal control of social phobia.

Amir et al. (1998), for example, have reached the conclusion that "The results of the present study are consistent with studies implicating cognitive biases in the maintenance of social phobia and lends support to the presence of yet another bias in generalized social phobias, interpretation bias" (p. 956). If "maintenance" is taken to mean acting as the controlling factor or the proximate (as opposed to the final) cause, such claims of causality bear a deeper examination. I shall, therefore, consider the studies making it in detail.

In the first such study (Hackmann et al., 1998), 30 socially phobic participants and 30 controls were asked to recall a recent episode of social anxiety and to describe it in detail ("as a film-scenario"). Subjects also had to rate to what extent they saw themselves through their own eyes on a seven-point scale. Socially phobic subjects reported more images and rated them more negatively. They described themselves more from an "observer's" vantage point than did controls. In contrast, socially phobic subjects realized as clearly as did the control subjects the distortions in their scenarios. Similarly, an interviewer rated scenarios from both groups equally.

Although, clearly, in this study socially phobic individuals tended to report "more imagery" (i.e. imagine or recall events in more vivid detail than did the control subjects), the meaning of the above finding is for the time being obscure. How this difference in degree between groups of experimental subjects supports the inference of the causal implication of cognitive factors in social phobia, remains baffling. After all, the same cognitive quality is found in both groups, albeit to a somewhat higher degree among socially phobic individuals. The contention of the authors, therefore, that "negative self-imagery plays an important role in the maintenance of social phobia" (p. 9), seems wholly unjustified.

The second study (Amir *et al.*, 1998) to be considered in this section was already described previously in another context. It concerns a comparison of the responses of (generalized) socially phobic subjects to the Interpretation Questionnaire (IQ) to those of two other groups of subjects (obsessive-compulsive disorder and normal controls).

The IQ is made up of 15 scenarios depicting direct social interactions and seven not requiring it. Three alternative outcomes/interpretations are provided and designated by definition as positive, negative and neutral. The subjects were asked to rank the likelihood that such an interpretation would come to mind in similar situations, as well as to rate on a seven-point scale how positive or negative such an outcome would be for them.

Two versions of the questionnaire were filled out: when thinking about oneself or when imagining a typical person.

Socially phobic individuals were predicted to be more likely to choose the negative possibility in social situations.

When the participants rated the questionnaires as if it concerned them, socially phobic individuals interpreted social situations more negatively than did the other participants; there were no differences regarding non-social situations. When rating the situations in general, no differences between the groups came to light, regardless of scenario (social or not).

Although on the face of it – given its elegantly controlled design – the study appears methodologically sound, some concerns about the nature of the data must be raised. The most pressing one is that, despite its reassuring name, we do not know what the IQ is actually measuring.

Let it be overlooked, for the sake of discussion, both the uncertainty as to what psychological quality the results (p. 950) really express, and the reservations about the transfigurations they underwent (subjects' rankings were transformed into interval or ratio-like scores and subjected to analysis of variance, followed by t-tests, p. 950). Let it be said that the socially phobic subjects have significantly more of this (hypothetical) quality than do the OCD and the normal subjects. Is one justified to speak of bias then? On what grounds? What is the normative unbiased response? Is it that of the normal subjects? After all they too exhibit the very same negative interpretations, although admittedly to a smaller degree. So do the OCD participants who report a similar propensity but to a higher degree, without turning into socially phobic individuals.

In a recent study, Taylor and Alden (2010) carried out two similar experiments with highly socially anxious students and with socially phobic participants; only the latter part will be reported.

Eighty subjects were randomly assigned to two experimental conditions: taking part in a simulated conversation with a confederate in the laboratory, while being prohibited from engaging in "safety-behaviors" (i.e. "subtle-avoidance") and taking part in a simulated conversation with a confederate in the laboratory, while being free to engage in "safety behaviors."

The experimental group prevented from engaging in "safety behaviors" was found on average to have less negative judgments of their performance than did the contrast group that was free do to so. The experimental participants' evaluation of their performance also accorded better with those of the independent observers and the confederates. Contrary to what might have been expected, however, there was no difference in the levels of subjective anxiety reported by both groups.

On the basis of the evidence the authors conclude: "Safety behaviors are causally involved in the persistence of negative social judgments hypothesized to be key factors in the maintenance of social anxiety disorder" (Taylor and Alden, 2010, p. 234).

These conclusions are wholly unwarranted. First of all and crucially, the fact that safety behaviors were either absent or present in the experimental conditions, did not make any difference to the reported anxiety levels. Secondly, while safety behaviors were presumably either present or absent, this difference in kind resulted only in a difference of degree in "judgmental bias" between the two experimental conditions. Notably, the differences between the means, although statistically significant, were not great (e.g. $p = 0.014$). That being the case, the likelihood of some overlap between the score distributions of the two groups is considerable.

In summary, the authors' double claim that "safety behaviors" cause "judgmental biases" that in turn maintain social phobia, cannot be justified by the evidence at hand.

In the final analysis, characterizing socially phobic individuals as tending to view social situations through the prism of a "negative interpretative bias," is no more than saying – figuratively – that they envisage these fearfully or that, ultimately, they are socially phobic. As to the proposition than these "biases" are the proximate cause of social phobia, if maintenance were defined as the effect exercised by a controlling factor, no support for it was in evidence in the experiments under review. All participants – not just the socially phobic – displayed a "negative interpretative bias" to some extent. Only the socially phobic, however, were socially phobic.

Discussion

Notwithstanding the insistent claims, no cognitive processes (or their configurations) uniquely characterizing socially phobic individuals have been identified. For this reason, socially phobic individuals cannot be characterized or identified in terms of these processes.

No wonder then, that no cognitive factor or process has been demonstrated to exercise a causal control over either the socially phobic pattern as a whole, or some of its features.

We remain in a quandary, however, as this whole line of research is laboring under a crippling handicap: namely, the absence of a formal definition of the main terms used within the context of the cognitive perspective.

What are cognitions in cognitive therapy? Whereas cognitive science construes cognition as "information-processing" (McFall and Townsend, 1998, p. 526), inferred from actions such as classification, detection, and so on, cognitive therapy represents cognitions either as things (something that one has) or subjective mental experiences (1998, p. 526). These are conceived of as accessible and quantifiable by "introspective" self-report methods. Thus, the uncertainty arising from measuring cognitive content or processes compounds further the theoretical ambiguity noted earlier. Moreover, many such instruments (e.g. the Interpretation Questionnaire – IQ – Amir *et al.*, 1998; the "Probability Cost Questionnaire" – PCQ – Foa, Franklin, Perry and Herbert, 1996) were constructed ad hoc. What do they measure?

While the theoretical construct is never defined, the participants' responses to the IQ, for example, are taken to be a reflection of their consciousness. Whereas only the responses (in this case presumably, the act of writing) can be observed, it is the thinking "behind" them – as it were – that is constantly alluded to in the text of the article. Responses to the IQ, or to any other such questionnaire, however, might be meaningful in different ways. An alternative interpretation of the responses would be to consider them social conduct, set in a particular and circumscribed social situation. Typically, the socially phobic individual is eager to satisfy important people (or anxious at the very least, not to provoke their displeasure). In this case, the experiment could be an exercise in self-description in reference to past and future actions, in terms molded by the social context of the experiment and constrained by the limited options provided by the experimental task.

Furthermore, the relationship between the laboratory task, where the participants indicate (e.g. on the PCQ) what they might do, and what actually takes place in their ordinary lives (external or ecological validity), remains uncertain.

In a similar vein, although the term is invoked frequently and assigned a causal role (see, e.g., MacLeod and Mathews, 2012, p. 210), no definition of what a "cognitive bias" might be was found in the numerous articles under review. Is bias defined relatively, in comparison to some standard (embodied by whom?) or absolutely, defined by formal rules of logic? Is a theoretical perspective or a philosophical outlook a bias? What of religious beliefs (e.g. reincarnation, refraining from harming animals or Judgment Day) – are these biased? Considering the possibility that different cultures have different systems of rationality (see Lukes, 2000), which would be normative and which biased? In the same vein, is the well-documented (Baron, 1988) propensity of most people to "jump to conclusions" and generalize from small unrepresentative samples or to make spurious predictions (e.g. about future conduct) from irrelevant bits of information (e.g. impressions during a brief interview, while flirt-ing) and other widespread irrationalities (Gardner, 1993), the norm or a bias? What of the well-known propensity of elected politicians to make preposterous promises before being elected and conversely, shy away from making hard choices when in office? Is this the result of a bias?

In general, "bias" has been used interchangeably with cognitive distor-tions, dysfunctional thoughts, assumptions or beliefs, cognitive structures or schemata and associative networks and encoding biases. Rough syno-nyms, however, do not make up for the lack of a definition of "cognitive bias," for the theoretical meaning of these terms is just as ambiguous.

Assertions that cognitive biases – whatever these may be – cause (main-tain) social phobia are frequently made. MacLeod and Mathews (2012), for example, concluded that the results of the studies they surveyed were "revealing the causal contributions made by specific types of cognitive bias to anxiety symptomatology" (p. 210).

These claims are, on the whole, unfounded. Over and above specific experimental manipulations, if the term "to maintain" were defined as the effect exercised by a controlling factor, no such demonstration was on offer. As seen previously, in all studies making such claims, socially phobic individuals showed the "cognitive process" allegedly being meas-ured to a higher degree. Thus, although Amir *et al.* (1998), for example, claimed that social phobia results from faulty cognitive processes, all participants in their study – not just the socially phobic participants – reported them to varying degrees (fig. 2, p. 951).

Similarly, while the socially phobic participants in Hackmann *et al.* (1998) did report "more imagery" (i.e. imagine or recall events in more vivid detail than did the control subjects), the control participants reported it too. Thus, the same cognitive process was found in both groups albeit – on average – to a somewhat higher degree in socially pho-bic participants.

How would such a difference in scale (between experimental groups), square with the proposition that: (1) it reflects a cognitive "bias" and furthermore; (2) it plays a causal role in social phobia? Need not effect be present, when the cause is manifest (and vice versa)? In light of the above, why were only the socially phobic participants socially phobic? Perhaps a counterargument to the objection could be that only a certain critical threshold of this factor is causal, but then what is it?

However that may be, given the great individual differences found on every dimension of social phobia, it is highly likely that some of the socially phobic participants would fall below such a hypothetical threshold, while some of the controls would score above it. Thus, the likelihood that some participants in all experimental groups overlap to some extent, further undermines the possibility that a cognitive factor – "bias," if that what it is – plays a causal role in social phobia.

Bias in this context, rather than referring to any process characterizing social phobia, fits much better the spurious and complacent conclusions drawn from statistical differences observed. It is consistent with the systematic singling out of one group of individuals, for basically a universal trait (subjectively reported). Thus, while reading the literature under review, one gradually forms the impression that "the cognitive-behavioral clinician merely assumes causality, without a quantitative theoretical model or empirical evidence; whatever behavior is observed must have resulted from a person's cognitions" (McFall and Townsend, 1998, p. 325). In this sense the conclusions are foreshadowed in the assumptions of the cognitive outlook; the experiments do not put its central theses to the test.

Regardless of its scientific status, the hypothesis of the cognitive causation of social phobia has a powerful appeal as a rationale for the "proper" kind of treatment. In keeping with this, cognitive approaches to treatment are seen as fixing the cognitive "apparatus" within the patient. Such a construal of treatment (i.e. as an antidote to a presumed "etiology") follows an idealized pattern established by the medical model of disease.

Evidence (drawn from clinical trials), however, does not offer much support for this supposed match between cognitive "etiology" and "therapy." As can be seen in Stravynski (2007, pp. 211–261), "cognitive" treatments neither affect hypothetical cognitive processes in a specific way, nor more so than supposedly non-cognitive treatments (including medication). Altogether, the "cognitive" changes observed in these studies were part of a general trend towards improvement. This makes the cognitive factors in question – correlates – features of social phobia, rather than its cause.

What conclusions can be drawn from this survey? Several possibilities need to be considered. First of all, it is likely that no typical "socially phobic" cognitive structure or process has been identified because there are no inherently socially phobic structures or processes "within" individuals exhibiting the broad socially phobic pattern of conduct. This would imply that socially phobic characteristics – cognitive and otherwise – are exacerbations of fundamentally normal responses, occurring within the normal range.

Ultimately – although this may not be entirely obvious at the present – there might be no socially phobic entity found in nature. Alternatively, social phobia as a "pragmatic" category (as suggested in Chapter 3), would neither be expected to have stable sharply defined features, nor be characterized by identical processes.

Secondly, it is possible that the conceptual foundations (i.e. Cartesian dualism) of this approach are unsound. In a "cognitively therapeutic" spirit, I shall briefly examine some of the conceptual assumptions undergirding the cognitive approach.

Within the cognitive perspective, words are used to denote an intangible reality. For instance, its central tenet is that people act on beliefs. But what is belief? Within the cognitive approach, it is, by definition, an inner state. But what could possibly be its referents (see McFall and Townsend, 1998, p. 317), to allow measurement?

A "belief can be articulated in words; it can be open to the bearer's awareness; and it can be manifested in action" (Lacey, 1995, pp. 70–71). None of these is, of course, the belief itself; this – if it may be said to exist other than metaphorically – remains inaccessible.

In cognitive therapy, beliefs are treated as fixed and stable features that can be measured and expressed in one value. Are they?

Jaundiced observers of the political scene, for example, would likely be under the impression that beliefs – at least in that arena – are held and discarded self-servingly. Politicians, however, are human (although some might deny it). Is this a general disposition?

Another (this time, historical) example might illuminate this theme. What were the wretched inhabitants of East Prussia thinking and believing in early January 1945, as the Soviet assault on Germany began? Fleeing in panic, or hiding desperately from a Red Army bent on revenge, they doubtless felt very sorry for themselves, believing they were simultaneously victims of their own government (that brought them to this pass) and of the invading "barbaric Asiatic hordes."

What did the same inhabitants, however, believe much earlier (since 1933 to be precise)? As the region most supportive of the Nazi movement in Germany, they doubtless rejoiced in its coming to power, and were amply rewarded for their steadfast support. The same inhabitants probably delighted in the swift suppression of the internal enemies of the regime, and rejoiced in its early triumphs.

Without doubt (it may be permitted to speculate), the inhabitants of East Prussia enjoyed quietly the satisfaction of belonging to a "master-race," as well as, more concretely, the spoils of plunder of the conquered countries of Europe, without giving much thought to the mass massacres, starvation and enslavement of the "inferior races" dwelling in Eastern Europe – as long as the war was proceeding successfully. What were they thinking at that time?

It seems that human beliefs and thinking, embedded as they are in behavior and circumstances (see Chapter 1), are far more supple and adjustable than cognitive theory would allow. Perhaps we are all politicians (in different degrees)?

Be that as it may, the conviction that we have a direct and unencumbered perception of our minds that can accurately articulated may be an illusion (see Gopnik, 1993; Sampson, 1981).

If belief, by contrast, were defined as a label applied to an extended pattern of behavior (i.e. an intricate process of acting as if), the postulated but intangible inner state becomes redundant (see Rachlin, 1992).

Nevertheless, in the cognitive approach, such inner states are abstracted from the living human organism taking part in dynamic relations with the (social) environment. Mental states are seen as elements in a self-contained structure of causes and effects, with conduct as its output. Agent and environment are seen as separable, with the environment a kind of stage on which a plot, dictated from within, unfolds. "The knower's psychological states, the ideas in his or her head, are held to be more important, more knowable, and more certain than any underlying material interests, social practices or objective properties of the stimulus situation" (Sampson, 1981, p. 731).

The practice of setting up a dichotomy between the actual display of behavior and the manner or the quality of its organization (thoughtfulness), has been criticized on philosophical grounds as an instance of a "category mistake." According to Ryle (1949), this logical fallacy consists in treating the label for a class of events, as if it were a member of that class. From this vantage point, the distinction between conduct and its organization might be likened to attempting to separate the choreography of a ballet (the complex interlocking sequence of steps) from the movements of the dancers, or the strategy from the armed forces striving to implement it.

The Cartesian dualistic philosophy (discussed in Chapter 1) in which the cognitive program is embedded separates the mind from the body and, in addition to making it a special substance, accords it a central role in human conduct. It also asserts a capacity – introspection – allowing humans to know their minds. This outlook, making its first appearance in the teachings of Pythagoras and later given a fuller development by Plato, has been rejected by numerous philosophers.

Nietzsche, for example, in keeping with Spinoza (see Schacht, 1995, pp. 167–186) integrated reason with other human powers, all rooted in the body.

In his *Treatise of Human Nature* ([1739]1961), Hume famously asserted that "Reason is and ought only to be the servant of the passions and can never pretend to any other office than to serve them" (Kemp Smith, 1941, p. 144). On this view, reasoning is limited to propositions that represent something else and may be true or false. Actions, by contrast, do not represent something else; they exist only by dint of being carried out. Conclusions and actions are therefore ontologically different; this is why "reason can never be a motive to an action" (Kemp Smith, 1941, p. 144).

Wittgenstein (1958) raised various objections to Cartesian dualism from the perspective of analytic philosophy (see Chapter 1). Most importantly, Wittgenstein called into question the notion that introspective practices penetrate some hidden inner realm. He held that invoking inner processes provides, at best, pseudo-explanations for conduct (Parker, 1996, p. 367). Rather, he considered the metaphorical descriptions of "inner states" as the presentation of criteria for further action (embedded in a certain cultural way of life). "Because life is lived in advance of itself, it is more plausible to understand talk of inner world as oriented towards impending action than as predications based on reference to internal states. In this way, language, as verbal gesture, grounds experience" (Davis, 1996, p. 95).

Similarly, Quine (1960) argued that language was crucial in establishing private experience and self-awareness, while being tied inextricably to the culture of the community of its users. Marx put it thus: "It is not the consciousness of men that determines their being, but, on the contrary, their social being that determines their consciousness."

These philosophical views, presented as an antidote to the conceptual confusions generated by Cartesian dualism, do not so much diminish thought as attempt to widen our conception of it – by anchoring it in social life.

Jones and Nisbett (1971) found that individuals believed that conjunctures of circumstances determined how they behaved. Observers, however, tended to impute these individuals' behavior to innate characteristics and habit. When trying to understand individuals we know little about (for lack of information or curiosity), we tend to attach inner causes to behavior. This is part of "folk psychology." Perhaps this practice has been elevated into the cognitive approach (Stich, 1983).

6 Causality at the interpersonal level: a multi-causal analysis

Causality at the interpersonal level of analysis

In Chapters 4 and 5, the view was put forward that long-standing attempts to identify a typical characteristic or malfunctioning – be it physical or mental – uniquely associated with social phobia and accounting for its allegedly abnormal anxiety, have not met with success.

Viewed narrowly and hopefully, this failure might yet be redeemed with more precise methods of measurement or new tools, regardless of the lack of clarity as to what is being searched for. Viewed skeptically, given the ambiguity of the concept of anxiety and the theoretical murkiness of its role, compounded by the reductive dualistic logic driving these research efforts, the quest is flawed and misguided. As such, it can only add to the conceptual confusion.

An alternative perspective on the question of what causes social phobia, is therefore called for. The presentation of such a perspective is the aim of this chapter. Needless to say, this alternative approach is compatible with the theoretical formulation of social phobia in Chapter 1 and its characterization in Chapter 3. This chapter completes the theoretical presentation of the interpersonal approach to social phobia, by outlining its analysis of causality.

An Aristotelian framework for causal analysis

The comprehensive explanatory analysis I shall put forward is embedded in the *hylomorphic* (*hylo* – form; *morph* – matter) world view, originating in Aristotle (see, e.g., Shields, 2007, pp. 53–63). This view rests on the thesis that everything in the world, including inanimate objects as well as live entities (plants, animals, humans), are made up of matter organized or structured in particular ways. Humans are made of the same fundamental materials as other animals or non-living things; the same quantum mechanical laws govern molecules within biological systems or inanimate nature.

In the hylomorphic view, the distinction between these natural entities is to be found at the level of their *organization*, not at the material level as such. It is the organization of organisms that endows them with life. Such organization allows them to have distinctive capabilities (e.g. motion, nourishment, sentience, development, reproduction, communication) and, in the case of humans, speech. In that sense, organization is not just a basic analytic principle, but a feature of the universe and has to be prior to matter, in the sense of a necessary condition. For matter is not self-organizing; structure is imposed on it. Hylomorphism admits several causal factors in its analysis. This allows (as shall be seen later) the consideration of various phenomena – including social phobia – as multi-causal. A comprehensive explanatory analysis must take into account all causal features.

The emphasis on organization and structure originates in Aristotle's biological outlook. Indeed, current biological descriptions of life resonate with hylomorphic notions.

Russell, Wolfe, Hertz, Starr and McMillan (2008, pp. 2–3), for instance, put it as follows.

Picture a lizard on a rock, slowly shifting its head to follow the movements of another lizard ... You know that the lizard is alive and that the rock is not. If you examine both at the atomic levels, however, you will find that the differences between them blur ... The differences between a lizard and a rock depend not only on the kinds of atoms and molecules present but also on their organization and their interactions.

The organization of life extends through several levels of a hierarchy. Complex biological molecules exist at the lowest level of organization, but by themselves these molecules are not alive. The properties of life do not appear until they are organized into cells ... A cell is the lowest level of biological organization that can survive and reproduce ... as long as it has ... appropriate environmental conditions. However, a cell is alive only as long as it is organized as a cell; if broken into component parts, a cell is no longer alive, even if the component parts are unchanged.

Life is an emergent property of the organization of matter into cells ... Plants and animals are multicellular organisms. Their cells live in tightly coordinated groups and are so interdependent that they cannot survive on their own ... Like individual cells, multicellular organisms have emergent properties that their individual components lack.

The next more inclusive level of organization is the population, a group of unicellular or multicellular organisms of the same kind that live together in the same place ... all the populations of different organisms that live in the same place form a community ... The next level, the ecosystem, includes the community and the nonliving environmental factors with which it interacts ... The highest level encompasses all the ecosystems of the world's waters, crust, and atmosphere. Communities, ecosystems, and the biosphere also have emergent properties.

The above excerpts leave no doubt that it is the organization that produces the functional unity of the living being and allows organisms to have a variety of capabilities (e.g. nourishment, movement, development, reproduction, sentience). The form or organization is inseparable from the material ingredients; the two are interdependent. One important ramification of this outlook is that every element has two kinds of properties; those related to the materials that compose them and properties emanating from their integration into a larger structure. In its modern definition, in terms of molecular biology (stretches of DNA), a gene is a sequence of nucleotides that have fundamental physical properties but acquire new characteristics by occupying a definite position on a particular chromosome. In its new status as an organic part of the cell, it is contributing to the functioning of the whole (see Rolston, 2006, p. 474).

In that sense, organisms are more than the sum of their parts; an entity is likely to have emergent properties subsequent to the integration of the various compositional elements. After all, being *organ*-ized means becoming an organ and thus an integral contributor to an organism's life activities, or, put differently, having a definite *function* within it.

In summary, cells, organs and organisms are complex self-organizing (and self-reproducing) units whose activities (i.e. living) are goal directed and, as such, admit of a teleological description.

Having shown the paramount importance of structuring and integrating the different parts of a living organism, let the focus be widened now to include the organism's characteristic activities. Crucially, these are displayed only within its habitat – its natural environment. The environment (physical and social) is an integral part of life, without which most activities would not take place, nor indeed be possible. Evolution, for example, is the result of both variations in the genotype and prevailing conditions in the environment. Flight is equally dependent on certain capacities and a narrow range of atmospheric conditions.

Having made the point, let me now turn the hylomorphic perspective to human life activities, namely the distinctively patterned ways in which humans interact with specific individuals, certain groups and with the social environment in general, as set in a particular way of life.

In the hylomorphic outlook, actions, experiences of sensations and feelings, thoughts and beliefs arise out of and are woven into extended patterns of environmental and social interactions, engaged in by an individual with others within a certain cultural context, woven into a way of life. By consequence, their occurrence is not confined to a private "inner theatre" intelligible only to the individual experiencing them. These interactional patterns and the emotions or beliefs that infuse them, are observable and in principle – but perhaps not always in practice – in full view. This would explain the fact that, for example, I may be flustered and in disarray, but to other people observing me, what I am about is limpidly clear. Nonetheless, errors occur when, for example, overly hasty and excessively hopeful conclusions are reached on a limited and irrelevant sample of behavior or utterances (e.g. promises, confidences). As the interactive pattern unfolds, how things stand becomes unmistakably obvious. The same applies to dissembling. Good acting ability may simulate the appropriate emotional interaction for a time, but it is likely to break down with a change of context, "off stage" as it were.

Furthermore, actions are not only bodily movements and corresponding physiological activation – although they do involve them. Actions require environmental settings to evoke and sustain them as well. Without the specific environmental and social setting, the action would not take place; it would be pointless and unintelligible otherwise. Thus, most psychological phenomena are set in complex relational patterns. Experiences, however private, are intricate and comprehensive responses to the world, set in social and therefore cultural context.

Similarly, these transactions structure and organize the neurophysiologic processes involved in implementing the activities of the individual (in the world). The activities of a living being as a whole, as well as the activities of the parts that make it up, are best understood functionally. All fit within a single hierarchical and unified structure, in the service of definite ends. There is an inextricable connection between structure and function; all organization is for the sake of something.

All psychological activities and experiences, in the hylomorphic outlook, are realized by the body or, to put it differently, constituted in matter. The complex processes of fearing, mourning and loving illustrate the embodiment that is central to this view. This is also true of imagining, desiring, hoping and pining. Moreover, "mental" states are functional states of the living material beings that realize them. To put it hylomorphically: all form is realized in matter. Unlike the putative Cartesian interaction between the mental and physical substances, all psychological activities, in the hylomorphic outlook, are firmly located in the physical world and compatible with it.

The fact that other non-human beings display some of the same patterns (e.g. fear, pleasure, attachment, playfulness) suggests that these complex activities may be realized by different bodily states. Furthermore, the fact that matter constituting the body also changes over a lifetime may imply that its various activities "are realized in some suitable matter" (Nussbaum and Putnam, 1992, p. 33) and that "the same activity can be realized in a variety of materials" (p. 33). To stretch this further, the hylomorphic outlook allows for the possibility that there is "no essential connection between a psychological state and any particular realization of it" (Cohen, 1992, p. 60). From a hylomorphic perspective, a narrowly materialist account cannot illuminate, let alone account for behavior. At best, it may specify some conditions necessary for its realization or coming into being.

To make patterns of activity intelligible, they are to be considered teleologically – in terms of their function in the setting in which they are displayed. Activities are understood best in terms of their function and the goals at which they are aimed, not in terms of the mechanics and the physiology involved. One talks of the ear or the eye in terms of their function, not what they are made of. In sum, definitions in the hylomorphic world view are all in terms of function flowing from a certain mode of organization, not of matter.

With this brief exposition of the hylomorphic framework as a backdrop, I shall now turn to the analysis of causality flowing from it and subsequently apply it to social phobia.

Causes

What constitutes a cause? The Aristotelian explanatory framework involves four analytical elements of causality or modes of understanding (Hocutt, 1974; Shields, 2007, pp. 36–97; Hankinson, 2009). We have already become acquainted with two of these: the material and the formal (i.e. organizational) elements or causes. The pair might be termed the internal causes. In our case, the material cause is the composition of the human body.

As to the formal cause, there are two organizational aspects. First of all, there is the "inner" organization of the living body at different levels (e.g. cells, tissue, organs, systems), the processes (physiology) and their coordination. Secondly, there is the patterning of life activities that the (whole) individual carries out in its environment, social and otherwise – let it be called the "outer" or interpersonal organization.

In this quest for an understanding of social phobia, I shall take the material and its "inner" organization for granted, as there is little reason to doubt their soundness (see Chapter 4). I shall, however, be far more interested in the formal cause in its second sense, that of the patterning of relationships socially phobic individuals establish with people in the various spheres of the social environment (see Chapters 1 and 3). I shall return to that theme below.

At another level of explanatory elements, one finds the efficient (or proximate) and final (or ultimate) causes. These might be termed the external causes. Outside the Aristotelian conceptual universe, probably only the efficient would be considered a cause.

In principle, an analysis of efficient causes yields an answer to the question of "how" did something occur, or what brought it about. The answer to the question is typically in terms of how one thing leads to another or how something works; it is therefore often "mechanical." In the Cartesian universe, there are only proximate causes. We have seen attempts to implement such causal analyses in Chapters 4 and 5.

Proximate causes, however, may vary in complexity from the limited (cause and effect) to the intricate (a cascading chain of causes and effects). To take a medical example (see Wong *et al.*, 2008), a patient's difficulty to keep balance owing to weakness in and poor coordination of his legs (ataxia) were traced – among several other possibilities – to neurological deficits.

A proximate analysis, however, could be also extended and become quite complex, as in this case. It starts from an analysis establishing that the ataxia is a result of neurological deficits, but does not stop there. What caused the neurological deficits? Tests showed that the deficits were the result of vitamin B_{12} deficiency. What of the deficiency itself? What led to it? It was discovered to be the consequence of an impoverished diet – consisting mostly of toasted oats cereals, bread and french fries.

The purely efficient causal analysis, concentrating on antecedent conditions to reveal how a certain state of affairs came about, as in the case illustration, hits rock bottom at this stage. Crucially, as to why the patient's nutritional pattern is so inadequate, an answer is beyond the scope of an analysis of efficient causes. In order to clarify this, there is no alternative but to search for final causes.

In contrast with an analysis of proximate causes, an analysis of final causes allows the answering of "why" questions. The answers that it provides to such questions are teleological (i.e. in terms of ends – see Garson, 2011 for teleological explanations in biology and Matthen, 2009 for teleology in Aristotelian thought).

An end serves as a linchpin to an overall pattern of activity, integrating sub-patterns that in turn structure various dynamic elements, all intertwined and integrated by their common purpose. Obviously, there is an intimate connection between the organization, in the sense of characteristic transactional patterns, and its function. Any organized activity must be for the sake of some end. Thus, "in a system with a certain goal, a form of behavior will occur because it brings about that goal" (Looren de Jong, 1997, p. 160).

The behavior of soldiers belonging to various military units attempting a pincer movement against their opponents, dancers each seemingly executing slightly different movements, over time integrating into small sections of dancers, coalescing in turn into a larger ballet movement, are examples of complex patterns that are woven, as it were, into a larger pattern extended in time and identified by their function. The functions of these patterns are the final causes of the behavior of the individual participants. Whereas the ballet (usually) unfolds predictably, the pattern of the two-pronged attack might be transformed while meeting resistance, or even become disorganized under the pressure of unexpected counter-attacks. The change in pattern would transform their function from, say, offensive to defensive or eliminate it altogether, in case of a rout – a disintegration of the military force. These examples illustrate the fact that final causes are to their effect, what a pattern is to its elements (Rachlin, 1992, p. 1372).

Whereas an efficient cause invariably precedes its effect, the effect of a final cause is folded into the cause (i.e. a pattern denoting an end). Such functions are relative to their surroundings and – as is the case with social phobia – when obviously enhancing security in a particular environment, they are not problematic in ascription. This is not always obviously the case. The final cause of a particular pattern of behavior might be understood only a considerable time after it took place. This will become evident when a pattern started in the past and extending into the future, as well as the context molding it, has become sufficiently pronounced and its function in the environment clear. *Ultimate causation is often a historically contingent process.*

The function of a larger pattern, into which a smaller pattern fits, might be considered the overarching ultimate cause, to which the final cause (i.e. the purpose) characterizing the sub-pattern considered by itself – contributes. Promoting and enhancing one's life might be regarded as the ultimate cause altogether, encompassing all other final causes (e.g. protection from harm).

Although formal causes take priority over material causes and ultimate causes over proximate ones, none of these perspectives by themselves provide a satisfactory and complete account. In that sense, material and proximate causes may be regarded as necessary – but not sufficient – conditions. Ultimately, the richest and most comprehensive understanding results from clarifying all explanatory perspectives – internal and external to the living organism.

As we have already dealt with the material and "inner" formal causes earlier, I shall now turn to the "outer" formal cause and to the efficient and final causes subsequently. These will be approached gradually.

At the interpersonal level of analysis, social phobia must arise out of the brute facts of being human and being a member of a society and a cultural community, and therefore, a way of life.

In addition to sociability, a key capacity necessary for social phobia is social fearfulness or anxiousness (used interchangeably), considered relationally. It is obvious from lived experience and observation that some dealings with others are threatening and induce fear. What characterizes these? As argued in Chapter 1, social anxiety conceived interpersonally, varies in lockstep with the parameters of power and status inherent in social transactions. Emphatically, these are relational or transactional notions – not individual attributes of the participants. These are the main parameters describing the dynamic transactions between two individuals or a pattern of relationships between an individual and others that form a group. The construct of power expresses ascendancy through the capacity to compel or to thwart, by threat or exercise of force. In part it is achieved by the ability to grant what is desired by another or deny it. In the end, intimidation relies on the ability to inflict pain and, ultimately, death.

In contrast, to accord status, is to elevate someone as possessing superior qualities (e.g. rank or charm, decisiveness, integrity) and treat them accordingly. Correspondingly, to suffer diminished regard, losing it altogether or worse, to be excluded from a group, is experienced painfully as loss (MacDonald and Leary, 2005).

Relationally, dominance and corresponding submission are intertwined; in humans such interactions are played out in sequences of carefully "choreographed" exchanges, framed by cultural norms. A fixed stare is met with lowered eyes and averted gaze, disparaging comments with bowed head; harsh criticisms are acknowledged blankly or with an ingratiating smile, a submissive posture and in softly spoken and apologetic tones. Dominance is recognized by deference; the dominant individual is not treated casually or ignored.

Relationally, inequality of power – be it through gradual erosion or precipitous loss, or previously established disparities of power threatening to reemerge – gives rise to fearful apprehension. The degradation of status, as manifested in the manner one is treated, is associated with shame (e.g. one is not up to standard) and humiliation (e.g. loss of respect).

The recognition of one's weakness in not having been able to prevent an injury or successfully counter it, opens up the possibility of similar defeats in future confrontations. It engenders caution: eschewing conflict and ingratiating appeasement if possible; submission if not. When the realization of cherished plans depends on those who pay little heed to one's well-being, or if one is coerced to engage in unwanted activities or withstand degrading treatment – one feels threatened, ashamed and humiliated. Such exchanges could equally involve menacing officials, a bullying superior, an overbearing brother or a flirtatious but fickle stranger.

Social fears are normal and commonplace (see Chapter 2). While exaggerated, overgeneralized and overextended in time, the social anxiousness of socially phobic individuals is undifferentiated from common social anxiety, although they seem to experience it more keenly. Qualitatively, it involves the same subjective experiences (e.g. focus on threat, suspiciousness, apprehension, worry); similar physical preparation towards the danger ahead (e.g. increased circulation of blood, tensing up of muscles) and self-protective responses when facing it (e.g. avoidance, immobility, submission, aggression). It is orchestrated by the same systems of emotional regulation in the brain. These very systems (as well as other activities of the brain) are stifled by real or fake (e.g. placebo) medication or other substances (e.g. alcohol, tea).

Normal fearful responses in a social context, arising out of an interpersonal insufficiency of power, are the necessary conditions for social phobia, making it possible. These two elements are elicited relationally by repeatedly engaging (literally or imaginatively) in dangerous transactions with threatening individuals or groups. Imaginative does not imply delusional; the terrorized citizens of dictatorships know well enough what boundaries are not to be crossed, without ever putting the issue to a precise test.

This analysis then makes clear that the circumstances in which the self-protective transactions take place, or are likely to take place, elicit fear. The fear-evoking situations therefore, constitute the proximate causes of both normal social anxiety and the defensive interpersonal patterns in which it is embedded. By extension and in aggregate, these are the proximate causes eliciting the various fearful patterns making up social phobia; these social occasions and the individuals in them, determine whether normal socially anxious, as well as socially phobic, episodes might take place and determine their extent.

The formal cause of social phobia is the predominantly powerless and defensively submissive interpersonal pattern described in detail in Chapters 1 and 3. The pattern shapes the socially phobic individuals' interactions with others (e.g. keeping a distance, avoiding frictions, remaining inconspicuous, being bland and having a deferential manner). This pattern also structures and integrates the various psychological and physical functions of the individual within the socially phobic mold. Thus, blushing, looking away, difficulty articulating words, inattention and memory lapses are so many facets – among others – that make up the overall socially phobic pattern.

While generally responding not dissimilarly on specific occasions when threatened and therefore in a fearful state, normal individuals are nevertheless not socially phobic. Crucially, over time and across situations, they do not display the interpersonal pattern of powerless self-protection inimical to satisfactory social functioning. The extended socially phobic relational pattern is enacted only by socially phobic individuals.

The ultimate cause of social phobia, then, is the defensive function of the overall pattern and most of the sub-patterns making it up; it is enacted by the socially phobic individual for the sake of self-protection from social injury (e.g. humiliation, lack of respect). Put differently, it is an interpersonal strategy of minimizing damage while navigating the treacherous currents of social life, in pursuit of various personal goals.

In the final analysis, social phobia is a multi-causal phenomenon. Namely, the events evoking the socially phobic responses (e.g. the fearsome encounters) act as the proximate cause. The socially phobic interpersonal organization (i.e. pattern) acts as the formal cause. The ultimate cause is intimately bound up with the formal cause; in a manner of speaking, the latter is the means to the former. The overall – self-protective – socially phobic pattern is to safety, what a piano is to music-making or a sharp knife's blade is to cutting – a means to an end.

In summary, the causes invoked in the above analysis are best seen as processes extended in time, rather than singular events narrowly and sharply demarcated.

Of the four causes, prominence was given in the above analysis to the formal and ultimate causes and to a lesser extent to the proximate ones. The material cause remained relatively undeveloped in our analysis, since, as can clearly be seen in Chapters 4 and 5, all life functions of socially phobic individuals are within a normal range.

For this reason, the crucial differences between socially phobic and normal individuals are in the formal (i.e. relational) and, by extension, in the final (i.e. in terms of goals) realms of causality. The material basis is the same, as are the proximate (i.e. evoking) circumstances.

The historic emergence of the socially phobic pattern

The overarching relational pattern – the formal cause – is the linchpin of the causal analysis of social phobia. On the one hand, it is evoked and further shaped by various menacing situations and transactions. On the other hand, out of these patterned transactions (seemingly characterized by weary distance keeping, intensely vigilant inactivity, stumbling performance and disarray) emerges an overall relational pattern, enacting a coherent and purposeful strategy of self-protection.

For the very reason of being a pivotal part of the explanatory framework, the presence of such an overall web of patterns raises a secondary question: how did it come about?

Theoretically, the interpersonal outlook would maintain that the fearful interpersonal pattern can only emerge historically (in an extended process, rather than being the consequence of a single predetermining factor or "traumatic" event). In this view, social phobia would emerge gradually, but not inevitably, in fits and starts, through idiosyncratic processes arising out of unique individual circumstances (at the same time, social and cultural). The socially phobic pattern would stabilize, intensify or atrophy gradually, in a constantly evolving process, as part of a life trajectory (see Rose, 1998).

Do the available facts accord with, or contradict this theoretical position? Be that as it may, an additional question is as follows: what factors might influence such a historic course? The following survey is an attempt to answer these queries. As much (theoretically speaking) rides on the answers, the survey is rather comprehensive.

A historic pattern may naturally be marked by the initial conditions of its coming into being. I shall first touch on these. The first factor to consider is whether a certain kind of "innate" endowment is conducive to social phobia. For this purpose, I have chosen "temperament" as a construct, purporting to describe a biological or constitutional endowment. The second factor to be considered is the caretakers of the young individual, constituting, as it were, the early social environment. Initial development may plausibly be seen as emerging out of the resulting transactions and related experiences.

Further possible environmental influences (e.g. family, peers and adverse life events) will be considered at a later stage.

Constitutional factors

Temperament

Certain psychological features exhibited by the infant may be taken as early expressions of inborn propensities. Such presumably enduring characteristics are considered as revealing of temperament. What is temperament?

A rather abstract definition would be that it is a hypothetical construct, linking early manifesting and enduring complex patterns of behavior to regulating systems in the brain (Reiss and Neiderhiser, 2000, p. 360). The most prominent perspectives on the matter are summarized in Goldsmith et al. (1987).

The operational definition of temperament found in the seminal work of Chess and Thomas (1987) is useful in illustrating the notion. In their original study, nine features (based on parental reports, not observation) were rated: activity level, regularity of biological functions, tendency towards approach or withdrawal, adaptability (over time; not a response to the new), intensity of reaction, threshold of responsiveness, distractibility, attention span and perseverance.

This multidimensional assessment gave rise to four temperamental categories. These were as follows:

1. "easy" temperament – positive in mood, regular in bodily functions, quickly adaptable;
2. "difficult" temperament – negative in mood, irregular bodily functions, slow to adapt, tends to withdraw from new situations, reacting with high emotional intensity;
3. "slow to warm up" temperament – similar to the latter but more placid;
4. "mixed" temperament – an undifferentiated category.

The key finding, that parents of the difficult children in that study were on the whole no different from parents of the other children, was interpreted as supporting the "temperamental" hypothesis.

To bring the issue closer to our concerns, the hypothetical tendency to reticence in encounters with unfamiliar individuals and unusual situations (so prominent in social phobia) has been put forward as evidence of such a temperamental trait. Thus, several authors (e.g. Rosenbaum et al., 1991) postulated a link between anxiety disorders in general (social phobia included) and a temperamental construct going by the name of "behavioral inhibition."

This trait, in all probability a rough equivalent of the "withdrawal" aspect of the "difficult" temperament in Chess and Thomas (1987), has been postulated to be a reflection of a lowered threshold to fearful stimuli in limbic and hypothalamic structures (see Kagan, Reznick and Snidman, 1987), themselves under genetic control.

Social phobia and "behavioral inhibition"

Before considering studies relating behavioral inhibition to social phobia, it is necessary to clarify further both this "temperamental" construct as well as its measurement.

"Behavioral inhibition" was validated in a series of four studies (Garcia Coll, Kagan and Reznick, 1984; Kagan, Reznick and Snidman, 1987, 1988; Kagan, 1989), all carried out in the Boston area. Garcia et al. (1984) is the seminal study involving 305 21–22-month-old children (all born in 1978). The children were selected after a brief telephone interview with the mother, either because of their pronounced tendency to withdraw from, or conversely, to seek out, encounters with unfamiliar children and adults.

Based on these telephone interviews, 56 children (of 305) were classified as inhibited and 104 as uninhibited; the remaining 145 of the middling kind lacking pronounced characteristics, were excluded. This is an important point of method, to which I shall return soon.

Of the chosen 160, the mothers of 117 children accepted to be tested with their offspring in the laboratory. After further observations, 33 were reclassified as inhibited and 38 as uninhibited, and 47 as neither. It is noteworthy, again, that only the most extreme cases were selected for study (see Garcia *et al.*, 1984, p. 1018).

Two "coders" (positioned behind a one-way mirror) observed mother and child interactions in several episodes:

1. *warm-up*: the subjects were greeted and briefed;
2. *free-play*: the mother was instructed neither to prompt the child to play, nor to initiate interactions with him or her;
3. *reaction to modeling*: the experimenter enacted several scenarios (talking on a toy phone, a doll cooking food and serving it to other dolls, three animals walking through a rainstorm ...);
4. *reaction to an unfamiliar adult*: a unfamiliar women entered the room sat down for 30 seconds without initiating contact; then, she called the child by name and asked him or her to perform three items taken out of Bailey's scale of mental development and left the room;
5. *reaction to an unfamiliar object*: the experimenter drew the curtains to reveal a robot; the child was encouraged to explore the robot and was shown how to switch on/off the lights fixed in its head; the experimenter switched on a recording and the voice came through a speaker in the robot's mouth; the child was again encouraged to explore the robot;
6. *separation from the mother*: the mother was motioned to leave the room for 3 minutes (when the child was playing); she came back immediately if the child started crying.

Throughout these scenarios, latency of the approach to the stranger or the robot, clinging to the mother, crying, fretting, withdrawal and vocalization of distress were rated. Additional measurements such as inhibition of play, apprehension and facial expressions were taken, without being further defined. This is rather problematic, as these measures are less obvious indicators of inhibition or lack thereof.

Based on the number of inhibited behaviors, "the index of behavioral inhibition" (IBI) was created; the children were classified as inhibited (9 and more), uninhibited (2 or less) and neither (3 to 8). These predetermined cut-off points were based on a pilot study.

The experiments were carried out again after three to five weeks with an overall reliability of .63. It is surprising in light of this figure to find that while the stability for the inhibited sub-group was .56, it was only .33 for the uninhibited. Nonetheless, most children – 68% of the inhibited and 82% of the uninhibited – retained their original classification at the second testing.

Parental ratings of the toddler's temperament were moderately correlated with the IBI (mother .54, father .49). By contrast, the correlations across episodes, were on average rather low −.27; subsequent ratings, tended to be even less consistent.

A second study (Kagan et al., 1987), including 120 children (21 months old and 31 months old) of which 60 were classified as inhibited and 60 uninhibited, overall replicated the results of Garcia Coll et al. (1984). The latter study, however, expanded physiological measurements (only heart rate was monitored in the first study). Larger pupil diameters, elevated levels of (morning) salivary cortisol and greater muscle tension (inferred indirectly, from the evidence of less variability in the pitch periods of single-word utterances spoken under stress) characterized the inhibited children.

These physiological peculiarities were essentially replicated in a third study (Kagan et al., 1988) including 58 subjects (28 inhibited, 30 uninhibited) 21 months old, 49 (26 inhibited, 23 uninhibited) 31 months old and 100 unselected subjects 14 months old.

The fourth study (reported piecemeal in Kagan, 1989; Kagan and Snidman, 1991a, 1991b) concerned the all-important question of whether inhibited and uninhibited profiles may be predicted from certain features of the infants' behavior, observed at 2 and 4 months of age, in various assessment situations. These included the following: one-minute of quiet with mother smiling; presentation of three-dimensional images; presentation of three mobiles; and playing a record with a female voice at different loudness levels. The variables rated were limb movement (flex–extend), arching of the back, tongue protrusions, motor tension in hands or limbs and crying. Four groups (94 subjects in total) were created on the basis of combinations of levels of motor activity and crying. The two contrast groups were made up of subjects high in motor activity and crying versus low in motor activity as well as in crying.

The children were reassessed at 9, 14 and 21 months for reactions to 16 situations representing unfamiliarity (see above) with fretting and crying as indices of fearful behavior. With the exception of crying, the whole gamut of behaviors presumably assessed was not reported in the results. This limits considerably the conclusions that can be drawn from them.

The main finding established links between a high degree of motor activity and crying on the one hand and fearful behavior (defined by crying and fretting again) on the other hand. Altogether, this is puzzling. The results seem to demonstrate the stability of the same behavior rather than providing support for the prediction of a type of conduct from altogether different features of behavior, which one might have expected. The fact that the inhibited and uninhibited profiles seemed to be stable over time cannot be seen as establishing them necessarily as predictors of "behavioral inhibition"; no evidence for this has been reported so far.

These studies gave rise to a series of other investigations that expanded but also challenged aspects of the construct. A detailed discussion may be found in Stravynski (2007, pp. 251–255).

Methodologically, the temperamental construct of "behavioral inhibition," while heuristically useful, is beset by several weaknesses. First of all, some evidence suggests that it is not uniformly constructed. Secondly, it is not entirely stable: over a third of the children identified as inhibited at 21 months of age become less inhibited in time. Thirdly, the behavioral tendency associated most closely with the construct is evident only in a small fraction of the children exhibiting the worst psychological and physiological features. Statistically, "behavioral inhibition" held up as a construct only in comparisons of extreme-scoring individuals from both ends of the distribution (10 percent each).

The case for "behavioral inhibition" would obviously have been far more convincing had the characteristic in question held up in comparison with the norm (average) characterizing the cohort. In actuality, the typically available study found none of the significant correlations in including the whole sample in the analysis. It is worth reiterating that significant results emerged only when comparing the most extreme 20% of the subjects found on both ends of the distribution.

These weaknesses notwithstanding, the possibility that social phobia might have a temperamental predisposition, evident at an early age (e.g. 21 months), must not be overlooked. Let me now turn to the studies that have investigated such possible links.

The main study exploring the link between "behavioral inhibition" in young children and anxious disorders in general (identified at an older age) was reported in Biederman et al. (1990).

The child subjects were drawn from three sources: (1) the cohort from the Garcia Coll et al. (1984) (so-called "epidemiologic" for including subjects from the general population) studies previously described (originally classified as inhibited n=22, uninhibited n=19; aged 7–8 years at the time of the study); (2) children of a group of panic disorder/agoraphobic patients in treatment (classified as inhibited n=18 or not inhibited n=12 at the age of 4–7 years); (3) children consulting the pediatric care service (undifferentiated n=20 at the age of 4–10 years), whose parents – it was assumed – were normal. "Diagnoses" (lifetime) were arrived at on the basis of interviews with the mothers.

No differences in prevalence rates of childhood avoidant disorder were found between the groups. When all anxiety disorders, however, were lumped together, a link between this wide category and "behavioral inhibition" was found in the sample of children of parents meeting criteria for panic disorder/agoraphobia but not in the "epidemiologic," that is, general population (Garcia Coll et al., 1984) sample. A study testing this link in children of socially phobic parents remains to be carried out.

From a different perspective, Rosenbaum et al. (1991) tested whether the family members (parents as well as siblings) of behaviorally inhibited subjects had a stronger propensity towards social phobia (and anxiety disorders in general).

The samples described in the previous study (Biederman et al., 1990) were amalgamated to create three groups: inhibited, uninhibited and normal controls. Parents of inhibited children had greater rates of (lifetime) adult social phobia (17.5%) compared with parents of uninhibited subjects (0%) and those of normal controls (3%). Conversely, parents of inhibited children also reported significantly higher rates of childhood avoidant disorder (15%), compared to none reported in the other groups.

The results regarding siblings, however, were disconcerting. Contrary to what might have been expected, none of the siblings of the inhibited subjects met criteria for avoidant disorder (this was also the case with the siblings of the normal controls) while 17% of the siblings of children in the uninhibited group did.

In a further analysis (Rosenbaum et al., 1992), the combination of both "behavioral inhibition" and an anxiety disorder in a child were found to be highly associated with a parent's anxiety disorder (88% vs. 32%). Statistically, however, the rate of anxiety disorders in parents of inhibited or uninhibited children was similar. In the case of (parental) social phobia, 50% of the inhibited children meeting criteria for anxiety disorders had such parents as compared with 9% in children classified only as behaviorally inhibited and 0% for the uninhibited children without anxiety disorders. These results if anything seem to diminish the role of "behavioral inhibition" in the development of social phobia as such.

This particular question was addressed specifically in Biederman et al. (1993). For this purpose, inhibited children with parents free of anxiety disorders (from the Kagan study) were compared to inhibited children whose parents met criteria for various anxiety disorders.

Overall, the results showed that a greater proportion of inhibited children of parents fulfilling criteria for anxiety disorders tended to meet criteria for anxiety disorders themselves (22% vs. 14%). Limiting this to avoidant disorder, the rates, although lower, were still in the same direction (17% vs. 9%). In a subsequent 3-year follow-up, the rate of inhibited children who developed avoidant disorder increased (from 9 to 28%). A similar trend (from 17 to 27%) was observed in the group of inhibited children whose parents fulfilled criteria for anxiety disorders. No such trend was observed among the uninhibited children.

Specific results concerning social phobia as such at the end of the follow-up, however, showed a different picture. Seventeen percent of the inhibited children in the "epidemiologic" sample (Garcia Coll et al., 1984) met criteria for social phobia but so also did 20% of the uninhibited children. In contrast, 23% of the inhibited children, whose parents met criteria for panic disorder/agoraphobia, were classified as socially phobic compared with 6% of the uninhibited children (p. 817, table 2). These results suggest that the clinical status of the parents – more than any other factor – acts as a powerful liability towards the social phobia of a child.

In a study testing whether behavioral inhibition predisposes specifically to social phobia or avoidant disorder of childhood (among other specific anxiety disorders), Biederman et al. (2001), compared 64 inhibited children to 152 non-inhibited children aged 2 to 6 years. Correspondence to defining criteria was established by means of the "Schedule for the affective disorders and schizophrenia for school-age-children-epidemiologic" version (Orvaschel, 1994) completed by the mother.

The prevalence of social phobia and avoidant disorder among the inhibited group was found to be significantly higher at 17% than that of the non-inhibited group at 5%, suggesting that behavioral inhibition may be associated with problems characterized by social anxiety in early childhood. The rather astonishing above result could be an artifact of the fact that the mothers filled out the "diagnostic" instrument, perhaps misidentifying a pre-existing tendency to withdrawal (i.e. behavioral inhibition) as a pattern of social phobia.

However, and statistical significance notwithstanding, it is difficult to imagine the meaning of designating a 4- or 5-year-old as socially phobic. The typical onset of social phobia is in adolescence; prevalence rising with age, as social demands increase (e.g. from 0.5% in 12–13-year-olds to 4% in 14–17-year-olds in Essau et al., 1999). Childhood social phobia, therefore, ought to be greeted with considerable skepticism.

In a 5-year follow-up of the Biederman et al. (2001) study, Hirshfeld-Becker et al. (2007) assessed the prevalence of social phobia in children between the ages of 7 and 11 years (average age was 9.6 years).

Two hundred and eighty-one children were included in the original study after undergoing the Kagan and Snidman (1991a) behavioral inhibition task protocol. At follow-up of the remaining 215 participants,

67 were considered behaviorally inhibited (the highest 20%) and 148 non-behaviorally inhibited.

A significantly higher proportion of the behaviorally inhibited group as compared to the non-inhibited group (22% vs. 11%) met DSM criteria for social phobia (as assessed using the K-SADS).

It is difficult to draw general conclusions from these studies for, with the exception of Biederman *et al.* (2001), they are marred by several important methodological flaws. First of all, most studies in this series deal with aggregates of multiple anxiety disorders (e.g. Biederman *et al.*, 1990; Rosenbaum *et al.*, 1991, 1992), as a meaningful single variable. This seems to be in part the direct consequence of the inadequacy of the sample size (e.g. n=31) that is often too small to enable meaningful distinctions between categories of anxiety disorders. The upshot is that the statistical analyses were often carried out on percentages calculated from small cells of subjects (e.g. 50% = two subjects out of four). Although this masks the underlying problem, the difficulty in drawing meaningful conclusions remains.

Secondly, and most importantly, all longitudinal studies have made use of the same original sample (of 41 subjects) described in Biederman *et al.* (1990). Thus, despite numerous publications and a variety of control-groups, all have used the same experimental cohort (Garcia Coll *et al.*, 1984). These can hardly be called independent replications.

Thirdly, whether the operational definition of "behavioral inhibition" was equivalent (they were clearly not the same) throughout the various studies is uncertain.

Finally, the parents in the control groups were assumed to be normal because they have not sought help (pediatric vs. psychiatric clinic). No screening was carried out to make sure that this is not the case.

For all the above reasons, an independent study of a different cohort carries much weight. Chronis-Tuscano *et al.* (2009) assessed 159 children (in Oregon, USA) by means of the Behavioral Inhibition Test (see Kagan and Snidman, 1991a) at 14 and 24 months and at the age of 4 and 7 years.

The final categorization (high-stable and low-unstable) using all four points in time was created by means of a latent class (a form of cluster) analysis. The low behaviorally inhibited group, however, included also the unstable subjects. Nonetheless, the groups were statistically distinct. The final analysis included 15 subjects in the high-stable group and 107 in the low-unstable group.

Follow-up assessments of the 122 remaining participants (mean age=15.5 years) by means of semi-structured interviews (K-SADS), established prevalence of social phobia.

A regression analysis found the difference (in terms of current prevalence of social phobia) between the two groups, namely 20% vs. 11%
or three out of 15 in the high-stable group, and 12 out of 107 in the
low-unstable group, not to be statistically significant. This lack of significance is telling; it suggests that the link between behavioral inhibition
and social phobia is weak, at best.

Possible precursors to the construct of "behavioral inhibition"

A longitudinal study by Kagan and Moss (1962) of social anxiety,
although not making use of the modern category of social phobia (it was
carried out between 1929 and 1959) seems most relevant as the descriptions of the children resemble the main features of the socially anxious
(1962, p. 174 and appendix 2, p. 296).

The main objective of this study (the Fels longitudinal program) was
to ascertain the stability of certain psychological characteristics, one of
them being passivity in the face of frustration. Passivity in this study
(1962, p. 51), defined as "the degree to which the child acquiesced or
withdrew in the face of attack or frustrating situations," appears to be the
rough equivalent of the construct of "behavioral inhibition" developed
later on (Kagan, 1989, p. 668).

The subjects (45 girls and 44 boys, offspring of 63 families) were
recruited into the study during the last trimester of the mother's pregnancy (between the years 1929 and 1939). Both children and mothers
were observed in various situations (at home, at school and at day-
camp), between the ages of 3 months and 14 years. The information was
extracted from detailed observation diaries. The remaining 71 subjects
were re-evaluated as adults (between the ages of 19 and 29), by means of
interviews and administered tests.

The most important finding was that passivity between the ages of
3 and 6 and 6 and 10 was significantly associated with social anxiety
in adulthood (r=. 41 and .46 respectively), but for men only. The same
results emerged when childhood behaviors (e.g. sudden crying, withdrawal from social interactions, seeking proximity to the mother) were
related to adult social anxiety in men (the only exception being withdrawal from social interaction for women). Conversely, social spontan-
eity (laughing, smiling, displaying eagerness to interact) in childhood
was inversely related to social anxiety in adulthood (r=−.45).

In conclusion, these early studies link manifestations of reticence and
safety seeking at an early age and social anxiousness in adulthood for men.

In the final analysis, considering the above-described studies and bearing in mind the various methodological weaknesses and contradictory

findings, it is difficult to maintain that "behavioral inhibition" and social phobia in adulthood are firmly associated.

This conclusion is consistent with the findings of Caspi, Moffitt, Newman and Silva (1996), who have failed to find a link between inhibited temperament as established at the third year of life and anxiety disorders at the age of 21. A particular significance attaches to the results of this longitudinal study. First of all, it followed a cohort from Dunedin, New Zealand, making it an independent investigation – unrelated to the project from Boston. Secondly, temperament was treated as a continuum and as a consequence was likely to have included subjects who were less extreme exemplars of inhibition. The Caspi et al. (1996) study provides a welcome counterpoint to the series issued from Boston, defining inhibition in the most restrictive way, while using for contrast the most extremely uninhibited subjects.

Potentially far more interesting – if fears rather than disorder entities are considered – was the observation by Garcia Coll et al. (1984) that "behavioral inhibition" is clearly associated with social fears. The stability of this association was much later demonstrated prospectively in a study (Schwartz, Snidman and Kagan, 1999) of 13-year-olds (drawn from the same original two cohorts), classified 12 years earlier as inhibited (n=44) and uninhibited (n=35). A significantly higher percentage (61% vs. 27%) of inhibited subjects reported a general discomfort in various social situations and interactions. Incongruously, inhibited subjects' concerns about performance in front of groups (e.g. public speaking) were no different (statistically) from those of the uninhibited subjects.

Altogether, temperament in the guise of "behavioral inhibition" can neither be considered a sufficient condition nor even a necessary one for the emergence of social phobia. As seen earlier, the link held true for only a fraction of inhibited individuals. Crucially, many individuals designated "uninhibited" also developed social phobia. This fact, more than anything, mitigates the role of temperamental factors in the development of social phobia. This does not, however, preclude it constituting a nonspecific liability, among others, towards social phobia.

Perhaps "if behavioral inhibition is a constitutional variable, it might be more appropriately considered a behavioral propensity towards social introversion" (Turner, Beidel and Wolff, 1996, p. 168). In this sense, "behavioral inhibition" is a facet – albeit considered in an extreme degree – of a common psychological or personality feature (or dimension) such as introversion (Eysenck and Eysenck, 1969). Introverted individuals have, by definition, a stronger propensity to behave defensively and react with greater alarm, that is, anxiously (Gray, 1970).

Environmental factors

However that may be, it stands to reason that the propensity to engage people defensively, or withdraw from social contacts altogether, would need a social environment in which such individuals over time repeatedly fail to adapt, for the maladjusted pattern of functioning to crystallize. It is, therefore, the social environment (the one the individual interacts with) and the way of life (social practices and cultural demands) the individual shares – rather than the temperamental propensity – that would probably constitute the amalgam of factors shaping the emergence of the full-blown socially phobic pattern.

Early social environment

The attachment relationship The attachment theory maintains that human infants especially (but also primates in general) are primed and driven to create attachment relationships. Specifically, the human infant has a set of pre-adapted behaviors that will unfold with maturation. These behaviors will be elicited when a suitable context (certain adults) will be available. Adults, in turn, are predisposed to respond to the infant by nurturing, vocalizing and touch. The attachment relationship organizes the infant's attachment behaviors (e.g. smiling, vocalizing and seeking closeness) around the caregiver. By 12 months of age, these behaviors are integrated into a well-established pattern and are used towards maintaining and reactivating contact with the caregiver. The attachment relationship remains as a backdrop, even when the infant is engaged (e.g. in exploration) elsewhere. When detecting a potential threat, the infant will seek safety in either proximity with the caregiver, or in reassurance at a distance.

While delineating the interpersonal and emotional vicissitudes of the attachment relationship, Bowlby (1981a) repeatedly emphasized its main function: protection from harm and survival.

To sum up, attachment is understood as a behavioral pattern or system, ensuring proximity to caregivers and by consequence their protection from danger. Attachment, therefore, is not a quality that an infant is endowed with, nor is it a hypothetical construct (e.g. anxiety) driving the infant to do anything. Furthermore, attachment as a relationship between an infant and a caregiver is the product of a history of interactions between the two participants, who – by means of this process – become emotionally *tied* to one another. For those so involved, for example, even brief separations are upsetting. Both fearfulness of separation as well as of strangers – that become rather pronounced in the second half of the first year of life – might be construed as part of the process of attachment, organized around a particular (usually mothering) figure.

It is noteworthy that the responses to both reunions and separations are patterned and highly organized, not haphazard. A typical sequence after a separation involves a period of protest, followed by a period of despair culminating in detachment (Sroufe and Waters, 1977). A prolonged separation, however, has a highly upsetting (i.e. emotionally intense and disorganizing) effect on the infant. This highlights the emotional importance of the attachment relationship.

Having clarified the concept of attachment, I can now discuss its measurement. A paradigm of assessment (the Strange Situation) to assess the attachment relationship was developed by Ainsworth, Blehar, Waters and Wall (1978) (see Sroufe, 1996, pp. 180–182 for a detailed description).

The procedure involves seven episodes after a caregiver and an infant enter a room containing various toys (1 min.):

1. The infant is allowed to play while the caregiver is seated in a chair nearby (3 min.);
2. A stranger comes in and sits quietly (1 min.), chats with caregiver (1 min.), engages the infant in play;
3. The caregiver leaves (3 min.) unless the stranger cannot calm down the upset infant;
4. The caregiver returns and the stranger leaves (3 min.);
5. The caregiver leaves the infant alone (3 min. or less);
6. The stranger returns and attempts to comfort the infant – if needed (3 min.);
7. The caregiver returns (3 min.).

Various doubts have been raised about the extent to which observations gathered by this method accurately reflected behavior in a natural (i.e. home) setting (see Lamb, Thompson, Gardner, Charnov and Estes, 1984 for a critique). Moreover, the fact that this method of assessment conflates both stranger and separation (steps 3 and 4) anxieties (see Marks 1987, p. 142) constitutes a serious flaw in the procedure. However that may be, the Strange Situation seems to have weathered the criticisms and withstood the test of time through extensive use (see Karen, 1998 for a survey of its use in various studies).

Based on observations during the Strange Situation assessment, three main patterns of attachment relationships have been identified: secure, anxious and avoidant (the following descriptions rely on Sroufe, 1996, pp. 182–185).

The securely attached infants willingly separate from the caregiver to become involved in play activities. They are not particularly apprehensive of a stranger. If distressed, they seek contact with the caregiver. In his or her presence they recover smoothly from a heightened and disorganized emotional state.

The anxiously attached infants, by contrast, are reluctant to explore and are wary of a stranger. They are quite upset by separations, and find it difficult to settle down, even when reunited with the caregiver.

The avoidantly attached infants separate rather easily to play. They are upset only when left alone, and, significantly, take little notice of the caregiver upon reunion and are not responsive to him or her.

Bowlby's (1981b) central hypothesis was that the availability and responsiveness of the caregiver (i.e. quality of care) are strong determinants of the kind of resulting attachment relationship. Theoretically, securely attached infants would have had histories of caregiver availability and responsiveness; avoidant infants, histories of unavailability and rejection on the part of the caregiver, while anxiously attached infants, histories of haphazardly available care and intermittently effective (i.e. reassuring) interventions on the part of the caregiver.

According to Bowlby (1981b), the intense separation anxiety and other fears exhibited by these infants are a reaction to the uncertainty of the availability of the caregiver in the face of a threat. Fearful behavior and proximity seeking have also a communicative function in alerting the caregiver to the distress of the infant and elicit his or her reassurance and assistance in calming the infant (emotional regulation in the terminology of Sroufe, 1996). Given that the caregiver cannot be counted on to attend to the needs of the infant when they arise, the infant will tend to intensify the signals in response to lower and lower thresholds of possibility of threat. As a consequence, the infant would be easily aroused, frequently distressed and not easily reassured.

It is interesting to note that infant temperament has not been shown to affect attachment directly, while seeming to influence the relationship in interaction with certain caregiver characteristics (e.g. maternal tendency to control; see Mangelsdorf, Gunnar, Kestenbaum, Lang and Andreas, 1990).

Is a particular pattern of attachment in infancy enduring? What are its long-term implications?

Clearly, a particular pattern of attachment in infancy does not directly lead to specific outcomes in adolescence or adulthood. Secure attachment does not ensure life without difficulties. In the face of such difficulties, however, securely attached children tend to display more resourcefulness, resilience and relational abilities. Conversely, anxious attachment in infancy does not by necessity lead to an anxiety disorder later on. Such a complex, disordered pattern of behavior would depend, in Bowlby's (1981b) formulation, "on an interaction between the organism as it has developed up to that moment and the environment in which it then finds itself" (p. 364). Theoretically, this implies that with the rise of new circumstances, past experiences would not simply vanish without trace, but would leave their mark on the process of adaptation through the remnants of the behavioral patterns that have been forged previously.

Validating research   The main ideas embedded in attachment theory were examined in an admirable longitudinal study carried out by the "Minnesota group for research on attachment." For descriptions of it, I rely mostly on Sroufe, Carlson and Shulman (1993) and Sroufe (1983). Two specific hypotheses were put to a test: first of all, that the psychological availability and responsiveness of the caregiver determines the quality of attachment; secondly, that the quality of attachment in turn influences the way a person deals with intimate relationships (e.g. dependency, nurturing, separations and loss; p. 47) and participates in social life.

Subjects were recruited before birth in 1974–1975 relying on 267 expectant mothers who were high-risk for difficulties in caretaking (low socioeconomic status, high-school dropouts, unmarried, unplanned pregnancy). In this ongoing longitudinal study the quality of attachment relationship was determined by the Strange Situation paradigm at the age of 12 and 18 months. Observations in the home were carried out in the first 6 months of age. Subsequently, the children were observed with their parent in the laboratory on several occasions as well as in various environments (e.g. school, summer camp) during childhood, adolescence and adulthood.

In what follows, I single out examples of behavior typical of the anxiously attached children (classified as such at 12 and 18 months of age) as they grew up, because of the striking resemblance of their conduct with the interpersonal features of social phobia. A comprehensive overview of this pattern of attachment may be found in Cassidy and Berlin (1994).

For example, as a group, anxiously attached 4-year-old girls were particularly withdrawn, passive, submissive and neglected by their peers. Furthermore, anxiously attached 4-year-olds were found to participate less in social activities. When they did, they were less dominant (the index included verbal and non-verbal observed behaviors) than the securely attached children.

In another study (Renken, Egeland, Marvinney, Mangelsdorf and Sroufe, 1989), a strong link between anxious attachment and passive withdrawal was established for 6- to 8-year-old boys in a school context. Thus, 58% of the passively withdrawn children were previously categorized as anxiously attached.

At summer camp anxiously attached 10- to 11-year-olds spent less time in group activities, and rarely initiated and structured group activities themselves. Groups of mostly securely attached children were involved in more elaborate play activities. When three or more anxiously attached children congregated, their activities had to be structured by a counselor. Left to their own devices, they would revert to uncoordinated and solitary types of activities performed in parallel (e.g. play on a swing). This illustrates the difficulties such children had in managing important aspects of social functioning such as fitting in and in establishing one's status (Sroufe *et al.*, 1993, pp. 330–331).

Another example of the tendency towards submissiveness of the anxiously attached children may be conveyed by observations of exploitative behavior among children attending the summer camp. In five dyads out of 19 observed, there was evidence of victimization (repetitive pattern of exploitation or physical or verbal abuse) of one child by another. In all cases, the victim was an anxiously attached child whereas the bullies were all avoidant; none of the bullies were anxiously (or securely) attached children.

Both examples illustrate to some extent how the complex pattern of behaviors of the anxiously attached children helped to shape the social environment in which they found themselves (see also Scarr, 1996). For example, teachers tended to be nurturing and controlling with the obedient and retiring anxiously attached children. By contrast, they were rejecting and punitive with avoidant children who tended to defiance.

Anxious attachment, social anxiety and social phobia Although not concerning social phobia as such, a study of social functioning and attachment (Bohlin, Hagekull and Rydell, 2000) carried out in Sweden, found that social anxiety was more severe among the anxiously attached than among securely and avoidantly attached 8- to 9-year-olds.

Only one study to my knowledge has linked anxious attachment in early childhood to anxiety disorders – with social phobia amongst them – at the age of 17.5 years (Warren, Huston, Egeland and Sroufe, 1997). The subjects were 172 17.5-year-olds, identified as socially phobic by means of a structured interview (the interviewers being blind to their attachment status that was determined at the age of 12 months by means of the Strange Situation 16 years earlier). In the final sample, 32 subjects were anxiously attached, 95 securely and 37 avoidantly attached.

The main finding was that a greater number of children meeting criteria for anxiety disorders were as infants identified as anxiously attached. The most prevalent anxiety disorder observed in that group was indeed social phobia (ten), followed by separation anxiety disorder (eight) and overanxious disorder (eight). Twenty-eight percent of the anxiously attached infants developed anxiety disorders in adolescence compared to 13 percent of the children who were not anxiously attached in infancy. Crucially, far more (40% vs. 28%) of the anxiously attached infants developed normally and reported no clinical problems when interviewed in adolescence. Perhaps the most theoretically meaningful result was that only anxious attachment (but not avoidant or secure attachment) in infancy was associated with social phobia (and other anxiety disorders) in late adolescence.

Remarkably, nurses' ratings of the newborn's temperament (defined as newborn crying, motor activity and relaxation when held) significantly predicted anxiety disorders (undifferentiated) in late adolescence.

The possible link between insecure attachment and temperament was examined by Manassis, Bradley, Goldberg, Hood and Swinson (1995). The subjects of the study were 20 children (aged 18 to 59 months) of 18 mothers meeting criteria for various anxiety disorders who were assessed for "behavioral inhibition" as well as "type of attachment," using the original assessment procedures described earlier. Sixteen out of 20 children were defined as insecurely attached and 15 as behaviorally inhibited, but no relationship was found between the two constructs. Surprisingly, only one of the children met DSM-III-R criteria for avoidant disorder.

In summary, anxious attachment (and significantly, only anxious attachment) at the age of 12 months was associated with the rather vast category of anxiety disorders (albeit with social phobia prominent amongst them) in late adolescence (17.5 years). In regression analysis, anxious attachment in infancy, predicted anxiety disorders – but not social phobia specifically – in adolescence, over and above other variables such as maternal anxiety and an array of variables indexing temperament. Nevertheless, it must be borne in mind that even a greater proportion of infants classified as anxiously attached did not develop an anxious disorder of any description by late adolescence.

In the final analysis, anxious attachment is best considered a liability towards social phobia, but not a sufficient or even a necessary aspect of its development.

Later environmental influences

In addition to attachment, other parental factors and the family overall have been considered as possible environmental influences over the development of social phobia. Peers and adverse life events have been studied to a lesser extent.

Family environment

Child rearing and other parental characteristics viewed retrospectively and prospectively in relation to social phobia/avoidant personality disorder A number of studies (see Stravynski, 2007, pp. 263–266 for a summary) queried socially phobic individuals (retrospectively) about their parents. The main framework for this line of research was Parker's (1979) model, situating parental influences on two dimensions: control and caring. Its main hypothesis combines "overprotection" with "low care."

The main finding was that socially anxious subjects tended to describe at least one of their parents as overprotective. This, however, was not exclusive to social phobia (Grüner, Muris and Merckelbach, 1999). Of greater consequence is the fact that the above self-reported results have been buttressed by observation of child–parent interactions by Hudson and Rapee (2001). Moreover, overprotection was shown to be a stable parental characteristic, true of mothers and fathers, and applied equally to all siblings (Hudson and Rapee, 2002).

This is confirmed in the only longitudinal study (Kagan and Moss, 1962) available, having the additional merit of being based on observation, rather than retrospective recall on the part of the subjects. Overprotectiveness on the part of mothers towards girls between the age of 0 and 3 years and boys between the ages of 6 and 10 years was associated with social anxiety in adulthood.

In most studies socially anxious subjects identified their parents as less caring or outright rejecting (parents were also described as shame or guilt engendering). In the dissenting study (Arbel and Stravynski, 1991) of that series, socially phobic/avoidant personality disorder participants stood out from the control group in mostly lacking positive experiences with their parents, rather than feeling rejected. This observation is bolstered by other studies (Stravynski, 2007, pp. 263–266) reporting less emotional warmth on the part of the parents of socially phobic individuals.

However, in Kagan and Moss (1962) hostility (including rejection) on the part of mothers towards girls between the ages of 0 to 3 years and boys between the ages of 6 and 10 years was negatively associated with social anxiety in adulthood.

Another important factor prominent in most studies is the relative isolation of the parents and the low sociability of the family (Stravynski, 2007, pp. 263–266). Similarly, in most studies testing this, parents were perceived as greatly concerned about the opinion of others (Stravynski, 2007, pp. 263–266).

In summary, a rather consistent link was established between social phobia and the retrospective perception of parents as being on the one hand overanxious and overprotective, and on the other hand, rather little or only intermittently involved with their child. The implications of such environmental features on the shaping of the socially phobic pattern (e.g. through modeling and encouraging self-protective patterns of behavior) are still to be elucidated. However, the haphazard care given often in response to self-dramatizing expressions of distress on the part of the child are well-known features of the anxious pattern of attachment. Finally, social phobia was rather consistently linked to membership of a rather isolated family, mindful of proprieties in relations with others.

Socially phobic parents   A number of studies (e.g. Fyer *et al.*, 1995; Tillfors, Furmark, Ekselius and Fredrikson, 2001) reported that a statistically significant (ranging from 15 to 26%) proportion of socially phobic individuals had socially phobic parents.

Although it stands to reason that parents may transmit their own patterns of behavior either directly (e.g. serving as an example, encouraging and discouraging certain behaviors) or indirectly (e.g. inculcating certain rules), nothing specific has been highlighted so far.

However, some general attitudes have been documented. Woodruff-Borden, Morrow, Bourland and Cambron (2002), for example, have found that parents with anxiety disorders tended to disagree with their children more, praise them less and ignore them more often than normal parents.

Furthermore, mothers with anxiety disorders granted less autonomy to their children. A gradation was established: anxious mothers of anxious children tended to restrict their autonomy more than did anxious mothers with non-anxious children. The latter acted like normal mothers in this respect (Whaley, Pinto and Sigman, 1999).

However dire the implication of having such a parent might be for some individuals, the explanatory value of this factor for the development of social phobia, in general, is bound to be limited. As only a fraction of socially phobic individuals had grown up with such a parent, the familial transmission of social phobia fails to account for the bulk of cases.

Parental influence facilitating the development of "behavioral inhibition" or moving away from it   That parents have such an influence is well documented in Kagan *et al.* (1987) as are the means they had deployed. In this study, inhibited children (at the age of 21 months) who became uninhibited later on (between the ages of 3.5 and 5.5 years) had mothers who introduced peers at home and encouraged their child to face up to stressful situations. Conversely, uninhibited children who became inhibited later on had mothers who encouraged greater caution.

In Chen *et al.* (1998), "behavioral inhibition" observed at 25 months was inversely correlated with acceptance and encouragement towards achievement and positively with protection and concern, in a sample of (non-Chinese) Canadians. Against theory, the correlations went in the opposite direction in a sample of Chinese from mainland China. For instance, whereas punishment was correlated with fostering "behavioral inhibition" in the Canadian sample, it was inversely correlated in the Chinese sample.

These cultural differences might be read as diminishing the importance of specific parental characteristics. As suggested by Leung, Heimberg, Holt and Bruch (1994), the sociability of the family (i.e. what is being done about the "behavioral inhibition"), rather than various general parental attitudes towards the child, may be the key determinant environmental factor in "behavioral inhibition."

Parental influences on the development of social behavior

In study of 42 grade-1 children, Putallaz (1987) examined a possible link between the behavior of mothers and the social behavior and social status of the children at school (defined as three positive nominations and ratings). After observing interactions of the children and their mothers, pairs of children and their mothers were created and the children observed at play together.

A positive association was found between a mother being disagreeable and demanding towards his or her child, and the child exhibiting a similar pattern of conduct towards his or her mother and the playmate.

Hypothetical social situations (e.g. trying to enter a group, bullying) were then presented to the subjects who had to say what they would do and then to the mothers who had to say what advice they would give to their child.

Mothers of higher-status children tended to advise their children to be more assertive in the face of, say, teasing, whereas the mothers of low-status children tended to advise them to seek the assistance of an adult. Similarly, higher-status children responded that they would join a group of unknown children during recess, whereas low-status children answered that they would play by themselves. It is interesting to note that an association was found between the mothers' advice and that of the children's hypothetical behavior in only one out of four experimental situations.

In a study from Australia (Finnie and Russell, 1988), 40 preschool children (5-year-olds) were observed at play by themselves. Then the mothers were instructed to bring their child to a room where two children were at play and help their child join in, in whatever way they can. The mothers of high-status children encouraged them to join in, stimulated exchanges between the children, and integrated the child without disrupting the ongoing play. In contrast, mothers of low-status children tended to involve themselves only with their own child while ignoring the others. Furthermore, they were complacent towards negative behavior on the part of their child.

In a similar study (Russell and Finnie, 1990) of 49 5-year-olds, children were divided (by their teachers) into popular, rejected and neglected categories. A mother would be asked to help their child to join two children already at play. Mothers of popular children were found to give more suggestions as to how to integrate the play activity, compared to mothers of rejected or neglected children. During the play period, mothers of popular children interfered less, whereas mothers of the other children tended to be more directive, authoritarian and disruptive. It appears that distinct patterns of behavior characterized the mothers of children belonging to different status categories.

Homel, Burns and Goodnow (1987) investigated the associations between parental membership in social networks and the children's friendship networks among 305 families from Sydney with 5- to 9-year-old children.

Overall, the more friends the parents had, the more sociable the children and the greater the number of their playmates. Furthermore, the subjects knew many children who were not acquainted with each other.

Family influences on socially phobic children

In the only study of its kind (carried out in Australia; Craddock, 1983), highly socially anxious undergraduates (whom the authors considered to be socially phobic) were compared to normal subjects in terms of the family systems in which they lived. A greater rate of families of socially anxious subjects compared to those of normal controls were characterized by high cohesion (strong bonding, limited autonomy) and high rigidity (enforced by authoritarian and rule-bound leadership), resulting in limited flexibility in terms of role relationships and shifts in power structure.

In a study investigating parental influences (Barrett, Rapee, Dadds and Ryan, 1996; Dadds, Barrett, Rapee and Ryan, 1996), 150 anxious children between the ages of 7 and 14 years (of whom 31 were considered to be socially phobic) were compared to normal children. The children as well as their parents were presented separately with various (mostly social) scenarios, and their responses regarding the behavior of the child in them were recorded. This was followed by a joint family discussion regarding appropriate responses to the situation that was observed.

The socially phobic children did not give more avoidant responses to hypothetical social situations than did the other children in the anxious group; but the anxious group overall reported a greater tendency for avoidance than did the normal subjects.

The mothers and fathers of socially phobic children, however, tended, more than other parents, to foresee avoidance of social situations on the part of their child. Following the family discussion, the rate of the children in the anxious group who predicted that they would tend to avoid social situations more than doubled, from 30 to 68%. In the normal group joint family discussions resulted in the opposite trend; responses involving avoidance dropped from 17 to 6%.

Both results powerfully illustrate the influence of parents in molding children's responses. Unfortunately, distinct results for socially phobic individuals were not provided; nor is it known how the verbal reports relate to what the participants actually do.

In summary, socially phobic individuals tended to originate from rigidly rule-bound families, tending to hamper autonomy and bolster (or at least not discourage) avoidance.

Peer environment

Socially anxious children and their peers

A question of interest in the developmental study of social phobia is whether typical relationships characterize the contact of "socially phobic"/socially anxious children. As, to my knowledge, no relevant studies with socially phobic subjects have been carried out, I will survey the available research with either socially anxious children or such adults describing their childhood retrospectively.

In Gilmartin (1987), two age groups (19–24 and 35–50) of individuals described as "shy with the opposite sex" were compared to a group (19–24) of self-confident subjects.

Shy subjects (of both age groups) reported a greater incidence of bullying by peers in childhood and adolescence than did the self-confident (94% and 81% vs. 0%), as well as being left out of sports activities at school and a dislike for rough games. Although this retrospective study cannot clarify whether the withdrawn behavior of the shy or the rejecting behavior of the peers comes first, it does highlight the vicious circle that characterizes such a relationship.

Two studies attempted to answer this query. In the first (La Greca, Dandes, Wick, Shaw and Stone, 1988), children aged 8 to 12 years were assessed in terms of their social anxiety and their "sociometric status." Children who were ignored by their peers were more socially anxious than children labeled "popular" and, crucially, were in some ways more anxious than children who attempted to socialize while being actively rejected.

In the second study (Walters and Inderbitzen, 1998) 1,179 adolescents were investigated. Those classified as submissive (i.e. easily pushed around) by their peers were characterized by the highest levels of social anxiety. Conversely, lower but equivalent levels of social anxiety characterized all other children, cooperative as well as dominant.

Social anxiety and status within peer groups (longitudinal studies)

In Hymel, Rubin, Rowden and Le Mare (1990), 155 8-year-olds (from Waterloo, Ontario) were followed and reassessed after 3 years. Measures included both observation of the child at play in the laboratory, assessment of classroom (shy, anxious) behavior by the teacher as well as peer assessment of social behavior (popularity, aggression and isolation) at school.

At the age of 8, no association was found between shy and anxious behavior and isolation, as determined by peers or observation. At the age of 11, however, an association between the above factors did emerge; anxious children who were ignored by peers (e.g. not chosen as playmates) were considered by teachers as shy.

Solitary play at the age of 8 did not predict shyness and anxiousness at the age of 11, but isolation at the age of 8 predicted (albeit weakly, r=.34) isolation at the age of 11 as well as shy and anxious behavior. Under regression analysis, however, none of these associations held. However that may be, being shy and anxious at the age of 8, predicted isolation at the age of 11. This would imply that the process of isolation starts with shyness and not the other way around.

In Vernberg, Abwender, Ewell and Beery (1992), 68 12- to 14-year-olds who had just moved to a new neighborhood were assessed at the beginning of a new school year in September, and then reassessed in November and May the following year. Self-report by the children of being rejected was correlated with self-reports of social anxiety. Social anxiety at the beginning of the study predicted (−.4) less companionship in subsequent assessments.

The above studies are contradicted to some extent by the findings of Olweus (1993) who focused on 15 out of a 71-strong sample of 16-year-olds who had been victimized by their peers at school. Victimized children were considered those identified (by both teachers and peers) as being persistently aggressed. No sequels to victimization in terms of differences in social anxiety at the age of 23 were found. Given the small number of subjects and the possibility of insufficient statistical power, these results must be approached with caution until further replication.

Social anxiety, social phobia and victimization

Slee (1994) administered questionnaires concerning bullying and social anxiety to 114 children of 11 years of age on average. Being a victim of bullying correlated significantly with fears of negative evaluation (.31 boys and .41 for girls).

Crick and Grotpeter (1996) studied the link between victimization and adjustment in terms of loneliness and social anxiety in 474 children (grades 3 to 6). Social anxiety, avoidance and loneliness could be predicted from self-reports of exclusion from groups or being belittled and denigrated. Being the target of overt aggression, however, did not increase predictive power. Lack of positive peer treatment was related to loneliness and social avoidance, but not social anxiety. Similar results were reported by Storch, Brassard and Masia-Warner (2003). Altogether, it is possible that victims exhibit a perceptible vulnerability (furtiveness?) and defenselessness that excites verbal aggression or violence in some children.

Craig (1998) studied 546 (grades 5 to 8) children who were divided into bullies, victims and comparison subjects according to cut-off scores on scales. Victims of bullying had the highest social anxiety scores.

In a meta-analytic study (Hawker and Boulton, 2000) the significance of the association between being victimized and social anxiety has been reconfirmed. However, the meaningfulness of this link is put in a proper perspective by the larger framework of this study. Thus, the statistical size of effect for social anxiety was the smallest, whereas the size of effect of the association between victimization and depression came out as the highest.

McCabe, Antony, Summerfeldt, Liss and Swinson (2003) asked socially phobic, obsessive-compulsive and panic disorder patients (26 of each) whether they were ever bullied or severely teased. Fully 92% of the socially phobic individuals reported such experiences, compared with 50% of the obsessional subjects and 35% of panic disorder subjects.

In summary, social anxiety is strongly associated with various behavioral strategies aiming at self-protection; avoidance, passivity and especially submission, are prominent. Whether victimization leads to anxiety, or something in the (e.g. fearful) behavior of the victim provokes aggression, remains unclear. It is possible that victimization is an indirect and spiraling process of vulnerability, stemming from a failure to integrate into a group, achieve standing amongst its members and benefit from its protection.

Adverse life events during childhood

In this section, I rely on retrospective studies in which socially phobic individuals were queried about various adverse events in their childhood.

Separation or loss of parent

In three studies (Tweed, Schoenbach, George and Blazer, 1989; Arbel and Stravynski, 1991; David, Giron and Mellman, 1995;), no greater association between separation and loss experiences for the socially phobic, compared to control groups, were reported. Bandelow *et al.* (2004), however, found more instances of socially phobic individuals being raised by foster parents as compared to controls.

It is interesting to note that Arbel and Stravynski (1991) found a greater fear of abandonment, without the actual event ever having taken place, reported by the socially phobic/avoidant personality disorder compared to normal controls. This was perhaps the outcome of an insufficiency of positive interactions, rather than of actual threats of abandonment.

Strife between parents

Magee (1999) found that witnessing chronic hostility and verbal aggression between parents was associated with higher risk of social phobia. Moreover, Bandelow *et al.* (2004) reported a considerable degree of actual violence (e.g. father beating mother – 18% vs. 2.5%) in families of socially phobic individuals. Such a familial context, where it occurs, might be related to the tendency towards appeasement and avoidance of conflict typical of the socially phobic.

Parental alcoholism

David *et al.* (1995) found an association between parental alcoholism and phobia (both social and agoraphobia); 35% of phobic subjects reported parental alcoholism compared with 8% in normal controls. Unfortunately, the results were not broken down and the rate among the socially phobic alone was not given.

Sexual and physical abuse

In four out of six studies available (Pribor and Dinwiddie, 1992; David *et al.*, 1995; Magee, 1999; Dinwiddie *et al.*, 2000), an association between some form of sexual coercion in childhood and adult social phobia was reported. Sexual abuse was detected by questions such as "Were you ever forced into sexual activity including intercourse?" Conversely, socially phobic individuals were less likely to have been sexually abused than those identified as having a panic disorder (Safren, Gershuny, Marzol, Otto and Pollack, 2002), while avoidant personality disorder was less associated with sexual abuse than all other personality disorders (Rettew *et al.*, 2003).

In a similar vein, Mancini, van Ameringen and MacMillan (1995) and Ernst, Angst and Földényi (1993) failed to find such an association. The latter finding has also the advantage of according with clinical experience.

Mancini *et al.* (1995) also failed to find a link between physical mistreatment while growing up and social phobia. In contrast, Bandelow *et al.* (2004) found a significant level of physical violence directed at the socially phobic individual from members of the family when compared with normal controls (e.g. father 50% vs. 29% or siblings 26% vs. 5%). A similar link was reported by Chartier, Walker and Stein (2001). These findings go against the grain of clinical experience.

In summary, it is exceedingly difficult to give due weight to the relative importance of the various and disparate factors surveyed earlier. Studies investigating the links between them and a range of "disorders" (social phobia included), however, set these in perspective. In Kessler, Davis and Kendler (1997), for instance, almost all types of childhood adversities predicted social phobia. However, the same types of adversities also predicted equally well or better many other disorders. Furthermore, none of the adversities resulted in the highest associations with social phobia. The presence of multiple adversities was interactive rather than additive, and resulted in a greater association. This finding suggests that the adverse factors are not discrete features, but, rather, elements that combine (partially or in totality) to form a general pattern of the environment in interaction with which the child develops.

General conclusion

The main conclusion that can be drawn from the overview of various factors, associated in time with social phobia, is that – by default – the forging of the socially phobic interpersonal pattern is a highly idiosyncratic and historically contingent process. In view of the paramount importance accorded to the socially phobic interpersonal pattern (the formal cause), within the interpersonal explanatory framework, the above conclusion corroborates the choice of the interpersonal level of analysis.

No single all-important factor, either innate or environmental, no one particular experience, unsettling as it might have been, leads inexorably towards social phobia. Neither temperament, nor parent–child relationships are determinant in the development of social phobia – although these might constitute a liability towards it. This is underscored by the fact that some of the children assumed to be the most at risk did not become socially phobic, whereas some of those considered least likely to develop social phobia did so.

Consistently with the above findings in longitudinal studies (see Stravynski, 2007, pp. 101–104), no developmental factor, singly or in combination, predicted the emergence of social phobia; only fully formed social phobia predicted social phobia later on.

It bears reiterating that no single factor, either constitutional or environmental, was found to be implicated in all (or most) cases of social phobia, and as such, constituted an indispensable condition for the development of the socially phobic pattern.

At the early stages of development, both "behavioral inhibition" and "anxious attachment" might represent a liability or a potential towards social phobia. Neither, however, constitutes a necessary condition for it. Other factors, aggravating the risk or attenuating it, are therefore of the utmost importance. What are these?

Most research has been concentrated on parents. It is perhaps a vestige of psychoanalytic teaching that accords the utmost importance to family life. As a matter of principle, parental influence is doubtless important. Parents inculcate rules of social behavior (e.g. the importance of propriety) and examples of a defensive social life (e.g. relative isolation). They encourage and reward certain behaviors but perhaps more importantly ignore most and punish others. The latter point may be relevant to the failure of extinction of social fears. Thus, little is known of particular patterns of punishment (e.g. types of punishment, their proportionality, etc.) and patterns of intimidation in the process of socialization of socially phobic individuals and the pattern of relationship (say between parent and child or certain peers) in which it is embedded (Kemper, 1978b, pp. 237–262). Furthermore, how much of this is generalized outside the home and how lasting such influences are is largely unknown.

However that may be, it is possible that altogether too much importance is accorded to parental influences at home, while neglecting the exceedingly important area of group socialization outside the home (see Deater-Deckard, 2001). This tends to become increasingly important with age, especially in the industrialized West. Arguably (see Harris, 1995), children learn separately how to behave at home, how to behave outside it and discern acutely the differences between the two. The consequences of behavior in each environment are plainly different. At home the child might be shown gratuitous signs of affection at times, praised for what is considered praiseworthy occasionally and scolded for misbehaving most of the time. Out of the home most appropriate behavior is ignored, misbehavior is at times rewarded and mistakes magnified and ridiculed. It is likely that much of the socialization in terms of enacting social roles and the transmission of culture are done outside the home and take place in peer groups (Harris, 1995).

To sum up, the overall findings reviewed in the second half of this chapter, concerning the emergence of the socially phobic pattern, fit comfortably with the theoretical outlook of the interpersonal approach and, in aggregate, provide it with supporting evidence.

Ultimately, the socially phobic pattern develops through an extended process of learning that, in dealings with powerful others, one does not count for much, as one's wishes and feelings are mostly ignored. Moreover, when at odds with such individuals, one is usually defeated or outdone. While engaging in such struggles, one's weaknesses (real and imaginary) are magnified and ridiculed, while strength and achievements are ignored and belittled.

Naturally, such likely prospects are viewed with increasing alarm and self-protective measures, aiming at minimizing the risks of being coerced, diminished or otherwise mistreated, emerge and begin to take hold. When these become habitual (i.e. stabilize or broaden), the embryonic socially phobic pattern begins to crystallize. Such a historic process is simultaneously interpersonal (i.e. social and cultural) and somatic (i.e. fearful), literally incorporating experience. It is consolidated when an individual systematically and repeatedly fails to engage various aspects of social life of his or her community in a participatory and assertive manner and instead responds both fearfully and defensively.

As the process is most probably an idiosyncratic and highly contingent one, only an outline may be provided; the various socially phobic individuals would correspond to it generally, but not in detail.

The distress occasioned by separation from a caregiver (age range between 8 and 24 months, peaking at 9 to 12 months; see Chapter 2) is in all likelihood the earliest form of powerlessness and social fear experienced by a child. A fear of strangers – prominent at about the same time – might be added to this. Speculatively speaking, this may be the first experience (there will be others) in the young individual's life as a supplicant, depending entirely on the goodwill of his or her caregivers, and later in life, on that of strangers. Such goodwill may at times falter or be altogether unavailable. A self-involved caregiver might not be very responsive to the insistent demands of the child and attend to it intermittently and inadequately – only when the child is very upset. Another parent might be quite anxious about and more concerned with diffusing various potential dangers (e.g. an infection or injury), than responding to the requests of the child. Conversely, a parent could be rather domineering and short-tempered, exasperated with the nagging child and terrifying it into submission. To the parents, the child may appear frustratingly difficult for being reticent about new situations and slow to adapt when in them, and altogether reacting with excessive emotional intensity. Situations outside the home (e.g. family gatherings, playground, kindergarten) where the child might be teased, ignored, punished or bullied, might evoke similar distress.

Over extended periods of time, from the interplay of various environmental (and therefore cultural) circumstances, the responses to long series of unresponsive, unrewarding social interactions or, worse, intimidating or wounding ones gradually coalesce into an overall defensive pattern. On the one hand, in emotional terms, it will be characterized by a high degree of vigilance to threat and physical activation in preparation against it, with some difficulties in modulating arousal. On the other hand and in interpersonal terms, it might involve distancing strategies such as outright avoidance or a precarious and passive manner of participation in social life, with a tendency to stay away from other children and from competitive group activities. Additionally, children who might have been ill-used (being mocked or rebuffed) at school, for example, would respond by means of acts of appeasement and submissiveness (e.g. giving no cause for offence, not leaving oneself open to rejection or ridicule by reaching out or showing off).

The fully formed socially phobic pattern is forged by adult demands made on the individual, by the way of life of his or her community. These crystallize in late adolescence or early adulthood; so does the onset of social phobia (see Stravynski, 2007, pp. 88–89).

Part IV

Applications of the interpersonal approach

7   Assessment and functional analysis

The assessment of social phobia was dealt with in a definitional sense in Chapter 3. In it, social phobia was framed as follows:

a fearful and powerless interpersonal pattern (constituted of various sub-patterns), protective against the threat of humiliation (either as public degradation or private personal rejection). The integrated pattern is abnormal in that it seriously compromises the ability of the individual to carry out desired personal goals and to participate fully in the life of the groups and communities to which she or he belongs.

Unlike the DSM-5 and ICD-10 criteria, this interpersonal definition puts in perspective the claim that "abnormality" or severity of anxiousness are the quintessence of social phobia. Rather, it makes fearfulness a feature permeating a defensive (and self-protective) interpersonal strategy that, as a collateral consequence, undermines social functioning. Viewed interpersonally, it is the self-protective relational pattern – not its accompanying anxiousness – that is uniquely socially phobic. Without minimizing the anxious distress experienced by the socially phobic, the main liability and abnormality of social phobia reside in their impaired participation in social life.

Starting from these premises, it was found in Chapter 2 that the assessment of anxiety – however defined and carried out – leaves much to be desired and only by a long stretch of the imagination can it be considered an assessment of social phobia. What, then, would be an adequate assessment from an interpersonal perspective?

Before answering that question, it would be useful, in the first place, to compare intrapersonal and interpersonal perspectives on assessment, and, secondly, to spell out first principles.

The assessment of social phobia, however construed, is of paramount importance both scientifically (as a means to identifying it and quantifying its main features and processes) and practically (to establish severity and gauge improvement). The availability of quite a few instruments claiming to accomplish that purpose – although on the face of it a boon – also offers grounds for concern, as indicative of the uncertainties surrounding such a deceptively simple activity.

The measurement of psychological factors is fraught with fiendish difficulties, mostly conceptual. The deceptive simplicity and ease of use of "psychological tests" are achieved by overlooking these.

Psychological measurement – in the absence of any external validating criterion – remains by necessity the measurement of a hypothetical construct (see Stravynski, 2007, pp. 77–83, for a comprehensive argument). Given this predicament, the validity of what is being measured remains uncertain and inextricably bound up with theoretical questions regarding the nature of the hypothetical construct itself. In this particular case, it is what theoretical construction to put on the psychological pattern of what is called "social phobia."

Naturally, different kinds of measurements will be devised depending upon whether social phobia is considered an instance of disordered anxiety or, alternatively, as has been argued in previous chapters, an interpersonal pattern. Depending on the theoretical path chosen, the main conceptual task becomes defining anxiety (and its disorder) in the former and interpersonal pattern (and abnormality) in the latter example. Most available measures, by contrast, reflect practical imperatives. While satisfying some standards of accuracy (i.e. reliability, internal cohesion), issues of validity are set aside. In that sense, the measures remain theoretically muddled and their possible meaning is anyone's guess.

This, for example, accounts for the fact that although a number of measurement instruments may have been devised with the intention of measuring the very same social anxiety or social phobia, by dint of having taken a different tack (of emphasizing one presumed feature over another), they are only moderately related (e.g. Stravynski, 2007, pp. 48–52).

Certain rather technical difficulties (e.g. poor agreement between assessors, loose associations between certain items and the rest) might be readily remedied with some tinkering, by devising more concrete or narrow indicators or eliminating poorly related items. Other problems concerning poor discrimination or conversely generalization (construct and external validity – see Stravynski, 2007, pp. 105–135), spring from what social phobia is presumed to be; these are not easily remedied and require a conceptual overhaul.

Furthermore, what exactly is to be measured and its meaning – given the intangible and protean nature of psychological qualities – is not obvious, even after protracted reflection. The deployment of various interactive patterns – social functioning – provides a ready-made example. Attempts at seductiveness or at reining-in resentment against those whom we feel have wronged us (for the sake of keeping the peace), for instance, are obviously woven into the very fabric of life. Although we are continuously interacting with others, these patterns are to some extent intangible and elusive for being fleeting, fluid and without clear boundaries, woven into other activities. Moreover, these are carried out repeatedly as variations on a theme and are consequently not easy to spot and quantify.

The wellsprings of measurement, therefore, are the a-priori ideas the measurers entertain regarding what is to be found in the segment of the natural world of interest to them. Despite appearances to the contrary, psychological measurement is always an exercise, at times artfully concealed, in theory (see Gould, 1981). The measurement of "intelligence" is a case in point (see Richardson, 2002).

Measurement: intrapersonal and interpersonal

It is useful to distinguish between two approaches to the measurement of social phobia, in keeping with the two approaches to the construal of social phobia described in Chapter 1. An intrapersonal approach to assessment would assume that socially phobic behavior is only a surface manifestation of anxiety – a hypothetical mental construct – itself powered by hidden psychological and biological processes, and driving conduct from within, as it were. In other words, socially phobic conduct is assumed (as it commonly is) to be a manifestation (e.g. "symptom") of a hypothetical defective mental or brain structure or process (e.g. disordered anxiety) endowed with agency. Philosophically, this view is intimately bound up with a reductionist and dualist outlook. Practically, this sort of assessment relies on a series of interrelated assumptions.

In self-report tests, scores across various domains and situations are summed up or averaged out into one number, disconnected from the numerous contexts and processes that yielded it, and presumed to be a valuation of a *uniform* and *stable* trait, which is located within the person. Moreover, it is presumed that the same trait (e.g. anxiety) is operative "within" all socially phobic persons, wide variations notwithstanding. Intrapersonal measurement may therefore be described as nomothetic and deductive, tending to generalize, so as to identify a unifying principle not necessarily obvious on an individual level.

The commonplace leap from the results of a "test" to the conclusion that it measures something concrete (albeit in the context of intelligence testing) moved Brigham (1930) to caution against "a naming fallacy which easily enables [us] … to slide mysteriously from the score of the test to the hypothetical faculty suggested by [the] name given in the test" (p. 130).

This caveat often goes unheeded. It is a curious fact of clinical life that the administration of a soberly or grandiloquently named scale often awakens a flight to credulity in clinicians, their patients (see Brigham, 1930), as well as the administrative consumers of their reports. It is assumed that the score settles the presence of social phobia and reveals its degree, as the thermometer does for temperature. Such credulity is unjustified, as what the questionnaires (or interviews) actually measure and with what degree of accuracy – in short their validity – is rather uncertain (Stravynski, 2007, pp. 105–135).

By contrast the interpersonal approach to measurement arises from a holistic and systemic (non-dualist and non-reductionist) outlook. It starts with the premise that the behavior or sets of activities of the whole individual, displayed in the settings and the interactions that give rise to them are the quintessence of being alive – and as such are the most valuable psychological material. Not least, all other psychological (e.g. emotional, cognitive) processes are seen as being realized within such activities and interactions; these psychological processes have no existence apart from the life activities of the individual. In other words, the relational patterns the (whole) individual engages in integrate structure and drive the activities of its different constituent elements and processes (e.g. emotion, thought).

In principle, patterned life activities in relation to the social and physical world are most of what can be known about a living organism (human and otherwise), but by no means all. Despair, deceit, sexual longing or seeking unity with the divine, for instance, may be glimpsed at through some activities (e.g. excessive alcohol consumption, lying, masturbation and prayer) but are not identical with these. Expiating guilt through self-torment or some redeeming activity, for instance, although likely to be both pervasive and extended, may pass undetected, having only tenuous connections with specific actions (self-denial, doing good).

Be that as it may, the interpersonal approach to measurement skirts the validity problems that beset intrapersonal measurement. Needless to say, it is not without its own difficulties.

Observing and measuring interpersonal behavior may appear relatively simple, as it is most of the time in the public domain. For the same reason, inferences about interpersonal activities might appear relatively straightforward. In application, however, this approach too, has its limitations. The clinician can carry out an assessment only "second-hand," as in interviews, with the concomitant dangers of retrospective bias, concealment and misunderstanding, for the same words do not always denote the same behavioral categories (i.e. mean the same thing).

Context (especially cultural), which frames conduct and makes it meaningful by highlighting its function, is even more difficult to pin down.

Additionally, what is of interest to the measurer may not easily be picked out of the stream of life. Patterns of behaviors of most interest in the study of social phobia (e.g. appeasing, dissembling fear, giving in or conversely resisting passively through procrastination) arise out of specific interactions and thus depend, to an extent, on other participants in it. These patterns, therefore, would not necessarily be dramatically expressed and draw attention to themselves. These might rather occur as a stream of subtle, barely discernible acts either of commission or of omission, intermittently emitted and difficult to spot in and of themselves, especially the latter.

Furthermore, these acquire meaning only in context and in relation to their function. As such, these would be intelligible to the actors (as in flirtation) and to a lesser degree to spectators, or would escape their notice altogether. This is especially true of the socially phobic way, so often characterized by – what seems to the observer – omissions and passivity, punctuated by evasiveness (i.e. intensely emotional silences while others communicate, not daring to act despite strongly desiring something).

Practically, assessment of social phobia interpersonally relies almost exclusively on what the patient reports either unaided – as in self-report questionnaires – or as elaborated through leading-questions and further interpreted by an interviewer. Interactions with the interviewer or simulation during an interview might be exceptions.

From an interpersonal point of view, filling out self-report scales or answering questions during an interview are not instances of pure self-observation or self-disclosure on the part of the subject, although in some instances they might be. As any human behavior, these confidences (as well as half-truths or outright confabulations) are firmly anchored in the context in which they occur, and are elicited by the exchanges (e.g. feeling humiliated by a condescending interviewer, eliciting the sympathy of an impressionable one) and simultaneously guided by goals of the individual in that context (e.g. seeking help collaboratively or conversely going through the motions manipulatively, in pursuit of compensation).

It bears keeping in mind that, because of the above-mentioned limitations of these commonplace psychological methods of measurement, social phobia may be easily simulated on tests (as may be other disorders or brain damage; see Faust, Hart, Guilmette and Arkes, 1988 for instruction and amusement) and dissembled on both questionnaire and interview. Most socially phobic individuals, moreover, are highly practiced and often successful dissemblers of some or all of their difficulties and related problems (e.g. drinking alcohol as self-medication), in some cases even from such privileged and keen observers as their spouses.

Interpersonal assessment – first principles

What would constitute an ideal interpersonal assessment? So as to set a lofty standard, we need not be hobbled by practical considerations. We can imagine (as we did in Chapter 1) that we are able to observe – undetected – anyone continuously, even in their most private and unguarded moments. Blessed with sufficient leisure and omniscience, exempt from all legal and moral constraints, we would observe a variety of activities, modulated by settings and time patterns set within a certain way of life.

If observation were carried out long enough, we would doubtless find that many patterns repeat themselves (e.g. making a living, fulfilling social roles, seeking excitement and pleasure or intimacy and wisdom or the sacred) and therefore become easier to identify. At some stage, under stable conditions, we would find that saturation has been reached, when no new information has been forthcoming. At this point, both personal and cultural patterns that have already begun to emerge earlier would consolidate, as various relational and broadly social activities would begin to coalesce in clusters and repeat themselves, some tightly woven into contexts and others in distal relation to them.

Of all the manifold aspects of human interactions, the dimension most relevant to our concerns would be social fearfulness; as a universal characteristic (see Chapter 2) it is a useful indicator. It is so because from an interpersonal point of view, social anxiety is rooted in fearful social behavior (understood as an extended pattern) and as such, a most useful index of defensiveness. As seen in Chapters 1 and 3, highly socially anxious individuals would be characterized by a fearful self-effacement, reticence and passivity. They would tend to keep a safe distance, but when obliged to take part and cornered, would typically choose conciliation and accommodation for fear of being snubbed or criticized. Needless to say, involvement in acrimonious exchanges could give cause for resentment and retaliation later on.

As previously mentioned from our continuous but unobtrusive observation of all social activities, extended fearful relational patterns would begin to emerge, coalesce in clusters and repeat themselves. We would then notice that these would be firmly anchored in certain social settings (e.g. institutions, the marketplace) and structured by social practices (e.g. acting deferentially towards superiors, keeping a distance from other employees) embedded in time cycles. Patterns could be relatively discrete and short (e.g. presenting a brief oral report at a meeting with other members of a team) or extended (e.g. the actual presentation preceded by numerous written versions, rehearsals accompanied by difficulties in concentrating on other tasks, disturbed sleep, intestinal cramps with diarrhea, etc.).

Within the activities dedicated to making a living, for example, patterns of exchanges would also repeat themselves at some stage, differentiated by the position of the interlocutors in the institutional hierarchy, and modulated, for instance, by their personal manner (e.g. encouraging or critical) and type of relationship (e.g. impersonal or personal). Thus, within this period, patterns of interaction might be further differentiated by whether the individual relates to others formally, as incarnating institutional roles within a hierarchical structure (e.g. chairing a meeting) or informally, as an individual one is acquainted with (e.g. exchanging office gossip).

Similarly, during non-working periods, activities would cluster in relation to various social contexts. Patterns of interactions related to securing and maintaining a dwelling place and to daily living (e.g. buying and preparing food) would be fairly repetitive and therefore well defined. Other patterns, less frequently manifest or in the extreme – mostly absent – may be usefully grouped under headings such as leisure, family life, intimacy (emotional and sexual) and friendships; patterns in these social domains would require longer periods of observation to emerge.

In summary, interpersonal assessment, in trying to capture what is unique and contingent about an individual life may be described as idiographic in orientation. It is also inductive, as it seeks to generalize from a multitude of individual occurrences and circumstances, taking into account all their infinite variety.

Within the context of the clinic where the socially phobic would be commonly seen, in view of practical, legal and ethical considerations, an interpersonal assessment is best carried out by means of a *continuous* self-observation by the patient. While accuracy might be an immediate concern, self-observation has several advantages. The individual is in the most privileged position to follow the thread running through various seemingly disparate actions involved in extended patterns (such as jovial friendliness or sidestepping confrontations) and to recognize their use. Furthermore, the features of the context (e.g. situation, individuals) evoking these, are plain to the self-observer.

Additionally, self-report covers areas of intimacy (e.g. cold and critical mother, petulant lover), out of reach to anyone but the participants, and covers reactions usually kept private (being reduced to tears, raging incoherently, sexual disappointment or fulfillment). Self-observation is at its best when a trusting collaborative relationship is established between patient and clinician. Unfortunately, this may seldom be entirely the case when such an assessment is carried out initially.

As we are interested in extended relational patterns, self-observation is to be continuous and could be organized in the following sequence.

First of all, individuals, situations and events evocative of anxiousness (embedded in fearful activities – see below) have to be identified and the severity of experienced anxiousness rated. This can be established by means of ratings on a subjective scale running from 0 (serene and peaceful) to 10 (terrified and panicky) with 5 indicating a moderate but not disabling level of anxiousness. Subjective gradations of severity are useful for analytical purposes (see the section on "functional analysis" below).

Secondly, the anchoring situations allow the teasing out of the activities (typically defensive) displayed in these (e.g. avoidance, escape, dissembling, propitiating, pacifying, submitting, currying favor and bristling with indignation). This information could be usefully elaborated and refined by judicial questioning from the clinician. Finally, it allows the establishment of relational patterns inferred across situations and specific behaviors.

An assessment comes to a natural end when new information is no longer forthcoming. Although recurring patterns are commonplace and to be expected, it goes without saying that stability could be disrupted by significant life changes occurring unexpectedly (e.g. change of management and reorganization at work, pregnancy and dissolution of an intimate relationship) all the same. For this reason, it is best for this type of assessment to be carried out uninterruptedly as long as the patient is in consultation.

The information gathered during the assessment period constitutes the raw material as it were, that needs, as in any intelligence activity – to be analyzed and interpreted. From this analytic process, a case formulation and subsequently, a treatment plan will emerge. The method by which this comes about – functional analysis – is presented below.

Functional analysis

Once the assessment is completed, a comprehensive picture of the main fearful interpersonal sub-patterns making up social phobia and set in social and interpersonal context ought to emerge. It will describe how and to what extent the set of activities called "social phobia" is enacted by a given individual under prevailing conditions. Crucially, if the conditions were to change, so would some of the sub-patterns and, consequently, the overall socially phobic pattern. The sub-patterns viewed in context, lend themselves readily to a reading of the function they fulfill. In other words, it allows the inferring of the relational purpose of the interpersonal conduct. To put it differently, it reveals for the sake of what the pattern is enacted.

In summary, this type of analysis allows the identification of two types of functions. First of all, it identifies the functional relationship between aspects of socially phobic behaviors and the specific situations and interactions they spring from. Secondly, it allows the consideration of various aspects of socially phobic behavior (displayed in context) purposefully (i.e. for the sake of which these are performed).

True understanding of a specific case of social phobia implies identifying what causes it. A functional analysis of the results of an interpersonal assessment allows one to do just that. This analytic framework is the application of the principles established in Chapter 6, where social phobia, conceived interpersonally, was considered from a multi-causal perspective.

In this analysis, three causal factors predominate. In Aristotelian terms, these are the proximate, the formal and the final or ultimate (see Table 7.1).

Translated into interpersonal terms, the situations prompting – and therefore controlling – the various fearful patterns making up social phobia constitute – in aggregate – its proximate or eliciting cause.

The interactional patterns or sets of activities typical of the socially phobic individuals' dealings with others, consisting of distance keeping and a prudent submissiveness (e.g. avoiding frictions, remaining inconspicuous, bland and deferential) are its formal or organizational cause. Overall and taken in abstract, the relational "forms" (patterns or sets) of activity in these interactions are predominantly ones of relative powerlessness (and therefore dependency), characterized by defensiveness and submissiveness.

The final or ultimate cause of social phobia is the manifest defensive and self-protective function of the overall pattern and most of the subpatterns making it up; it is enacted by the socially phobic individual for the sake of keeping safe from public and private humiliations. Put differently, the socially phobic pattern enacts an interpersonal strategy of minimizing risk and damage, while navigating the menacing aspects of social life (e.g. coercion, criticism, conflict, condescension, rejection and being ignored).

The proximate (or eliciting) cause may be seen as relatively independent from the socially phobic individual. After all – to take two examples – people occupying powerful positions within social institutions or highly sought-after individuals (surrounded by admirers vying to gain their

Table 7.1. *Causal elements*

Proximate	Formal	Ultimate
Eliciting situations, events	Patterns of fearful interpersonal behavior	Inferred function (purpose)

Table 7.2. *Functional analysis: Case A*

Situations	Sub-patterns of interpersonal behavior (anxiousness level)	Function
Parent–teachers meetings	Blushing; submissive posture; says little (8)	Self-protection (against being in the wrong and subsequent criticism)
Well-lit spaces	Freezing; says little (8)	Self-protection (against blushing and being mocked)
Outings with husbands, friends and spouses	Wears turtle neck blouses; large sunglasses; eats cold food; no alcohol; says little (9)	Self-protection (against reddening, blushing and being teased)
Initiating contact, promoting friendship, participating in conversation	Avoids; does not participate (6)	Self-protection (against indifference or rejection)
Bullying by a brother, being ignored by mother	Defenceless, submissive (7)	Self-protection (against escalating confrontation)

favor), exist and relate to the world independently of the socially phobic individual, when he or she come into their orbit.

By contrast, the formal cause – the organization of the overall relational pattern – is enacted by the socially phobic individual and, as such, is tightly bound with its purpose (the ultimate cause). In this sense, the overall socially phobic relational pattern, as well as its constituting sub-patterns and elements, are a means to an end.

The interpersonal assessment described earlier, if tabulated (see Tables 7.2–7.4), provides all the necessary elements to deduce the above-mentioned causes of social phobia operative in each case.

The column on the left lists all the fearsome situations evoking a state of anxiousness. These could be arranged in different forms. First of all and perhaps most usefully, it would list situations in a descending

Table 7.3. *Functional analysis: Case B*

Situations	Sub-patterns of interpersonal behavior (anxiousness level)	Function
Meeting with clients or representatives	"Freezing," passive conciliation (9)	Self-protection (not letting himself be open to questioning; criticism)
Overseeing wayward employees	Avoids confrontation; takes over instead (7)	Self-protection (sidestepping exercising authority; an embarrassing scene)
Crowded and hot spaces (family gatherings, social functions)	Passive and vigilant (7)	Self-protection (refrains from drawing attention to himself)
Being teased	Passive; pretending not to have heard (7)	Self-protection (not drawing attention to himself; avoiding a confrontation he cannot win)
When wife is domineering or critical	Flees and avoids confrontation; is resentful and feels low when by himself (6)	Self-protection (against a bruising confrontation he cannot win)

Table 7.4. *Functional analysis: Case C*

Situations	Sub-patterns of interpersonal behavior (anxiousness level)	Function
Public speaking as an expert	Enacts role poorly: avoids contact with audience; speaks quickly and inaudibly; articulates badly (9)	Self-protection (from challenges; flees as soon as possible)
Dealing with individuals in positions of authority	Submissive: passive, soft-spoken, inarticulate; gazes down (7)	Self-protection (deflects criticism, sarcastic comments)
Writing a document for public consumption	Avoids; procrastinates (5)	Self-protection (from coming criticism)
Women he finds attractive	Avoids; flees (5)	Self-protection (against confusion and appearing ridiculous; pre-empts indifference, rejection)
Wife engages in activities he finds objectionable	Avoids confrontation; resents her; retaliates surreptitiously (4)	Self-protection (against angry exchanges and being disregarded subsequently)

hierarchy of anxiety ratings. If such a hierarchy obtains, it may suggest the situational dimension, most likely modulating the intensity of fearfulness. This identifies the eliciting (proximate) cause of social phobia in each case.

The central column lists patterns of activities enacted anxiously, taking place in or in reference to the situations and therefore evoked by these. The interpersonal patterns may range from keeping a distance (e.g. sitting as far away from the lecturer as possible) to passive participation (e.g. grinning nervously; remaining silent, chin down, while being bullied) or active interactions (e.g. trying to be amusing; ingratiatingly offering to be of service). These sub-patterns of social phobia allow the identification of the organizational (formal) cause of social phobia (i.e. the relational pattern) in each case.

The column on the right lists the presumed function of the behavior in the context of the situation and the relational dynamic enacted within it. Typically, the function would be defensive and self-protective. It would be – if at all possible – one of vouchsafing safety by keeping away from danger. As life necessities (e.g. ensuring a livelihood; finding a partner) dictate some degree of participation, the socially phobic pattern of conduct may be said to be performed for the sake of minimizing the risk of social harm (e.g. being snubbed, overtly criticized or involved in conflicts inviting retaliation). This identifies the purposeful (ultimate) cause of social phobia in each case.

In summary, the functional analysis allows the deduction of two functions linking all factors of causality. First of all, it connects triggering circumstances with certain socially phobic responses. Formulated in terms of causality, it links the evocative circumstances to a manner of organization for dealing with these. Secondly, it joins a system of organization of behavior – to its purpose – as a means to an end.

I shall use cases A, B and C from Chapter 3 to illustrate the application of functional analysis. This analysis allows the identification of the causalities operating in each case of social phobia. In the interest of ease of reading, the cases are reproduced below.

Application of functional analysis: case descriptions   A is a 36-year-old homemaker and a mother of two children aged 12 and 7 years. When consulting, she reports dreading going to parent–teacher meetings at school and to outings with her husband's friends and their wives. In company, especially when seated at a table in a well-lit room, she feels trapped and longs to escape. While trying to endure it, she feels remote and unfocused, attending to the conversation and participating only fitfully. She feels most threatened by the possibility of being addressed, doubting that she could respond appropriately without betraying her disarray and blushing. While dreading such a possibility, in a state of mounting tension, she experiences an oppressive sensation in her chest that makes it difficult to breathe, and occasionally has intestinal cramps followed by diarrhea. Normally, her social life is restricted to the home and family, and she stays away from the above-mentioned threatening situations, whenever possible.

When going out, she takes considerable precautions against the possibility of being seen blushing (i.e. flushing spread over portions of the face, neck and chest). To minimize the likelihood of this happening, she accepts only invitations to events taking place outdoors. These she attends wearing turtleneck blouses, wide-brimmed hats and large sunglasses, eating only cold food and declining alcoholic drinks. She does, however, take fitness classes without too much difficulty, as she is surrounded by relative strangers, unconcerned with her presence.

She worked briefly in a clerical capacity before marrying, and had found doing anything in the presence of others difficult; dealings with persons in position of authority were particularly disconcerting.

She finds her married life satisfactory and her husband supportive and understanding. She feels confident with him and able to express her point of view.

In private life – with the exception of her husband – she has difficulties initiating or maintaining a conversation, expressing an opinion or receiving a compliment for fear of blushing, even with familiar persons. Furthermore, she complains of being unable to set limits to the interference of different family members who tend to take decisions affecting her, without prior consultation.

She feels incapable of developing new contacts and friendships, although she would like to.

In retrospect, her difficulties began in early adolescence when her early sexual maturity set her apart from classmates who teased her. The repeated taunts provoked blushing that in turn intensified the teasing. It was then that she started wearing loose-fitting turtleneck blouses and found speaking in class increasingly difficult, although she tended to be self-effacing even beforehand.

These long-standing difficulties were exacerbated by the death of her father three years before consulting. She was very attached to him and still feels his loss very keenly. She finds her mother by contrast, cold, harsh and controlling.

B is 41-year-old married father of two children aged 16 and 14 who dreads business-related meetings with clients and/or their representatives, particularly when he is the center of attention. In such encounters, he attends to what is being said erratically and is sometimes hard put to come up with appropriate answers, especially when challenged. Ahead of such meetings, his heart races, pressure builds up in his chest and he feels hot, sweaty and flushed.

During meetings, he dreads the possibility that the other participants find him nervous and insecure and possibly incompetent. To avoid confrontations, he tends to adopt a conciliatory posture towards wayward clients (e.g. delays in payments, rude and unappreciative comments). He can, however, become disproportionately angry after long periods of self-restraint. While at times longing to escape this part of his life, he feels compelled by necessity to soldier on, hoping to expand his business.

Occasionally in the past, when put on the spot in front of many people, he experienced episodes of panic that rendered him speechless. Although milder fluctuating instances of these difficulties had occurred before, they have been exacerbated in the last few years by his attempts to shift his business from individual customers to companies. He finds dealing with representatives of companies or their management more difficult, as their negotiating tactics are harsher and at times underhand.

He finds leading his company and overseeing his employees trying, although to a lesser extent. He lurches from being over-controlling and irritable, to ignoring non-pressing issues (e.g. overseeing the training of employees) that demand attention nevertheless. Since the shift in his customers began, he had felt increasingly anxious and low, sleeping poorly.

On the advice of a friend, he has made a point of attending social functions with a potential for business contacts. During these events, he keeps mostly to himself and is ill-at-ease. When seated at a table, he remains silent, speaking only when addressed directly. He perseveres, although no business opportunities have materialized.

These anxieties also extend to his personal life. He is apprehensive of social situations in crowded and hot spaces (e.g. family celebrations), during which he is tied down to one spot, unable to get away without being noticed. Frequent family gatherings make him uncomfortable, as he hardly participates in the jovial bantering and dreads being made fun of by the more boisterous members. When such teasing takes place, he remains silent and looks away, hoping his discomfort will pass unnoticed. Although he would prefer not to attend such get-togethers, he has so far resisted the temptation.

Although he gathers that his wife has an inkling of his suffering, he has never mentioned it. He is reticent to confide in her – convinced she will not understand and will think less of him. Although he appreciates her as a capable and confident person, she overwhelms him at times. On occasion, he finds her disregard for his views or her outspoken comments to be bruising. When this takes place, he feels low and withdraws, sulking for days.

The "anti-depressant" medication prescribed by his physician, while taking the edge off his anxious distress, does not meaningfully improve his overall condition.

He describes himself as having always been timid. His mother worried about everything, while his father was a harsh authoritarian. Although quiet and withdrawn, he demanded strict obedience and imposed collective punishments on the children. The patient was scared of his father, who would violently strike his turbulent brother (who nevertheless remained defiant).

He became self-conscious in his teens because of acne; he would repeatedly examine his face for new eruptions and would be upset about his appearance. Consequently, he missed classes and failed several courses; this excluded the possibility of pursuing a higher level of studies.

C is a man of 42, married and father of two children, who works in the public sector. He is ambitious to make the most of the expertise in his field he has developed, but held back and troubled by the public speaking that this entails.

On such occasions, he is intermittently seized by panic, feeling uncertain about where he is, unable to articulate, hands unsteady, legs weak, heart pounding, flushed and in a sweat. When in front of an audience, he feels uncertain and imagines being sized up and found wanting as pretentious and not convincingly competent. The size of the audience and the presence of figures of authority are aggravating factors. By contrast, he is generally comfortable in small groups or with individual interlocutors. However, he is intimidated by self-assured individuals in positions of authority or women he finds attractive, and shrinks in their presence and finally withdraws.

Although still suffering and struggling (and therefore seeking help), he describes himself as much better now than he was years ago, since he is able to present in public, however inadequately.

Nevertheless, the weeks preceding a presentation are a torment to him. He experiences a fluctuating and at times disorganizing level of anxiousness without let up. While in the grip of this, he cannot concentrate on anything else and engages repeatedly in the preparation and constant revisions of his texts and supporting graphics. The typically successful conclusion of the presentation brings only brief relief, as he finds many faults in it and himself. He experiences a lesser degree of dread when engaged in the task of producing written material; he imagines how it will be read by others, who undoubtedly will find it incomprehensible and intellectually shoddy. Such activity consumes an inordinate amount of time, in part because it is typically interspersed with periods of procrastination.

Since his early days at school, he found it impossible to answer the teacher when questioned; feeling trapped, he would become "paralyzed and incoherent." Nevertheless, he was a very good student, especially in scientific subjects, but had great difficulty in writing essays or compositions, which proved a major handicap at university.

He describes himself as always having been rather inhibited. Despite his powerful physique, he let himself be mistreated by other children at school and was terrorized by threats made by a classmate with a reputation for delinquency.

His father was a tough manual laborer who set great store by force and aggressive self-assertion. He found his son woefully lacking in these manly qualities and treated him brutally and with derision. A forceful and turbulent sister won the father's approval, while the patient tried to keep out of their way. His mother was a fearful and sickly individual who paid little attention to him and wished not to be disturbed.

Results of functional analyses   The functional analyses of the three cases are summarized in Tables 7.2 to 7.4.

Overall and in every case, the eliciting causes evocative of socially phobic reactions were social situations requiring satisfactory transactions with powerful and demanding – and therefore potentially dangerous – individuals. The situations were of two kinds.

First of all, there were situations involving *impersonal* transactions during which complementary social roles had to be enacted. All these took place in the public domain and institutional settings. All three cases struggled to enact their role as an office clerk (A), salesman/business-owner (B) or lecturer (C), requiring satisfactory interactions with their counterparts – office manager, clients/employees, lecture organizers and audience.

Secondly, situations involving social roles and interactions of a *personal* kind: with friends, family, spouses. Some of these took place in public (e.g. family gathering in a restaurant) but others were in private (e.g. at home).

Altogether, the social situations determined whether the socially phobic reaction would occur or not. No socially phobic behavior and related experiences occurred without these contexts and conversely, the occurrence of such events never failed to trigger a socially phobic response. The presence of aggravating factors (e.g. bright lighting, warm temperature, number of participants, size of room) and their degree, modulated the extent of the socially phobic response (i.e. how extended or severe it was).

As to the formal or organizational cause, in all three cases, the relational sub-patterns observed were overall ones of relative powerlessness (distancing, submissiveness) and dependency (i.e. being at the sufferance of others). Keeping away from menacing settings, if possible, was the general tendency. It was mostly in evidence in personal and private situations, where the consequences of exercising such an option were neither costly, nor followed by immediate consequences. In impersonal and public situations (e.g. the marketplace), tied to making a living, it was only taken up by A – a woman – who practically and culturally could opt for a life of a homemaker. The men (B and C), egged on by necessity but also ambition, had to soldier on while yearning – some of the time – to be released from continuing service "in the trenches." In situations (either personal or impersonal) that could not be avoided – at least not constantly – camouflage and dissimulation, combined with a passive and limited degree of participation, were displayed by all three.

The only impersonal public activity in which A took part was meeting with teachers in her role of mother and therefore overseer of the children's education. This she did as a deferential and passive recipient of the teacher's observations and opinions.

The activities of both B and C in the public domain were, by contrast, directed towards securing a livelihood and gaining recognition (the two were mutually reinforcing). Analytically, these may be separated in two: the performance of the specific task at hand, while enacting the social role in which the action is embedded (e.g. giving out a ticket and being a policeman, repairing a car and being a mechanic, reaching a verdict and being a judge). The distinction between the two becomes readily apparent, if we assess each as an extended pattern.

Both B and C began preparations for their respective public appearances long before these were due. B prepared budgets and plans while C went over the text of his presentations (weeks before). Both revised their documents repeatedly, trying to anticipate likely reactions and eliminate sources of criticism (mistakes, "overcharging") and contentious issues (taking critical stances towards accepted practices and received ideas). Both attempted to rehearse their respective presentations, while focusing on potential pitfalls. These activities were carried out in a state of mounting anxiousness and its concomitants – distractedness, irritability, insomnia and intestinal cramps.

While the anxious presentation in public was beginning to crystallize far in advance of the public performance itself, no obvious elements of the public social role both B and C embodied could be observed beforehand. B allowed his employees a great deal of autonomy and what he did not trust them to do satisfactorily, he did himself. Most public dealings with customers were delegated to others. The exercise of authority by B was very muted and haphazard. When feeling beleaguered, he would retreat from his company office to his office at home.

Exercise of authority and self-presentation in that light was limited on the part of C; it was not necessary or required in his regular position. When not presenting, he was affable, seemingly always in good humor and circumspect, studiously avoiding rubbing up others the wrong way.

In both cases, the task to be performed (presentation of a business proposal and a lecture) – despite misgivings – was always ultimately accomplished (albeit with some help of medication that took the edge off the jitteriness).

The enactment of the social role (a provider of expert service, a lecturer), however, by both B and C was mostly absent. When made, it appeared feeble – as if not daring to stake the claim to authority and defend possible challenges to it. Both would dress down, had a slightly hunched posture and assumed a very modest demeanor. The preliminary contact with their audience was very brief: B only greeted the other participants while C busied himself with the audio-visual equipment. Both attempted to conclude their activity as quickly as possible. During the performance itself, both B and C would look only at their papers, and would go through the presentation at a breathless speed, poorly articulating their speech and barely audible. Both had difficulty in grasping the commentaries addressed to them and felt trapped (while longing to escape). Negotiating (in the case of B) and answering questions (both B and C) was carried out in a similar fashion.

It is worthwhile pointing out what did not take place or what was omitted. Neither of them controlled nor attempted to set the agenda and thereby dominate the proceedings (as could have been appropriate in a lecturing context – the case of C) or take advantage of the position of a client to negotiate a favorable deal (the case of B). The desire to bring the session to a speedy conclusion – as the driving concern – brought out limited and rigid responses, not necessarily to B's advantage.

In summary, taking into account situations both of an impersonal nature in the public domain as well as those of a personal kind, cautious and powerless submissiveness and prudential risk-management through the regulation of time of exposure to danger, proximity to it and invisibility (e.g. eschewing any provocation), were the most frequent sub-patterns making up the overall socially phobic pattern, as seen in all three cases. Crucially, the socially phobic pattern and its component parts were always enacted in a state of anxiousness. Within the evoking situations, neither the defensive interpersonal patterns nor fearfulness were manifest in isolation.

The hypothesis that the formal cause of social phobia resides in a powerless/submissive interpersonal pattern, set within a risk-minimizing strategy, is bolstered by the absence of powerful/dominating behavior in all cases. Seeking attention (in dress or manner), taking initiative or charge, acting boisterously or seductively, being judgmental or dismissive, making demands or issuing threats (by bluster or hint) – taken as examples – were not in the repertoire of these individuals. Nonetheless, on occasion – after extended periods of bullying or harassment – flashes of anger would be occasionally directed at their tormentors by B (e.g. non-payment of bills) and C in the public domain, but not at their spouses. Such outbursts served defensive ends; these were not modes of domination in the service of gaining power, for the sake of mastering the situation.

The ultimate cause of social phobia emerges clearly from the generalization of all the interpersonal sub-patterns mentioned so far; these are performed for the sake of self-protection. The inference that the socially phobic pattern, in all three cases, was performed in the pursuit of safety is unlikely to be controversial. It was most obviously so in situations that were avoided; remaining in a safe haven, at a remove from danger, is self-explanatory. Passive participation in social events, punctuated by withdrawals, was also self-protective as a means of abstaining from drawing unwished-for attention.

The feeble performances of B and C as actors of social roles and performers in set pieces, enacted in the public arena while muddling through their respective tasks, is more difficult to characterize in terms of ultimate causes. The tasks were doubtlessly performed for the sake of making a living. The performances in both cases, while diminished, were not wholly disrupted. Although undermined by a distractedness borne of simultaneously attempting to conceal the fearful over-arousal (shaky hands, unsteady voice, reddening of the face, sweat) and attending to the business at hand, the performance, although stumbling, would nonetheless achieve its ostensible aims.

Both B and C systematically abstained from making a claim to stature and expertise before, during and after engaging in the specific display of knowledge and related activities they were sought after or hired to do. In that sense, both enacted poorly the public social role from which their activities emanated. From the interpersonal perspective, such an omission or absence is best interpreted as self-effacement. It is purposeful in being enacted for the sake of safety. Such an unassuming manner is less liable to draw attention and provoke challenges, which both B and C felt unable to beat back and successfully overcome, with their status undiminished or even enhanced. In both cases, the goal of relative safety was being achieved relationally, by means of submissiveness (as lack of dominance) and powerlessness (in the sense of relying on others for being spared and left unharmed).

In sum, in the functional analyses above, both the performance of specific tasks and the social role from which these emanate are understood interpersonally, as enacting a submissive and powerless strategy. This relational pattern is enacted in both public and private spheres of social life, although some of the specific actions or elements making up the pattern in every situation are different, for being flexibly adjusted.

This defensive activity is often enacted in a heightened state of anxiousness – a mixture of alarm, vigilance, preparedness and exertion. Defensive activity and fearfulness are inseparable. Fluctuating anxiousness is a dynamic process, closely attuned to and reflecting variations in the maneuvering of the individual in the face of ceaselessly evolving threatening circumstances. In sum, anxiousness, in the face of menacing circumstances, flags self-protective activities.

As to the purposeful nature of these relational patterns, the principle is worth reiterating: interpersonal conduct and its relational function are interdependent; neither can be meaningfully separated from the other. The former is performed for the sake of the latter. The submissive and powerless pattern is enacted for the relative safety it confers, in other words, self-protection.

Functional analysis as a stepping stone to treatment

Assessment provides the raw material, as it were, for functional analysis. A functional analysis, while useful in itself, may serve as a stepping stone to treatment. In such a role, it allows the elaboration of the content of an individualized treatment intervention, made to measure. Additionally, it provides a productive framework for generating working hypotheses to guide treatment. How is this achieved?

Setting objectives and targeting the means for attaining them   Broadly speaking, judging from our functional analyses of cases A, B and C, it has been found that the extended socially phobic pattern, enacted by each, is a network of interpersonal conduct characterized by withdrawn and submissive behavior, with manifest powerlessness – all deployed defensively and self-protectively. The treatment implication of such a construction is an overhaul of the interpersonal socially phobic pattern.

In idealized terms, it ought to change from an interpersonal defensive strategy (e.g. distance keeping, refraining from provocation, pacifying)

Table 7.5. *Content of treatment: Case A*

Problem areas Setting: Social role	Targeted patterns of behavior	Function
Impersonal		
Dealing with school staff as a parent	Enquiring; making observations; expressing opinions and appreciation of the teacher's efforts	Acting independently: participating on equal footing; taking charge of children's education
Going out (e.g. picnic, restaurant) with her husband's acquaintances and friends	Greeting people she meets; addressing people sitting next to her; thanking the organizers of the event	Pursuing autonomous goals; participating in creating and maintaining networks of friends
Personal		
Initiating and promoting contacts with those she wishes to befriend	Expressing desire for friendship; organizing meetings and social exchanges	Pursuing autonomous goals; creating friendships apart from husband
Being ignored by her brother and mother in important decisions (e.g. inheritance)	Insisting on being consulted; threatening with non-collaboration, if ignored	Acting powerfully: asserting herself to achieve equal footing and demand respectful treatment (from relatives)

to participation in social life with a greater variety of means (e.g. self-expression). Altogether, goals other than safety should predominate. Participation implies cooperation, in other words, properly enacting a variety of complementary social roles, both public and private, some formal and others informal.

As the organization of relationships is transformed by degrees from defensive harm prevention to active participation in social life, so will the corresponding aims change. These will shift gradually from the socially phobic self-protection to greater self-realization, as an active participant in the life of the community. How can such a project of self-transformation be aided?

Two considerations are paramount. First of all, alternative *patterns* of interpersonal behavior need to be planned and established; these will not emerge spontaneously by dint of having reached the conclusion of their desirability. Such goals effectively will dictate the *content* of treatment. This will be elaborated below, as the final ramification of the functional analysis undertaken earlier. Secondly, the issue of how best to promote the process of self-transformation – in a practical sense – is important in itself. This topic will be dealt with in Chapter 8.

Table 7.6. *Content of treatment: Case B*

Problem areas Setting: Social role	Targeted patterns of behavior	Function
Impersonal		
Meeting with clients as expert and businessman	Taking charge of the meeting; dressing up	Acting powerfully: enacting confidently the role of expert and businessman-owner
	Emphasizing the strengths in his proposal; anticipate weaknesses from client's point of view	
	Admitting ignorance or justified criticism	
	Taking time to consider; do not reply immediately	
Overseeing employees	Creating regular meetings with concrete feedback and monitoring of performance	Acting authoritatively: enacting confidently the role of manager-owner
Personal		
Being teased during family gatherings	Expressing displeasure: telling the person (in private) "I do not find the joke funny"	Acting powerfully: putting an end to an irritant
Wife being critical and demanding	Agreeing if she is justified; rejecting what she says if disagreeing with it, without any justification	Acting independently and firmly

As illustrations, Tables 7.5–7.7 describe the objectives and the means to attain them in cases A, B and C.

In all three, objectives in the public arena – deemed more urgent (and more distressing) – preceded those in private life. Impersonal relations are broadly distinguished from personal relationships.

In all three cases, the general and most important objectives in the public domain were to enact a social role that broadly fits the social rules governing such processes and institutions (while acknowledging a scope for individual interpretations).

The goals in the private arena focused on insisting on a respectful treatment from significant others (e.g. spouses and family), and, simultaneously, starting a process of challenging the current marital or family arrangements. The isolated A was the exception, in having to focus on initiating contacts.

All objectives, either impersonal or personal in nature, were seen as being attainable by means of greater self-assertion (power) and self-reliance (autonomy). In terms of organizational (powerlessness) and purposeful (self-protection) causes of social phobia, these patterns are

Table 7.7. *Content of treatment: Case C*

Problem areas Setting: social role	Targeted patterns of behavior	Function
Impersonal Public speaking in his area of expertise	Taking change: dressing up; describing his professional trajectory; addressing the audience and organizers	Acting powerfully: drawing attention to one's strong points Creating a memorable
	Preparing a text to support speaking (short sentences, frequent punctuations – pauses)	learning experience with the audience
	Speaking slowly; articulating precisely; using silence (e.g. when presenting figures)	
	Engaging the audience frequently (questions)	
Personal His wife ignores his opinion or wishes	Expressing disappointment and stressing objections to what she did	Acting powerfully: being judgmental

mirror images of social phobia. As such, they are meant to undo the formal and ultimate causes of social phobia.

Finally, it is important to note that although reducing anxiousness is a paramount therapeutic objective, it is not targeted as such. The reason for this is that fearfulness, construed interpersonally, arises out of the relationship between the self-protective patterns and the menacing social contexts. In that sense anxiousness is a by-product of that interaction.

If – as a consequence of therapy – the defensive interpersonal patterns of powerlessness and dependency shrink, to be replaced by alternative relational modes (e.g. greater assertiveness and independence) better suited to participation in social life, the factors sustaining anxiousness would weaken or dissipate. Under such conditions, fearfulness is expected to dwindle in vigor and perhaps become an occasional occurrence of itself.

8   Treatment: undoing and overhauling social phobia

"Oh human nature! You have been born to fly! Why fail and fall at merely puffs of wind?"

Dante

Viewed interpersonally, social phobia is a long-standing overall pattern (or network) of fearful sub-patterns, typically characterized by prudent distance keeping, and, when engaged in interactions, by submissiveness and general powerlessness. Fearfulness and interpersonal patterns are but two analytic aspects of what is an integrated activity, involving the whole human individual.

The menacing social and cultural circumstances in which these fearful relational patterns are enacted highlight their purposeful nature: self-protection against public degradation and personal rejection. Cultivating a meek and entertaining manner, hiding signs of tremulousness, steering clear of contentious issues or giving offence, refraining from participating in competitive activities or declaring one's suit, are all examples of self-protective sub-patterns, enacted for the sake of minimizing the risk of coming to grief.

In keeping with this perspective, overcoming social phobia, be it in terms of weakening its hold, diminishing its extent, or its complete undoing, requires the dissolution of some, most or, better still, all the self-protective sub-patterns (making up the overall socially phobic web of patterns). This objective requires an overhaul in social functioning, as well as resetting goals towards which new relational patterns are directed.

Since the socially phobic commonly seek help for a host of ills (related to different aspects of their anxiousness), is it not sidestepping the main complaint?

Anxiousness was construed previously (Chapters 1 and 3) as arising out of the relationship between self-protective patterns and menacing social contexts. Anxiousness is therefore a by-product of that interaction. As such, intense fearfulness arises out of, and may be read as indicative of, extensive powerlessness and therefore vulnerability, in the face of a grave threat. Little anxiousness, however, may reflect successful distance keeping from the menacing situation rather than – interpersonally – the ability and the resolve to confront it (taking appropriate action in pursuit of either one's best interest, doing the right thing or any deliberately chosen goal). Anxiousness or fearfulness in the interpersonal view is a by-product of a dynamic interaction, sensitive to both behavior and context. The more powerless and defensive the interpersonal pattern of behavior in the face of the most menacing social context (e.g. large formal gathering graced by imposing and powerful authorities), the greater the fearfulness.

For the above reasons, the interpersonal approach does not specifically target the state of anxiousness, although diminishing it is an important goal. During successful therapy, as self-protective patterns wither and are replaced by interpersonal patterns allowing greater and better enactment of social roles (and therefore participation in social life), diminished fearfulness would occur naturally. It would come about as a collateral result from such interpersonal transformation.

What does the transformation amount to? Ideally imagined, the former socially phobic individual, instead of passively living at the margins, would become more venturesome, actively seeking out opportunities. Once spotted, these would be engaged in judiciously, mixing prudence with dash and daring. Initial setbacks, rather than failures, would be considered natural consequences of probing unchartered territory, providing useful information – albeit gained at high cost. Such stumbling would provide a necessary pause for rethinking one's way, in a process of building up towards a desired goal.

Within social settings, social roles would be embraced and the mode of relating to others would expand considerably. Such a forthright manner would range from submissive to dominant modes of behavior, playful or earnest, wielded flexibly as occasion – dictated by various social circumstances and roles – demands. Life lived in this way is not particularly menacing and requires a modicum of self-protection. This could take both defensive and offensive forms. A necessary measure of security would be found in solid (rather than precarious) memberships in various groups and cooperative participation in activities of the community to which the individual belongs. Anxiety, under such circumstances, would be expected to fluctuate mostly within the "normal" (i.e. low levels) range, punctuated by occasional flare-ups when engaging in high-risk activities (e.g. confrontations with serious consequences). These would subside rapidly as conflict is resolved or other high-stakes activities unwind one way or the other.

The realization of such a highly ambitious therapeutic program is unlikely, at least in its entirety, within a relatively brief period of time. Nonetheless, it is worthwhile setting out an ideal towards which the application of the interpersonal approach would be striving. Not least, this ideal would also be useful in marking the culmination of a trajectory, along which the therapeutic effort ought to be moving.

The process of becoming socially phobic was construed developmentally (as an idiosyncratic, historically contingent creation, continually coming into being). In a like fashion, the reversal of this trend, culminating in the undoing of social phobia, needs to be construed as an extended process; one devoted to the cultivation and elaboration of interpersonal patterns of conduct, that could be described as the mirror image of social phobia. Fearful distance keeping, submissiveness and powerlessness for the sake of harm avoidance need, by degrees, to give way to greater and better (e.g. in enacting social roles) participation in social life.

How is this to be achieved? The interpersonal approach involves applying certain principles, rather than following a recipe with set ingredients, tools and techniques. What are these principles?

Unraveling the causes of social phobia

Any attempt to counteract abnormality must, first and foremost, do away with what causes it. In keeping with the interpersonal analytic framework elaborated previously (in Chapter 6), the socially phobic pattern may be understood as the consequence of several causes. To reiterate: the cause underpinning all other causes is the purposeful nature of the comprehensive socially phobic pattern in terms of self-protection. Thus, the function of the various strands of the socially phobic pattern – manifestly performed for the sake of minimizing the risk of private rebuff, as well as public loss of face and standing – is the ultimate cause of social phobia.

This self-protective purpose is pursued and realized by means of a fearful relational pattern. It is prominently characterized by keeping to a safe perimeter, and in dangerous encounters, by submissiveness and powerlessness. Understood as a form of organization or a strategy, it is the formal cause of social phobia.

Finally, the situations that prompt fearful reactions and self-protective activities are the proximate causes of social phobia.

Whereas the formal cause and the ultimate cause are integrated and are enacted by the socially phobic individual, the proximate cause is largely independent of him or her. I shall consider the causes in an ascending order of importance.

Undoing the proximate cause – changing the social environment

Such causal analysis opens up the possibility of changes of social environment as a means towards eliminating certain proximate causes and thereby undermining aspects of social phobia. Not all public activities are equally important and their attendance meaningful. Some activities of this kind may have been imposed by interfering (and at times well-meaning) relatives or friends. Drastic restructuring could be envisaged in the public and occupational sphere (e.g. law can be practiced in various ways, not only by pleading in court) and to a lesser degree in private life (e.g. living separately from a demanding elderly mother).

Although as a matter of potentiality always worth considering, in most cases, the practicality of improving social phobia by means of intervening in the proximate causes (by substituting some environments), would be limited. Changing employer while keeping the same occupation would already have been tried, usually with minimal benefit, as the demands made on the socially phobic employee would remain roughly similar.

Undoing the formal cause – changing the relational pattern

Practically, the greatest potential in unraveling social phobia lies in dissolving the formal cause, by striving to alter the manner in which socially phobic individuals relate to others and, consequently, their functioning.

The fully integrated socially phobic pattern is a generalization or an abstraction. It identifies the extended web or network of various sub-patterns, arising and subsiding with the occurrence of various social circumstances. Tangibly, the socially phobic pattern is made up of sub-patterns enacted on various occasions. Prudent distance keeping, making oneself inconspicuous, deceptive dissembling, as well as submissiveness and powerless dependence, are enacted through interpersonal sub-patterns. For social phobia to weaken or wither, the fearful sub-patterns making up the socially phobic web have to be transfigured.

The process of therapeutic change involves discarding (rapidly or gradually) grossly self-protective (and, as such, self-centered) relational patterns, while simultaneously fashioning more courageous ways of participating and mastering unpredictable, fearsome interactions. This needs to be followed by cultivating new habits (of seeking opportunities of furthering one's goals by means of collaborative, yet self-assertive, ways of transacting with others).

Although traditionally identified as "treatment or therapy," the process – in the broadest sense – is educational. As such, it is formative rather than curative. It resembles learning to meditate, swim, cook or dance, far more than taking antibiotic medication (for bacterial infection) or undergoing surgery (for obstructed blood vessels). Its greatest affinity is with any serious attempt to transform one's way of life.

Such a process concerns refashioning long-standing habits (e.g. acting deferentially), breaking habitual patterns (e.g. finding refuge in non-committal silence) and evolving new forms of conduct (e.g. speaking in a forthright manner, taking on positions of responsibility). Ultimately and at another level – when anxiousness has subsided and is no longer the main consideration – it involves a different kind of living, an extended process of furthering projects and their realization. None of these many-stranded activities can be episodic; by necessity, these range over long stretches of time.

Content   The patterns of conduct singled out for building up (for being incompatible with social phobia) constitute the content of therapy. Overall, these will be non-defensive ways of transacting with others. From a social life predicated on maximizing safety and minimizing harm, it will be refocused on the pursuit of the patient's social objectives. For the sake of this, first of all, all distance keeping (avoiding, fleeing) has to cease. Secondly, when in social settings, non-defensive new patterns of conduct have to be developed. These would mostly seek to replace passive attendance and submission by active and appropriate participation. Overall it would mean enhancing interpersonal power and independence, both exercised in a collaborative manner and pressed into service for the sake of an increased and better participation. This also allows, by degrees, taking greater advantage of the increased social opportunities available.

Practically, treatment goals are best ordered in terms of the severity of impairment in social functioning, in descending order; those resulting in the most severe consequences, are best dealt with first. Typically, the most acute distress and the greatest impairment is manifest in the public domain. Most likely it will involve difficulties in assuming a social role enacted in public, usually, but not exclusively in occupational contexts. Acting as a best man at a wedding (a public role in a private context) presents an almost insurmountable challenge to the socially phobic individual. The least acutely problematic, but nonetheless insidiously troublesome relationships would prevail in the private domain. These may involve crippling, long-standing arrangements for the sake of keeping the peace and pacifying overbearing and at times irate acquaintances, friends and family relations of varying degrees of intimacy.

Starting from an initial state of fleeing danger or fearful submission when this is impossible, what ought treatment to aim at?

I shall argue that, ideally, the best outcome would be midway between fearful withdrawal on the one hand, and reckless social involvement, on the other. In keeping with an Aristotelian conception of virtue (Shields, 2007, pp. 323–326), I shall advocate the fashioning (by degrees) of a mid-point position that could be described as one of courageous determination. Such a stance, mindful of context and circumstances, despite a certain degree of fear and apprehension, enables the deliberate choice of action to be performed, or stand to be taken. In other words, it helps to define, in specific circumstances, what needs to be done, for the right kind of reason.

Regardless of the specific issues tackled in each case and across areas of social functioning (e.g. public or private), the trajectory of socially phobic individuals, throughout the therapy process, is similar. Within an interpersonal space (as seen in Figure 1.1, Chapter 1), defined by power and mode of relating, it would have as its starting point the margins of the respectfully/submissive quadrant (where these characteristics are highly pronounced). By means of small increments in powerful behavior, it would move towards the center of all quadrants, where all characteristics are finely poised. The evidence for this is discussed later.

In lock step with the gradual withering of self-protective patterns, a parallel reduction in various parameters of fearfulness commonly takes place.

In summary, the treatment proceeds as a gradual process of fashioning self-assertive yet collaborative ways of relating to others and simultaneously discarding grossly self-protective (and, as such, self-centered) ones. It does this through a process of better enacting social roles and perhaps taking on new ones. In that respect, it is useful to distinguish between social areas of functioning; namely, between activities in public and private domains of life. In the former case, formal social roles are enacted in transactions taking place in settings framed by relatively rigid rules (e.g. laws); in the latter, informal personal transactions take place against a flexible array of rules, allowing much variation on similar themes (e.g. friendship, courtship).

A most useful perspective on dealing with the content of treatment as well as structuring its process (to be presented next), is the dramaturgical one. It was first outlined in Chapter 1, in the context of an analysis of the functioning of the socially phobic. Applied to treatment, it would direct the clinician to insert the targeted interactional patterns of behavior within the enactment of a role (e.g. public speaker but also member of an association, friend, spouse and father) that best fits the social and cultural context of the individual.

In the interest of ease of exposition, it may be useful to recap the dramaturgical perspective.

As its name implies, it considers social life from the vantage point of a theatrical performance. Performances are viewed as depending largely on context, the performers on stage, as it were, addressing an audience. Performances, on this view, emerge from interactions with others and are constantly modified in light of the ongoing dynamic transactions. These principles are on display in the procession of different *personae* one adopts in the course of a day or a lifetime. Needless to say, although this perspective illuminates human social life, it is partial and limited. Theoretically, an additional account of self is necessary for a complete understanding of personhood (see Harré, 1991b).

Within the dramaturgical framework, role means both a *part* in a play as well as a *script*, supplying the words and other non-verbal actions. The theatrical outlook also illuminates other aspects of social life, such as choice of costumes and venue, preparations (e.g. rehearsals), and the distinction between "front-stage" and "back-stage" conduct. These are highly useful notions in treatment.

In a practical vein, four main considerations guiding the build-up of a performance have been found valuable. First of all and most importantly, the patterns of behavior singled out for being built up and encouraged are best identified as an element of the performance of a social role, in interaction with corresponding social roles enacted by other individuals. Secondly, it is helpful to define a desired outcome (function) that requires acting in a manner (a pattern of conduct) likely to lead towards it. Thirdly, it is imperative to stay in character, so as not to make the role incoherent. Fourthly, an issue of some importance in the case of the reflexively self-effacing socially phobic is to consider how to project the appropriate social status in one's appearance as well as manner of conduct.

In therapy, as in theatre and life, the importance of body movement in the projection of emotion cannot be overestimated. Both theatrical experience and experimental studies suggest that an emotion can be communicated in modulating three non-verbal features: posture, facial expression and breathing pattern (see Bloch, Orthous and Santibanez, 1987; Bloch, 1986). This knowledge can be readily applied. Courageous determination, for example, would involve a straight (perhaps military bearing) posture, a direct gaze combined with a quietly confident facial expression, and a rather slow and deliberate pattern of speech (and attendant breathing) with pauses between sentences. The process of building up a social role, especially one involving public speaking, is much helped bearing in mind the three parameters. Among these, slowing down and steadying the breathing rhythm while speaking seem the most important (see Homma and Masaoka, 2008, p. 1013; Bloch, Lemeigan and Aguilera-Torres, 1991).

In sum, the choice of a theatrical metaphor as a frame for the various therapeutic goals and their enactment – besides its heuristic value as rich source of ideas – has also the not negligible practical merit of being immediately intelligible to the socially phobic individual seeking help.

Process As for practical skills, so for self-transformation – people learn by practicing. No one is born knowledgeable or good, but many people are. Bravery is fostered by displaying courageous actions; independence, by autonomous self-assertion. It goes without saying that learning to behave differently is not just emulating somebody or following a formula. To perfect any skill, one needs to understand the considerations framing the conduct and guide oneself accordingly, in purposeful action. Furthermore, to achieve a proficient level, one must strive to improve, learning from blunders and mishaps and studying the activities of masters. In that sense, any complex goal-directed behavior, interpersonal or otherwise, emanates intelligence. In the words of a Chinese proverb:

> I hear and forget.
> I see and remember
> I do and I understand.

The practical steps that move the process of learning along may be ordered according to several levels of intervention.

First of all, a strategic shift from defensive self-protection to engaging all social possibilities (e.g. accepting all invitations, joining all available social activities; no longer taking precautions towards dissimulating blushing or voice or hand tremor). This may have to be implemented gradually.

Secondly, when the strategic shift begins to consolidate, tactical advantages need to be sought out. Practically, it means the gradual deployment of the behaviors targeted as the means towards advancing the therapeutic goals, in appropriate spheres of activity. Typically, the greatest impairments and fears are manifest in occupational circumstances, where social roles are warped by being enacted defensively and therefore inadequately. Positive change in this area makes the greatest difference; it boosts morale and sets the stage for subsequent attempts in other spheres of life.

This level of intervention is appropriate when the requisite behaviors (e.g. initiating a social activity) or their constituent elements (e.g. directing the gaze at the interlocutor, speaking slowly and enunciating clearly) are already in use by the socially phobic in other contexts. Under such circumstances, the role of the therapist consists mostly in guiding and encouraging the enactment of a certain scenario, as described earlier in the theatrical section. This could involve preparing a certain set of phrases as well as actions, in specific circumstances. This context needs to be elaborated as involving definite individuals, their social roles and previous relationships. The intended goal of the activity, and the likely reactions to it, need also be borne in mind.

When targeted, this set of actions would be assigned as "homework," to be tried out in between sessions (e.g. when entering the room where the meeting is held, approach each of the participants, greet them and present yourself by giving your name and your role in the organization).

Thirdly, it may be considered necessary to develop ways of acting not in the repertoire of the socially phobic individual (e.g. responding with fortitude to a refusal or to being corrected; giving generous praise; or expressing tenderness). Such actions are pivotal in the interpersonal approach. These would typically combine an increase in social power and a lessening of a submissively respectful diffidence (e.g. taking on the role of an educator while presenting in public; refusing unwelcome requests without pretexts and/or apologies; taking charge). These rather complex patterns of behavior, probably never attempted before by the socially phobic individual, would need to be built up gradually. This is best done on an individual basis, not generically, taking into account the specific circumstances and persons involved, while offering the socially phobic individual guiding rules framing such activities.

It is useful (conditions permitting) to demonstrate several ways in which these may be put to use, according to circumstances. It shows that the same effect may be achieved by different means. This would be followed by asking the socially phobic individual to enact the most likely scenario briefly, offering constructive feedback (see below), and re-enacting the scene again in light of the feedback. Alternative, less likely scenarios (e.g. point blank refusal) could be prepared in a similar fashion. Such a procedure has been applied successfully in a variety of clinical settings: small groups, individual sessions, with confederates involved occasionally (e.g. to simulate an audience) or even without any other participants.

Schematically presented, and framed by the principles presented in the theatrical section, the process would flow through the following steps.

First, "instructions" are given. These would describe the targeted behavioral pattern, its purpose and intended effect (function). These are best provided in the mode of a script, identifying the social roles of each participant, with specific "lines" agreed upon, and followed by instructions for the role's enactment within a specific situation.

Second, a demonstration ("modeling") either by the therapist or another patient (if such is available) is made of how to perform the particular social action targeted. Several demonstrations are better than one, as these make clear that the same purpose (function) may be achieved by various means.

Third, the patient simulates ("role rehearsal") the targeted behavior with the therapist or other participants, if available. This is best done in very short segments, keeping to a specific set of "instructions."

Fourth, "feedback" is given. This allows the therapist (and other participants) to praise positive features of the performance and the (complete or partial) achievement of the intended effects; it also leaves room for suggested improvements, by pinpointing specific sub-behaviors. The feedback may be divided into verbal and non-verbal aspects. If the verbal (i.e. the lines to be spoken) is well prepared in advance, most feedback would concern the para-verbal (e.g. tone of voice, enunciation, pace) and the non-verbal aspects of performance (e.g. posture, facial expression and breathing pattern).

This prompts another "role-rehearsal", followed by "feedback." Usually, at least two simulations are necessary to develop and organize the various elements involved in a rather complex behavior, fit to be tried out in real life.

Fifth, "homework" – targeted behaviors practiced to a satisfactory level of performance within sessions are assigned as "homework" tasks to be performed in real life, between sessions. These are the bedrock of therapy and not negotiable, as practicing would be when learning to play a musical instrument. As will be seen later, the performance of interpersonal tasks in real-life situations is the single most important element in the course of such a treatment.

For both practical and symbolic reasons, tasks assigned as homework are reviewed (on the basis of self-monitoring records; see below) at the beginning of the following session and if proven helpful, further improved.

Sixth, "self-monitoring" – patients are asked to note daily the frequency of each target's performance and to rate the subjective level of anxiety experienced during each performance; these would be discussed at the beginning of the next session.

To sum up, this process of change is guided throughout by considerations of gradually, but persistently, moving the patient in an interpersonal space from a position of relative insufficiency of power (e.g. evasiveness, submissiveness) and correspondingly low standing (e.g. behaving ingratiatingly), to a self-sufficiency of power (enough to pursue one's goals) and a greater independence (autonomy) as to the opinions of others.

To reiterate: in the interpersonal approach, anxiousness is viewed as a facet of an insufficiency of power, combined with low standing. With the rise of greater self-determination, the fearful state of alarm accompanying self-protection would be expected to be much reduced in scope and gradually match normal patterns of responding in similar circumstances.

Undoing the ultimate cause – from fearful self-protection to cheerful self-creation

If considered a disorder of anxiety, the best possible outcome of a course of therapy for social phobia would be remission, signifying that the individual who underwent treatment no longer meets the defining (e.g. DSM-5) criteria for social phobia. Typically, this would combine a less severe anxious distress with a diminished tendency to avoid social situations.

On the interpersonal view, although beneficial, this is a rather limited outcome, as it affects mostly the defensive distance keeping inherent in social phobia. It is likely that when entering social situations, the powerless/dependent interpersonal behavior characterizing the socially phobic would persist. After all, such a relational manner is a long-standing habit and is unlikely to disappear and give way to adaptive social functioning of itself.

Viewed interpersonally, the absence of social phobia would imply a greater ability to venture out of a safety zone, to act more powerfully and independently, and to enact social roles prolifically and with greater poise.

Although highly desirable, in practice, the usual outcome is likely to be more limited. Although distress and psychopathology that have cast a dark shadow may have shriveled or outright vanished, what kind of life can be expected to emerge once the individual is again under sunny skies?

Reasoning theoretically, the intimate link between the fearfully submissive and powerless socially phobic manner of relating (formal cause) and its self-protective function (ultimate cause) would suggest that, in general, the weakening of the former would result in the decline of the latter. All the same, experience shows that it usually happens only partially (i.e. in relation to the narrow socially phobic pattern alone). Why is that so?

Social life, viewed panoramically, is an all-encompassing interpersonal network of patterns, ranging over many relational spheres, exceeding the reach of social phobia by far. Many of the facets prominent and troublesome in social phobia are invisibly and insidiously woven into the fabric of numerous relationships and are enacted (or refrained from being expressed) for the same self-protective motives. To reiterate, despite the shrinking of the overarching socially phobic pattern or its dissolution, the now far-less-pronounced tendency towards self-protection does not disappear altogether. Correspondingly, remnants of powerlessness, such as passivity (e.g. resisting others' initiatives but not offering alternatives) and dependency (e.g. keeping taking medication as a safety net), linger on.

To sum up, although partially uprooted, aspects of defensiveness (seen as a risk-minimizing strategy) still exert a pervasive influence – perhaps in an attenuated form – in many spheres of social life. Furthermore, the fact that the formerly socially phobic individual continues to function within the same social networks and most likely with the same individuals, will exert pressure towards maintaining relationships as they have been in the past.

It is useful to ask again: does life, freed from the stultifying embrace of social phobia, blossom spontaneously? Would the shrinking of the state of abnormality or even its complete demise give rise, by itself, to a different, purposeful outlook to the now diminished and partially discarded striving for safety?

Experience shows that it is not likely. Although the quest for safety would have weakened, and the ability to display self-assertion and enhanced involvement with other people strengthened, the life of even the formerly socially phobic remains somewhat restricted, defined by rigidities borne of long-standing habits of prudence, passivity and dependence. Seen clinically, this suggests that a generalization of the benefits of therapy to other spheres of life – although hoped for – is not automatic and needs to be promoted actively.

Where possible, treatment that reaches an advanced stage (when fearful submission is gradually replaced by a more determined self-assertion and greater self-regard) may benefit from actively applying the same approach to other situations, where anxious distress is less pervasive and therefore outside the boundaries of what was initially considered the socially phobic pattern. Such expansion of the therapeutic goals benefits from being actively sought out. In the aid of such activism, it is worthwhile elaborating an alternative, forward-looking strategy or "ideology" to replace the "therapeutic" one (of diminishing harm and relieving suffering) that has been guiding the treatment so far. Such an outlook, in terms of a life worth living and pursuing (an antithesis to social phobia), could be one of "flourishing" (e.g. Keyes, 2007), the Aristotelian definition of a good life. Such a pursuit requires highly developed virtues of reasoning (choices are fashioned through reasoned discussion) and character (e.g. fortitude), not least taking responsibility for forging such virtues, as well as for one's life in general.

All human change is achieved through patient nursing of habit development; in principle all aspects of our humanity may and ought to be cultivated. Whether to evolve or stagnate is a personal responsibility. Especially when embarking on a process of self-cultivation, one must guard against the normal inclination of swerving from one extreme (e.g. passive resignation) to another (e.g. implacable hostility) and steer a middle course. Speaking the truth, in the right context and for the right reasons, when conduct, emotion and thought are in harmony (e.g. integrity), is an example of poise and deliberate temperance.

The formerly socially phobic, particularly, benefit from attending to self-reliance (autonomy) for the sake of self-definition and ultimately self-creation (power). Self-determination need not necessarily mean an egocentric approach, involving only self-interest promoted by narrow calculation. It suggests, rather, cultivating an independence of outlook and means, to allow the widest range of choices and commitments in living one's life. Human relatedness is crucial to a life worth living. While relationships based on mutual interest are a necessity and in their own way rewarding, those turning on mutual appreciation and regard are particularly satisfying. The ability to create and sustain such relationships is precious.

As the ultimate cause is the cause of causes, such an outlook – with its emphasis on "flourishing" – provides a coherent vision and framework, acting as an organizing principle for the sake of a worthwhile life freely chosen, with its necessary attendant relational patterns and their corresponding emotions.

Illustrative cases

It is clear from the description of the interpersonal approach applied to the treatment of social phobia that it is an amalgam of analytic principles, rather than a set technique or formula. Viewed from the interpersonal vantage point, there is no generic social phobia, but a variety of socially phobic individuals. While the categorical term "social phobia" inevitably (and wrongly) hints at a monolithic pattern, the various facets or processes making up social phobia range widely. Although there are decided trends, these represent likelihoods, rather than set facts. The interpersonal approach, therefore, is most meaningfully tailored to individual specifications. The treatment process is illustrated – in outline – by the three cases already encountered in Chapter 7. Their assessment and functional analysis were described in Tables 7.1–7.3. The analysis subsequently yielded treatment plans described in Tables 7.4–7.6. The actual treatments are described below. Additional descriptions of treatment, involving other case studies treated by a similar approach, may be found in Stravynski, Arbel, Lachance *et al.* (2000).

Case A

A agreed, at the outset of her treatment, to the principle that staying away from social activities had to cease, although the actual implementation might be gradual or even piecemeal. As a consequence, she was to accept all invitations outright, although actual participation could be reconsidered or even (under certain circumstances) cancelled at a later stage.

Since this raised the possibility that she might blush, a non-defensive manner of carrying on had to be devised that was practicable in most situations (personal and impersonal), whether she acted in a private or a public capacity. In case of blushing, two possibilities were put forward. First of all, if no remarks were made, she was to carry on as if nothing had happened: neither fleeing to the restrooms, nor offering excuses or explanations. Secondly, if comments about her blushing were made, she was to say: "So what?"

As is typical of such cases, she never blushed throughout treatment and subsequent follow-up. She quickly reported dropping levels of anxiousness in social situations during which she was encouraged to speak and circulate, while engaging with various individuals. Nonetheless, throughout the treatment period, an apprehensive discomfort continued to build up before each social activity. These, however, expanded considerably, as indoor activities and those where hot food was served were no longer ruled out. Towards the end of the treatment period (of 12 weekly sessions), she spent a day at a friend's house and participated in a Christmas party at her husband's place of work. Both activities were enjoyed and not just endured.

The treatment period ended with the preparation and rehearsal of a statement to her brother, putting him on notice that she would no longer tolerate decisions (affecting her) taken without prior consultation and approval. To her surprise, the brother acquiesced and explained away what happened before as a misunderstanding.

During the follow-up period, however, it soon became clear that the brother did not keep his commitment and, after a further confrontation, she cut off contact with him.

A parent–teacher meeting was prepared and rehearsed, emphasizing that it was an exchange to be held between a mother and a teacher. While both were concerned about the progress and the welfare of the child at school, as a mother, she had the duty and the authority that came with it of overseeing the child's upbringing. In keeping with this, a scenario of active participation was devised: after listening to the teacher's evaluation, she would ask a few questions and express both satisfaction (about progress) and reservations (about lack of it) and thank the teacher for her efforts.

Despite apprehensions beforehand, the actual meeting went well and she gradually became involved in a group of parents active in the school. In a complete reversal of what she would have done in the past, on her own initiative, A asked that the graduation day ceremony of her younger child be moved, so that she would be able to attend it.

During the follow-up period, she increasingly went out with women friends and ate hot meals (sometimes accompanied by alcohol) without difficulty. Also, she gradually changed her wardrobe from turtlenecks to blouses and dresses, some relatively revealing and low cut.

While her husband praised her progress, she felt that he had become more jealous and even prone to demanding reassurance that she was not about to leave him. Nevertheless, their intimacy had deepened and they spent much more time in each other's company and talking to each other. Dancing lessons were in the offing.

Towards the end of the 1-year follow-up, she decided to look for a part-time clerical position and an interview was outlined (including the strengths and weaknesses she could bring to the job) without being rehearsed. Although she was not selected, A was proud of having been short-listed and intended to persist.

Finally, A organized a party involving some 50 participants to celebrate her daughter's confirmation. Although a twinge of concern would occasionally rise up ahead of social activities, she pursued them deliberately and once in the thick of action, experienced little discomfort. At the 1-year follow-up, concerns about blushing had vanished. At this stage, A no longer met the criteria defining social phobia.

Case B

B agreed at the outset to accept all social invitations in his private life and to attend all business-related meetings (as opposed to sending underlings). As treatment progressed, he gradually upgraded his wardrobe to broadly fit the dress code prevailing among his clients and their representatives.

During meetings, he was particularly anxious about what he felt were insinuations of inflated and unnecessary costs or other underhand dealings on his part. Point-blank requests to justify some expenses or their extent were even more menacing. During such confrontations, he would at times experience rapid surges of anxiety (panic) that left him shaken and speechless. The "anti-depressant medication" (which he had been taking for two years prior to therapy) made him feel safer in that it "took the edge off" his highly aroused state. It did not, however, suppress the anxious state sufficiently to allay concerns about whether it attracted notice.

To turn around his defensive manner of participating in the meetings ("waiting to be hit" and "hiding"), it was suggested that he come to a meeting as if he were hosting it, among other activities, proposing or actually setting an agenda. It was agreed that the first item would be a brief presentation of the proposed project – justifying the choice as offering the best value for money – with cheaper or more costly alternatives mentioned in passing. The second item would be an explanation of the budget and the third, taking questions. Such a set agenda, it was felt, would create a structure and set a certain procedure and discipline that would reduce disruptive interruptions. In the face of these, he was not to answer, but say: "Please let me finish. I will answer questions later."

Several scenarios concerning exchanges were envisaged as most likely: (1) if he could not give an answer on the spot, he would admit ignorance without any pretexts, and promise to check the facts and give a speedy reply; (2) all quibbles about expenses would be answered – if applicable – from "best value for money" or the "lowest cost" perspective, depending on the clients' preferences; (3) possibilities that he never envisaged would be answered: "You are bringing up a good point, let me consider it and give you a reply later."

The scenarios were not rehearsed, but put into practice immediately by B. Although there was a lag in improvement in levels of anxiousness (that fell only gradually), within a number of weeks B felt more in command of the situation ("knowing what to do"). He was less preoccupied with what the other participants thought of him and whether his appearance betrayed his nervousness. B found it helpful to be reminded that he was the owner and the representative of a company and during the meetings – usually held at the clients' offices – on duty. His goal in taking part – it was argued – was to promote his business interests by providing the services his clients were seeking. Conversely, he did not attend the meetings in a private capacity (he was not engaging in courtship in the hope of winning affection or pleading for favors as a supplicant).

Soon after, of his own initiative (although this was not targeted in treatment), he ceased taking part in meetings of various business networks in which he found no interest, but for a long time attended for fear of mockery and criticism on the part of some of his relatives, who set great store by such memberships. It was decided that if queried about it, he would say "I did not find these meetings useful," without apology or justification.

At a later stage, a new manner of relating to his employees – compatible with his role in the company – was introduced. When displeased, instead of either fuming in silence or (rarely) storming out in a fit of anger (leaving the site or shutting himself up in his office), he was encouraged to say "I am not happy with this," and subsequently offer a reasoned criticism (not necessarily on the spot).

Conversely, he was guided to express satisfaction and compliment the worker(s) when a job was well done – something he never did before. He did not, however, take up a suggestion to set up regular meetings with employees (for the sake of a systematic monitoring of performance). The active management of workers remained fitful. Similarly, the training of employees for specific tasks or projects remained unsystematic and, when attempted, fell into disuse shortly after. Nonetheless, the company seemed to have functioned reasonably well without it.

Most of B's efforts throughout treatment were invested in getting contracts and he blossomed rather quickly into the role of expert provider of specialized services, handling his clients confidently and impersonally with only occasional bouts of anxiousness (followed by anger) with particularly difficult (i.e. aggressively disrespectful) clients.

Things progressed more slowly in his personal life, perhaps because the scope for either distance keeping and avoidance or passive participation was greater and the penalties for such defensiveness – unlike in business life – distant and intangible.

In this sphere, he agreed to start attending his children's after-school activities (e.g. hockey games, musical recitals). This was something he had stopped doing, to his great regret, in the year before the consultation, when there was a marked deterioration in his phobic fears and his mood darkened. As he feared that parents he knew might notice his discomfort, it was agreed that he would "go on the offensive" by taking the initiative to approach and greet anyone he knew. Although he was immediately able to go through the motions, he continued to worry about the fact that he was hot and his hands clammy; he was especially concerned that this might provoke unfavorable comments. These fears subsided gradually, and he was encouraged to address other parents as well.

At family gatherings, he felt very tense about the propensity of one of his relatives to tease him directly or make jokes about him indirectly. During these moments, he would sit stony-faced, pretending not to hear and would look away.

As a solution to this oft-occurring situation, it was suggested that: (1) while at the table, he gaze at this relative with an expression of displeasure; (2) after the meal, he approach the relative and say that "I do not find your jokes about me amusing. I wish you would stop it."

Although the relative feigned amusement in reaction to B's outspoken request, he never went back to the teasing/joking banter. Conversely and unsurprisingly, his manner towards B became more friendly and deferential.

In his private life, the most painful situations for B involved his wife. She tended to give him orders, preceded by criticisms of his different shortcomings. This was tackled during follow-up, when the acute distress related to his business activities had abated and his functioning in the public arena was at its peak. Although he would not necessarily carry out the command (at least not when requested), he would feel cruelly wronged and would brood about it, becoming increasingly upset. He would finally withdraw into solitary activities and silence that could last days. During this time, he would feel low and diffusely anxious, but not angry. However, when going over these incidents in therapy, resentment was palpable.

As a manner of handling this, it was suggested that the response be divided in two parts. Immediately, regardless of the manner in which the request was made, he was to say: "I'll see when I can do it." Later, when a suitable moment for calm conversation would come up, he was to say – as the case may be – either: "You said that I ... I disagree with that [if he did]" without offering any excuses or justifications, or: "You said that I ... after thinking about it, I find that you were right [if he agreed that the criticism was justified]. I'll pay more attention to it in the future."

This transformation in his responses had an immediate effect on his interactions with his wife. Her manner became less fierce and her requests softer and more tentative. The greatest gain was that she became more respectful of his moments of leisure, when he enjoyed being at peace and doing nothing. In the past, these were the prime times for asking him to take care of all kinds of chores as "he had nothing to do." At this stage, B no longer satisfied the criteria defining social phobia. Of his own initiative, he consulted his family physician so as to gradually stop the "anti-depressant" medication he had been taking for more than three years.

It was felt that this rapid turn of events, at the end of the follow-up, was propitious for the development a greater intimacy in the couple, thereby enriching the marriage. Surprisingly, this notion was greeted in lukewarm fashion by B. Although he agreed that complimenting his wife occasionally would be a good thing to do, "it wasn't him." For the same reason, he dismissed the possibility of offering her a gift as a symbolic

gesture of appreciation. Similarly, he was unable to see the point in con-
fiding in her about his past problems and how the therapy – of which she
was aware – had helped him. He was skeptical about whether "she would
understand."

Case C

Unlike A and B, C repeatedly pointed out that he sought help for public
speaking only, considering the rest of his life and functioning unproblem-
atic. Since this activity was not part of what he did for a living – and hence
not a necessity – it was first suggested that he might consider giving it
up. C adamantly refused, emphasizing that he was strongly committed to
acting as a speaker. Despite the acutely prolonged distress occasioned by
the activity and the preparations for it, he found the recognition inherent
in being solicited by various institutions (for an expertise he had developed for the training of personnel), deeply gratifying.

In preparation for treatment, it was argued that, in view of the formal setting where the speaking activity usually took place, his "informal
approach" – a lame, humorous manner in the service of "establishing a
rapport" – needed to be reconsidered.

First of all, his role was recast as an educator and his activity branded
pedagogy (not entertainment). The rather formal settings (e.g. small lecture halls) in which he had to perform, lent themselves well to the establishment of a strictly ranked pedagogy: he was to learn speaking from the
lectern, as it were.

Secondly, it was agreed that he needed a costume – as in the theatre –
that would provide a cue for what his role was when he walked into the
lecture hall, even before mounting the podium or uttering a word.

Thirdly, his performance, from his entry on stage to the end, was
divided in two: introduction and lecture. An initial introductory phase,
clearly distinct from the actual lecture, would allow him to take charge,
so as to set the stage. He would address the audience and the organizers formally, greet them, describe his credentials and background and,
finally, how he intends to proceed. No self-deprecating jokes or other
attempts at humor were allowed.

As to the lecture, he was asked to prepare a text that, in addition to
having the appropriate content, would lend itself comfortably to speaking. A singing metaphor was used throughout to aid the phrasing. To this
end, only short sentences were chosen, with frequent punctuation, allowing pauses for breathing.

When a text was created to the above specifications, a trial presentation was simulated, beginning with the introduction. In the course of the

rehearsals, the text was constantly modified (as in the process of composition for the voice) to fit even better with the requirement of speaking slowly, articulating precisely and – as in singing – using moments of silence for emphasis and phrasing.

This aspect was the most difficult for C to master and initial set-backs (accompanied by impatient self-blaming) were frequent. Nevertheless, the new sober and formal manner of introducing the presentation, although initially alien and artificial in his eyes, was instantly helpful and set the stage for a more measured and relaxed performance of public speaking.

With the final text in hand, C was ready for a dress rehearsal. New role-playing was conducted with the therapist modeling ways of presenting the introduction as well as fragments from the presentation proper. For the sake of projecting the appropriate emotional state (courageous determination was chosen), in addition to the slow pace of speaking and clear enunciation, a straight posture was encouraged as well as gazing at the audience during pauses in speech and returning – unhurriedly – to the presentation. Although this was not explicitly a therapeutic goal, C commented that as the result of the preparations, the quality of delivery was much improved and even the content of the presentation was far better structured and therefore easier to follow.

The immediate result was a much shortened and less acute anxious state during the periods preceding presentations. While episodes of panic never occurred during the treatment period, fluctuating anxiousness at a more moderate (less disorganizing levels) persisted. Overall, anxiousness gradually abated, lagging characteristically the major changes in the manner of relating to others, displayed in a variety of specific situations.

By the end of a 1-year follow-up, C no longer fulfilled criteria for social phobia.

In C's initial estimation public speaking was his only difficulty. As he improved, it became apparent, in the later stages of therapy, that he was now troubled by his wife's tendency to disregard some of his wishes, stated or not. In the past, he seemed to have been little troubled by it, discounting the incidents as unimportant, in the interest of "keeping the peace." At this stage of therapy, he became acutely conscious of being ignored and resented it.

It was agreed to add this issue to the goals of therapy and attempt to resolve it by acting in a decisive manner. He was to approach his wife during a quiet moment and tell her: "I was disappointed that you did ... despite the fact that I asked you not to. Could we agree that when something concerns us both, nothing be done about it one-sidedly?"

Although C was indecisive and found it difficult to identify the right moment, when he actually spoke to her, he was only mildly apprehensive.

His wife's reaction was positive as to the principle (unlike what he had expected) – to which she wholeheartedly agreed – but she denied having violated it. Although he felt that she was making efforts and the frequency of "being ignored" did diminish to an extent, his sensitivity to these slights was actually on the rise. While he veered between passive resentment and episodic boldness, her propensity to deny or rationalize what she did remained unchanged and it now irritated him. As the follow-up period approached its end, discord was simmering and C's dissatisfaction with this aspect of his marriage persisted.

Unlike the case of B, where a newly found assertiveness triggered a smooth process of mutual readjustment in marital life, in the case of C it seemed to have upset long-established power relations and unleashed conflict. Although increasing frictions, this challenge of past crippling arrangements could arguably be seen as a higher level of functioning on the part of C. It was a transition from a passively submissive or at most reactive, to an actively assertive, pattern of conduct. Be that as it may, only the latter puts an individual on the path to greater autonomy in the realization of one's life goals.

Outcome

Are the results achieved (with the cases described earlier) typical? In other words, what are the effects of the interpersonal approach to the treatment of social phobia? Before delving into the studies carried out to put this to the test, it is well to bring to the fore a salient point about social phobia and to establish some standards by which to judge results. These will be useful also in comparing the effects of the interpersonal approach to other available treatments, guided by very different – explicit or implicit – theoretical considerations.

A most important feature of social phobia, when considering the effects of treatment, is its chronicity (see Stravynski, 2007, pp. 113–114). Tantalizingly, "epidemiological" studies estimate rates of prevalence of social phobia (at the time of the investigation) to be lower by far than those reported over the "lifetime." Overlooking the possibility that this gap is an artifact of how lifetime "diagnoses" are arrived at, it would seem that natural social processes leading to remission would account for the difference. Examples of such extended events would be as follows: crossing paths with an ardent and enterprising admirer; working for a demanding but sympathetic overseer; and being thrown by fate into a group with a strong "esprit de corps."

No evidence of such benign processes can be seen, however, in the lives of patients seeking help, perhaps because they are, for the most part, little capable of responding to, let alone taking advantage of, such naturally occurring social opportunities. Social phobia typically crystallizes as a pattern in adolescence (in the face of increasingly insistent social and interpersonal demands of adulthood). It remains among the most chronic problems seen in the clinic (see Stravynski, 2007, pp. 113–114). Help is often sought long after the onset of problems. In the two studies presented below, the phobic problem is on average of 25 years duration.

Outcome studies need, at a minimum, to meet certain requirements that provide as much guarantee as can be had for the relative soundness of the results. These standards, however, do not necessarily vouchsafe the conclusions drawn from them; interpretations need to be judged on their own merits.

Studies included below conform to the following requirements:

1. The sample included socially phobic participants exclusively. As the onset of social phobia is typically in late adolescence, all treatment studies concerned adult patients only.
2. Clinical status, either before or after treatment, was determined by recognized defining criteria (e.g. DSM-IV), not cut-off points on some scale.
3. The assessment battery included multiple measures of outcome. As the psychometric characteristics of individual measures often leave much to be desired, a convergence of outcome of all or most measures enhances confidence in the validity of the results.
4. The study design included more than one experimental condition (and therefore random assignment of patients to them). Such "controlled" studies either contrast the experimental treatment with a well-established treatment of known outcome (that serves as benchmark), or an experimental condition that simulates a treatment, without offering its substance (e.g. "placebo").

Placebo (from the Latin *placere*, literally "to please") refers to the historically observed fact that dealings between individuals culturally recognized as healers and cure-seeking sufferers soothe suffering and stimulate the organism's potential for self-healing. It might be argued that, until the twentieth century, all medical treatment that did not injure the patient (unlike purging, bleeding) consisted of inert remedies and the attendant social rituals performed in appropriate settings (Wootton, 2007).

Such simulation of treatment, to have an effect, must be intelligible to the patient in culturally sanctioned terms of reference (see Moerman, 2002). Shamanic rituals aiming to appease offended spirits (incantations, amulets, potions), for example, would be meaningless to most Western patients. Exorcism, however, may exert a powerful effect on a Western faithful (e.g. Barlow, Abel, and Blanchard, 1977).

The average Western patient, on the other hand, responds powerfully to medical authority and, it is to be hoped, to its healing rituals (establishing diagnosis; running tests; prescribing pills; performing surgery) (see, e.g., Finkler, 1994) embedded in a shared outlook ("medical science"), construing the living organism as a machine and inadequate functioning – as its breakdown (in our case, of the brain or the mind).

Whereas "placebo" – seen narrowly – can have a precise meaning in the context of pharmacotherapy (pharmacologically inert but otherwise identical-looking pills *and* a similar mode of prescription and administration), its implementation within the study of psychological treatment is ambiguous. No psychological experimental condition is entirely inert; all exercise some influence. Is the administration of relaxation training (Manzoni, Pagnini, Castenuovo and Molinari, 2008), to take it as an example, a treatment or the equivalent of the pharmacological placebo procedure?

Being admitted to a treatment program and put on a waiting list (after extensive intake interviews and the administration of various psychological measurements) is perhaps the best psychological control available in the case of social phobia. It is the closest equivalent to the medical "placebo" effect. It combines inactivity with the expectation of future benefits of expert ministrations. It is suitable, for, unlike episodes of depression which are often self-limiting, social phobia – at least among those seeking treatment – runs an undeviatingly chronic course.

Standards of improvement

Three potential strands of outcome are relevant to social phobia and may be reported:

1. Reduction in subjective distress in, and avoidance of anxiety-evoking situations, is the most common index. This is usually taken as the primary measure of improvement. It is the natural upshot of the commonly held intrapersonal notion that social phobia is primarily a "disorder" of social anxiety. Needless to say, such a notion is at variance with the interpersonal outlook.

2. Improvement in social functioning (i.e. the manner in which the patient participates in social life, assumes roles and fits in – see Beattie and Stevenson, 1984). Such measures would be congenial to the interpersonal outlook, but are seldom encountered. This is odd in view of the fact that impaired social functioning is at the heart

of social phobia and a defining criterion (although not a necessary one) in DSM-5 and ICD-10. It is without a doubt a reflection of the principal role accorded to anxiety in the intrapersonal understanding of social phobia. All impairments and disabilities are understood as flowing from it.

3. Improvement in clinical status (i.e. remission). As the best result possible, from a clinical point of view, its meaningfulness is obvious and beyond challenge. Most importantly, it sets an absolute standard. Improvements in social anxiety and social functioning, by contrast, are relative to pre-treatment levels. Such gains, although ostensibly "significant" by statistical standards, are not obvious and might be modest from the point of view of the difference they make to patients' lives. Rates of remission are rarely reported and indeed might be a tall order, considering the chronicity of social phobia (seen in the clinic) and the relative short duration of treatment (about which later). In such circumstances, remission (as outcome) is quite a remarkable achievement.

The outcome of the interpersonal approach: clinical aspects

Short and medium term: results at the end of treatment and at the 1-year follow-up Two formal studies assessed the short- and middle-term effects of the interpersonal approach.

In the first study (Stravynski, Arbel, Bounader et al., 2000), 68 socially phobic individuals were assigned to either a waiting list or to two group treatments, based on the interpersonal approach. Both focused on improving social functioning (by means of switching from self-protection to participation), either with or without social skills training. Both treatments included 12 weekly sessions, followed by two additional trimonthly sessions during the first 6 months of the follow-up. Sixty participants completed treatment and 59 completed a 1-year follow-up.

While no clinically meaningful change was observed during the waiting period, a statistically significant and equivalent lessening of anxious distress, avoidance and better functioning in numerous facets of social life were noted in both treatment conditions (after treatment and maintained over the follow-up).

Clinically, the most important finding was the continuing and steady improvement in remission rates; this was equivalent in both treatment conditions (see Figure 8.1). At the end of treatment, 29% of the participants, on average, no longer met criteria for social phobia. The remission rate rose to 49% at the 6-month follow-up. Fully 60% of the patients

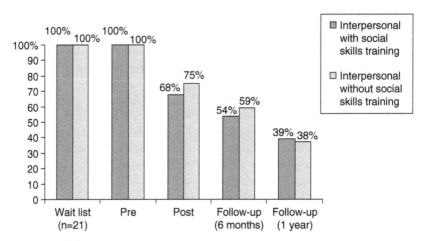

Figure 8.1. *Proportion of patients meeting DSM-IV criteria for social phobia (from Stravynski, Arbel, Bounader et al., 2000)*

no longer fulfilled criteria for social phobia at the end of the 1-year follow-up.

The primary purpose of the second study, Stravynski, Arbel, Gaudette and Lachance, 2013a) was to dismantle the interpersonal approach, as means towards identifying its active ingredients. To this end, 102 socially phobic individuals (DSM-IV) were randomly assigned to three treatment-conditions, all based on the interpersonal approach and geared towards improving social functioning. The first two were conducted in small groups, either with or without training (discussion only) during the sessions, with interpersonal "homework" tasks performed in between sessions. The third treatment condition consisted of brief individual meetings with a therapist, who only oversaw patients' performance of interpersonal "homework" tasks. Twenty participants were put on a waiting list and then reassigned at random.

Seventy-six completed treatment and 67 completed a 1-year follow-up. All treatments were administered in 14 sessions in total, with each participant receiving the same amount of focused attention (20 minutes per session approximately).

While no clinically meaningful change was noted during the waiting period, a statistically significant and equivalent improvement obtained in all treatment conditions. Notable benefits were in terms of reduced anxiety, avoidance and general psychopathology and better social functioning that maintained over the 6-month and 1-year follow-ups.

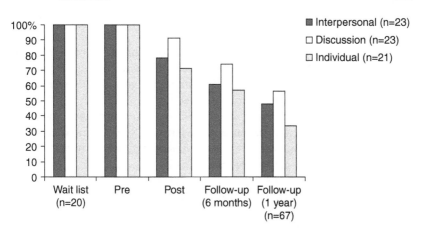

Figure 8.2. *Proportion of patients meeting DSM-IV criteria for social phobia (from Stravynski, Arbel, Gaudette and Lachance, 2013a)*

Most meaningfully, a continuing and equivalent improvement in remission rates was noted (see Figure 8.2); there were no statistical differences in the rates between the experimental treatment conditions at any point. On average, then, 25% of the patients were in remission at the end of treatment and 36% at the 6-month follow-up. At the 1-year follow-up, however, 54% no longer fulfilled criteria of social phobia.

Is the interpersonal approach enhanced by medication? Combinations are favored by many clinicians, and not least, in vogue with patients. In Stravynski, Amado, Lachance, Sidoun and Todorov (2013b) the question was put to a test. Fifty-nine socially phobic participants were randomly assigned to 14 sessions of the interpersonal approach, either with or without medication (paroxetine); 48 completed treatment and follow-up of up to 1 year.

On average, significant and equivalent improvements in severity of anxiety and social functioning were reported by both patients and clinicians (following brief interviews at the end of treatment and at 6- and 12-month follow-ups. In sum, the addition of medication to the interpersonal approach did not enhance its effects.

While clinically disappointing, this result is consistent with the outcomes of similar combinations, as applied to a variety of anxiety disorders (e.g. Black, 2006; Pontoski and Heimberg, 2010). Conceptually, however, the results are far from meaningless. They suggest that the reduction in fearfulness achieved collaterally, by the shift from self-protective and defensive relational patterns to participatory ones, fostered by the interpersonal approach, is not meaningfully affected by an additional chemical dampening of the nervous systems, involved in emotional regulation.

In summary, the rather rapid dissolution of long-standing (on average 25 years duration) self-protective relational patterns, accompanied by considerable reductions in anxious distress, provide the interpersonal approach to treatment with strong support.

The interpersonal approach is made-to-measure for each individual case. As implemented in various variants, it yields similar results. Outcome is equivalent, with or without modeling, role-play and feedback, administered in groups or individually. The practice of targeted behaviors between sessions, by contrast, remained a crucial ingredient (see also Stravynski, Lesage, Marcouillet and Elie, 1989). While all other elements may be trimmed or added according to circumstances, putting into practice newly evolved non-defensive patterns of conduct in one's dealings with relevant people, in appropriate settings, cannot be dispensed with.

A simultaneous combination of medication (at least paroxetine or the SSRIs) did not enhance the interpersonal approach in Stravynski, Amado et al. (2013). This disappointing outcome is generally consistent with the results of similar attempts of combining psychological and pharmacological approaches. It argues for skepticism in the face of an enduring unjustifiable enthusiasm for combinations among clinicians and patients. The only exception to this rule is the study reported by Blanco et al. (2010). In it, 128 socially phobic patients were assigned to either phenelzine alone (n=35), cognitive behavior group therapy (CBGT) alone (n=34), their combination (n=32) and a placebo pill (n=27).

Rates of those were much improved (as defined by CGI=1; 2010, p. 288) at the 3-month follow-up, as follows: combined 47%, medication alone 22%, CBGT alone 8% and placebo 7%. Strikingly, only the combined condition yielded results significantly different from placebo.

These outcomes are disconcerting and give pause in regard to the relative poor showing of CBGT. In contrast to the results reported in Blanco et al. (2010), cognitive therapy (that might be considered a form of exposure) has been shown in numerous studies to be an effective method of anxiety reduction in social phobia (see Stravynski, 2007, pp. 291–299). If only for this reason, further research is needed.

The interpersonal approach to treatment lends itself well to small groups (five to six participants) led by a therapist and co-therapist; it usually involves a short and intensive course of therapy, lasting 12–14 sessions (up to 28–30 hours). It must be conceded forthwith that, clinically speaking, such a structure and duration is arbitrary and more in harmony with research rather than clinical reasoning, seeking to demonstrate effectiveness and efficiency simultaneously. Needless to say, within the interpersonal framework for therapy presented in this chapter, even individuals who no longer meet criteria for social phobia (and from a biomedical standpoint, enjoy a clean bill of health) may still benefit from an active and lengthy follow-up. For many, it is essential in shepherding the intricate transition from a self-protective to a self-determining mode of interpersonal relationships in general and all it implies for their lives. Similarly, a generalization from gains in settings dealt with in therapy, to other spheres of life, needs to be promoted actively. It does not occur automatically.

The interpersonal approach to treatment is not exclusively bound to the group format, and can be applied individually. As a matter of fact, in Stravynski, Arbel *et al.* (2013), the individual condition resulted in the highest rate of improvement by any standard (see Figure 8.1 earlier); these differences, however, were not statistically significant. The efficiencies gained through the group format are to some extent offset by a higher dropout rate (typically 20 percent).

Most importantly, as can be seen in the next section, gains achieved in the medium term hold firmly in the long haul.

Long term: results after an 8- to 15-year follow-up Long-term follow-ups were carried out (Gibbs, Stravynski, and Lachance, 2013) among available participants from the two outcome trials described earlier (Stravynski, Arbel, Bounader *et al.* 2000; Stravynski, Arbel, Gaudette *et al.*, 2013a). These involved 36 participants in the Stravynski, Arbel, Bounader *et al.* (2000) study and 22 participants in the Stravynski, Arbel, Gaudette *et al.* (2013a) study. Altogether, the rate of inclusion in the long-term follow-up was on average 55 percent of the patients available for assessment. Most participants were assessed between 11 and 15 years after the end of treatment in Stravynski, Arbel, Bounader *et al.* (2000) and between 8 and 10 years in Stravynski, Arbel, Gaudette *et al.* (2013).

It is encouraging to note that the remission rates among participants from both studies continued to rise when compared to those observed at the 1-year follow-up. Fully 78% of the participants in the Stravynski, Arbel, Bounader *et al.* (2000) study and 77% in Stravynski, Arbel, *et al.* (2013) trial were in remission (on average) 12 years after the end of their treatment in the former study, and 10 years after the end of their treatment in the latter study. These remission rates were a significant increase from the roughly 55–60% remission rates observed at the 1-year follow-up.

Taken together, these results suggest that the interpersonal approach to treatment, at its best, induces dynamic and gradually expanding improvements of degree, which ultimately become improvements in kind, gradually transfiguring the social life of the participant. Furthermore, the dissolution of the socially phobic pattern, once achieved, seems durable at the very least. An echo of this is heard in the stable drops of reported levels of anxiousness on the one hand and in improved social functioning on the other hand.

The reduction in anxiousness may be expressed, either in relative terms (as a *statistically* significant gain in comparison with pre-treatment levels), or in absolute terms (as a *clinically* significant or meaningful correspondence to a benchmark of "normal" anxiety levels).

In the latter sense, of most interest is the rate of participants who could be considered as having made a meaningful (i.e. clinically significant) improvement by absolute standards. Coincidence or not, the proportion of participants reporting normal levels of anxiety at the long–term follow-up, was almost identical at 54–55 percent (Gibbs *et al.*, 2013) in both (Stravynski, Arbel, Bounader *et al.* 2000; Stravynski, Arbel *et al.*, 2013a) studies.

It should be remembered that within the interpersonal approach, the conceptual link between remission and lesser improvement and severity of anxiousness is not direct (and simple), as it is within an intrapersonal outlook. Anxiety, considered intrapersonally, is a trait – a stable state of the organism – driving socially phobic behavior. By definition, socially phobic conduct would imply high and uniform levels of anxiety. Clinical experience and evidence from pre-treatment assessments suggest that this is hardly the case. Rather, anxiousness is very much situational and, as such, fluctuating and variable.

Within the interpersonal approach, anxiousness is construed as arising dynamically from the interaction of the relatively powerless (e.g. submissive) behavior of the socially phobic, with the relatively powerful behavior of others, acting in a menacing (social and cultural) context. Such a conception accounts for the great variation in anxiousness reported by the same person, in different situations.

As may be gathered from the above definition, the key to interpreting therapeutic progress, within the interpersonal approach, is social functioning and not anxiety levels as such. These would be relative to the quantity and quality of social functioning and have no independent and absolute meaning in themselves. For example, it is conceivable that, in the course of therapy, improvement may be accompanied by rising levels of anxiousness and conversely, regression by a weakening trend of anxiousness.

Thus, in a positive therapeutic development, a continued expansion of social activity, combined with greater risk taking, may result in greater vulnerability and therefore higher levels of anxiousness – initially. As appropriate participation (e.g. adequately enacting a social role) gradually replaces self-protectiveness, levels of anxiousness will drop. In the context of a limited therapeutic outcome, with social functioning restricted to well familiar and predictable interactions, nothing much would give rise to anxiety – unless stepping out of these narrow boundaries becomes necessary or envisaged.

It is worth noting that no significant differences, in terms of severity of reported anxiety, were found between those in remission and those still meeting DSM-IV criteria for social phobia, at the long-term follow-up (Gibbs *et al.*, 2013). Clearly, social phobia is not synonymous with high anxiety levels, or a particularly "disordered" kind of anxiety. Nor is the absence of socially phobic conduct characterized by great serenity. In light of this result, in particular, it is difficult to maintain – theoretically – that anxiety drives social phobia.

In terms of validity, the results concerning anxiety and social functioning at long-term were largely consistent with the gains reported at the 1-year follow-up involving the full sample of participants in the original studies. These encouragingly suggest that, despite the constraints of being able to retrace only a part of the original participants, of whom only a fraction agreed to participate in the long-term follow-up, the resulting outcomes may be deemed not unrepresentative.

The outcome of the interpersonal approach: theoretical aspects

Theoretically, the interpersonal approach to treatment, described earlier, would predict that overall, and regardless of the specific relational problems tackled in each case, and the areas of social functioning (e.g. public or private) eliciting these, the trajectory of socially phobic individuals throughout the therapy process (within an interpersonal space defined by power and mode of relating) would be expected to follow the same path. This would have as its starting point the margins of the respectfully/ submissive quadrant (where these characteristics are highly pronounced) and move, by means of small increments in powerful behavior, towards the center of all quadrants, where all characteristics are finely poised.

That prediction is borne out by Kyparissis, Stravynski and Lachance (2013b). In this study, 85 patients, treated by the interpersonal approach described earlier, filled out an Interpersonal Circumplex (see Plutchik and Conte, 1997) type of measure, adapted from the Interpersonal Check List (Laforge and Suczek, 1955) on four occasions: before and

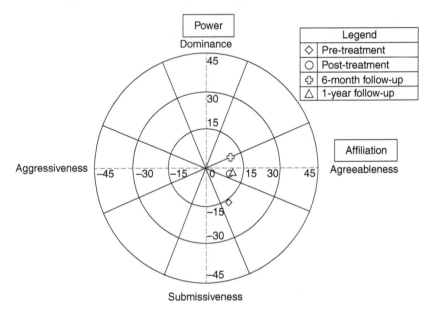

Figure 8.3. *Mean interpersonal axes scores at the pre-treatment, post-treatment, 6-month and 1-year follow-ups, plotted onto the Interpersonal Circumplex*

after treatment, and at 6- and 12-months follow-up. The answers to 88 interpersonal statements were subsequently arranged in a two-dimensional interpersonal space reflecting power and affiliation. Each axis was defined by two ends: dominance–submissiveness and aggressiveness–agreeableness. Combinations of the two are divided into octants. The results may be seen in Figure 8.3.

Consistent with theory, the main change in time was on the power axis. Specifically, participants reported a significant lessening in their powerlessness after the end of treatment. The improvement was maintained over follow-ups of 6 and 12 months. Meaningfully, and in absolute terms, a change in kind was reported. Starting from a relative (non-adaptive) position of powerlessness at the end of treatment, patients leapt to the adaptive area in the center of the Circumplex, shifting from being relatively less powerless to becoming more powerful at the 6-month follow-up.

Specifically, the participants became less submissive over time; significant differences were observed at post-treatment and these gains maintained during follow-up. Within the shrinking of the submissive patterns, significant reductions in the areas of modesty/self-effacement, docility/dependence and mistrust took place after treatment and remained stable

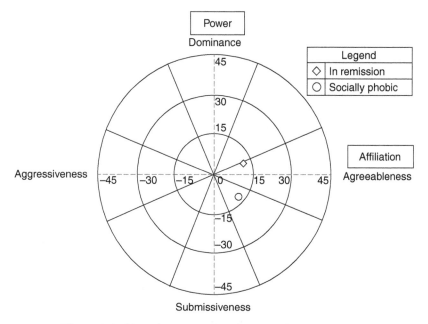

Figure 8.4. *Mean interpersonal axes scores of patients either in remission or still socially phobic at the 1-year follow-up, plotted onto the Interpersonal Circumplex*

Note: The symbol associated with each group is depicted in the legend.

thereafter. These changes dovetail closely with the therapeutic approach described earlier. It is interesting to note that the shrinking of submission, when all participants are included in the analysis, did not give rise to dominance.

The distinction between changes reported by patients who were in remission as compared to those still fulfilling criteria for social phobia at the 1-year follow-up, however, qualify the above result and provide a further test of the theory. The results may be seen in Figure 8.4.

As would have been expected, patients who were no longer socially phobic reported significantly more powerful interpersonal behavior than did those who were still socially phobic. In absolute terms, while both sets of patients were in the adaptive area, those no longer socially phobic were in positive territory, suggesting that they shifted from being less powerless (as were those still socially phobic) to being more powerful (i.e. generating powerful behavior in their social lives). Specifically, those in remission were less submissive and less modest/self-effacing than were their (still) socially phobic counterparts.

No significant changes occurred on the affiliation axis as a whole. Specific changes, however, suggested a more self-assertive and confident manner of relating to others. Consequently, patients tried less hard to please but also (perhaps being less vulnerable) were less critical/hostile and aggressive. These results provide further support to the interpersonal formulation of social phobia and its application to treatment.

Finally, in parallel with the diminishing powerlessness (or rallying of power), corresponding drops in levels of anxiousness were reported. As anxiousness – seen interpersonally – is embedded in powerlessness in the face of threatening social situations, the above result provides indirect support to the theory. The interpersonal approach to treatment, after all, makes no attempt to reduce anxiety as such.

The process of change, delineated in abstract conceptual terms in Kyparissis et al. (2013b), is rendered more palpable by a detailed series of cases studied by Amado (2005). In a first "anthropological" phase, with an emphasis on ecological validity, four socially phobic individuals were studied in their natural environment, while carrying out their normal activities. Two shy and two normal individuals served as control participants.

Information was obtained by means of in-vivo observation, diaries and interviews with each participant, as well as two informants who knew them well. The spheres of social life covered by the study were as follows: work, friends and leisure, family and marital relations. In other words, the social functioning under observation spanned both social activities conducted formally and in public settings, as well as varying degrees of private life, conducted rather informally, sometimes in public sometimes in private intimacy.

Overall, the socially phobic tended towards evasiveness, fleeing or avoiding situations, whenever possible. When feeling compelled to take part in an activity or remain in a situation, their presence was muted and self-effacing.

When pushed into a corner and elusive tactics to no avail, the socially phobic subject could become belligerent, as a last resort. This bout of aggressiveness, however, was quick to fizzle out and seemed defensive rather offensive in nature. It was a means towards putting an end to acrimonious exchanges and to disengage, rather than towards intimidating, for the sake of domination.

Altogether, the frequency of use of self-protective patterns was found to be in proportion to the degree of formality of the setting, and in inverse proportion to the degree of intimacy of the relationship, with the people involved.

In a second phase, the socially phobic patients were treated by the interpersonal approach during a 14-session course of treatment.

Towards the end of treatment, the various self-protective patterns began to erode. Evasive distance keeping was on the wane, while participatory involvement and self-assertive conduct were on the rise. As a result of greater forthrightness and expressivity, conflict situations were better handled, and, consequently, fewer defensive outbursts of aggressiveness and subsequent sulkiness were observed.

In the main, the conduct of the socially phobic became more like that of the normal and the shy (who were also observed during the naturalistic pre-treatment phase), in that they sought out others and engaged them, rather than observing social life passively, from the removes of a safety zone.

Formal public settings, requiring the performance of formal social roles, however, remained an area of vulnerability, where anxiously self-protective behavior would intermittently resurface.

Theoretically, anxiousness is linked to interpersonal defensiveness. During successful treatment, defensiveness crumbles as it is replaced by more powerful behavior, deployed for the sake of a greater and better participation. It would be predicted that such structural changes in interpersonal behavior would be followed, although in a lagging fashion, by a reduction in the levels of attendant anxiousness. This process delineated in Stravynski, Grey and Elie (1987) corroborates this hypothesis.

The outcome of the interpersonal approach in comparison

As social phobia is commonly construed as an abnormal anxiety state or anxiety disorder, most treatments devised for it seek to alleviate anxiety. Consistent with this outlook, the primary outcome in most studies is reduction in anxiety. While the treatments achieve significant improvements relative to pre-treatment levels, it remains generally unknown how meaningful these are in absolute terms, in reference, for example, to normal functioning.

However it may be, by this standard, the interpersonal approach matches or exceeds the improvements reported with other psychological treatments (see Stravynski, 2007, pp. 289–334). In relative terms, in Stravynski, Arbel, Bounader et al. (2000), for example, 60% of the patients reported more than 50% improvement in the tendency to avoid, while 40% reporting this (considerable) magnitude of reduction in the intensity of anxious distress.

In absolute terms, the proportion of participants rating their anxiety at "normal" levels was 64% at the end of treatment and 50% at the 1-year follow-up in Stravynski, Arbel, Bounader et al. (2000). The corresponding proportions were 70% and 85% in Stravynski, Arbel et al. (2013a).

In summary, the relative and absolute sets of results, in terms of anxiety reduction, suggest that the interpersonal approach meaningfully reduces anxiety (although within its own terms of reference, it is not the chief goal of therapy).

The goal of therapy in the interpersonal approach is the shrinking and weakening of defensive and self-protective interpersonal patterns. In that sense, and clinically speaking, the best quantifiable result is remission; this encapsulates both manageable levels of anxiety and a relatively unimpaired social functioning. Defined as the failure to satisfy the defining criteria of social phobia, remission sets an absolute standard. By contrast, statistically significant changes relative to pre-treatment levels are likely to be modest in terms of the difference they make to patients' lives.

To my knowledge, only one study (Clark et al., 2006) is comparable, in this respect, to the outcome issued from the interpersonal approach. Clark et al. (2006) assigned 62 socially phobic patients to 14 weekly sessions of either cognitive therapy (CT) (n=21), exposure (Ex) with applied relaxation (n=21) or a waiting list (WL) (n=20). Remission rates at the end of treatment were: 86% for CT, 45% for Ex and 5% for the WL.

Some of these results give rise to puzzlement. First of all, CT typically results in outcomes similar to exposure (not necessarily remission) (see Stravynski, 2007, pp. 291–299). That CT in Clark et al. (2006) would induce a remission rate double that of Ex is singular and would need to be reconfirmed. Finally, the fact that 5% of the patients on the WL remitted spontaneously goes against the grain; it makes one wonder about the severity of social phobia of the study participants.

All the same, the rates of remission issued from the outcome of the interpersonal approach, on average (roughly 50–60%), match the average (about 65%) reported by Clark et al. (2006), in a similar time frame.

Practically speaking, attempts to change aspects of social functioning are found in other treatment approaches, either deliberately or inadvertently. For example, "cognitive therapy," although conceptually concerned with remedying beliefs and thought processes – construed as the causal factors maintaining anxiety – guides patients to drop "safety behaviors," and to attend to interactions with other people and to be themselves (e.g. Clark et al., 2003). Speculatively speaking, it is possible that these "activating procedures," shorn of their theoretical rationale, prod socially phobic patients into a more outgoing and participatory mold, and thereby help directly in improving social functioning and diminishing anxiety.

The fact that this was found to be the case, in the context of the "cognitive therapy" of depression (Jacobson *et al.*, 1996), is suggestive.

The same principle may be operative in the application of "interpersonal therapy" to the treatment of social phobia. Developed for depression and reliant on a psychodynamic (i.e. an intrapersonal) conceptual analysis, "interpersonal therapy" is concerned with the exploration of interpersonal difficulties in four areas: grief, "role dispute" (i.e. conflict), "role transition" (i.e. grown children leaving home) and "interpersonal deficits" (i.e. isolation). How such explorations are applied to the treatment of social phobia is unclear. Needless to say, the self-labeling of the therapy as "interpersonal" is incongruous, from the perspective of the interpersonal approach articulated in this book, as it is not concerned with interactions between persons in the social environment.

Regardless of the ambiguity of its key constructs (e.g. "role insecurity"), the therapy leads to a significant reduction of anxiety and improvement in social functioning (Borge *et al.*, 2008; Lipsitz *et al.*, 2008), equivalent to that obtained with cognitive therapy. One is tempted to speculate that this has much to do with the "encouragement of emotional expression ... and of social activity" (Stangier, von Consbruch, Schramm and Heidrich, 2010, p. 290).

Conclusion

The interpersonal approach to treatment, presented in this chapter, was molded by two decisions taken in earlier chapters. Firstly, the received notion of social phobia as anxiety disorder (or disease) was rejected as theoretically unsound and empirically unsubstantiated. Secondly, the act of rejection gave rise to an alternative – interpersonal – formulation of social phobia. This led to a corresponding causal analysis. This understanding of social phobia as multi-causal provides the framework that organizes the interpersonal approach to undermining and undoing social phobia.

For all intents and purposes, this approach seeks to shrink and subsequently dissolve defensive interpersonal patterns, and the self-protective goals they are aiming at. This is achieved by means of a process (best described as one of learning) of building up and improving social functioning for the sake of a greater and better (especially in terms of enactment of social roles) participation in social life. Such participation ranges from the impersonal (in the public domain) to the personal (in intimate circumstances).

The treatment process is created jointly and cooperatively. The therapist brings to it the explanatory framework, the interpersonal functional analysis, and as an upshot, interpersonal objectives and realistic means for their achievement. The therapist also oversees the process of learning empathetically, by organizing a sequence of "educational" experiences. Structuring and pacing these, as well as providing an example and encouragement, help to adjust the process to fit individual circumstances, character and abilities.

The socially phobic individual must bring to this encounter a serious involvement and a determination to turn his or her life around. The sorts of changes pursued during therapy – as with any skill – require a certain initial fortitude, followed by constant practice, for the sake of honing and improving the pattern of conduct. The ambitious might even try excelling at it.

Formulated theoretically, relative powerlessness and defensiveness gradually diminish and turn into a relatively powerful involvement and cooperation. Out of the interpersonal transformation arise emotional changes and a transfigured outlook. Greater and better participation give rise to a concomitant drop in fearfulness and apprehensiveness, followed by greater confidence and poise.

When put to a test in controlled trials, an intensive but relatively short-term (14 sessions) application of the interpersonal approach yields most promising outcomes. Bearing in mind the average 25-year duration of social phobia among the participants, the interpersonal approach results in a remission rate of between 50 and 60 percent at the 1-year follow-up. Most gratifyingly, these results remain (at least) stable at up to 15 years' follow-up.

Although results for the sake of intelligibility have been presented in terms of remission rates, the interpersonal approach is not curative in its orientation. Formulated in terms of current clichés, it does not so much care to cure "mental illness," as it seeks to promote "mental health." This much is apparent from the fact that it does not focus on the anxious distress – the chief complaint of most socially phobic individuals. Rather, it promotes competence, involvement in social life and, within it, a cooperative autonomy – all crucial ingredients for "constructive social development and personal well-being" (Ryan and Deci, 2000, p. 68).

Part V

Conclusions

"The empiricist thinks he believes only what he sees, but he is much better at believing than at seeing."

Santayana

9   Concluding remarks

Conceptual foundations

My declared aim at the outset was to provide the best explanatory framework for social phobia. I argued that the means to that end was to construe social phobia interpersonally. This required the fashioning of an alternative psychology to serve as the foundation for the subsequent interpersonal analysis and formulation. It is useful to summarize this alternative psychology; it provides the foundations for the conclusions to follow. By way of contrast, a brief outline of the received – non-interpersonal – view is necessary.

Psychology viewed *intrapersonally* deals with the "mental," delineating and studying various hypothetical constructs (e.g. intelligence, anxiety) and processes, allegedly exerting a causal control over behavior. In this view, the world – social and otherwise –is but a backdrop or a stage for the enactment of various scenarios essentially dictated from within. As the neat parceling out between "genetic and environmental" factors in twin studies illustrates, no interaction is assumed to occur between the two (see Richardson, 2000, pp. 65–69). States of mind, for this and other reasons, are considered stable and unvarying features, and may therefore be meaningfully captured by one score (e.g. intelligence; see Richardson, 2002). Meaning, in this rather implacably mechanical universe, is assigned solipsistically, from within. For example, the unsteady and sweaty hands of which the socially phobic complain are considered to be "symptoms" of anxiety, no more meaningful than coughing and sneezing in the case of a respiratory tract infection.

Furthermore, many in this field of inquiry nurture a deep suspicion that these "states of mind" sit on top of a rich vein of biological substratum (genetically transmitted, it goes without saying) to be mined and processed subsequently. In the fullness of time, it is permitted to hope, the mental will be re-transcribed into the neuro-chemical and, ultimately, the physical, perhaps in terms of elementary particles.

The anthropological psychology, which has been put forward as a foundation for the interpersonal perspective, rejects the above principles, namely dualism and reductionism – perhaps, simplified outrageously. The bedrock of its skepticism is the questioning of "mind" as an independent "agent," as well as doubting that mind is really the brain in disguise.

In their stead, it suggests understanding the undivided living human individual as an active participant in a social and cultural way of life, carried out in a certain social and cultural environment. Such a premise makes an intrapersonal or individualistic account, either in terms of mind or body, unintelligible.

Persons are whole and unified organisms. Human activities, notably speech, are actions in the world and not an expression of an inner realm. Nothing hidden from view (but observable privately) goes on "behind" the behavior.

Rather, in life's activities, all human powers combine together in a meaningful way. Human conduct is permeated with thought and suffused with emotion; these are manifest in it, and can be divorced from behavior only speculatively. There are no separate faculties. Rather, people can only behave emotionally, intelligently, and so on. These capacities (intelligence, emotion) of the living human being are not independent, but overlap and shade off into each other. The whole living being is involved in every experience, and putting it figuratively, the whole living being and the world embrace and intertwine.

Most importantly, humans are sociable beings and live their lives through relationships with others. Human relationships are embedded in larger societal and cultural systems. These encompass language, ideas about the nature of the universe, a system of morals often embedded in a religious outlook, political and economic organization, kinship, dress, diet, rites of passage, and so on.

A mode of life is a system of relationships, exhibiting regularities of patterns and configurations of social conduct, organized by a formal framework. The system is evident from the fabric of human existence within it. A way of life is thus, simultaneously, the extent of its practices and the norms governing it.

Psychological processes are attuned to circumstances and change in lock step with these; psychological processes cannot be formulated independently of interpersonal and sociocultural considerations.

The conduct of people in times of war is a case in point. Killing (murder) is a rare phenomenon; yet it becomes casual when ordinary men (soon women too?) are put in uniform, given weapons and organized in military units under orders to kill the enemy (see Browning, 1993, and Bartov, 2001 for examples). Such a dramatic change in behavior is inconceivable and unaccountable from an intrapersonal point of view (an epidemic of brain malfunctioning? a breakout of biased homicidal cognitions?). It becomes intelligible only within the framework of societal mass processes, embedded in particular cultures. Such licenced and "acceptable" killing is perpetrated out of loyalty to the community and society and on its behalf, as it were; the group is the killing organization.

Meanings attached to conduct, therefore, are social and cultural. Individuality is a variation on these common themes. The same underhand conduct may be considered admirable (e.g. cunning) and a matter of pride in one segment of society, while taken to be despicable and demeaning (and therefore shameful) in another. Finally, such a psychology views all human attributes dynamically, as emerging out of a ceaseless dialectical interaction with their social environment and fashioned by it. Last but not least, all life activities – including those of the socially phobic – are senseless, unless understood purposefully (see Campbell, 2010), as having a function within a specific form of life (considered empathetically).

For all the above reasons (see Putnam, 1994, for a systematic argument), I took the anthropological psychology underpinning the interpersonal approach, linking the active (undivided) individual to his or her social and cultural environment, to be an autonomous domain – irreducible to other levels of inquiry. Psychology on this view, while grounded in the physical make up and organization of persons as well as their emergent powers, is not determined by it, as it depends also on external conditions.

The fact that humans have historically functioned in such a variety of social arrangements and cultures (e.g. Chinese communism, US capitalism in the twentieth century), under propitious (e.g. peaceful cooperation and prosperity) and inimical conditions (e.g. war-time devastation and want), suggests the possibility that multiple psychological attributes may be realized by different configurations of lower level biological structures, as called for by environmental conditions. Vast individual differences may also be seen as an illustration of this possibility.

Fearfulness, for example, is not realized in identical fashion physiologically and anatomically. It cannot be identified from a set pattern of brain activity. The amygdala – a brain structure active in fear states – is also involved in other emotional responses, apparently as a function of the intensity of any stimulation – pleasant (e.g. erotic) or aversive (e.g. menacing – see Hamann, 2005, p. 288).

For these reasons, anxiousness may be best considered a variable functional psychological state, evoked by specific circumstances, rather than a definite physiological or biochemical entity. In a similar vein, evolution, for example, depends on variations in the genotype but also on the environment. In that sense, the evolutionary process, while conforming to the laws of physics and chemistry, cannot be deducible or predicted from these laws (Putnam, 1994).

As I recapitulate the various themes taken up throughout the book, much will be found that is compatible with the above first principles and very little that constitutes a serious challenge.

What is social phobia and what is its nature?

Although considering social phobia a *disorder* of anxiety might appear plausible on the strength of the complaints of those who are seeking help, the evidence in support of it is slim at best.

However defined and measured (usually as a lay construct, quantified subjectively), in absolute terms, no specific sort of socially phobic (or abnormal social) anxiety has been identified. Palpitations, trembling and sweating, for example, taken to be indicative of anxiety, are reported not only by the socially phobic but also by various other categories of individuals (e.g. normal, shy, other disorders).

In quantitative terms, no specific demarcation point cuts off abnormal social anxiety from the normal sort. Thus, although socially phobic individuals typically rate themselves subjectively as more anxious than do normal individuals, the difference between the two is one of degree, rather than of kind. This also applies to the various subtypes of social phobia. Additionally, if intermediate degrees of severity (subclinical fears) are taken into account, the results become consistent with a continuum of social fears, with the socially phobic (as a group), at its high end.

However, when what are considered physiological indices of anxiety are objectively measured in the laboratory (admittedly evoked by somewhat artificial social tasks), the differences – significant on the continuum of subjective anxiety – blur (e.g. Gerlach *et al.*, 2001) and in some studies vanish altogether (e.g. Edelmann and Baker, 2002). Objectively then, the distinction between socially phobic and normal individuals is not to be found in anxiousness; it lies elsewhere.

In a survey conducted by Stein *et al.* (1994), 85 percent of the 519 participants (a sample representative of the population of Winnipeg) identified public speaking – a typical socially phobic concern – as the worst situation in terms of "nervousness." While the degree of distress varied, it is obvious that "nervousness" in such a social situation is the norm. Musicians and singers for instance, commonly report "stage fright" (performance anxiety) and so do other artists.

Thus, anxiousness in social settings, unlike social phobia, is commonplace. It is prefigured to some extent in childhood, increasingly evident in adolescence and fully manifest in adulthood, evoked by dealings with authorities and a variety of socially competitive activities. Given its ubiquity, social anxiety could plausibly be considered an adaptive mechanism, conferring a protective advantage from an evolutionary point of view (see Gilbert, 2001). Social anxiety or sensitivity (Stravynski et al., 1995b) about evoking displeasure in others is protective of the individual and doubtless plays a role in reducing strife and, hence, increases cohesion within the group. Viewed from that vantage point, the maladaptive interpersonal pattern of social phobia might be seen as the extended misuse of highly adaptive, short-term defensive tactics.

In sum, nothing in terms of anxiety suggests that the socially phobic are obviously abnormal. It is not revealed in any specific comparison, whether the anxious responses are conceived narrowly (e.g. tremor, pallor, sweat) or broadly (e.g. avoidance, hiding, immobility). Nor are the threatening social situations (evoking these) unusual or abnormal. The differences that have been identified (in self-reported subjective distress) are exacerbations (at times extreme) of apparently normal tendencies. If this conclusion is warranted, it follows that social phobia cannot be characterized in terms of anxiety alone. Pondering information concerning anxiety, as such, would not allow the identification or prediction of social phobia or other anxiety states, normal or abnormal.

Is social phobia then, although not necessarily a disorder of anxiety as such, a disorder nevertheless? If disorder is taken as the equivalent of disease, defined concretely rather than figuratively, the notion itself does not withstand critical scrutiny, nor is there compelling evidence to shore it up.

In most respects, the bulk of the results surveyed in Chapter 4 are consistent with the fact that on any measure – be it neurotransmission or brain activity – the socially phobic are far more alike their normal counterparts than different from them. Altogether, and this time in absolute terms, no major structural, neuro-chemical or endocrine abnormalities associated with social phobia have come to light (Stravynski, 2007, pp. 143–167).

If social phobia cannot be regarded as a disorder/disease of anxiety, is at least considering it as a natural kind – as the classification manuals seem to be doing – justified? On current evidence, some aspects of social phobia (that stand up fairly well) provide a qualified support for its being a coherent construct. Thus, the socially phobic pattern seems to be identified reliably in interviews. Social phobia is associated consistently with more severe difficulties in a greater number of social situations and a poorer social functioning. Finally, social phobia has a fairly distinctive age of onset and a fairly equal sex distribution; it typically precedes other disorders (e.g. anxiety, affective) with which it has strong affinities.

Unfortunately, these observations are not enough to ground a hypothetical construct and much evidence questions the validity of social phobia as an entity. The most damning is that no specific factors, on any level of analysis (social, cognitive, biological, developmental), have been shown to be associated reliably with social phobia. Furthermore, social phobia has strong links with other putative entities with pronounced anxious features (e.g. agoraphobia, anorexia/bulimia, depression) as well as various personality disorders. This raises the possibility that social phobia, far from being an independent, sharply defined entity, has rather porous borders, and constitutes a possible element in an even larger and perhaps unstable pattern, forming and reforming, in response to evolving life circumstances.

What then are the unique characteristics of social phobia, allowing its characterization in these terms? A related question concerns the nature of social phobia or its identity; namely, what is it an instance of?

Social phobia can be described distinctively in interpersonal terms. The main interpersonal patterns making up social phobia are best seen as a host of tactics, organized as elements in a defensive strategy, having as an aim self-protection from bruising interactions. To this end, risk taking is minimized by keeping a safe distance from (dangerous) social events whenever possible; when necessary, social activities are engaged in with fearful submission and passive dependence (refraining from any provocation as it were).

In aggregate, and abstracted from the specific transactions with a myriad of social dangers personified by individuals and settings, social phobia is a fearful and relatively powerless web of interpersonal patterns (constituted of various sub-patterns), protective against the threat of humiliation (either as public degradation or private personal rejection).

Humiliation is experienced when one is treated brutally or hurtfully as an impostor, as it were, pretending to be what one cannot possibly be, laying claim to an undeserved dignity of membership or status.

The integrated, socially phobic pattern is abnormal for two reasons. First of all, it is grievously upsetting and distressing. Secondly, it seriously compromises the ability of the individual to carry out desired personal goals and to participate fully in groups, institutions and communities.

Every socially phobic individual exhibits this fearful pattern (characterizing only social phobia), with "avoidant personality disorder" probably being its most severe manifestation.

Fearfulness – the all-purpose state of alarm, permeating the defensive behavior and arising out of its interaction with the menacing social context, undergirds the self-protective tactics (distancing, evasiveness, submissiveness), while readying the individual to respond to further threats that may arise. Anxiousness arises with, and is involved in shaping the interpersonal self-protective activity, while sustaining the process of its unfolding.

While the socially phobic differ markedly from normal individuals, it is not so much in terms of the anxiety reactions associated with and directed towards specific transactions (e.g. being under scrutiny), but cumulatively, as a sequence of various fearful self-protective patterns of conduct, displayed at different times, in various spheres of social life. Only the socially phobic enact the overall pattern. The various elements constituting it, both interpersonal and emotional, are within normal range.

What is the nature of social phobia or, put differently, what is its identity? It is easiest to start with what it is not.

Social phobia is not demonstrably an entity, let alone a disease entity, existing independently of the social and cultural world, stably coherent within, with a core of necessary properties, and well differentiated from other entities near (i.e. other anxiety or personality disorders) or far (i.e. normality). Nor are the socially phobic – the members of this putative category – identical. Social phobia is characterized by a great heterogeneity, both in degree but also in kind, especially when it is associated with other co-occurring disorders or some of their features (e.g. inordinate concerns about appearance).

Moreover, every feature of social phobia can be located on a continuum; an exacerbation of, but in continuity with, normality. None is a unique characteristic of social phobia.

In purely scientific terms then, no compelling argument justifies considering social phobia a categorical entity, as its taxonomic classification currently implies.

In the final analysis, and bearing in mind all the above considerations, it is most fitting to consider social phobia as a pragmatic category. The main strength of this kind of category is flexibility and therefore usefulness, both practical and theoretical. The designation of pragmatic category fits comfortably with the reality of social phobia.

First of all, such a category acknowledges that the membership within it is distributed on a continuum, varying in degree of resemblance, with no members necessarily identical. Furthermore, such a category itself is located on a continuum with normality, with distinctions at times blurred and made on practical grounds (i.e. social functioning).

Secondly, it accommodates a dynamic social phobia, extended in time and permanently in flux, both in terms of the elements making up the various interpersonal patterns, as well as the web of patterns constituting the overall social phobic cluster – in relation to specific situations and life circumstances.

Finally, a pragmatic category is rich in theoretical potential, as it admits the possibility of different ways of conceptualizing the nature of social phobia. Casting social phobia in relational, rather than medical terms, for example, frees social phobia from the straitjacket of being cast in the mold of a stable and unvarying medical "condition," inviting a quest for "etiology" (the touchstone that will resolve all perplexities and presumably establish what social phobia is "really" like).

A pragmatic approach to the identity of social phobia, by being unprejudiced, allows the relative merits of different perspectives, the interpersonal, but also others, to be judged by the only standard that matters – their explanatory power; the ability to integrate most – if not all – known facts about social phobia.

What causes social phobia?

It is commonly considered (e.g. in the DSM-5) that socially phobic behavior stems from abnormal levels (or kind) of anxiety. An attempt to understand social phobia as a disease or a "disorder" implies the identification of the processes causing such allegedly abnormal anxiety. Within such an outlook prevails "an intuitive concept of disorder that underlies medical judgment and is widely shared by health professionals – that the symptoms of disorder are due to an internal process that is not functioning as expected (i.e. an internal dysfunction)" (Wakefield *et al.*, 2002, p. 380).

On this view, anxiety is the expression of the dysfunction of certain (unknown) regulatory mechanisms within the individual; social phobia, then, would be its ultimate consequence.

The quest for the inner sources of "abnormal" anxiety is in part vitiated by the fact that the anxiousness experienced by the socially phobic is very much of the common or garden variety – undistinguished and indistinguishable from any other kind.

Be that as it may, in current practice, malfunctioning processes would be envisaged as either physical (typically "neurophysiologic") or "mental" (as in mental disease) – however defined. This is in keeping with the reductionist construal of the human, made up of a machine-like body (Taylor, 1970, p. 62; Shepherd, 1993, p. 569), within which dwells a non-material "ghostly" mind.

In both domains, causality is envisaged as an antecedent event (Taylor, 1970, p. 49), a transmittal of force (or its failure) from one contiguous element to another. The action of each element is explained by the "force" exerted by the element lower down the chain of transmission. Although in the material domain a mechanical system is literally possible, in the "mental realm" the chain can only be metaphorical, with expectations, intentions, interpretations, and so on acting as figurative links in a chain and metaphorically satisfying the requirement of contiguity. Social phobia then, construed as a faulty mechanism, would be the result of defects in, malfunction of, or altogether a breakdown of such an orderly transmission.

The search for bodily and "mental" malfunctioning as a cause of "anxiety" – that potent, but insubstantial hypothetical entity with agency – that, in turn, is the cause of social phobia, has generated elaborate research programs. These are highly valuable, allowing the evaluation not only of concepts and underlying assumptions, but also of the evidence to which they give rise.

The causal view of the bodily (i.e. biomedical) outlook on social phobia may be summarized by two interlinked propositions postulating the following:

1. the anxiety driving the socially phobic pattern of behavior is caused by unspecified (molecular or cellular) events in particular regions of the brain of the individual exhibiting it;
2. something coded in the genes of the individual displaying the socially phobic pattern predisposes him or her to such a brain malfunction.

Neither hypothesis has been corroborated.

First of all, altogether no specific neurobiology, let alone "pathophysiology," of social phobia has been brought to light. The socially phobic, therefore, cannot be identified or characterized in these terms. The intense reactivity of the "fear-network" is hardly exclusive to social phobia (see Gorman *et al.*, 2000). Moreover, all such reactions fall within the normal range. The state of overexcitement of the brain, then, is associated with social phobia not specifically, but indirectly, as an instance of intense fearfulness. An intensified brain activity is involved in and sustains the active process of fearing of the whole living organism (human or otherwise) in the face of threat, be it phobic or not. Such activity is a facet or a correlate of social phobia; it can hardly be considered its cause.

Similarly, no clear association between genes encoding for functional proteins of different monoaminergic systems and social phobia was established. These findings are consistent with results from a host of neurotransmission studies in which no major abnormality in monoaminergic function could be detected.

All in all, no systematic evidence supporting the hypothesis that social phobia (as a fully fledged pattern of conduct) might be transmitted genetically has been brought to light. Furthermore, the fact that social phobia is to a high degree associated with numerous co-occurring disorders (see Stravynski, 2007, pp. 105–111) makes the hypothesis that all are under specific and separate genetic control quite implausible.

If no evidence of disease in the socially phobic brain (body) has come to light, could it be lodged in the socially phobic mind? Notwithstanding the insistent claims that studies "revealing the causal contributions made by specific types of cognitive bias to anxiety symptomatology" (MacLeod and Mathews, 2012, p. 210) abound, the overall evidence does not support that conclusion.

First of all, no cognitive processes (or their configurations) uniquely typifying socially phobic individuals have been identified. In that sense, social phobia can neither be characterized nor predicted in terms of such processes, for these processes are non-specific and widely shared.

Secondly, no cognitive factor or process has been shown to exercise a causal control over anxiousness or the socially phobic pattern as a whole, and to be in evidence in every socially phobic individual. Such control would imply a tight link between cause and effect. Statistical differences, notwithstanding, all groups, the socially phobic as well as contrast participants, exhibited similar cognitive processes but to differing degrees. While the socially phobic reported a higher degree of these widely shared cognitive features, it is baffling that only the socially phobic participants were socially phobic. Need not effect be present when the cause is manifest and vice versa? As there typically were considerable overlaps between the groups, it is implausible that causality depended on the reaching of a certain threshold.

In summary, the non-specific cognitive processes associated with social phobia are its correlates. As co-occurring features, these are manifest to varying degrees in various individuals and probably absent in some. These, therefore, can hardly be claimed to cause either the anxiety that allegedly drives social phobia or cause social phobia directly.

The main implication of these results, issued from the two strands of reductive dualism, is that social phobia is not reducible to sub-personal units of analysis. First of all, no sub-personal essence or process uniquely characterizes social phobia, allowing it to be described in those terms, or predicting it from such information. Secondly, no dimension or feature of social phobia, on any level of analysis, exercises a controlling effect on social phobia as a whole.

Knowing something about these processes does not contribute much, if at all, to an understanding of social phobia.

If these conclusions are accurate, the quest for understanding of social phobia is, in all likelihood, hindered by remaining in the narrow confines of a reductive dualistic logic. Applied as it is to the ambiguous construct of anxiety, with its theoretically murky causal role, such a quest is flawed and misguided. Persisting in this way, while perhaps contributing yet more information, clarifies little. In terms of understanding, however, it thickens the conceptual confusion.

As an alternative, the interpersonal approach offers a viable causal analysis, endowed with considerable explanatory power (about which more later). Its cornerstone is the fact that social phobia can be characterized and uniquely described in interpersonal terms. Indeed, social phobia can only be described in such terms. As was discussed earlier, attempts to describe social phobia as being prey to anxiety, for example, founder; social phobia is made intelligible only in interpersonal terms.

The causal analysis compatible with an interpersonal perspective borrows from Aristotle and relies on his hylomorphic world view. In this analysis, social phobia is a multi-causal phenomenon.

Social phobia can only be manifested by an embodied human being, endowed with typical human powers. This is the material cause of social phobia. Although a necessary condition, there is nothing distinctively socially phobic about this.

I shall now turn to the main factors germane to the causal analysis of social phobia. The settings, events and individuals (all evoking socially phobic responses) act as the proximate cause. These fearsome situations exercise control over the socially phobic web of patterns and actualize these interpersonal patterns. Aspects of the overall pattern come to the fore when the proper (i.e. menacing) environmental conditions are present. The socially phobic reactions (e.g. fearful vigilance, procrastination) are in abeyance in their absence. Crucially, the behaviors of the socially phobic, as well as those of their interlocutors (in the fearsome situations), are intertwined and determine dynamically each other. Altogether, the socially phobic interpersonal conduct is intelligible only in its environmental context.

The socially phobic interpersonal organization (or relational pattern) with the social world serves as the formal cause. It is best likened to a strategy, integrating the various sub-patterns (characteristically vigilant distance keeping whenever possible, submissive dependence, if not) or relational tactics in the repertoire of the socially phobic. Anxiousness within this framework is the emotional tenor pervading the (fearful) interpersonal activities. It is a process inherent in the socially phobic behavior and oriented towards the threatening circumstances that evoke it.

The ultimate cause – the function of behavior – specifies its purpose. Put differently, it identifies for the sake of what the socially phobic sequence of actions is performed. It makes the socially phobic exertions meaningful. Living organisms, from bacteria to socially phobic humans, cannot be understood fully without considering their activities functionally or purposefully (Campbell, 2010). The ultimate cause is obviously intimately bound up with the formal cause; in a manner of speaking, the latter is the means to the former. As the relational means deployed by the socially phobic are predominantly cautiously defensive, it can be rather safely inferred that this is done for the sake of self-protection from social injury (e.g. being ignored, snubbed, criticized, mocked).

This analytic framework integrates the most important aspects of social phobia and thereby clarifies it. The multiplicity of analytical perspectives brings one closer to the reality of social phobia. Not least, this analysis makes socially phobic conduct meaningful.

Finally, although not being, strictly speaking, part of the causal analysis, it is relevant to ask how the extended socially phobic interpersonal pattern – the formal cause – comes about. The answer, within the interpersonal perspective, is that its origins are historic, involving a process contingent on various circumstances and vicissitudes. Crucially, this interactive historic trajectory is undetermined by any single factor, constitutional (e.g. temperamental) or environmental. Understanding how the individual interpersonal pattern develops historically illuminates the workings of the formal cause. It also sheds light on social phobia as a whole.

Applications

Nothing is more practical than a good theory. The interpersonal framework has two practical repercussions. First of all, given an appropriate assessment, it allows a causal analysis of *every case* of social phobia. Secondly, such an analysis provides the foundation, as well as practical guidelines, for efforts to undermine, disintegrate and ultimately overhaul the socially phobic relational pattern, together with its self-protective function. This is achieved best by fostering new relational patterns, incompatible with the fearful defensiveness characterizing social phobia. Namely, these would combine a courageous self-assertion on the one hand and cooperation on the other. Both are combined in the interest of a greater and better (mastering and enacting social roles) involvement in social life.

The explanatory range of the interpersonal theory of social phobia

What is wrong with the socially phobic?

Knowledgeable observers (Frances and Widiger, 2012 – involved in the making of the DSM-IV) of psychiatric classification – consider the "classification of mental disorders" as "no more than a collection of fallible constructs that seek but never find an elusive truth" (p. 113). The "DSM does its job reasonably well if it is applied properly and its limitations are understood" (p. 113).

Unfortunately, this is not quite how these constructs are used. On the one hand, the "diagnostic entities" satisfy the desire to "explain" suffering by labeling it, while providing the necessary communication tools. These are doubtless the legitimate uses alluded to earlier (p. 113). On the other hand, these constructs are anchoring research. In that context, the entities listed in diagnostic manuals (social phobia amongst them), are treated as independent and mutually exclusive disease entities or "mental disorders," as if possessing stable essential characteristics, in evidence in everyone so afflicted. Furthermore, the validity of these entities is taken for granted and unquestioned, unleashing the quest to establish their "etiology," the elusive presumed malfunctioning.

When applied to social phobia, the explanatory power of the disease/ disorder perspective is exceedingly narrow and rather impoverished, as it relies on anxiety alone – its only explanatory concept. Anxiety may be deep, but it does not reach far.

Putting aside all quibbles about its validity and measurement, the perspective of social phobia as an anxiety disorder assumes a stable level of "abnormal" anxiety, generated by malfunctioning inner mechanisms or processes. Such an outlook provides no account of the fluctuating degrees of anxiety experienced by a socially phobic individual in the course of their days, let alone the great individual variability in anxiety rates among the socially phobic as a group.

Furthermore, as the anxiousness of the socially phobic is of an undifferentiated sort, found in varying degrees in different populations, how would anxiety result in social phobia in one case, panic in another, and combine social phobia with obsessive-compulsive disorder in a third? Why does anxiousness rise to a feverish pitch in normal individuals on occasion (e.g. as a wedding day approaches) and subside subsequently, without making them socially phobic?

To take the argument further, the disease/disorder framework also fails to explain how a nominally independent socially phobic entity, driven by anxiety, co-occurs ("co-morbid") in meaningful rates with other supposedly mutually exclusive entities, belonging to the vast category of anxiety disorders and, apparently, driven by the very same anxiety.

And what of the very high prevalence of social anxieties in other – non-anxiety – disorders (e.g. body dysmorphic and bulimic)? How can it be contended, in terms of anxiety alone, that these rather socially anxious individuals are not socially phobic? The claim that anxiety is the factor explaining social phobia is scarcely defensible.

All these baffling conundrums dissipate, as dew in the sunshine, within the interpersonal explanatory framework.

Under the interpersonal conception, fluctuations of anxiousness arise out of the (typically defensive) relational patterns deployed and oriented towards menacing social settings and other participants. As both the evoking situations and the evoked states of preparedness (directed at these), change constantly, so do the levels of anxiousness attending these efforts. Within the interpersonal explanatory framework, a steady level of abnormal anxiety is scarcely conceivable.

The high degree of variability of fearfulness is foretold by the fact that although social phobia is characterized by a risk-minimizing defensive interpersonal strategy (aiming at self-protection), the actual overall pattern (i.e. the strategy) differs from person to person in terms of the sub-patterns (i.e. the actual tactics) that it fields. These differences are tied to individual life circumstances, and therefore to specific situations evoking the socially phobic responses. These, in turn, emerge from the historic trajectory, during which the socially phobic pattern, with all its elements, was – and continues – to be forged. Socially phobic conduct and its anxious emotional face are meaningful only in an interpersonal context; each co-varies with the other.

In epidemiological studies (Stravynski, 2007, pp. 105–112), social phobia is found to have close links with other hypothetical entities with pronounced anxious/affective features (e.g. panic, anorexia/bulimia nervosa, body dysmorphic disorder, alcoholism and depression). This is baffling if social phobia is considered a self-contained entity. Is the socially phobic "patient" so debilitated that he or she is prone to various other diseases?

The anomaly of "co-morbidities" among social phobia and other "disorders" is easily resolved within the interpersonal perspective. Within the interpersonal explanatory framework, these are not considered mutually exclusive and independent natural entities, but rather abnormal inter-personal patterns of conduct – pragmatic constructs – best understood functionally, as self-protective. Endowed with permeable boundaries and sharing a common purpose, their co-occurrence is easily assimilated. These become additional tactics, within a wider strategic web.

Seen in this light, panic (i.e. intense surges of anxiousness) or other fearful patterns (e.g. agoraphobia – stay close to one's base of safety or trusted companions) simply widen the range of the self-protective pattern or strategy of social phobia and complement it, in keeping with particular evoking circumstances.

The taking of prescribed medication, or dosing oneself with alcohol, may be seen as additional self-protective measures, seeking to control anxiousness and diminish vulnerability – a second line, in a staggered defensive strategy.

Intermittent or chronic depressed mood (with attendant self-blame) and withdrawal from social life accompany the setbacks and disappointments of the socially phobic. The same is true of any "disfigurement" (e.g. acne or pregnancy) that might attract malicious attention. Thus, lying low and licking one's wounds, when predators are on the prowl, is best construed as a third such – figurative – line of defense.

From the interpersonal perspective, social phobia as a pragmatic construct admits wide variations; it may be construed narrowly or widely. At its minimal incarnation, the difficulty in social functioning encompasses one situation only (e.g. pleading in court, lecturing). At its most expansive, social phobia is an idiosyncratic and loosely defined multi-tiered protean pattern extended in time, accompanied by myriad manifestations, arising in particularly trying social and cultural circumstances. Conceivably, social phobia may fade out of existence under particularly favorable circumstances and be resurrected as these deteriorate.

At the extreme, in certain ways of life, even persons with the greatest liabilities (e.g. temperamental) would not become socially phobic, as the necessary circumstantial conditions would be lacking. The orthodox Jewish way of life described in Greenberg and Witztum (2001) illustrates this. As marriages are arranged, women are confined to the private sphere. Their range of responsibilities (running the household and raising children), brings them in contact mostly with other women and a narrow family circle; social phobia, among women in such a cultural context, is hardly imaginable.

Conversely, in extraordinary reversals of fortune, even the most unlikely individual – once powerful and mighty – may display socially phobic conduct.

A historic anecdote shines a light on this. Field Marshal Wilhelm Keitel, an artillery officer during World War I, was between the years 1938 and 1945 the head of the German Armed Forces High Command. From late 1941, he was second only to Adolf Hitler in the military hierarchy. In that capacity he issued, among others, the order that unleashed a wave of murderous terror in the German occupied parts of the Soviet Union – as a method of pacification.

In the early hours of May 9, 1945, as the surviving highest ranking member of the pulverized German military, Keitel was brought to Soviet-occupied Berlin for the formal signing of the act of capitulation, before the assembled representatives of the high-command of the Soviet and Western allies. Now a prisoner of war, surrounded by victorious enemies, he struggled to maintain a dignified bearing. Not unlike the socially phobic in the limelight, surrounded by unsympathetic observers (e.g. his salute went unanswered), he was rattled, tense and speechless, with red blotches on his face. As his facial muscles kept twitching, he could not keep his monocle in place; his hand shook while holding the pen. A year later he was tried and hanged for war crimes.

In the interpersonal causal analysis, as this case so dramatically illustrates, the menacing setting is an indispensable element of causality. A threatening social situation is necessary to elicit a response from the socially anxious or the socially phobic; the two are intertwined and form a unity.

Social phobia, by definition, involves anxious distress and an impaired functioning. When the socially phobic are compared to normal individuals, in terms of anxiety and other features (e.g. social skills), although statistical differences are found between the groups, the socially phobic responses lie within the normal range, if not outright within the norm (e.g. in physiological terms).

The "normality" of the socially phobic features on the one hand, and the "abnormality" of the overall socially phobic functioning on the other, constitutes a paradox. Needless to say, it is uncongenial to the view that social phobia is a disorder caused by an inner malfunctioning. These facts, by contrast, fit well within the interpersonal perspective and lose thereby their "paradoxical" significance.

The social behavior and the attendant anxiousness of the socially phobic individual, observed in one situation at one point in time, as they are in experimental settings, are indeed not dissimilar from the range of forms of conduct exhibited by normal persons in similar circumstances. Differences, if found, are those of degree.

Social phobia studied "off-stage" – in its natural habitat – reveals a very different reality. In this, differences in degree, as well as differences in kind, are in evidence. If one steps back – figuratively speaking – from the experimental situation so as to take in a broader view, over time larger and more meaningful units of behavior and emotion – recurring patterns – will emerge. Altogether, the cumulative social functioning of socially phobic individuals, involving numerous patterns of behavior, extended in time and ranging over various situations, is likely to be wholly different from that of normal persons. Such a wider pattern of patterns for instance, might include, in addition to typical ways of behaving (e.g. pliant and ingratiating – acts of commission), also failures to act (e.g. approach an attractive person) or outright avoidance (e.g. ignore invitations – acts of omission). This set pattern of conduct would be combined with tentative wavering between various courses of action, without committing oneself definitively to any. It is only the larger pattern, in which numerous sub-patterns are embedded – although varying in particulars from individual to individual – that would characterize social phobia. Consequently, the overall socially phobic pattern is likely to be distinct from the normal one in functionality. This combines both differences in degree (e.g. fewer initiatives, less risk-taking) and in kind (i.e. predominance of powerlessness such as self-effacement, appeasement).

The difference between the normal and the socially phobic pattern of interpersonal conduct could also be formulated in terms of purposefulness. While normally goals are variable and encompass a wide range of possibilities, those of the socially phobic are narrow and stark – mostly self-protection from humiliation. These may overshadow all spheres of life. Most activities, social and otherwise, by involving prudent distance keeping, submissiveness and dependency are geared towards its realization.

In studies of predictive validity (Stravynski, 2007, pp. 101–104), little predicts social phobia. This seems in contradiction with what might be expected of an anxiety disorder caused by an inner malfunctioning.

The fact that only full-blown social phobia predicts social phobia later on, corroborates the interpersonal explanatory framework. Only fully formed social phobia predicts social phobia – the abnormal pattern. It reiterates the normality of the socially phobic features, with the upshot that its abnormality is functional. Moreover, it suggests that social phobia is undetermined by any intrapersonal characteristic. Rather, it requires "propitious" circumstances to emerge and persist. There is no accounting for social phobia without social settings; the fearful interpersonal responses characterizing social phobia are evoked and molded by these.

In summary, conceptual coherence of seemingly disparate facts is only achieved theoretically (see Murphy and Medin, 1985), by means of the interpersonal outlook. Altogether, it seems that the interpersonal perspective on social phobia is far closer to reality than the received view of social phobia as an anxiety disorder.

The causes of social phobia and their link to treatment

All approaches considering social phobia a disorder/disease share implicitly the view that social phobia is the result of "abnormal" anxiety. Both reductive dualisms – the bodily and the mental – locate the anxiety-generating putative processes within the individual.

In principle, can both claims to having unveiled (or caught a glimpse of) the cause of social phobia be valid? One way of reconciling the two is to argue that each is a transcription of "anxiety" in different terms, on different levels of analysis. In that sense, it is no more than pointing to anxiety – but naming it in different languages.

Otherwise, and especially in relation to treatment, the two are mutually exclusive. If social phobia were construed as a neurological disease of sorts, it would not be expected to be accompanied by specific belief systems and thought processes, let alone purposeful and coherent functioning. But, then, how is it that the socially phobic improve under psychological ministrations such as cognitive therapy, allegedly designed to improve their thinking? Brain "malfunctions" (e.g. Alzheimer's disease; Wernicke-Korsakoff syndrome) are not known to respond to psychological interventions aimed at promoting rational reasoning.

On the other hand, and now looking at causality and treatment from a different angle, if cognitive "biases" generate anxiety, how can medication correct these biases (see Stravynski, 2007, pp. 216–218), while stifling anxiety?

Altogether, the equivalent anxiety reduction in the short term that was achieved under both approaches (Stravynski, 2007 pp. 289–334) questions the causal analysis of each. Unsurprisingly, as was discussed in Chapters 4 and 5, neither causal claim is corroborated by the evidence at hand. How, then, do both approaches achieve the anxiety reduction at which they are aiming?

As is obvious from pharmacological studies, part of the answer must be the, far-from-negligible, "placebo" effect. However, as the outcomes from pharmacological treatment typically exceed this, and the improvements flowing from psychological treatment are durable, there is clearly more to the operations of these treatments than placebo. These will be presented shortly below.

Coming back to the "placebo" effect, neither reductive approach (be it physical or "mental") comes to grips with the not insignificant improvement achieved under "placebo" conditions – at least as long as the mock treatment lasts. However defined, how would a simulacrum of treatment affect brain malfunction or distorted cognitive processes? In the reductive analysis of causality, either bodily or mentally, the nature of "placebo" and how one is to understand its effects are not satisfactorily explained (see Benedetti, 2009). It is swiftly clarified within the interpersonal framework.

In view of the incongruities between the rival reductionist views of causality, it is surprising – theoretically speaking – that their radically different methods of treatment result in equivalent outcomes.

Furthermore, the inconsistencies of at least some of the results issued from treatment with the theoretical model underpinning it (e.g. cognitive improvements arising from purely pharmacological treatment) create a bewildering mixture of ideas and facts. One way of stemming the confusion is to ignore the awkward facts. Another is to seek a better theoretical formulation.

All these disparate facts find their rightful place and coalesce into a meaningful whole within the interpersonal theoretical framework. These will be taken up in turn.

Understood interpersonally, socially phobic responses overall consist in distance keeping and submissive relational patterns, enacted fearfully and oriented towards menacing social settings and other participants. Their chief end is self-protection. Anxiousness is part and parcel of defensive relational activity, as directed at the interpersonal threat.

Far from correcting alleged malfunctioning, pharmacological treatments achieve anxiety reduction by interfering rather broadly (by various chemical ways with varying qualitative results) with the brain, among others but not exclusively – dampening the activity of the systems involved in emotional regulation. This stifles some of the normal processes sustaining the fear response (but also depression, pain and others), while inadvertently interfering with other processes in the brain, with various undesired consequences ("secondary effects").

When medication is stopped, but the socially phobic relational pattern remains intact and the menacing circumstances in place, anxiousness, according to the theory, will surge back. Indeed, it does. The benefits of medication in social phobia last only as long as it is taken.

As to cognitive therapy, regardless of its theoretical rationale, in practice it guides the patient (wittingly or not) to attempt to undermine certain elements of the general socially phobic pattern. This certainly applies to gross defensive sub-patterns such as outright avoidance and other self-protective measures. In cognitive therapy the patient is encouraged to seek out and confront fear-evoking situations (so as to test their cognitions). As a consequence of diminishing avoidance, a reduction of anxious arousal is achieved. From the interpersonal perspective, it is the dissolution of at least some of the patterns of self-protection that underlies the durability of the reduced anxiety associated with this treatment. The outcome from pharmacological treatment, where it is not, provides a stark contrast.

"Interpersonal therapy" (not to be confused with the interpersonal approach to treatment described in this book) provides another example of encouraging results achieved by practices consistent with the principles of the interpersonal approach, as presented in Chapter 8, but unrelated to its own theoretical rationale. Developed for depression and reliant on a psychodynamic (i.e. an intrapersonal) conceptual analysis, "interpersonal therapy" is concerned with the exploration (within sessions) of difficulties (e.g. "role insecurity") in four areas: grief, "role dispute" (i.e. conflict), "role transition" (i.e. grown children leaving home) and "interpersonal deficits" (i.e. isolation). Incongruous with its theoretical rationale, emotional expression and social involvement are encouraged (e.g. Stangier et al., 2010, p. 290).

From the perspective of the interpersonal approach presented in this book, it is these suggestions that are the active ingredient and the most helpful part of the therapy. For even a partial shedding of the crudest self-protective patterns (e.g. avoidance, vigilant distance keeping) would result in a lessening of anxiety.

In all three examples given (pharmacological, "cognitive" and "interpersonal" therapies), the therapeutic rationales, based on causal analysis of dubious validity, are best interpreted as rhetorical devices that are functionally identical, although different and contradictory in content. Their usefulness is in the sensible encouragement – if only partial and intuitive, without the benefit of a systematic theoretical analysis – towards weakening the socially phobic interpersonal pattern and encouraging self-assertion and cooperation in its stead. If such changes obtain, weaker anxiousness, in accord with the interpersonal perspective, would follow.

It is unclear as to what aspect of reality the unfortunate and misleading term "placebo" refers. Given the range of activities (sham operations, inert pills, exorcism, prayer, shamanic rituals) and contexts (the clinic, congregation of the faithful at holy sites of pilgrimage) in which it is operative, as well as the wide variety of suffering and ailments (among others: pain, insomnia, emotional distress, cardiovascular and gastrointestinal disorders – see Benedetti, 2009) that are responsive to it, the common element is situated in the culturally determined, relational domain. The fact that a "placebo," when taken as a "drug," boosts physical performance (e.g. in sporting activities), but has undesirable side-effects when taken as a "medication," locates it firmly in a way of life.

In sum and interpersonally speaking, "placebo" in the context of the treatment of social phobia designates the transaction between individuals in the role of sufferer, with individuals designated as culturally sanctioned healers, operating in approved cultural settings. Relationally, it is a transaction between the relatively powerless and afflicted – supplicants as it were – and the powerfully "well-connected," who have acquired mastery of seemingly occult forces, as understood in a certain social and cultural context.

Making authoritative pronouncements, explaining to the help-seeker his or her predicament in culturally intelligible terms, prescribing medication or other activities (e.g. tasks) are all elements of such transactions. The titles, the diplomas on display, the costumes (e.g. the white coat and stethoscope) and the pills serving as a prop – if available – dramatize the enactment of the relationship. The mixture, relationally speaking, is a potent brew. The socially phobic tend to submissive dependency and respond powerfully to authority.

In the best case, it induces confidence and a willingness to be guided. This relational pattern, if put to good use, allows the start of a cooperative relationship, supporting the transition from fearful self-protection towards a more courageous self-sufficiency.

In the worst case, it induces a hopeful but dependent passivity, leaving the socially phobic relational pattern intact. As soon as this kind of treatment (e.g. medication) ends, relapse occurs.

Not unlike the interpersonal perspective, Benedetti (2009) deems the "psychosocial context" (pp. 32–34) the crucial factor for generating "placebo" effects.

In sum, the interpersonal perspective encompasses and sheds light on all facts concerning social phobia. Not least, by integrating these within a consistent theoretical framework and tracing their interrelationships, these facts are rendered meaningful.

Beyond social phobia, the explanatory range of the interpersonal perspective may be extended as well to the understanding of other abnormalities (e.g. depression).

Another example of the potential of this extension is problematic – dysfunctional – sexuality. It lends itself easily (especially the male variety) to a reductive formulation, involving the body alone. In that view, erectile problems, for example, stem from difficulties in blood flow – a case of defective plumbing, as it were. Before being taken over by urology and making them organic, sexual dysfunctions were understood as "psychogenic" – the consequence of troubled minds.

From reasoning by now well rehearsed, the interpersonal approach rejects both reductive views, and seeks to understand sexuality relationally, set in a cultural framework. The sexual response or lack of it, not unlike fearfulness or grief, is strongly embodied. It is embedded in and emerges from patterns of seductive and erotic interpersonal behavior, directed at an enticing and responsive partner. In short, it is created and sustained relationally, in a social and cultural context.

This conception was put to a test involving a particular population: sexually dysfunctional men who also had great difficulties in creating and maintaining intimate relationships. Relationally – to simplify – they tended to be either overbearing and insensitive, or passive and oversensitive. Both types, rather than concentrating on the rewards and progress of the relationship in the present, were in dread of the moment of truth looming in the future. Summoned on stage, as it were, there would be no turning back from performing to a critical audience.

In Stravynski et al. (1997), 69 sexually dysfunctional single men were randomly assigned to treatment focusing on either their sexual dysfunction, their interpersonal problems in courtship and intimacy, or a combination of both. All patients were interviewed and examined by an internist, to rule out organic problems underlying the sexual dysfunctions.

As could be expected, both conditions that focused on improving the interpersonal functioning of the men resulted in far greater rates of stable relationships. As to sexual functioning, the interpersonal condition alone achieved the greatest improvement (albeit statistically similar to the combined). Fully 80 percent of the men who received no guidance or treatment addressing their sexual dysfunction, no longer fulfilled the criteria for sexual dysfunction at the 1-year follow-up. By contrast, only 40 percent of those treated for their sexual difficulties alone were in remission at the same time.

As in social phobia, self-protective patterns (either offensive or defensive) generated anxiousness likely to be inimical to naturally occurring and normal sexual functioning. As in the treatment of social phobia, building up cooperation – in this case in intimacy – resulted in diminished anxiousness and enhanced erotic and sexual collaboration and satisfaction.

Other problems, for example, depression or psychogenic vomiting in the context of social phobia, have responded favorably to the interpersonal approach (e.g. Stravynski, 1983; Stravynski, Verrault, Gaudette, Langlois, et al. 1994).

Overcoming social phobia

The reductive approaches to treatment seek to fix the alleged malfunctioning processes, either in the brain or the mind, so as to reduce the abnormal anxiety – the putative cause of social phobia. When the anxiety comes down to a manageable level – so the reasoning goes – adequate social functioning, hitherto inhibited, will be released.

This assumption is unwarranted, both on empirical (i.e. the evidence is tenuous – see Stravynski, 2007, pp. 289–334) and on conceptual grounds. Acting submissively and defensively (e.g. appeasing for the sake of keeping the peace), is a long-standing habit, at this stage probably functionally independent and only loosely related to specific levels of anxiety. Acting powerfully (e.g. voicing discontent and demanding satisfaction; acting flirtatiously and flouting all propriety; lying blatantly and defiantly) was never in the repertoire of such individuals.

When the social anxiousness of the socially phobic weakens in intensity, under medication, for example, the grossest self-protective patterns (e.g. avoidance, fleeing, keeping a safe distance) totter a bit, but rarely collapse (Stravynski, 2007, pp. 289–334). All the same, self-protection (as a ruling purpose and the driving force shaping the appropriate relational pattern), is likely to remain unaffected. Accordingly, the comprehensive socially phobic relational pattern remains, in the main, intact (pp. 289–334).

In sum, interacting with others in a powerful (i.e. self-assertive) yet cooperative manner, while enacting a variety of social roles, is something that a socially phobic individual has little or no experience of doing. In all likelihood, it needs to be built up.

This is where the interpersonal approach steps in. From that vantage point, as the overall socially phobic relational web is broken up into sub-patterns, the main trends are easier to spot.

First of all, prudent distance keeping is exercised whenever possible. Secondly, when active participation is required, submissive engagement comes to the fore. These are the main interpersonal tactical maneuvers, all enacted fearfully. Combined with others (e.g. non-committal equivocation), these forge an overall anxious relational strategy of relative powerlessness (e.g. seeking not to displease or antagonize) and dependency (e.g. seeking approval), enacted for the sake of self-protection from bruising and ultimately humiliating encounters.

Although the complaints of those who seek help are in terms of anxious distress, the interpersonal approach seeks to undo social phobia by overhauling the socially phobic defensive interpersonal pattern. This is done sequentially, by tackling selectively its main constituting elements. The practical goal is to undermine the structure, in the most effective manner. This is done by reconfiguring old habits into new patterns if possible, and forging altogether new ways of being, for the sake of improved participation. As the defensive patterns useful only for self-protection fall into disuse, fearfulness diminishes. As social life becomes less of a threatening environment, teeming with unforeseeable dangers, and more of a treasure house where many opportunities are to be found, anxiousness stabilizes, becomes restricted and normalizes.

The newly developed and still evolving interpersonal tactics leading to this are the mirror image of social phobia. Instead of operating behind a safe perimeter, the socially phobic individuals are encouraged to act boldly and firmly. Furthermore, they are incited to seek out settings where the action crucial to the furthering of their interests or the realization of their life plans takes place. Within the proper context, self-assertion, tempered by the reciprocity and cooperation required within any given social role, is encouraged.

When tested, as a relatively short-term treatment program of 14 sessions, the interpersonal approach (see Chapter 8) resulted in highly positive outcomes.

First of all, it yielded, on average, statistically significant and clinically meaningful reductions in reported anxiety levels, comparable to those achieved with either medication or psychological approaches aimed specifically at anxiety reduction.

Secondly, significant and meaningful improvements in social functioning were reported, both in the public arena as well as in the private domain. Both social functioning, together with the lessening in anxiousness that followed, continued, in general, to improve (albeit at a lighter pace) throughout the early stages of follow-up and reached a plateau about 1 year after the end of treatment.

Finally and most importantly, within that relatively short period, the interpersonal approach achieved a remission rate of between 50% and 60%. Gratifyingly, on the whole, these results continued to improve to reach a rate of 77% or, at the very least, remained stable for up to a period of 15 years' follow-up.

Practically, this demanding approach, relying strongly on patient cooperation in terms of homework tasks, may not be for everybody. About 20% of the initial participants tended to drop out.

In treatment, especially one without a preset and limited number of sessions, once the ability to function in the most pressing of circumstances (usually related to making a living) has been improved and a modicum of poise gained, a broader vision of therapy opens up and beckons. A useful way of characterizing the continuing guided program of self-transformation proposed by the interpersonal approach – and much liked by patients – is in terms of a quest for autonomy.

Interpersonally, autonomy is fostered by a process of learning, involving the taking of many small independent steps. It requires both doing and understanding – of the principles involved. Once grasped, it needs to be practiced relentlessly, as if mastering a skill, aspiring to do better and better. The quest might involve striking out in several, ultimately overlapping trajectories.

The first, and the foundation for the rest, may be described as self-mastery (e.g. acting courageously in fearsome circumstances) and self-sufficiency (e.g. acting for the right reasons, looking out for opportunities). The most important task is to forge a coherence of impulse, feeling and thought within oneself and unite it with resolute action. At its best, the actor and the act are one and indivisible.

The second trajectory may be described as the path of self-determination. It involves on the one hand, conspicuously and concretely, self-assertion in speech and action. On the other hand, more subtly and less obviously, it includes the choice of one's own identity, with the concomitant rejection of identities insinuated or imposed by others. Speaking interpersonally, it signifies actively seeking to integrate communities of choice, while moving away from others to which one has little allegiance.

Finally, it involves self-creation – a permanent and all-embracing activity of constant renewal. This has as the main goal becoming more the person one would like to be and mastering one's life, by attempting to realize cherished dreams.

As such, these elements of autonomy are fertile ground for fruitful and rewarding collaboration in co-creation. In the public sphere, it permits acting in various capacities – some necessary, others of choice. In private life, it makes possible the forging of the indispensable intimate bonds of love and friendship.

On a different plane, the quest for autonomy, as a set of ideals, is unlikely to be realized fully or may suffer setbacks. Nonetheless, even the partial pursuit of these is worthy and useful as an antidote to social phobia. Such activity points away from self-protection and mere survival, towards richer possibilities of a meaningful life worth living.

References

Adams, H. B. (1964). "Mental illness" or interpersonal behavior? *American Psychologist*, 19, 191–197.

Ainsworth, M. D. S., Blehar, M. C., Waters, E., and Wall, S. (1978). *Patterns of attachment: a psychological study of the Strange Situation*. Hillsdale, NJ: Lawrence Erlbaum.

Alden, L. E. (2005). Interpersonal perspectives on social phobia. In: W. R. Crozier and L. E. Alden (eds.), *The essential handbook of social anxiety for clinicians* (pp. 167–192). Chichester: Wiley.

Alden, L. E., and Taylor, C. T. (2004). Interpersonal processes in social phobia. *Clinical Psychology Review*, 24, 857–882.

Amado, D. (2005). *Existe-t-il un pattern de comportements spécifique aux phobiques sociaux? Une étude ethnographique*. Doctoral dissertation. Montreal, QC: University of Montreal.

American Psychiatric Association (APA) (1994). *Diagnostic and statistical manual of mental disorders* (4th edn., DSM-IV). Washington, DC: APA.

(2013) *Diagnostic and statistical manual of mental disorders* (5th edn., DSM-5). Arlington, VA: APA.

Amir, N., Foa, E. B., and Coles, M. E. (1998). Negative interpretation bias in social phobia. *Behaviour Research and Therapy*, 36, 945–957.

Anderson, E., Ruck, C., Levebratt, C., Hedman, E., Schalling, M., Lindefors, N., Eriksson, E., Carlbring, P., Andersson, G., and Furmark, T. (2013). Genetic polymorphisms in monoamine systems and outcome of cognitive therapy for social anxiety disorder. *PLOS ONE*, v. 8, e79015.

Andreasen, N. C. (1984). *The broken brain: the biological revolution in psychiatry*. New York: Harper & Row.

Andrews, G., Stewart, G., Allen, R., and Henderson, A. S. (1990). The genetics of six neurotic disorders: a twin study. *Journal of Affective Disorders*, 19, 23–29.

Angell, M. (2011). The illusions of psychiatry. *The New York Review of Books*, July 14.

Arbel, N., and Stravynski, A. (1991). A retrospective study of separation in the development of adult avoidant personality disorder. *Acta Psychiatrica Scandinavica*, 83, 174–178.

Arrindell, W. A., Pickersgill, M. J., Merckelbach, H., Ardon, M. A., and Cornet, F. C. (1991). Phobic dimensions III: factor analytic approaches to the study of common phobic fears. *Advances in Behaviour Research and Therapy*, 13, 73–130.

286

Atmaca, M., Sirlier, B.,Yildirim, H., and Kayali, A. (2011). Hippocampus and amygdalar volumes in patients with somatization disorder. *Progress in Neuro-Psychopharmacology and Biological Psychiatry*, 35, 1699–1703.

Bailer, U. F., Frank, G. K., Henry, S. E., Price, J. C., Meltzer, C. C., Weissfeld, L., ... Kaye, W. H. (2005). Altered brain serotonin 5-HT1A receptor binding after recovery from anorexia nervosa measured by positron emission tomography and [carbonyl11C]WAY-100635. *Archives of General Psychiatry*, 62, 1032–1041.

Bandelow, B., Charima Torrento, A., Wedkin, D., Brooks, A., Hajak, G., and Ruther, E. (2004). Early traumatic life events, parental rearing styles, family history of mental disorders, and birth factors in patients with social anxiety disorder. *European Archives of Psychiatry and Clinical Neuroscience*, 254, 397–405.

Barash, D. P. (1977). *Sociobiology and behavior.* New York: Elsevier.

Barber, B. (1957). *Social stratification: a comparative analysis of structure and process.* New York: Harcourt, Brace, & World.

Barendregt, M., and van Rappard, J. F. H. (2004). Reductionism revisited: on the role of reduction in psychology. *Theory and Psychology*, 14, 453–474.

Barkan, T., Hermesh, H., Marom, S., Gurwitz, D., Weizman, A., and Rehavi, M. (2006). Serotonin uptake to lymphocytes of patients with social phobia compared to normal individuals. *European Neuropsychopharmacology*, 16, 19–23.

Barker, R. G. (1968). *Ecological psychology: concepts and methods for studying the environment of human behavior.* Stanford, CA: Stanford University Press.

Barlow, D. H., Abel, G. G., and Blanchard, E. B. (1977). Gender identity change in a transsexual: an exorcism. *Archives of Sexual Behavior*, 5, 387–395.

Baron, J. (1988). *Thinking and deciding.* Cambridge University Press.

Barrett, P. M., Rapee, R. M., Dadds, M. M., and Ryan, S. M. (1996). Family enhancement of cognitive style in anxious and aggressive children. *Journal of Abnormal Child Psychology*, 24, 187–203.

Bartov, O. (2001). *The eastern front 1941–45: German troops and the barbarisation of warfare.* London: Palgrave Macmillan.

Baur, V., Hänggi, J., Rufer, M., Delsignore, A., Jäncke, L., Herwig, U., and Brühl, A. B. (2011). White matter alterations in social anxiety disorder. *Journal of Psychiatric Research*, 45, 1366–1372.

Beattie, M., and Stevenson, J. (1984). Measures of social functioning in psychiatric outcome research. *Evaluation Review*, 8, 631–644.

Beck, A. T. (1976). *Cognitive therapy and the emotional disorders.* New York: International Universities Press.

Beck, A. T., Emery, G., and Greenberg, R. L. (1985). *Anxiety disorders and phobias: a cognitive perspective.* New York: Basic Books.

Beeman, W. O. (1993). The anthropology of theatre and spectacle. *Annual Review of Anthropology*, 22, 369–393.

Beidel, D. C., Rao, P. A., Scharfstein, L., Wong, N., and Alfano, C. A. (2010). Social skills and social phobia: an investigation of DSM-IV subtypes. *Behaviour Research and Therapy*, 48, 992–1001.

Beidel, D. C., and Turner, S. M. (1997). At risk for anxiety: I. Psychopathology in the offspring of anxious parents. *Journal of the American Academy of Child and Adolescent Psychiatry*, 36, 918–924.

Beidel, D. C., Turner, S. M., and Morris, T. L. (1999). Psychopathology of childhood social phobia. *Journal of the American Academy of Child and Adolescent Psychiatry*, 38, 643–650.

Bell, C., Bhikha, S., Colhoun, H., Carter, F., Frampton, C., and Porter, R. (2013). The response to sulpiride in social anxiety disorder: D2 receptor function. *Journal of Psychopharmacology*, 27, 146–151.

Bell-Dolan, D. J., Last, C. G., and Strauss, C. C. (1990). Symptoms of anxiety disorders in normal children. *Journal of the American Academy of Child and Adolescence Psychiatry*, 29, 759–765.

Benedetti, F. (2009). *Placebo effects: understanding the mechanisms in health and disease*. Oxford University Press.

Benedetti, F., Mayberg, H. S., Wager, T. D., Stohler, C. S., and Zubieta, J.-K. (2005). Neurobiological mechanisms of the placebo effect. *The Journal of Neuroscience*, 25, 10390–10402.

Bennett, M. R., and Hacker, P. M. S. (eds.) (2003). *Philosophical foundations of neuroscience*. Oxford: Blackwell.

Bergner, R. M. (1997). What is psychopathology? And so what? *Clinical Psychology: Science and Practice*, 4, 235–248.

Bernstein, P. L., and Strack, M. (1996). A game of cat and house: spatial patterns and behaviour of 14 domestic cats in the home. *Anthrozoos*, 9, 25–39.

Bez, Y., Yesilova, Y., Kaya, M. C., and Sir, A. (2011). High social phobia frequency and related disability in patients with acne vulgaris. *European Journal of Dermatology*, 21, 756–760.

Biddle, B. J. (1986). Recent developments in role theory. *Annual Review of Sociology*, 12, 67–92.

Biederman, J., Hirshfeld-Becker, D. R., Rosenbaum, J. F., Hérot, C., Friedman, D., Snidman, N., ... Faraone, S. V. (2001). Further evidence of association between behavioral inhibition and social anxiety in children. *American Journal of Psychiatry*, 158, 1673–1679.

Biederman, J., Rosenbaum, J. F., Bolduc-Murphy, E. A., Faraone, S. V., Chaloff, J., Hirshfeld, D. R., and Kagan, J. (1993). A 3-year follow-up of children with and without behavioral inhibition. *Journal of the American Academy of Child and Adolescent Psychiatry*, 32, 814–821.

Biederman, J., Rosenbaum, J. F., Hirshfeld, D. R., Faraone, S. V., Bolduc, E. A., Gersten, M., ... Reznick, J. S. (1990). Psychiatric correlates of behavioral inhibition in young children of parents with and without psychiatric disorders. *Archives of General Psychiatry*, 47, 21–26.

Black, D. W. (2006). Efficacy of combined pharmacotherapy and psychotherapy versus monotherapy in the treatment of anxiety disorders. *CNS Spectrums*, 11, 29–33.

Blair, K., Geraci, M., Devido, J., McCaffrey, D., Chen, G., Vythilingam, M., ... Pine, D. S. (2008). Neural response to self- and other referential praise and criticism in generalized social phobia. *Archives of General Psychiatry*, 65, 1176–1184.

Blair, K., Shaywitz, J., Smith, B. W., Rhodes, R., Geraci, M., Jones, M., ... Pine, D. S. (2008). Response to emotional expressions in generalized social phobia and generalized anxiety disorder: evidence for separate disorders. *American Journal of Psychiatry*, 165, 1193–1202.

Blair, K. S., Geraci, M., Hollon, N., Otero, M., DeVido, J., Majestic, C., Jacobs, M., Blair, R. J., and Pine, D. S. (2010). Social norm processing in adult social phobia: atypically increased ventromedial frontal cortex responsiveness to unintentional (embarrassing) transgressions. *American Journal of Psychiatry*, 167, 1526–1532.

Blair, K. S., Geraci, M., Korelitz, K., Otero, M., Towbin, K., Ernst, M., ... Pine, D. S. (2011). The pathology of social phobia is independent of developmental changes in face processing. *American Journal of Psychiatry*, 168, 1202–1209.

Blair, K. S., Geraci, M., Otero, M., Majestic, C., Odenheimer, S., Jacobs, M., ... Pine, D. S. (2011). Atypical modulation of medial prefrontal cortex to self-referential comments in generalized social phobia. *Psychiatry Research*, 193, 38–45.

Blanco, C., Heimberg, R. G., Schneier, F. R., Fresco, D. M., Chen, H., Turk, C. L., ... Liebowitz, M. R. (2010). A placebo-controlled trial of phenelzine, cognitive behavioral group therapy, and their combination for social anxiety disorder. *Archives of General Psychiatry*, 67, 286–295.

Blashfield, R. K., and Livesley, W. J. (1991). Metaphorical analysis of psychiatric classification as a psychological test. *Journal of Abnormal Psychology*, 100, 262–270.

Blier, P., and Abbott, F. V. (2001). Putative mechanisms of action of antidepressant drugs in affective and anxiety disorders and pain. *Journal of Psychiatry and Neuroscience*, 26, 37–43.

Bloch, S. (1986). Modèles effecteurs des émotions fondamentales: relation entre rythme respiratoire, posture, expression faciale et expérience subjective. *Bulletin de Psychologie*, 39, 843–846.

Bloch, S., Lemeignan, M., and Aguilera-Torres, N. (1991). Specific respiratory patterns distinguish between basic emotions. *International Journal of Psychophysiology*, 11, 141–154.

Bloch, S., Orthous, P., and Santibañez-H, G. (1987). Effect of patterns of basic emotions: a psychophysiological method for training actors. *Journal of Social and Biological Structures*, 10, 1–19.

Bohlin, G., Hagekull, B., and Rydell, A. M. (2000). Attachment and social functioning: a longitudinal study from infancy to middle childhood. *Social Development*, 9, 24–39.

Boissy, A. (1995). Fear and fearfulness in animals. *The Quarterly Review of Biology*, 70, 165–191.

Bond, R., and Smith, P. R. (1996). Culture and conformity; a meta-analysis of studies using Asch's line judgement task. *Psychological Bulletin*, 119, 111–137.

Borge, F.-M., Hoffart, A., Sexton, H., Clark, D. M., Markowitz, J. C., and McManus, F. (2008). Residential cognitive therapy versus residential interpersonal therapy for social phobia: A randomized clinical trial. *Journal of Anxiety Disorders*, 22, 991–1010.

Bowlby, J. (1981a). *Attachment and loss*. Harmondsworth: Penguin Books.

(1981b). *Separation: anxiety and anger*. Harmondsworth: Penguin Books.

Boysen, G. A. (2007). An evaluation of the DSM concept of mental disorder. *The Journal of Mind and Behavior*, 28, 157–173.

Bradshaw, J., and Cameron-Beaumont, C. (2000). The signalling repertoire of the domestic cat and its undomesticated relatives. In: D. C. Turner and

P. Bateson (eds.), *The domestic cat: the biology of its behaviour* (2nd edn.) (pp. 67–94). Cambridge University Press.

Brambilla, P., Barale, F., Caverzasi, E., and Soares, J. C. (2002). Anatomical MRI findings in mood and anxiety disorders. *Epidemiologia e Psichiatria Sociale*, 11, 88–99.

Bremner, J. (2004). Brain imaging in anxiety disorders. *Expert Review of Neurotherapeutics*, 4, 275–284.

Brigham, C. C. (1930). Intelligence tests of immigrant groups. *Psychological Review*, 37, 158–165.

Brinkmann, S. (2011). Dewey's neglected psychology: rediscovering his transactional approach. *Theory and Psychology*, 21, 298–317.

Brissett, D., and Edgley, C. (eds.) (1990). *Life as theatre: a dramaturgical sourcebook*. New York: Aldine de Gruyter.

Brown, A. M., and Crawford, H. J. (1988). Fear Survey Schedule-III: oblique and orthogonal factorial structures in an American college population. *Personality and Individual Differences*, 9, 401–410.

Brown, G. W. (1996). Genetics of depression: a social science perspective. *International Review of Psychiatry*, 8, 387–401.

Browning, C. R. (ed.) (1993). *Ordinary men: Reserve Police Battalion 101 and the final solution in Poland*. New York: HarperCollins.

Brühl, A. B., Rufer, M., Delsignore, A., Kaffenberger, T., Jäncke, L., and Herwig, U. (2011). Neural correlates of altered general emotion processing in social anxiety disorder. *Brain Research*, 1378, 72–83.

Bryant, G., and Trower, P. E. (1974). Social difficulty in a student sample. *British Journal of Educational Psychology*, 44, 13–21.

Budd, M. (1989). *Wittgenstein's philosophy of psychology*. London: Routledge.

Buss, D. (1990). The evolution of anxiety and social exclusion. *Journal of Social and Clinical Psychology*, 9, 196–201.

Cacioppo, J. T., Bernston, G. G., Sheridan, J. F., and McClintock, M. K. (2000). Multilevel integrative analyses of human behavior: social neuroscience and the complementing nature of social and biological approaches. *Psychological Bulletin*, 126, 829–843.

Caetano, S. C., Fonseca, M., Hatch, J. P., Olvera, R. L., Nicoletti, M., Hunter, K., … Soares, J. C. (2007). Medial temporal lobe abnormalities in pediatric unipolar depression. *Neuroscience Letter*, 427, 142–147.

Campbell, D. W., Sareen, J., Paulus, M. P., Goldin, P. R., Stein, M. B., and Reiss, J. P. (2007). Time-varying amygdala response to emotional faces in generalized social phobia. *Biological Psychiatry*, 62, 455–463.

Campbell, R. (2010). The emergence of action. *New Ideas in Psychology*, 28, 283–295.

Canetti, E. (1981). *Crowds and power*. Harmondsworth: Penguin.

Carrithers, M. (1992). *Why humans have cultures: explaining anthropology and cultural diversity*. Oxford University Press.

Caspi, A., Moffitt, T. E., Newman, D. L., and Silva, P. A. (1996). Behavioral observations at age 3 years predict adult psychiatric disorders. *Archives of General Psychiatry*, 53, 1033–1039.

Cassidy, J., and Berlin, L. J. (1994). The insecure/ambivalent pattern of attachment: theory and research. *Child Development*, 65, 971–991.

Chamberlain, M. (2007). *Old wives tales: the history of remedies, charms and spells.* London: Tempos.

Chandler, D. G. (1966). *The campaigns of Napoleon.* New York: Simon & Schuster.

Chartier, M. J., Walker, J. R., and Stein, M. B. (2001). Social phobia and potential childhood risk-factors in a community sample. *Psychological Medicine,* 31, 307–315.

Chavira, D. A., Stein, M. B., and Malcarne, V. L. (2002). Scrutinizing the relationship between shyness and social phobia. *Journal of Anxiety Disorders,* 16, 585–598.

Chen, X., Hastings, P. D., Rubin, K. H., Chen, H., Cen, G., and Stewart, S. L. (1998). Child-rearing attitudes and behavioral inhibition in Chinese and Canadian toddlers: a cross-cultural study. *Developmental Psychology,* 34, 677–686.

Chess, S., and Thomas, A. (1987). *Origins and evolution of behavior disorders.* Cambridge, MA: Harvard University Press.

Chisholm, J. S. (1999). *Death, hope and sex.* Cambridge University Press.

Chorpita, B., and Barlow, D. (1998). The development of anxiety: the role of control in the early environment. *Psychological Bulletin,* 124, 3–21.

Chou, K.-L. (2009). Social anxiety disorder in older adults: evidence from the National Epidemiologic Survey on alcohol and related conditions. *Journal of Affective Disorders,* 119, 76–83.

Chronis-Tuscano, A., Degnan, K. A., Pine, D. S., Perez-Edgar, K., Henderson, H. A., Diaz, Y., ... Fox, N. A. (2009). Stable early maternal report of behavioral inhibition predicts lifetime social anxiety disorder in adolescence. *Journal of American Academy of Child and Adolescent Psychiatry,* 48, 928–935.

Churchland, P., and Haldane, J. (1988). Folk psychology and the explanation of human behaviour. *Proceedings of the Aristotelian Society,* 62, 209–254.

Clark, D. M. (1999). Anxiety disorders: why they persist and how to treat them. *Behaviour Research and Therapy,* 37, S5–S27.

Clark, D. M., Ehlers, A., Hackmann, A., McManus, F., Fennell, M., Grey, N., ... Wild, J. (2006). Cognitive therapy versus exposure and applied relaxation in social phobia: a randomized controlled trial. *Journal of Consulting and Clinical Psychology,* 74, 568–578.

Clark, D. M., Ehlers, A., McManus, F., Hackmann, F., Fennell, M., Campbell, H., ... Louis, B. (2003). Cognitive therapy vs Fluoxetine plus self-exposure in the treatment of generalized social phobia (social anxiety disorder): a randomized placebo controlled trial. *Journal of Consulting and Clinical Psychology,* 71, 1058–1067.

Clark, D. M., and Steer, R. A. (1996). Empirical status of the cognitive model of anxiety and depression. In: P. Salkovskis (ed.), *Frontiers of cognitive therapy* (pp. 75–96). New York: Guilford Press.

Clark, D. M., and Wells, A. (1995). A cognitive model of social phobia. In: R. G. Heimberg, M. R. Liebowitz, D. A. Hope, and F. R. Schneier (eds.), *Social phobia: diagnosis, assessment, and treatment: theoretical and empirical approaches* (pp. 69–93). New York: Guilford Press.

Cleckley, H. (1941). *The mask of sanity.* St Louis, MO: Mosby.

Clinical Practice Guidelines (2006). Social anxiety disorder. *Canadian Journal of Psychiatry,* 51, 355–415.

Coen, E. (1999). *The art of the genes: how organisms make themselves.* Oxford University Press.

Cohen, M. (1992). Hylomorphism and functionalism. In: M. C. Nussbaum and A. Oksenberg Rorty (eds.), *Essays on Aristotle's De Anima* (pp. 57–74). Oxford University Press.

Colloca, L., and Benedetti, F. (2005). Placebos and painkillers: is mind as real as matter? *Nature Reviews Neuroscience*, 6, 545–552.

Conquest, R. (1990). *The great terror: a reassessment.* New York: Oxford University Press.

Conrad, P. (2007). *The medicalization of society: on the transformation of human conditions into treatable disorders.* Baltimore, MD: Johns Hopkins University Press.

Cooney, R. E., Atlas, L. Y., Joormann, J., Eugène, F., and Gotlib, I. H. (2006). Amygdala activation in the processing of neutral faces in social anxiety disorder: is neutral really neutral? *Psychiatry Research*, 148, 55–59.

Corner, P. (2002). Italian fascism: whatever happened to dictatorship? *Journal of Modern History*, 74, 325–351.

Costafreda, S. G., Brammer, M. J., David, A. S., and Fu, C. H. (2008). Predictors of amygdala activation during the processing of emotional stimuli: a meta-analysis of 385 PET and fMRI studies. *Brain Research Reviews*, 58, 57–70.

Costello, C. G. (1982). Fears and phobias in women: a community study. *Journal of Abnormal Psychology*, 91, 280–286.

Cottingham, J. (1978). "A brute to the brutes?": Descartes' treatment of animals. *Philosophy*, 53, 551–559.

(1999). *Descartes.* London: Routledge.

Cox, B. J., MacPherson, P. S. R., and Enns, M. W. (2005). Psychiatric correlates of childhood shyness in a nationally representative sample. *Behaviour Research and Therapy*, 43, 1019–1027.

Craddock, A. E. (1983). Family cohesion and adaptability as factors in the aetiology of social anxiety. *Australian Journal of Sex, Marriage and Family*, 4, 181–190.

Craig, W. M. (1998). The relationship among bullying, victimization, depression, anxiety and aggression in elementary school children. *Personality and Individual Differences*, 24, 123–130.

Crews, F. (2007). Talking back to Prozac. *The New York Review of Books*, December 6.

Crick, N. R., and Grotpeter, J. K. (1996). Children's treatment by peers: victims of relational and overt aggression. *Development and Psychopathology*, 8, 367–380.

Crippa, J. A. S., de Lima Osorio, F., Del-Ben, C. M., Filho, A. S., da Silva Freitas, M. C., and Loureiro, S. R. (2008). Comparability between telephone and face-to-face Structured Clinical Interview for DSM-IV in assessing social anxiety disorder. *Perspectives in Psychiatric Care*, 44, 241–247.

Cronbach, L. J., and Meehl, P. E. (1955). Construct validity in psychological tests. *Psychological Bulletin*, 56, 81–106.

Dadds, M. R., Barrett, P. M., Rapee, R. M., and Ryan, S. (1996). Family process and child anxiety and aggression: an observational analysis. *Journal of Abnormal Child Psychology*, 24, 715–734.

Danti, S., Ricciardi, E., Gentili, C., Gobbini, M. I., Pietrini, P., and Guazzelli, M. (2010). Is social phobia a "mis-communication" disorder? Brain functional connectivity during face perception differs between patients with social phobia and healthy control subjects. *Frontiers in Systems Neuroscience*, 4, 152.

Dar-Nimrod, I., and Heine, S. J. (2011). Genetic essentialism: on the deceptive determinism of DNA. *Psychological Bulletin*, 137, 800–818.

David, D., Giron, A., and Mellman, T. A. (1995). Panic-phobic patients and developmental trauma. *Journal of Clinical Psychiatry*, 56, 113–117.

Davis, S. (1996). The cosmobiological balance of the emotional and spiritual worlds: phenomenological structuralism in traditional Chinese medical thought. *Culture, Medicine, and Psychiatry*, 20, 83–123.

Dawkins, R. (1976). *The selfish gene*. Oxford University Press.

de Coppet, D. (ed.) (1992). *Understanding rituals*. London: Routledge.

Deater-Deckard, K. (2001). Recent research examining the role of peer relationships in the development of psychopathology. *Journal of Child Psychology and Psychiatry*, 42, 565–579.

Delap, L. (2011). *Knowing their place: domestic service in twentieth-century Britain*. Oxford University Press.

Delgado, M. R., Olsson, A., and Phelps, E. A. (2006). Extending animal models of fear conditioning to humans. *Biological Psychology*, 73, 39–48.

Dewar, K., and Stravynski, A. (2001). The quest for biological correlates of social phobia: an interim assessment. *Acta Psychiatrica Scandinavica*, 103, 244–251.

Dewey, J. (1930). *Human nature and conduct*. New York: The Modern Library.

Dinwiddie, S., Heath, A. C., Dunne, M. P., Bucholz, K. K., Madden, P. A. F., Slutske, W. W., … Martin, N. G. (2000). Early sexual abuse and lifetime psychopathology: a co-twin-control study. *Psychological Medicine*, 30, 41–52.

Donkin, R. (2000). *Blood, sweat and tears: the evolution of work*. London: Texere.

Dörner, D., and Schaub, H. (1994). Errors in planning and decision-making and the nature of human information processing. *Applied Psychology: An International Review*, 43, 433–453.

Douglas, A. R., Lindsay, W. R., and Brooks, D. N. (1988). The three systems model of fear and anxiety: implications for assessment of social anxiety. *Behavioural Psychotherapy*, 16, 15–22.

Doyle, W. (2010). *Aristocracy*. Oxford University Press.

Ducat, J. (1974). Le Mépris des hilotes. *Annales: Économies, Sociétés, Civilisations*, 29, 1451–1464.

Edelmann, R., and Baker, S. (2002). Self-reported and actual physiological responses in social phobia. *British Journal of Clinical Psychology*, 41, 1–14.

Edwards, C., Heiblum, M., Tejeda, A., and Galindo, F. (2007). Experimental evaluation of attachment behaviors in owned cats. *Journal of Veterinary Behavior*, 2, 119–125.

Eifert, G. H., and Wilson, P. H. (1991). The triple response approach to assessment: a conceptual and methodological reappraisal. *Behavioral Research Therapy*, 29, 283–292.

El-Islam, M. F. (1994). Cultural aspects of morbid fears in Qatari women. *Social Psychiatry and Psychiatric Epidemiology*, 29, 137–140.

Elias, N. (1987). On human beings and their emotions: a process-sociological essay. *Theory, Culture and Society*, 4, 339–361.

Emerson, R. M. (1962). Power-dependence relations. *American Sociological Review*, 27, 31–41.

294   References

Epstein, S. (1972). The nature of anxiety with emphasis upon its relationship to expectancy. In: C. D. Spielberger (ed.), *Anxiety: current trends in theory and research* (pp. 292–337). New York: Academic Press.

Eren, I., Tukel, R., Polat, A., Karaman, R., and Unal, S. (2003). Evaluation of regional cerebral blood flow changes in panic disorder with Tc99m-HMPAO SPECT. *Psychiatry Research*, 123, 135–143.

Ernst, C., Angst, J., and Földényi, M. (1993). The Zurich Study: XVII. Sexual abuse in childhood, frequency and relevance for adult morbidity data of a longitudinal epidemiological study. *European Archives of Clinical Neuroscience*, 242, 293–300.

Essau, C. A., Conradt, J., and Petermann, F. (1999). Frequency and comorbidity of social phobia and social fears in adolescents. *Behaviour Research and Therapy*, 37, 831–843.

Evans, K. C., Wright, C. I., Wedig, M. M., Gold, A. L., Pollack, M. H., and Rauch, S. L. (2008). A functional MRI study of amygdala responses to angry schematic faces in social anxiety disorder. *Depression and Anxiety*, 25, 496–505.

Eysenck, H. J., and Eysenck, S. B. J. (1969). *Personality structure and measurement.* London: Routledge & Kegan Paul.

Fan, D. (2007). Towards complex holism. *Systems Research and Behavioral Science*, 24, 417–430.

Fang, A., and Hofmann, S. G. (2010). Relationship between social anxiety disorder and body dysmorphic disorder. *Clinical Psychology Review*, 30, 1040–1048.

Faria, V., Appel, L., Ahs, F., Linnman, C., Pissiota, A., Frans, O., … Furmark, T. (2012). Amygdala subregions tied to SSRI and placebo response in patients with social anxiety disorder. *Neuropsychopharmacology*, 37, 2222–2232.

Faust, D., Hart, K., Guilmette, T. J., and Arkes, H. R. (1988). Neuropsychologists' capacity to detect adolescent malingerers. *Professional Psychology: Research and Practice*, 19, 508–515.

Fernandez, K. C., and Rodebaugh, T. L. (2011). Social anxiety and discomfort with friendly giving. *Journal of Anxiety Disorders*, 25, 326–334.

Fesser, E. (2005). *Philosophy of mind.* Oxford: Oneworld.

Finkler, K. (1994). Sacred healing and biomedicine compared. *Medical Anthropology Quarterly*, 8, 178–197.

Finnie, V., and Russell, A. (1988). Preschool children's social status and their mother's behavior and knowledge in the supervisory role. *Developmental Psychology*, 24, 789–801.

Foa, E. B., Franklin, M. E., Perry, K. J., and Herbert, J. D. (1996). Cognitive biases in generalized social phobia. *Journal of Abnormal Psychology*, 105, 433–439.

Fodor, J. (1983). *The modularity of mind.* Cambridge, MA: The MIT Press.

Frances, A., Mack, A. H., First, M. B., Widiger, T. A., Ross, R., Forman, L., and Davis, W. W. (1994). DSM-IV meets philosophy. *The Journal of Medicine and Philosophy*, 19, 207–218.

Frances, A. J., and Widiger, T. (2012). Psychiatric diagnosis: lessons from the DSM-IV past and cautions for the DSM-5 future. *Annual Review of Clinical Psychology*, 8, 109–130.

Freitas-Ferrari, M. C., Hallak, J. E. C., Trzesniak, C., Santos Filho, A., Machado-de-Sousa, J. P., Chagas, M. H. N., … Crippa, J. A. S. (2010). Neuroimaging in social anxiety disorder: A systematic review of the literature. *Progress in Neuro-Psychopharmacology and Biological Psychiatry*, 34, 565–580.

Friman, P. C., Hayes, S. C., and Wilson, K. G. (1998). Why behaviour analysts should study emotion: the example of anxiety. *Journal of Applied Behavior Analysis*, 31, 137–156.

Furmark, T., Tillfors, M., Everz, P. O., Marteinsdottir, I., Gefvert, O., and Fredrikson, M. (1999). Social phobia in the general population: prevalence and sociodemographic profile. *Social Psychiatry and Psychiatric Epidemiology*, 34, 416–424.

Furmark, T., Tillfors, M., Garpenstrand, H., Marteinsdottir, I., Langstrom, B., Oreland, L., and Fredrikson, M. (2004). Serotonin transporter polymorphism related to amygdal excitability and symptom severity in patients with social phobia. *Neuroscience Letters*, 362, 189–192.

Fyer, A. J., Mannuzza, S., Chapman, T. F., Martin, L. Y., and Klein, D. F. (1995). Specificity in familial aggregation of phobic disorders. *Archives of General Psychiatry*, 52, 564–573.

Garcia Coll, C., Kagan, J., and Riznick, J. S. (1984). Behavioral inhibition in young children. *Child Development*, 55, 1005–1019.

Gardner, S. (1993). *Irrationality and the philosophy of psychoanalysis*. Cambridge University Press.

Garner, M., Baldwin, D. S., Bradley, B. P., and Mogg, K. (2009). Impaired identification of fearful faces in generalized social phobia. *Journal of Affective Disorders*, 115, 460–465.

Garson, J. (2011). Function and teleology. In: S. Sarkar, and A. Plutynski (eds.), *A companion to the philosophy of biology* (pp. 525–549). Oxford: Blackwell.

Gatherer, D. (2010). So what do we really mean when we say that systems biology is holistic? *BMC Systems Biology*, 4, 1–12.

Gee, B. A., Antony, M. M., and Koerner, N. (2012). Do socially anxious individuals fear embarrassment by close others? Development of the Fear of Embarrassment by Others Scale. *Personality and Individual Differences*, 52, 340–344.

Gelernter, J., Page, G., Stein, M., and Woods, S. (2004). Genome-wide linkage scan for loci predisposing to social phobia: evidence for a chromosome-16 risk locus. *American Journal of Psychiatry*, 161, 59–66.

Gelder, M., Gath, D., Mayou, R., and Cowen, P. (1996). *Oxford textbook of psychiatry*. Oxford University Press.

Gentili, C., Bobbini, M. I., Ricciardi, E., Vanello, N., Pietrini, P., Haxby, J. V., and Guazzelli, M. (2008). Differential modulation of neural activity throughout the distributed neural system for face perception in patients with social phobia and healthy subjects. *Brain Research Bulletin*, 77, 286–292.

Gentili, C., Ricciardi, E., Gobbini, M. I., Santarelli, M. F., Haxby, J. V., Pietrini, P., and Guazzelli, M. (2009). Beyond amygdala: default mode network activity differs between patients with social phobia and healthy controls. *Brain Research Bulletin*, 79, 409–413.

Gerlach, A. L., Wilhelm, F. H., Gruber, K., and Roth, W. T. (2001). Blushing and physiological arousability in social phobia. *Journal of Abnormal Psychology*, 110, 247–258.

296   References

Gerth, H., and Mills, C. W. (1953). *Character and social structure*. New York: Harcourt, Brace, & World.

Getty, J. A. (1999). Samokritika rituals in the Stalinist central committee, 1933–38. *Russian Review*, 58, 49–70.

Gibbs, D., Stravynski, A., and Lachance, L. (2013). The interpersonal approach to the treatment of social phobia: an 8 to 15-year follow-up. (Forthcoming.)

Gier, N. F. (1980). Wittgenstein and forms of life. *Philosophy of the Social Sciences*, 10, 241–258.

Gilbert, P. (2001). Evolution and social anxiety: the role of attraction, social competition, and social hierarchies. *The Psychiatric Clinics of North America*, 24, 723–751.

Gilmartin, B. G. (1987). Peer group antecedents of severe love-shyness in males. *Journal of Personality*, 55, 467–489.

Glassman, M. (2000). Mutual-aid theory and human development: sociability as primary. *Journal for the Theory of Social Behaviour*, 30, 391–412.

Goffman, E. (1956). *The presentation of self in everyday life*. New York: Doubleday.

Goldin, P. R., Manber, T., Hakimi, S., Canli, T., and Gross, J. J. (2009). Neural bases of social anxiety disorder: emotional reactivity and cognitive regulation during social and physical threat. *Archives of General Psychiatry*, 66, 170–180.

Goldin, P. R., Manber-Ball, T., Werner, K., Heimberg, R., and Gross, J. J. (2009). Neural mechanisms of cognitive reappraisal of negative self-beliefs in social anxiety disorder. *Biological Psychiatry*, 66, 1091–1099.

Goldsmith, H. H., Buss, A. H., Plomin, R., Rothbart, M. K., Thomas, A., Chess, S., ... McCall, R. B. (1987). What is temperament? Four approaches. *Child Development*, 58, 505–529.

Goodwin, D. W. (1986). *Anxiety*. New York: Oxford University Press.

Gopnik, A. (1993). How we know our minds: the illusion of first-person knowledge of intentionality. *Behavioral and Brain Sciences*, 16, 1–14.

Gorenstein, E. E. (1992). *The science of mental illness*. San Diego, CA: Academic Press.

Gorman, J., Kent, J., Sullivan, G., and Coplan, J. (2000). Neuroanatomical hypothesis of panic disorder, revised. *American Journal of Psychiatry*, 157, 493–505.

Gould, J. L., and Grant Gould, C. (2007). *Animal architects: building and the evolution of intelligence*. New York: Basic Books.

  (2012). *Nature's compass: the mystery of animal navigation*. Princeton, NJ: Princeton University Press.

Gould, S.-J. (1981). *The mismeasure of man*. New York: Norton.

Gray, J. A. (1970). The psychophysiological basis of introversion–extraversion. *Behaviour Research and Therapy*, 8, 249–266.

Gray, J. A., and McNaughton, N. (2004). *The neuropsychology of anxiety: an enquiry into the function of the septo-hippocampal system*. Oxford University Press.

Green, L. (1994). Fear as a way of life. *Cultural Anthropology*, 9, 227–256.

Greenberg, D., Stravynski, A., and Bilu, Y. (2004). Social phobia in ultra-orthodox Jewish males: culture-bound syndrome or virtue? *Mental Health, Religion, and Culture*, 7, 289–305.

Greenberg, D., and Witztum, E. (eds.) (2001). *Sanity and sanctity: mental health work among the ultra-orthodox in Jerusalem*. New Haven, CT: Yale University Press.

Griesinger, W. (1845). *Die Pathologie und Therapie der psychischen Krankheiten für Aerzte und Studirende*. Amsterdam: Bonset.

Grüner, K., Muris, P., and Merckelbach, H. (1999). The relationship between anxious rearing behaviors and anxiety disorders symptomatology in normal children. *Journal of Behavior Therapy and Experimental Psychiatry*, 30, 27–35.

Gullone, E., and King, N. J. (1993). The fears of youth in the 1990s: contemporary normative data. *The Journal of Genetic Psychology*, 154, 137–153.

(1997). Three-year follow-up of normal fear in children and adolescents, aged 7 to 18 years. *British Journal of Developmental Psychology*, 15, 97–111.

Gündel, H., Wolf, A., Xidara, V., Busch, R., and Ceballos-Baumann, A. O. (2001). Social phobia in spasmodic torticollis. *Journal of Neurology, Neurosurgery, and Psychiatry*, 71, 499–504.

Gursky, D. M., and Reiss, S. (1987). Identifying danger and anxiety expectancies as components of common fears. *Journal of Behavior Therapy and Experimental Psychiatry*, 18, 317–324.

Hacker, P. M. S. (1996). *Wittgenstein: mind and will* (Vol. IV). Oxford: Blackwell.

(1997). *Wittgenstein: on human nature*. London: Phoenix.

(2004). The conceptual framework for the investigation of emotions. *International Review of Psychiatry*, 16, 199–208.

(2007). *Human nature: the categorical framework*. Oxford: Blackwell.

Hackmann, A., Surawy, C., and Clark, D. (1998). Seeing yourself through others' eyes: a study of spontaneously occurring images in social phobia. *Behavioural and Cognitive Psychotherapy*, 26, 3–12.

Hagstrum, J. T. (2013). Atmospheric propagation modeling indicates homing pigeons use loft-specific infrasonic "map" cues. *The Journal of Experimental Biology*, 216, 687–699.

Hallam, R. (1985). *Anxiety: psychological perspectives on panic and agoraphobia*. New York: Academic Press.

Hamann, S. (2005). Sex differences in the responses of the human amygdala. *The Neuroscientist*, 11, 288–293.

Hankinson, R. J. (2009). Causes. In: G. Anagnostopoulos (ed.), *A companion to Aristotle* (pp. 213–229). New York: Wiley-Blackwell.

Hare, R. D. (1993). *Without conscience: the disturbing world of the psychopaths among us*. New York: Guilford.

Harré, R. (1991a). *Physical being: a theory for a corporeal psychology*. Oxford: Blackwell.

(1991b). The discursive production of selves. *Theory and Psychology*, 1, 51–63.

Harris, J. R. (1995). Where is the child's environment? A group socialization theory of development. *Psychological Review*, 102, 458–489.

Harvey, J. M., Richards, J. C., Dziadosz, T., and Swindell, A. (1993). Misinterpretation of ambiguous stimuli in panic disorder. *Cognitive Therapy and Research*, 17, 235–248.

Haslam, N. O. (1998). Natural kinds, human kinds, and essentialism. *Social Research*, 65, 291–314.

Hawker, D. S. J., and Boulton, M. J. (2000). Twenty years' research on peer victimization and psychosocial maladjustment: a meta-analytic review of cross-sectional studies. *Journal of Child Psychology and Psychiatry*, 41, 441–455.

Hawley, P. H. (1999). The ontogenesis of social dominance: a strategy-based evolutionary perspective. *Developmental Reviews*, 19, 97–132.

Hayano, F., Nakamura, M., Asami, T., Uehara, K., Yoshida, T., Roppongi, T., ...
Hirayasu Y. (2009) Smaller amygdala is associated with anxiety in patients
with panic disorder. *Psychiatry and Clinical Neurosciences*, 63, 266–276.

Heerey, E. A., and Kring, A. M. (2007). Interpersonal consequences of social
anxiety. *Journal of Abnormal Psychology*, 116, 125–134.

Heils, A., Teufel, A., Petri, S., Stober, G., Riederer, P., Bengel, D., and Lesch, K.
(1996). Allelic variation of human serotonin transporter gene expression.
Journal of Neurochemistry, 66, 2621–2624.

Heimberg, R. G. (1994). Cognitive assessment strategies and the measurement
of outcome of treatment for social phobia. *Behaviour Research and Therapy*,
32, 269–280.

Heimberg, R. G., Hope, D. A., Dodge, C. S., and Becker, R. E. (1990). DSM-
III-R subtypes of social phobia: comparison of generalized social phobics
and public speaking phobics. *Journal of Nervous and Mental Disease*, 178,
172–179.

Heiser, N. A., Turner, S. M., Beidel, D. C., and Robertson-Nay, R. (2009).
Differentiating social phobia from shyness. *Journal of Anxiety Disorders*, 23,
469–476.

Henderson, L. J. (1935). Physician and patient as a social system. *The New
England Journal of Medicine*, 212, 819–823.

Herry, C., Ferraguti, F., Singewald, N., Letzkus, J. J., Ehrlich, I., and Lüthi, A.
(2010). Neuronal circuits of fear extinction. *European Journal of Neuroscience*,
31, 599–612.

Hinde, R. A. (1976). On describing relationships. *Journal of Child Psychology and
Psychiatry*, 17, 1–19.

(1987). *Individuals, relationships and culture: links between ethology and the social
sciences*. Cambridge University Press.

Hirshfeld-Becker, D. R., Biederman, J., Henin, A., Faraone, S. V., Davis, S.,
Harrington, K., and Rosenbaum, J. F. (2007). Behavioral inhibition in preschool children at risk is a specific predictor of middle childhood social anxiety: a five-year follow-up. *Journal of Developmental and Behavioral Pediatrics*,
28, 225–233.

Hocutt, M. (1974). Aristotle's four becauses. *Philosophy*, 49, 385–399.

Hoes, M. J. (1986). Biological markers in psychiatry. *Acta Psychiatrica Belgica*,
86, 220–241.

Hofmann, B. (2002). On the triad disease, illness and sickness. *Journal of Medicine
and Philosophy*, 27, 651–673.

Hofmann, S. G., Korte, K. J., and Suvak, M. K. (2009). The upside of being
socially anxious: psychopathic attributes and social anxiety are negatively
associated. *Journal of Social and Clinical Psychology*, 28, 714–727.

Hofmann, S. G., and Roth, W. T. (1996). Issues related to social anxiety among
controls in social phobia research. *Behavior Therapy*, 27, 79–91.

Holmes, R. (1985). *Acts of war: the behaviour of men in battle*. New York: Free Press.

Homel, R., Burns, A., and Goodnow, J. (1987). Parental social networks and
child development. *Journal of Social and Personal Relationships*, 4, 159–177.

Homma, I., and Masaoka, Y. (2008). Breathing rhythms and emotions. *Experimental Physiology*, 93, 1011–1021.

Hope, D. A., Rapee, R. M., Heimberg, R. G., and Dombeck, M. J., (1990). Representations of the self in social phobia: vulnerability to social threat. *Cognitive Therapy and Research*, 14, 177–189.

Howarth, E. (1980). Major factors of personality. *Journal of Psychology*, 104, 171–183.

Hudson, J. L., and Rapee, R. M. (2001). Parent–child interactions and anxiety disorders: an observational study. *Behaviour Research and Therapy*, 39, 1411–1427.

(2002). Parent–child interactions in clinically anxious children and their siblings. *Journal of Clinical Child and Adolescent Psychology*, 31, 548–555.

Huizinga, J. (1955). *Homo ludens*. Boston, MA: Beacon Press.

Hume, D. ([1739]1961). *A treatise of human nature*. London: Dent.

Humphrey, N. K. (1976). The social function of intellect. In: P. P. G. Bateson, and R. A. Hinde (eds.), *Growing points in ethology* (pp. 303–317). Cambridge University Press.

Hunt, N., and McHale, S. (2005). The psychological impact of alopecia. *British Medical Journal*, 331, 951–953.

Hyman, S. E. (2007). Can neuroscience be integrated into the DSM-V? *Nature Reviews*, 8, 725–732.

Hymel, S., Rubin, K. H., Rowden, L., and LeMare, L. (1990). Children's peer relationships: longitudinal prediction of internalizing and externalizing problems from middle to late childhood. *Child Development*, 61, 2004–2021.

Illbruck, H. (2012). *Nostalgia: origins and ends of an unenlightened disease*. Evanston, IL.: Northwestern University Press.

Insel, T. R., and Quirion, R. (2005). Psychiatry as a clinical neuroscience discipline. *Journal of the American Medical Association*, 294, 2221–2224.

Irle, E., Ruhleder, M., Lange, C., Seidler-Brandler, U., Salzer, S., Dechent, P., … Leichsenring, F. (2010). Reduced amygdalar and hippocampal size in adults with generalized social phobia. *Journal of Psychiatry and Neuroscience*, 35, 126–131.

IsHak, W. W., Bokarius, A., Jeffrey, J. K., Davis, M. C., and Bakhta, Y. (2010). Disorders of orgasm in women: a literature review of etiology and current treatments. *Journal of Sex Medicine*, 7, 3254–3268.

Ishiguro, H., Arinam, I. T., Yamada, K., Otsuka, Y., Toru, M., and Shibuya, H. (1997). An association study between a transcriptional polymorphism in the serotonin transporter gene and panic disorder in a Japanese population. *Psychiatry and Clinical Neurosciences*, 51, 333–335.

Izard, C. E., and Youngstrom, E. A. (1996). The activation and regulation of fear and anxiety. *Nebraska Symposium on Motivation*, 43, 1–59.

Jackson, R. A. (1971). Peers of France and princes of the blood. *French Historical Studies*, 7, 27–46.

Jacobson, N. S., Dobson, K. S., Truax, P. A., Addis, M. E., Koerner, K., Gollan, J. K., … Prince, S. E. (1996). A component analysis of cognitive-behavioral treatment for depression. *Journal of Consulting and Clinical Psychology*, 64, 295–304.

James, B. (1997). Social phobia: a debilitating disease with a new treatment option – based on presentations at the XXth Congress of the Collegium Internationale Neuro-Psychopharmacologicum. *International Clinical Psychopharmacology*, 12, S1.

Jaworski, W. (2011). *Philosophy of mind*. Chichester: Wiley.

Jones, E. E., and Nisbett, R. E. (1971). *The actor and the observer: divergent perceptions of the causes of behaviour*. Morristown, NJ: General Learning Press.

Jost, J. T. (1995). Toward a Wittgensteinian social psychology of human development. *Theory and Psychology*, 5, 5–25.

Kachin, K. E., Newman, M. G., and Pincus, A. L. (2001). An interpersonal problem approach to the division of social phobia subtypes. *Behavior Therapy*, 32, 479–501.

Kagan, J. (1989). Temperament contributions to social behavior. *American Psychologist*, 44, 668–674.

Kagan, J., and Moss, H. A. (1962). *Birth to maturity: a study in psychological development*. New York: Wiley.

Kagan, J., Reznick, J. S., and Snidman, N. (1987). The physiology and psychology of behavioral inhibition in children. *Child Development*, 58, 1459–1473.

  (1988). Biological bases of childhood shyness. *Science*, 240, 167–171.

Kagan, J., and Snidman, N. (1991a). Infant predictors of inhibited and uninhibited profiles. *Psychological Science*, 2, 40–44.

  (1991b). Temperamental factors in human development. *American Psychologist*, 46, 856–862.

Kagan, J., and Zentner, M. (1996). Early childhood predictors of adult psychopathology. *Harvard Review of Psychiatry*, 3, 341–350.

Karen, R. (1998). *Becoming attached: first relationships and how they shape our capacity to love*. New York: Oxford University Press.

Keedwell, P., and Snaith, R. P. (1996). What do anxiety scales measure? *Acta Psychiatrica Scandinavica*, 93, 177–180.

Keegan, J. (1988). *The mask of command*. Harmondsworth: Penguin.

Keller, J., Shen, L., Gomez, R. G., Garrett, A., Solvason, H. B., Reiss, A., and Schatzberg, A. F. (2008). Hippocampal and amygdalar volumes in psychotic and nonpsychotic unipolar depression. *American Journal of Psychiatry*, 165, 872–880.

Kelman, H. C., and Hamilton, J. L. (1989). *Crimes of obedience: toward a social psychology of authority and responsibility*. New Haven, CT: Yale University Press.

Keltner, D., Buswell, B. N. (1997). Embarrassment: its distinct form and appeasement functions. *Psychological Bulletin*, 122, 250–270.

Kemp Smith, N. (1941). *The philosophy of David Hume*. London: Macmillan.

Kemper, T. D. (1978a). *A social interactional theory of emotion*. New York: Wiley.

  (1978b). A social interactional theory of emotions. In: M. Lewis and J. M. Haviland-Jones (eds.), *Handbook of emotions* (pp. 45–58). New York: Guilford Press.

  (2000). Social models in the explanation of emotions. In: M. Lewis and J. M. Haviland-Jones (eds.), *Handbook of emotions* (pp. 45–58). New York: Guilford Press.

Kemper, T. D., and Collins, R. (1990). Dimensions of microinteraction. *American Journal of Sociology*, 96, 32–68.

Kendell, R. E. (1986). What are mental disorders? In: A. M. Freedman, R. Brotman, I. Silverman, and D. Hutson (eds.), *Issues in psychiatric classification: science, practice and social policy.* New York: Human Sciences Press.

(1989). Clinical validity. *Psychological Medicine,* 19, 45–55.

Kendler, K. A., Neale, M. C., Kessler, R. C., Heath, A. C., and Eaves, L. J. (1992). The genetic epidemiology of phobias in women: the interrelationship of agoraphobia, social phobia, situational phobia, and simple phobia. *Archives of General Psychiatry,* 49, 273–281.

Kennedy, J., Neves-Pereira, M., King, N., Lizak, M., Basile, V., Chartier, M., and Stein, M. (2001). Dopamine system genes not linked to social phobia. *Psychiatric Genetics,* 11, 213–217.

Kenny, A. (1995). *The metaphysics of mind.* Oxford University Press.

(2005). *Wittgenstein.* Oxford: Blackwell.

Kershaw, I. (1993). "Working towards the Führer." Reflections on the nature of the Hitler dictatorship. *Contemporary European History,* 2, 103–118.

Kessler, R. C., Davis, C. G., and Kendler, K. S. (1997). Childhood adversity and adult psychiatric disorder in the US national comorbidity survey. *Psychological Medicine,* 27, 1101–1119.

Keyes, C. L. M. (2007). Promoting and protecting mental health as flourishing. *American Psychologist,* 62, 95–108.

Kiernan, V. G. (1988). *The duel in European history: honour and the reign of aristocracy.* Oxford University Press.

King, W. L. (1993). *Zen and the way of the sword.* Oxford University Press.

Kirsch, I., Moore, J., Scoboria, A., and Nicholls, S. S. (2002). The emperor's new drugs: an analysis of antidepressant medication data submitted to the U.S. Food and Drug Administration. *Prevention and Treatment,* 5, 1–11.

Klein, G. (2008). Naturalistic decision making. *Human Factor,* 50, 456–460.

Klumpp, H., Angstadt, M., Nathan, P. J., and Phan, K. L. (2010). Amygdala reactivity to faces at varying intensities of threat in generalized social phobia: an event-related functional MRI study. *Psychiatry Research,* 183, 167–169.

Klumpp, H., Angstadt, M., and Phan, K. L. (2012). Insula reactivity and connectivity to anterior cingulate cortex when processing threat in generalized social anxiety disorder. *Biological Psychology,* 89, 273–276.

Kumar, V., Abbas, A., Fausto, N., and Aster, J. (2010). *Robbins and Cotran pathologic basis of disease* (8th edn.). Philadelphia, PA: Elsevier.

Kupiec, J.-J. and Sonigo, P. (2000). *Ni Dieu ni gène: pour une autre théorie de l'hérédité.* Paris: Seuil.

Kyparissis, A., Stravynski, A., and Lachance, L. (2013a). Is social phobia characterized by a distinct interpersonal pattern? A comparison between social phobic, single sexually dysfunctional, and normal individuals. (Under review.)

(2013b). Does an interpersonal approach to treatment improve the dysfunctional interpersonal pattern in social phobia? A one-year follow-up. (Under review.)

La Greca, A. M., Dandes, S. K., Wick, P., Shaw, K., and Stone, W. L. (1988). Development of the Social Anxiety Scale for Children: reliability and concurrent validity. *Journal of Clinical Child Psychology,* 17, 84–91.

Lacey, H. (1995). Teleological behaviorism and the intentional scheme. *Behavioral and Brain Sciences,* 18, 134–135.

Lader, M., and Marks, I. M. (1971). *Clinical anxiety*. New York: Grune and Stratton.

LaForge, R., and Suczek, R. F. (1955). The interpersonal dimensions of personality: III. An interpersonal check list. *Journal of Personality*, 24, 94–112.

Laird, J. D. (2007). *Feelings: the perception of self*. Oxford University Press.

Lamb, M. E., Thompson, R. A., Gardner, W. P., Charnov, E. L., and Estes, D. (1984). Security of infantile attachment as assessed in the "Strange Situation." *Behavioral and Brain Sciences*, 7, 127–171.

Lane, C. (2008). *Shyness: how normal behavior became a sickness*. New Haven, CT: Yale University Press.

Lanzenberger, R. R., Mitterhauser, M., Spindelegger, C., Wadsak, W., Klein, N., Mien, L. K., ... Tauscher, J. (2007). Reduced serotonin-1A receptor binding in social anxiety disorder. *Biological Psychiatry*, 61, 1081–1089.

Lanzenberger, R., Wadsak, W., Spindelegger, C., Mitterhauser, M., Akimova, E., Mien, L. K., ... Kasper, S. (2010). Cortisol plasma levels in social anxiety disorder patients correlate with serotonin-1A receptor binding in limbic brain regions. *International Journal of Neuropsychopharmacology*, 13, 1129–1143.

Laufer, N., Maayan, R., Hermesh, H., Marom, S., Gilad, R., Strous, R., and Weizman, A. (2005). Involvement of GABAA receptor modulating neuroactive steroids in patients with social phobia. *Psychiatry Research*, 137, 131–136. Erratum in: *Psychiatry Research* (2006); p. 30; 144, 95.

Laufer, N., Zucker, M., Hermesh, H., Marom, S., Gilad, R., Nir, V., ... Rehavi, M. (2005). Platelet vesicular monoamine transporter density in untreated patients diagnosed with social phobia. *Psychiatry Research*, 136, 247–250.

Leary, M. R. (1983). Social anxiousness: the construct and its measurement. *Journal of Personality Assessment*, 47, 66–75.

Ledeneva, A. (2008). Blat and Guamxi: informal practices in Russia and China. *Comparative Studies in Society and History*, 50, 118–144.

Lederman, R. J. (1989). Performing arts medicine. *New England Journal of Medicine*, 320, 221–227.

LeDoux, J. (1996). *The emotional brain*. New York: Simon and Schuster.

Leray, E., Camara, A., Drapier, D., Riou, F., Bougeant, N, Pelissolo, A., ... Millet, B. (2011). Prevalence, characteristics and comorbidities of anxiety disorders in France: results from the "Mental Health in General Population" Survey (MHGP). *European Psychiatry*, 26, 339–345.

Lesch, K., Bengel, D., Heils, A., Sabol, S., Greenberg, B., Petri, S., ... Murphy, D. (1996). Association of anxiety-related traits with a polymorphism in the serotonin transporter gene regulatory region. *Science*, 274, 1527–1531.

Leung, A. W., Heimberg, R. G., Holt, C. H., and Bruch, M. A. (1994). Social anxiety and perception of early parenting among American, Chinese American and social phobic samples. *Anxiety*, 1, 80–89.

Levenson, M. R. (1992). Rethinking psychopathy. *Theory and Psychology*, 2, 51–71.

Levin, A. P., Saoud, J. B., Strauman, T., Gorman, J. M., Fyer, A. J., Crawford, R., and Liebowitz, M. R. (1993). Responses of generalized and discrete social phobics during public speaking. *Journal of Anxiety Disorders*, 7, 207–221.

Levitt, E. E. (1980). *The psychology of anxiety*. Hillsdale, NJ: Lawrence Erlbaum.

Lewis, A. (1967). Problems presented by the ambiguous word "anxiety" as used in psychopathology. *The Israel Annals of Psychiatry and Related Disciplines*, 5, 105–121.

Liberzon, I., and Phan, K. (2003). Brain-imaging studies of posttraumatic stress disorder. *CNS Spectrums*, 8, 641–650.

Liebowitz, M. R., Gorman, J., Fyer, A., and Klein, D. (1985). Social phobia: review of a neglected anxiety disorder. *Archives of General Psychiatry*, 42, 729–736.

Lilienfeld, S. O., and Marino, L. (1995). Mental disorder as a Roschian concept: A critique of Wakefield's "harmful dysfunction" analysis. *Journal of Abnormal Psychology*, 104, 411–420.

Lima, S. L., and Dill, L. M. (1989). Behavioural decisions made under the risk of predation: a review and prospectus. *Canadian Journal of Zoology*, 68, 619–640.

Lipowski, Z. J. (1989). Psychiatry: mindless or brainless, both or neither? *Canadian Journal of Psychiatry*, 34, 249–254.

Lipsitz, J. D., Gur, M., Vermes, D., Petkova, E., Cheng, J., Miller, N., ... Fyer, A. J. (2008). A randomized trial of interpersonal therapy versus supportive therapy for social anxiety disorder. *Depression and Anxiety*, 25, 542–553.

Lochner, C., Hemmings, S., Seedat, S., Kinnear, C., Schoeman, R., Annerbrink, K., ... Stein, D. J. (2007). Genetics and personality traits in patients with social anxiety disorder: a case-control study in South Africa. *European Neuropsychopharmacology*, 17, 321–327.

Looren de Jong, H. (1997). Some remarks on a relational concept of mind. *Theory and Psychology*, 7, 147–172.

Lorenzetti, V., Allen, N. B., Fornito, A., and Yücel, M. (2009). Structural brain abnormalities in major depressive disorder: a selective review of recent MRI studies. *Journal of Affective Disorders*, 117, 1–17.

Lourenço, O. (2001). The danger of words: a Wittgensteinian lesson for developmentalists. *New Ideas in Psychology*, 19, 89–115.

Lukes, S. (2000). Different cultures, different rationalities? *History of the Human Sciences*, 13, 3–18.

MacDonald, G., and Leary, M. R. (2005). Why does social exclusion hurt? The relationship between social and physical pain. *Psychological Bulletin*, 131, 202–223.

MacLeod, C. (1991). Clinical anxiety and the selective encoding of threatening information. *International Review of Psychiatry*, 3, 279–292.

MacLeod, D., and Mathews, A. (2012). Cognitive bias modification approaches to anxiety. *Annual Review of Clinical Psychology*, 8, 189–217.

Madrick, J. (2011). *Age of greed: the triumph of finance and the decline of America, 1970 to the present*. New York: Alfred A. Knopf.

Magee, W. J. (1999). Effects of negative life experiences on phobia onset. *Social Psychiatry and Psychiatric Epidemiology*, 34, 343–351.

Malcolm, N. (1977). The myth of cognitive processus and structures. In: T. Mischel (ed.), *Cognitive development and epistemiology* (pp. 385–392). New York: Academic Press.

Manassis, K., Bradley, S., Goldberg, S., Hood, J., and Swinson, R. P. (1995). Behavioural inhibition, attachment and anxiety in children of mothers with anxiety disorders. *Canadian Journal of Psychiatry*, 40, 87–92.

Mancini, C., van Ameringen, M., and MacMillan, H. (1995). Relationship of childhood sexual and physical abuse to anxiety disorder. *Journal of Nervous and Mental Disease*, 183, 309–314.

Mandelstam, N. (1970). *Hope against hope*. New York: Atheneum.

Mangelsdorf, S., Gunnar, M., Kestenbaum, R., Lang, S., and Andreas, D. (1990). Infant proneness-to-distress temperament, maternal personality and mother–infant attachment: associations and goodness of fit. *Child Development*, 61, 820–831.

Manzoni, G. M., Pagnini, F., Castelnuovo, G., and Molinari, E. (2008). Relaxation training for anxiety: a ten-year systematic review with meta-analysis. *BMC Psychiatry*, 8, 1–12.

Marks, I. M. (1987). *Fears, phobias and rituals*. New York: Oxford University Press.

Matthen, M. (2009). Teleology in living things. In: G. Anagnostopoulos (ed.), *A companion to Aristotle* (pp. 335–347). Oxford: Blackwell.

Mayr, E. (1974). Behavior programs and evolutionary strategies. *American Scientist*, 62, 650–659.

Mazower, M. (2002). Violence and the state in the twentieth century. *American Historical Review*, 107, 1158–1178.

McCabe, R. E., Antony, M. M., Summerfeldt, L. J., Liss, A., and Swinson, R. P. (2003). Preliminary examination of the relationship between anxiety disorders in adults and self-reported history of teasing or bullying experiences. *Cognitive Behaviour Therapy*, 32, 187–193.

McCauley Ohannessian, C., Lerner, R. M., Lerner, J. V., and von Eye, A. (1999). Does self-competence predict gender differences in adolescent depression and anxiety? *Journal of Adolescence*, 22, 397–411.

McFall, R. M., and Townsend, J. T. (1998). Foundations of psychological assessment: implications for cognitive assessment in clinical science. *Psychological Assessment*, 10, 316–330.

McFall, R. M., Treat, T. A., and Viken, R. J. (1998). Contemporary cognitive approaches to studying clinical problems. In: D. K. Routh and R. J. De Rubeis (eds.), *The science of clinical psychology* (pp. 163–197). Washington, DC: American Psychological Association.

McGinn, C. (1982). *The character of mind*. Oxford University Press.

McLellan, D. (1975). *Marx*. Glasgow: Collins.

McLemore, C. W., and Benjamin, L. S. (1979). Whatever happened to interpersonal diagnosis? *American Psychologist*, 34, 17–34.

McNeil, D. W., Turk, C. L., and Ries, B. J. (1994). Anxiety and fear. In: V. S. Ramachandran (ed.), *Encyclopedia of human behaviour*, Vol. I (pp. 151–167). La Jolla, CA: Academic Press.

Mead, G. H. (1934). *Mind, self and society*. Chicago, IL: University of Chicago Press.

Medawar, P. B. (1977). Unnatural science. *The New York Review of Books*, 3, 13–18.

Meichenbaum, D. (1977). *Cognitive-behavior modification: an integrative approach*. New York: Plenum Press.

Melke, J., Landen, M., Baghei, F., Rosmond, R., Holm, G., Bjorntorp, P., ... Eriksson, E. (2001). Serotonin transporter gene polymorphisms are associated with anxiety-related personality traits in women. *American Journal of Medical Genetics*, 105, 458–463.

Mersch, P. P. A., Hildebrand, M., Mavy, E. H., Wessel, L., and van Hout, W. J. P. J. (1992). Somatic symptoms in social phobia: a treatment method based on rational emotive therapy and paradoxical interventions. *Journal of Behavior Therapy and Experimental Psychiatry*, 23, 199–211.

Michels, R., Frances, A., and Shear, M. K. (1985). Psychodynamic models of anxiety. In: A. H. Tuma and J. D. Maser (eds.), *Anxiety and the anxiety disorders* (pp. 595–609). Hillside, NJ: Lawrence Erlbaum.

Mill, J. S., (2002). *A system of logic*, Honolulu, HI: University Press of the Pacific.

Millan, M. (2003). The neurobiology and control of anxious states. *Progress in Neurobiology*, 70, 83–244.

Millon, T., and Martinez, A. (1995). Avoidant personality disorder. In: W. J. Livesley (ed.), *The DSM-IV personality disorders* (pp. 218–233). New York: Guilford Press.

Mineka, S., and Kihlstrom, J. (1978). Unpredictable and uncontrolled aversive events and experimental neurosis. *Journal of Abnormal Psychology*, 85, 256–271.

Moelk, M. (1944). Vocalizing in the house-cat: a phonetic and functional study. *The American Journal of Psychology*, 57, 184–205.

Moerman, D. E. (2000). Cultural variations in the placebo effect: ulcers, anxiety, and blood pressure. *Medical Anthropology Quarterly*, 14, 51–72.

Moerman, D. (2002). *Meaning medicine and the placebo effect*. Cambridge University Press.

Mooij, A. (1995). Towards an anthropological psychiatry. *Theoretical Medicine*, 16, 73–91.

Morey, L. C. (1991). Classification of mental disorder as a collection of hypothetical constructs. *Journal of Abnormal Psychology*, 100, 289–293.

Morey, R. A., Gold, A. L., LaBar, K. S., Beall, S. K., Brown, V. M., Haswell, C. C., ... Mid-Atlantic MIRECC Workgroup. (2012). Amygdala volume changes in posttraumatic stress disorder in a large case-controlled veterans group. *Archives of General Psychiatry*, 69, 1169–1178.

Mousnier, R. (1969). *Les hiérarchies sociales de 1450 à nos jours*. Paris: Presses Universitaires de France.

Moynihan, R. (2003). The making of a disease: female sexual dysfunction. *British Medical Journal*, 326, 45–47.

(2010). Merging of marketing and medical science. *British Medical Journal*, 341, 698–701.

Moynihan, R., Heath, I., and Henry, D. (2002). Selling sickness: the pharmaceutical industry and disease mongering. *British Medical Journal*, 324, 886–891.

Murphy, G. L., and Medin, D. L. (1985). The role of theories in conceptual coherence. *Psychological Review*, 92, 289–316.

Murphy, N., and Brown, W. S. (eds.) (2007). *Did my neurons make me do it?* New York: Oxford University Press.

Muris, P., Merckelbach, H., Meesters, C., and van Lier, P. (1997). What do children fear most often? *Journal of Behavior Therapy and Experimental Psychiatry*, 28, 263–267.

Naimark, N. M. (2002). *Fires of hatred: ethnic cleansing in twentieth-century Europe*. Cambridge, MA: Harvard University Press.

Nakao, T., Sanematsu, H., Yoshiura, T., Togao, O., Murayama, K., Tomita, M., ... Kanba, S. (2011). fMRI of patients with social anxiety disorder during a social situation task. *Neuroscience Research*, 69, 67–72.

Nardi, A. E., Lopes, F. L., Freire, R. C., Veras, A. B., Nascimento, I., Valença, A. M., ... Zin, W. A. (2009). Panic disorder and social anxiety disorder subtypes in a caffeine challenge test. *Psychiatry Research*, 169, 149–153.

Nelson-Gray, R. O. (1991). DSM-IV: empirical guidelines from psychometrics. *Journal of Abnormal Psychology*, 100, 308–315.

Newell, R., and Marks, I. (2000). Phobic nature of social difficulty in facially disfigured people. *British Journal of Psychiatry*, 176, 177–181.

Nickell, P. V., and Uhde, T. W. (1995). Neurobiology of social phobia. In: R. G. Heimberg, M. R. Liebowitz, D. A. Hope, and F. R. Schneier (eds.), *Social phobia: diagnosis, assessment, and treatment*. New York: Guilford Press.

Noble, D. (2006). *The music of life: biology beyond the genome*. Oxford University Press.

(2008). Prologue: Mind over molecule: activating biological demons. *Annals of the New York Academy of Sciences*, 1123, xi–xix.

Noyes, R., and Hoehn-Saric, R. (1998). *The anxiety disorders*. Cambridge University Press.

Nussbaum, M. (1978). *Aristotle's De Motu Animalium*. Princeton, NJ: Princeton University Press.

Nussbaum, M. C., and Putman, H. (1992). Changing Aristotle's mind. In: M. C. Nussbaum, and A. Oksenberg Rorty (eds.), *Essays on Aristotle's De Anima* (pp. 27–56). Oxford University Press.

Nutt, D., Bell, C., and Malizia, A. (1998). Brain mechanisms of social anxiety disorder. *Journal of Clinical Psychiatry*, 59, 4–11.

Oatley, D., and Jenkins, J. M. (1992). Human emotions: function and dysfunction. *Annual Reviews in Psychology*, 43, 55–85.

Ohayon, M. M., and Schatzberg, A. F. (2010). Social phobia and depression: prevalence and comorbidity. *Journal of Psychosomatic Research*, 68, 235–243.

Ohman, A. (2000). Fear and anxiety: evolutionary, cognitive and clinical perspective. In: M. Lewis and J. M. Haviland-Jones (eds.), *Handbook of emotions* (pp. 573–593). New York: Guilford Press.

Ollendick, T. H., Matson, J. L., and Helsel, W. J. (1985). Fears in children and adolescents: normative data. *Behaviour Research and Therapy*, 23, 465–467.

Ollendick, T. H., Neville, J. K., and Frary, R. B. (1989). Fears in children and adolescents: reliability and generalizability across gender, age and nationality. *Behaviour Research and Therapy*, 27, 19–26.

Olweus, D. (1993). Victimization by peers: antecedents and long-term outcomes. In: K. H. F. Rubin and J. B. Asendorf (eds.), *Social withdrawal, inhibition and shyness in childhood*. Hillsdale, NJ: Lawrence Erlbaum.

Orvaschel, H. (1994). *Schedule for affective disorders and schizophrenia for school-age children–epidemiologic version (K-SADS-E)* (5th edn.). Fort Lauderdale, FA: Nova Southeastern University, Center for Psychological Studies.

Pallister, E., and Waller, G. (2008). Anxiety in the eating disorders: understanding the overlap. *Clinical Psychology Review*, 28, 366–386.

Papadimitriou, G. N., and Linkowski, P. (2005). Sleep disturbance in anxiety disorders. *International Review of Psychiatry*, 17, 229–236.

Parker, G. (1979). Reported parental characteristics of agoraphobics and social phobics. *British Journal of Psychiatry*, 135, 555–560.

Parker, I. (1996). Against Wittgenstein: materialist reflections on language in psychology. *Theory and Psychology*, 6, 363–384.

Parkinson, B. (1996). Emotions are social. *British Journal of Psychology*, 87, 663–683.

Paxton, R. O. (2004). *The anatomy of fascism*. New York: Knopf.

Pedersen, D. (2002). Political violence, ethnic conflict, and contemporary wars: broad implications for health and social well-being. *Social Science and Medicine*, 55, 175–190.

Pélissolo, A., André, C., Moutard, Martin, F., Wittchen, H. U., and Lépine, J. P. (2000). Social phobia in the community: relationship between diagnostic threshold and prevalence. *European Psychiatry*, 15, 25–28.

Phan, K. L., Fitzgerald, D. A., Nathan, P. J., and Tancer, M. E. (2006). Association between amygdala hyperactivity to harsh faces and severity of social anxiety in generalized social phobia. *Biological Psychiatry*, 59, 424–429.

Phan, K. L., Orlichenko, A., Boyd, E., Angstadt, M., Coccaro, E. F., Liberzon, I., and Arfanakis, K. (2009). Preliminary evidence of white matter abnormality in the uncinate fasciculus in generalized social anxiety disorder. *Biological Psychiatry*, 66, 691–694.

Phemister, P. (2006). *The rationalists: Descartes, Spinoza and Leibniz*. London: Polity.

Pinto, A., and Phillips, K. A. (2005). Social anxiety in body dysmorphic disorder. *Body Image*, 2, 401–405.

Pleskac, T. J., and Busemeyer, J. R. (2010). Two-stage dynamic signal detection: a theory of choice, decision time, and confidence. *Psychological Review*, 117, 864–901.

Plomin, R., DeFries, J. C., and McClearn, G. E. (1990). *Behavioral genetics*. New York: W.H. Freeman.

Plutchik, R., and H. R. Conte (eds.) (1997). *Circumplex models of personality and emotion*. Washington, DC: American Psychological Association.

Pollard, C. A., and Henderson, J. G. (1988). Four types of social phobia in a community sample. *The Journal of Nervous and Mental Disease*, 176, 440–445.

Pontoski, K. E., and Heimberg, R. G. (2010). The myth of the superiority of concurrent combined treatments for anxiety disorders. *Clinical Psychology: Science and Practice*, 17, 107–111.

Poulton, R., Trainor, P., Stanton, W., McGee, R., Davies, S., and Silva, P. (1997). The (in)stability of adolescent fears. *Behaviour Research and Therapy*, 35, 159–163.

Pribor, E. F., and Dinwiddie, S. H. (1992). Psychiatric correlates of incest in childhood. *American Journal of Psychiatry*, 149, 52–56.

Purdon, C., Antony, M., Monteiro, S., and Swinson, R. P. (2001). Social anxiety in college students. *Journal of Anxiety Disorders*, 15, 203–215.

Putallaz, M. (1987). Maternal behavior and children's sociometric status. *Child Development*, 58, 324–340.

Putman, D. (1997). Psychological courage. *Philosophy, Psychiatry, and Psychology*, 4, 1–11.

Putnam, H. (1994). Reductionism and the nature of psychology. In: H. Putnam, *Words and life* (pp. 428–440). Cambridge, MA: Harvard University Press.

Quadflieg, S., Mohr, A., Mentzel, H. J., Miltner, W. H., and Straube, T. (2008). Modulation of the neural network involved in the processing of anger prosody: the role of task-relevance and social phobia. *Biological Psychology*, 78, 129–137.

Quine, W. (1960). *Work and object*. Cambridge, MA: MIT Press.

Rachlin, H. (1992). Teleological behaviorism. *American Psychologist*, 47, 1371–1382.

Rachlin, H., Battalio, R., Kagel, J., and Green, L. (1981). Maximization theory in behavioural psychology. *Behavioral and Brain Sciences*, 4, 371–388.

Rapee, R. M., Mattick, R., and Murrell, E. (1986). Cognitive mediation in the affective component of spontaneous panic attacks. *Journal of Behaviour Therapy and Experimental Psychiatry*, 17, 245–253.

Reiss, D., and Neiderhiser, J. M. (2000). The interplay of genetic influences and social processes in developmental theory: specific mechanisms are coming into view. *Development and Psychopathology*, 12, 357–374.

Rendle, M. (2008). The problems of "becoming Soviet": former nobles in Soviet society, 1917–41. *European History Quarterly*, 38, 7–33.

Renken, B., Egeland, B., Marvinney, D., Mangelsdorf, S., and Sroufe, L. A. (1989). Early childhood antecedents of aggression and passive-withdrawal in early elementary school. *Journal of Personality*, 57, 257–281.

Rettew, D. C., Zanarini, M. C., Yen, S., Grilo, C. M., Skodol, A. E., Shea, T., ... Gunderson, J. G. (2003). Childhood antecedents of avoidant personality disorder: a retrospective study. *Journal of American Academy of Child and Adolescent Psychiatry*, 42, 1122–1130.

Richardson, K. (2000). *The making of intelligence*. New York: Columbia University Press.

(2002). What IQ tests test. *Theory and Psychology*, 12, 283–314.

Riis, O., and Woodhead, L. (2010). *A sociology of religious emotion*. Oxford University Press.

Robins, E., and Guze, S. B. (1970). Establishment of diagnostic validity in psychiatric illness: its application to schizophrenia. *American Journal of Psychiatry*, 126, 983–987.

Rodebaugh, T. L., Weeks, J. W., Gordon, E. A., Langer, J. K., and Heimberg, R. G. (2012). The longitudinal relationship between fear of positive evaluation and fear of negative evaluation. *Anxiety, Stress and Coping: An International Journal*, 25, 167–182.

Rodrigues, S. M., LeDoux, J. E., and Sapolsky, R. M. (2009). The influence of stress hormones on fear circuitry. *Annual Review of Neuroscience*, 32, 289–313.

Rolston, H. (2006). What is a gene? From molecules to metaphysics. *Theoretical Medicine and Bioethics*, 27, 471–497.

Romm, K. L., Mell, I., Thoresen, C., Andreassen, O. A., and Rossberg, J. I. (2012). Severe social anxiety in early psychosis is associated with poor premorbid functioning, depression, and reduced quality of life. *Comprehensive Psychiatry*, 53, 434–440.

Rose, S. (1995). The rise of neurogenetic determinism. *Nature*, 373, 380–382.

(1998). *Lifelines: biology beyond determinism*. Oxford University Press.

Rose, R. J., and Ditto, W. B. (1983). A developmental-genetic analysis of common fears from early adolescence to early adulthood. *Child Development*, 54, 361–368.

Rose, S., Kamin, L. J., and Lewontin, R. C. (1984). *Not in our genes: biology, ideology and human nature.* Harmondsworth: Penguin Books.

Rosen, J. B., and Schulkin, J. (1998). From normal fear to pathological anxiety. *Psychological Review,* 105, 325–350.

Rosenbaum, J. F., Biederman, J., Bolduc, E. A., Hirshfeld, D. R., Faraone, S. V., and Kagan, J. (1992). Comorbidity of parental anxiety as risk for childhood-onset anxiety in inhibited children. *American Journal of Psychiatry,* 149, 475–481.

Rosenbaum, J. F., Biederman, J., Hirshfeld, D. R., Bolduc, E. A., Faraone, S. V., Kagan, J., ... Reznick, J. S. (1991). Further evidence of an association between behavioral inhibition and anxiety disorders: results from a family study of children from a non-clinical sample. *Journal of Psychiatry Research,* 25, 49–65.

Ross, D. (1995). *Aristotle.* London: Routledge.

Rothgerber, H. K. (1997). External intergroup threat as an antecedent to perceptions of in-group and out-group homogeneity. *Journal of Personality and Social Psychology,* 73, 1206–1212.

Rubinstein, D. (1986). Wittgenstein and social science. In: S. Shanker (ed.), *Ludwig Wittgenstein: critical assessments* (pp. 290–311). London: Croom Helm.

Rudder Baker, L. (1984). On the very idea of a form of life. *Inquiry,* 27, 277–289.

Russell, A., and Finnie, V. (1990). Preschool children's social status and maternal instructions to assist group entry. *Developmental Psychology,* 26, 603–611.

Russell, B. (1958). *The will to doubt.* New York: Philosophical Library.

Russell, J. J., Moskowitz, D. S., Zuroff, D. C., Bleau, P., Pinard, G., and Young, S. N. (2011). Anxiety, emotional security and the interpersonal behavior of individuals with social anxiety disorder. *Psychological Medicine,* 41, 545–554.

Russell, P. J., Wolfe, S. L., Hertz, P. E., Starr, C., and McMillan, B. (2008). *Biology: the dynamic science.* Belmont, CA: Brooks/Cole.

Rutter, M., and Plomin, R. (1997). Opportunities for psychiatry from genetic findings. *British Journal of Psychiatry,* 171, 209–219.

Ryan, R. M., and Deci, E. L. (2000). Self-determination theory and the facilitation of intrinsic motivation, social development, and well-being. *American Psychologist,* 55, 68–78.

Ryle, G. (1949). *The concept of mind.* London: Hutchinson.

Sadeghi-Nejad, H., and Watson, R. (2008). Premature ejaculation: current medical treatment and new directions. *Journal of Sex Medicine,* 5, 1037–1050.

Safren, S. A. Gershuny, B. S., Marzol, P., Otto, M. W., and Pollack, M. H. (2002). History of childhood abuse in panic disorder, social phobia and generalized anxiety disorder. *The Journal of Nervous and Mental Disease,* 190, 453–456.

Salekin, R. T., Trobst, K. K., and Krioukova, M. (2001). Construct validity of psychopathy in a community sample: a nomological net approach. *Journal of Personality Disorders,* 15, 425–441.

Samochowiec, J., Hajduk, A., Samochowiec, A., Horodnicki, J., Stepien, G., Grzywacz, A., and Kucharska-Mazur, J. (2004). Association studies of MAO-A, COMT, and 5-HTT genes polymorphisms in patients with anxiety disorders of the phobic spectrum. *Psychiatry Research,* 128, 21–26.

Sampson, E. E. (1981). Cognitive psychology as ideology. *American Psychologist*, 36, 730–743.

Sapolsky, R. M. (1992). Behavioral endocrinology. In: J. B. Becker, M. Breedlove, and D. Crews (eds.), *Behavioral endocrinology* (pp. 287–324). Cambridge, MA: MIT Press.

Sarbin, T. R. (1964). Anxiety: reification of a metaphor. *Archives of General Psychiatry*, 10, 630–638.

    (1986). Emotion and act: roles and rhetoric. In: R. Harré (ed.), *The social construction of emotions*. Oxford: Blackwell.

Sareen, J., Campbell, D. W., Leslie, W. D., Malisza, K. L., Stein, M. B., Paulus, M. P., ... Reiss, J. P. (2007). Striatal function in generalized social phobia: a functional magnetic resonance imaging study. *Biological Psychiatry*, 61, 396–404.

Sawaoka, T., Barnes, R. D., Blomquist, K. K., Masheb, R. M., and Grilo, C. M. (2012). Social anxiety and self-consciousness in binge eating disorder: associations with eating disorder psychopathology. *Comprehensive Psychiatry*, 53, 740–745.

Scarr, S. (1996). How people make their own environments: implications for parents and policy makers. *Psychology, Public Policy, and Law*, 2, 204–228.

Schacht, R. (ed.) (1995). *Making sense of Nietzsche: reflections timely and untimely*. Champaign, IL: University of Illinois Press.

Schatzki, T. R. (1996). *Social practices: a Wittgensteinian approach to human activity and the social*. Cambridge University Press.

    (2000). Wittgenstein and the social context of an individual life. *History of the Human Sciences*, 13, 93–107.

Scheman, N. (1996). Forms of life: mapping the rough ground. In: H. Sluga, and D. G. Stern (eds.), *The Cambridge companion to Wittgenstein* (pp. 383–410). Cambridge University Press.

Schmidt, S., Mohr, A., Miltner, W. H., and Straube, T. (2010). Task-dependent neural correlates of the processing of verbal threat-related stimuli in social phobia. *Biological Psychiatry*, 84, 304–312.

Schneier, F. R., Abi-Dargham, A., Martinez, D., Slifstein, M., Hwang, D. R., Liebowitz, M. R., and Laruelle, M. (2009). Dopamine transporters, D2 receptors, and dopamine release in generalized social anxiety disorder. *Depression and Anxiety*, 26, 411–418.

Schneier, F. R., Liebowitz, M., Abi-Dargham, A., Zea-Ponce, Y., Lin, S., and Laruelle, M. (2000). Low dopamine D2 receptor binding potential in social phobia. *American Journal of Psychiatry*, 157, 457–459.

Schneier, F. R., Martinez, D., Abi-Dargham, A., Zea-Ponce, Y., Simpson, H. B., Liebowitz, M. R., and Laruelle, M. (2008). Striatal dopamine D2 receptor availability in OCD with and without comorbid social anxiety disorder: preliminary findings. *Depression and Anxiety*, 25, 1–7.

Schneier, F. R., Pomplun, M., Sy, M., and Hirsch, J. (2011). Neural response to eye contact and paroxetine treatment in generalized social anxiety disorder. *Psychiatry Research*, 194, 271–278.

Scholing, A., and Emmelkamp, P. M. G. (1993). Cognitive and behavioural treatments of fear of blushing, sweating or trembling. *Behaviour Research and Therapy*, 31, 155–170.

Schopenhauer, A. (2001). *Parerga und Paralipomena*, Vol. II (ch. XXXI, section 396). Oxford University Press.

Schwartz, C. E., Snidman, N., and Kagan, J. (1999). Adolescent social anxiety as an outcome of inhibited temperament in childhood. *Journal of the American Academy of Child and Adolescent Psychiatry*, 38, 1008–1015.

Schwartz, S. (2002). Separation anxiety syndrome in cats: 136 cases (1991–2000). *Journal of the American Veterinary Medical Association*, 220, 1028–1033.

(2003). Separation anxiety syndrome in dogs and cats. *Journal of the American Veterinary Medical Association*, 222, 1526–1532.

Scott, R. A. (2010). *Miracle cures: saints, pilgrimage, and the healing powers of belief.* Berkeley, CA: University of California Press.

Scott, S. (2005). The red, shaking fool: dramaturgical dilemmas in shyness. *Symbolic Interaction*, 28, 91–110.

(2006). The medicalisation of shyness: from social misfits to social fitness. *Sociology of Health and Illness*, 28, 133–153.

Scull, A. (2011). *Madness: a very short introduction.* Oxford University Press.

Searle, J. R. (1994). Animal minds. *Midwest Studies in Philosophy*, XIX, 206–219.

(1995). *The construction of social reality.* New York: Free Press.

Sebag Montefiore, S. (2003). *Stalin: in the court of the red tsar.* London: Weidenfeld & Nicolson.

Sehlmeyer, C., Schöning, S., Zwitserlood, P., Pfleiderer, B., Kircher, T., Arolt, V., and Konrad, C. (2009). Human fear conditioning and extinction in neuroimaging: a systematic review. *PLOS One*, 4, e5865.

Serpell, J. A. (1996). Evidence for an association between pet behaviour and owner attachment levels. *Applied Animal Behaviour Science*, 47, 49–60.

Sheehan, D. V. (1986). *The anxiety disease.* New York: Scribner's.

Shepherd, M. (1993). The placebo: from specificity to the non-specific and back. *Psychological Medicine*, 23, 569–578.

Shields, C. (2007). *Aristotle.* London: Routledge.

Shin, L., Wright, C., Cannistraro, P., Wedig, M., McMullin, K., Martis, B., … Rauch, S. (2005). A functional magnetic resonance imaging study of amygdala and medial prefrontal cortex responses to overtly presented fearful faces in posttraumatic stress disorder. *Archives of General Psychiatry*, 62, 273–281.

Shorter Oxford English Dictionary (1972). Oxford University Press.

Shott, S. (1979). Emotion and social life: a symbolic interactionist analysis. *American Journal of Sociology*, 84, 1317–1334.

Shumyatsky, G. B., Malleret, G., Shin, R.-Y., Tokizawa, S., Tully, K., Tsvetkov, E., … Bolshakov, V. Y. (2005). Stathmin, a gene enriched in the amygdala controls both learned and innate fear. *Cell*, 123, 697–709.

Sidanius, J., and Pratto, F. (1999). *Social dominance: an intergroup theory of social hierarchy and oppression.* New York: Cambridge University Press.

Sipila, T., Dananen, L., Greco, D., Donner, J., Silander, K., Terwilliger, J. D., … Hovatta, I. (2010). An association analysis of circadian genes in anxiety disorders. *Biological Psychiatry*, 67, 1163–1170.

Skre, I., Onstad, S., Torgersen, S., Lygren, S., and Kringlen, E. (1993). A twin study of DSM-III-R anxiety disorders. *Acta Psychiatrica Scandinavica*, 88, 85–92.

Slee, P. T. (1994). Situational and interpersonal correlates of anxiety associated with peer victimization. *Child Psychiatry and Human Development*, 25, 97–107.

Sobel, V. (2009). *Febris erotica*. Seattle, WA: University of Washington Press.

Sofsky, W. (1997). *The order of terror: the concentration camp*. Princeton, NJ: Princeton University Press.

Spence, D. (2014). Bad medicine: the rise of duloxetine. *British Medical Journal*, 348, 39.

Spence, S. H., Rapee, R., McDonald, C., and Ingram, M. (2001). The structure of anxiety symptoms among preschoolers. *Behaviour Research and Therapy*, 39, 1293–1316.

Spitzer, R., and Endicott, J. (1978). Medical and mental disorder: proposed definition and criteria. In: R. L. Spitzer, and D. F. Klein (eds.), *Critical issues in psychiatry* (pp. 15–39). New York: Raven Press.

Sprigge, T. L. S. (1984). *Theories of existence*. Harmondsworth: Penguin.

Srinivasan, A. (1983). The Hindu temple-dancer: prostitute or nun? *Cambridge Anthropology*, 8, 73–99.

Sroufe, L. A. (1996). *Emotional development: the organization of emotional life in the early years*. Cambridge University Press.

(1997). Psychopathology as an outcome of development. *Development and Psychopathology*, 9, 251–268.

(1983). Infant caregiver attachment and patterns of adaptation in preschool: the roots of maladaptation and competence. In: M. Perlmutter (ed.), *Development and policy concerning children with special needs*. Minnesota Symposia on Child Psychology, Vol. XVI (pp. 41–83). Hillsdale, NJ: Lawrence Erlbaum.

Sroufe, L. A., Carlson, E., and Shulman, S. (1993). Individuals in relationships: development from infancy through adolescence. In: D. C. Funder, R. Parke, C. Tomlinson-Keesey, and K. Widaman (eds.), *Studying lives through time: approaches to personality and development* (pp. 315–342). Washington, DC: American Psychological Association.

Sroufe, L. A., and Waters, E. (1977). Attachment as an organizational construct. *Child Development*, 48, 1184–1199.

Stangier, U., Esser, F., Leber, S., Risch, A. K., and Heidenreich, T. (2006). Interpersonal problems in social phobia versus unipolar depression. *Depression and Anxiety*, 23, 418–421.

Stangier, U., Von Consbruch, K., Schramm, E., and Heidenreich, T. (2010). Common factors of cognitive therapy and interpersonal psychotherapy in the treatment of social phobia. *Anxiety, Stress and Coping*, 23, 289–301.

Statman, D. (2000). Humiliation, dignity and self-respect. *Philosophical Psychology*, 13, 523–540.

Stein, D. J., and Bouwer, C. (1997). Blushing and social phobia: a neuroethological speculation. *Medical Hypotheses*, 49, 101–108.

Stein, D. J., Ipser, J. C., and van Balkom, A. J. (2009). Pharmacotherapy for social anxiety disorder (review). *The Cochrane Library*, 1, 1–64.

Stein, M., Chartier, M., Hazen, A. L., Kozak, M., Tancer, M. E., Lander, S., Furer, P., Chubaty, D., and Walker, J. (1998). A direct-interview family study of generalized social phobia. *American Journal of Psychiatry*, 155, 90–97.

Stein, M., Chartier, M., Kozak, M., King, N., and Kennedy, J. (1998). Genetic linkage to the serotonin transporter protein and 5HT2A receptor genes excluded in generalized social phobia. *Psychiatry Research*, 81, 283–291.

Stein, M. B., Walker, J. R., and Forde, D. R. (1994). Setting diagnostic thresholds for social phobia: considerations from a community survey of social anxiety. *American Journal of Psychiatry*, 151, 408–412.

(1996). Public-speaking fears in a community sample: prevalence, impact on functioning and diagnostic classification. *Archives of General Psychiatry*, 53, 169–174.

Stevens, S., Hofmann, M., Kiko, S., Mall, A. K., Steil, R., Bohus, M., and Hermann, C. (2010). What determines observer-rated social performance in individuals with social anxiety disorder? *Journal of Anxiety Disorders*, 24, 830–836.

Stich, S. (1983). *From folk psychology to cognitive science*. Cambridge, MA: MIT Press.

Stopa, L., and Clark, D. M. (1993). Cognitive processes in social phobia. *Behaviour Research and Therapy*, 31, 255–267.

Storch, E. A., Brassard, M. R., and Masia-Warner, C. L. (2003). The relationship of peer victimization to social anxiety and loneliness in adolescence. *Child Study Journal*, 33, 1–18.

Stravynski, A. (1983). Behavioral treatment of psychogenic vomiting in the context of social phobia. *Journal of Nervous and Mental Disease*, 171, 448–451.

(2007). *Fearing others: the nature and treatment of social phobia*. Cambridge University Press.

Stravynski, A., Amado, D., Lachance, L., Sidoun, P., and Todorov, C. (2013b). An interpersonal approach to the treatment of social phobia with and without medication (paroxetine): short and long-term effects. (Unpublished data.)

Stravynski, A., Arbel, N., Bounader, J., Gaudette, G., Lachance, L., Borgeat, F., ... Todorov, C. (2000). Social phobia treated as a problem in social functioning: a controlled comparison of two behavioural group approaches. *Acta Psychiatrica Scandinavica*, 102, 188–198.

Stravynski, A., Arbel, M., Gaudette, G., and Lachance, L. (2013). Dismantling an interpersonal approach to the treatment of social phobia. (Under review.)

Stravynski, A., Arbel, N., Lachance, L., and Todorov, C. (2000). Social phobia viewed as a problem in social functioning: a pilot study of group behavioural treatment. *Journal of Behavior Therapy and Experimental Psychiatry*, 31, 163–175.

Stravynski, A., Basoglu, M., Marks, M., Sengun, S., and Marks, I. M. (1995a). The distinctiveness of phobias: a discriminant analysis of fears. *Journal of Anxiety Disorders*, 9, 89–101.

Stravynski, A., Basoglu, M., Marks, M., Sengun, S., and Marks, I. M. (1995b). Social sensitivity: a shared feature of all phobias. *British Journal of Clinical Psychology*, 34, 343–351.

Stravynski, A., Gaudette, G., Lesage, A., Arbel, N., Petit, P., Clerc, D., ... Sidoun, P. (1997). The treatment of sexually dysfunctional men without partners: a controlled study of three behavioural group approaches. *British Journal of Psychiatry*, 170, 338–344.

Stravynski, A., Grey, S., and Elie, R. (1987). Outline of the therapeutic process in social skills training with socially dysfunctional patients. *Journal of Consulting and Clinical Psychology*, 55, 224–228.

Stravynski, A., Lesage, A., Marcouiller, M., and Elie, R. (1989). A test of the therapeutic mechanism in social skills training with avoidant personality disorder. *The Journal of Nervous and Mental Disease*, 177, 739–744.

Stravynski, A., Verreault, R., Gaudette, G., Langlois, R., Gagnier, S. and Larose, M. (1994). The treatment of depression with group cognitive – behavioural therapy and imipramine. *Canadian Journal of Psychiatry*, 39, 387–390.

Strohman, R. C. (2000). Organization becomes cause in the matter. *Nature Biotechnology*, 18, 575–576.

Sullivan, G. M., Oquendo, M. A., Simpson, N., Van Heertum, R. L., Mann, J. J., and Parsey, R. V. (2005). Brain serotonin1A receptor binding in major depression is related to psychic and somatic anxiety. *Biological Psychiatry*, 58, 947–954.

Sullivan, H. G. (1953). *The interpersonal theory of psychiatry.* New York: Norton.

Sutterby, S. R., and Bedwell, J. S. (2012). Lack of neuropsychological deficits in generalized social phobia. *PLOS ONE*, 7, e42675.

Svyantek, D. J., and Brown, L. L. (2000). A complex-systems approach to organizations. *Current Directions in Psychological Science*, 9, 69–74.

Szasz, T. (1987). *Insanity: the idea and its consequences.* New York: Wiley.

Tancer, M. E., Lewis, M., and Stein, M. (1995). Biological aspects. In: M. Stein (ed.), *Social phobia: clinical and research perspectives* (pp. 229–257). Washington, DC: American Psychiatric Press.

Taylor, C. (1970). The explanation of purposive behaviour. In: R. Borger and F. Cioffi (eds.), *Explanation in the behavioural sciences* (pp. 49–79). Cambridge University Press.

Taylor, C. T., and Alden, L. E. (2010). Safety behaviors and judgmental biases in social anxiety disorder. *Behaviour Research and Therapy*, 48, 226–237.

Thomas, K., Drevets, W., Dahl, R., Ryan, N., Birmaher, B., Eccard, C., ... Casey, B. (2001). Amygdala response to fearful faces in anxious and depressed children. *Archives of General Psychiatry*, 58, 1057–1063.

Thompson, E. (2007). *Mind in life.* Cambridge, MA: Harvard University Press.

Tiihonen, J., Kuikka, J., Bergstrom, K., Lepola, U., Koponen, H., and Leinonen, E. (1997). Dopamine reuptake site densities in patients with social phobia. *American Journal of Psychiatry*, 154, 239–242.

Tillfors, M. (2004). Why do some individuals develop social phobia? A review with emphasis on the neurobiological influences. Review. *Nordic Journal of Psychiatry*, 58, 267–276.

Tillfors, M., Furmark, T., Ekselius, L., and Fredrikson, M. (2001). Social phobia and avoidant personality disorder as related to parental history of social anxiety: a general population study. *Behaviour Research and Therapy*, 39, 289–298.

Torgersen, S. (1983). Genetic factors in anxiety disorders. *Archives of General Psychiatry*, 40, 1085–1089.

Townsend, J., and Altshuler, L. L. (2012). Emotion processing and regulation in bipolar disorder: a review. *Bipolar Disorders*, 14, 326–339.

Turner, D. C. (2000). The human-cat relationship. In: D. C. Turner and P. Bateson (eds), *The domestic cat: the biology of its behaviour* (2nd edn.) (pp. 193–206). Cambridge University Press.

Turner, S. M., Beidel, D. C., and Wolff, P. L. (1996). Is behavioral inhibition related to the anxiety disorders? *Clinical Psychology Review*, 16, 157–172.

Tweed, J. L., Schoenbach, V. J., George, L. K., and Blazer, D. G. (1989). The effects of childhood parental death and divorce on six-month history of anxiety disorders. *British Journal of Psychiatry*, 154, 823–828.

Tyrer, P. (1985). Neurosis divisible? *Lancet*, 23, 685–688.

van der Wee, N. J., van Veen, J. F., Stevens, H., van Vliet, I. M., van Rijk, P. P., and Westenberg, H. G. (2008). Increased serotonin and dopamine transporter binding in psychotropic medication-naive patients with generalized social anxiety disorder shown by 123I-beta-(4-iodophenyl)-tropane SPECT. *Journal of Nuclear Medicine*, 49, 757–763.

Vernberg, E. M., Abwender, D. A., Ewell, K. K., and Beery, S. H. (1992). Social anxiety and peer relationships in early adolescence: a prospective analysis. *Journal of Clinical Child Psychology*, 21, 189–196.

Vidal-Naquet, P. (1992). *Assassins of memory*. New York: Columbia University Press.

Vogel, S. (2012) *The life of a leaf*. Chicago, IL: University of Chicago Press.

Wakefield, J. C., Pottick, J. J., and Kirk, S. A. (2002). Should the DSM-IV diagnostic criteria for conduct disorder consider social context? *American Journal of Psychiatry*, 159, 380–386.

Walsh-Bowers, R. (2006). A theatre acting perspective on the dramaturgical metaphor and the postmodern self. *Theory and Psychology*, 16, 661–690.

Walters, K. S., and Inderbitzen, H. M. (1998). Social anxiety and peer relations among adolescents: testing a psychobiological model. *Journal of Anxiety Disorders*, 12, 183–198.

Warren, S. L., Huston, L., Egeland, B., and Sroufe, L. A. (1997). Child and adolescent anxiety disorders and early attachment. *Journal of the American Academy of Child and Adolescent Psychiatry*, 36, 637–644.

Watson, D. R., Bai, F., Barrett, S. L., Turkington, A., Rushe, T. M., Mulholland, C. C., and Cooper, S. J. (2012) Structural changes in the hippocampus and amygdala at first episode of psychosis. *Brain Imaging and Behavior*, 6, 49–60.

Webster's New Collegiate Dictionary (1962). Springfield, MA: G. and C. Merriam.

Westenberg, P. M., Drewes, M. J., Goedhart, A. W., Siebelink, B. M., and Treffers, P. D. A. (2004). A developmental analysis of self-reported fears in late childhood through mid-adolescence: social evaluative fears on the rise? *Journal of Child Psychology and Psychiatry*, 45, 481–495.

Whaley, S. H., Pinto, A., and Sigman, M. (1999). Characterizing interactions between anxious mothers and their children. *Journal of Consulting and Clinical Psychology*, 67, 826–836.

Wicker, A. W. (2002). Ecological psychology: historical contexts, current conception, prospective directions. In: R. B. Bechtel and A. Churchman (eds.), *Handbook of environmental psychology* (pp. 114–126). New York: Wiley.

Wijeratne, C., and Manicavasagar, V. (2003). Separation anxiety in the elderly. *Journal of Anxiety Disorders*, 17, 695–702.

Williams, J. H. G. (1998). Using behavioural ecology to understand depression. *British Journal of Psychiatry*, 173, 453–454.

Wilshire, B. (1982). *Role playing and identity: the limits of theatre as metaphor.* Bloomington, IN: Indiana University Press.

Winch, P. (1977). *The idea of a social science and its relation to philosophy.* London: Routledge.

Wittchen, H. U., Stein, M. B., and Kessler, R. C. (1999). Social fears and social phobia in a community sample of adolescents and young adults: prevalence, risk factors and co-morbidity. *Psychological Medicine*, 29, 309–323.

Wittgenstein, L. (1958). *Philosophical investigations.* Oxford: Blackwell.

Wong, C. L., Van Spall, H. G. C., Hassan, K. A., Coret-Simon, J., Sahlas, D. J., and Shumak, S. L. (2008). A young man with deep vein thrombosis, hyper-homocysteinemia and cobalamin deficiency. *Canadian Medical Association Journal*, 178, 279–281.

World Health Organization (1992). *The ICD-10 classification of mental and behavioural disorders.* Geneva: W.H.O.

Woodruff-Borden, J., Morrow, C., Bourland, S., and Cambron, S. (2002). The behavior of anxious parents: examining mechanisms of transmission of anxiety from parent to child. *Journal of Clinical Child and Adolescent Psychology*, 31, 364–374.

Yoon, K. L., Fitzgerald, D. A., Angstadt, M., McCarron, R. A., and Phan, K. L. (2007). Amygdala reactivity to emotional faces at high and low intensity in generalized social phobia: a 4-Tesla functional MRI study. *Psychiatry Research*, 154, 93–98.

Wootton, D. (2007). *Bad medicine: doctors doing harm since Hippocrates.* Oxford University Press.

Zachar, P. (2001). Psychiatric disorders are not natural kinds. *Philosophy, Psychiatry and Psychology*, 7, 167–182.

Zurcher, L. A. (1983). *Social roles: conformity, conflict and creativity.* London: Sage.

Index